Princeton Theological Monograph Series

Dikran Y. Hadidian

General Editor

30

CALVIN'S CONCEPT OF THE LAW

CALVIN'S CONCEPT
OF
THE LAW

I. John Hesselink

PICKWICK PUBLICATIONS
ALLISON PARK, PENNSYLVANIA

Copyright © 1992 by I. John Hesselink

Published by

Pickwick Publications
4137 Timberlane Drive
Allison Park, PA 15101-2932

Printed in the United States of America

Library of Congress Cataloging-in-Publication Data

Hesselink, I. John, 1928-
    Calvin's concept of the law / I. John Hesselink.
        p.   cm. -- (Princeton theological monograph series ; 30)
    Includes bibliographical references.
    ISBN 1-55635-007-4
    1. Calvin, Jean, 1509-1564--Contributions in concept of law.
    2. Law (Theology)--History of doctrines--16th century.   I. Title.
    II. Series.
    BT96.2.H48   1992
    241'.2--dc20   91-45745
                                                                            CIP

To the memory of my two Swiss mentors and friends, Karl Barth and Emil Brunner, neither of whom totally agreed with the contents of this work but both of whom were constantly supportive and encouraging .

CONTENTS

PREFACE

This work represents a revision, reduction, and refinement of my Basel University doctoral dissertation of 1961: *Calvin's Concept and Use of the Law.* Lest the mention of a dissertation frighten away some prospective readers, the following points may be reassuring: 1) In the main text I have translated all quotations from other languages. 2) This work, though still substantial, is shorter than the original, partially because I have reduced the number of footnotes as well as cut out some extraneous material. 3) Most importantly, I think most readers, including non-theologians and non-Calvin scholars, will find the style very readable.

There has been a very lively and encouraging interest in Calvin's life, work, and thought in the last twenty-five years. The annual Calvin bibliographies by Peter De Klerk in the *Calvin Theological Journal* (since 1971, usually in the November issue) give ample evidence of that.

However, given the importance of the subject, it is surprising that so little research has been done on Calvin's view of the law. One will find in Calvin bibliographies several essays which deal with one aspect or another of Calvin's approach to the law such as his treatment of natural law or the decalog. There have also been a few dissertations dealing with some aspect of Calvin's doctrine of the law which are cited in my Introduction, but no comprehensive treatment of Calvin's concept of the law has yet appeared. Hence this study still fills a gap, despite the proliferation of Calvin studies in the last three decades.

The danger in attempting a comprehensive study like this is that some aspects of the subject cannot be covered in the depth and thoroughness they deserve. For example, there are a number of monographs on Calvin's view of natural law as well as a few full-scale treatments of that subject. Since the particular focus of this work is the third use of the law (as a norm and guide for the believer), it might seem ad-

ix

visable to skip that subject; but that is not possible if one is to gain an adequate understanding of Calvin's doctrine of revealed law.

On a more personal note, I must express my regrets for the fact that it has taken so long to make this work available in published form. Over the years I have received a number of requests for the dissertation. It has been utilized by several scholars who have had access to the dissertation in a few select libraries here and abroad, but its general unavailability has been a source of frustration to others.

It should also be noted that parts of this work have appeared in modified form as essays in symposia and Festschriften. Where that is the case, I have indicated that at the appropriate place with a footnote.

A word about translations. I have used the standard English translations of Calvin's works, generally preferring the more recent translations to the older, e.g., the McNeill-Battles edition of the *Institutes* rather than the older translations of Allen and Beveridge, and the Torrance edition of the New Testament commentaries to the old Edinburgh edition. In every case, however, I have checked the translations with the original Latin and French editions as found in the *Calvini Opera* (which is part of the larger *Corpus Reformatorum*) and *Opera Selecta*. However, I have modified the translations occasionally for the sake of greater consistency and where a more literal translation may serve to make a point. In the case of translations from German, French, and Dutch works the translations are my own, although in some cases I have had the translations checked by specialists in those languages.

Finally, I come to that delightful but difficult part of the preface to a book where one acknowledges mentors, friends, and colleagues who have inspired, guided, encouraged, and assisted in other ways in a major effort of this sort. One cannot list them all, but I must begin with my professor of theology as a student at Western Seminary, Professor Emeritus M. Eugene Osterhaven. He introduced me in a serious way to Calvin and has continued through the years to be a wonderful source of inspiration and encouragement. I count it a singular honor to have succeeded him as the Albertus C. Van Raalte Professor of Systematic Theology at Western Seminary.

Next in line would have to be the incalculable debt I owe to my two great Swiss mentors, Karl Barth and Emil Brunner. I came to know Professor Brunner during the first years of my missionary career in Japan (1953-55) when he was a visiting professor at the International Christian University in Tokyo. We became good friends at that time and our friendship deepened during the years I studied in Basel (1958-61), despite the fact that I had elected to pursue my graduate studies with Karl Barth! (Brunner had already retired, so there was no possibility of continuing my studies with him.) Professor Barth was my *Doktorvater*, i.e., dissertation advisor, and was the most genial and delightful mentor and guide one could hope for. Neither he nor Professor Brunner agreed with all my interpretations, but both were unstinting in their encouragement and assistance, which included the loan of many of their volumes of the *Corpus Reformatorum*.

I am also grateful to other Basel University professors who played a special role in my doctoral program: Professor of Ethics, Hendrik van Oyen, the second reader of my dissertation; Professor of Church History, Ernst Staehelin, my examiner in that field; and Professor of New Testament and Early Christianity, Oscar Cullmann, who was my examiner in New Testament and also my "host" in the *Theologisches Alumneum*, the venerable international student house where I spent my first semester in Basel. He, and particularly his sister, Fräulein Loulou Cullmann, were my first—and only—mentors in German, which I had never studied formally

Then there are the many friends—all of them Calvin scholars—who graciously read my dissertation and offered encouragement along with helpful suggestions. They include the late Dr. Wilhelm Niesel of the *Theologische Hochschule* in Wuppertal; Hendrikus Berkhof, Professor Emeritus of the University of Leiden; T. F. Torrance, Professor Emeritus of New College, the University of Edinburgh; Edward A. Dowey, Jr. and David Willis, respectively Professor of Historical Theology and Systematic Theology at Princeton Theological Seminary; David Little, Professor of Ethics at the University of Virginia; Herbert W. Richardson, Professor of Theology at St. Michael's College, The University of Toronto; and especially the late Ford Lewis Battles, who closed out his career at Calvin College and Seminary, and Brian Gerrish, Professor of Historical Theology at the Divinity School of the University of Chicago, for these friends in particular continued to press me to get this work published.

I am also very thankful to Dikran Y. Hadidian, General Editor of Pickwick Publications, for his patience and perseverance. He was promised this manuscript a long time ago but never gave up on me. I would also like to thank his wife, Jean, for her assistance in this project. I am also indebted to a faculty colleague, Professor Robert A. Coughenour, who kindly read through the whole manuscript and caught many errors and made helpful stylistic suggestions, and to emeritus Professor Richard C. Oudersluys for invaluable assistance in proofreading.

Finally, special thanks to Mrs. Marilyn Essink, our faculty secretary, who typed much of the manuscript not only with her usual accuracy and carefulness, but also with an admirable spirit, and also to Mrs. Anna Donkersloot, who took over this task at a crucial juncture and typed the last three chapters, and finally my wife, Etta, who typed the original dissertation.

I. John Hesselink January, 1992
WesternTheological Seminary

INTRODUCTION

The popular image of Calvin, which continues to persist despite considerable evidence to the contrary, is that of a cold, logical systematician who stressed the sovereignty of God and taught a deterministic doctrine of double predestination. He is further characterized as the dour, relentless reformer of Geneva who burned Servetus. This grim caricature is then often concluded by noting that with Calvin the Bible became a literalistically interpreted lawbook. He is hence dismissed as a "law-teacher" (*Gesetzlehrer*) who knew little of the love and grace of God as revealed in Jesus Christ[1]

Much of this image is based on myth, falsehood, and prejudice and has been thoroughly refuted by Calvin research in the last half century.[2] As a result, the older portrayals of Calvin and his work by the Catholics, F. W. Kampschulte and Imbart de la Tour, and the Jew, Stephan Zweig, are no longer taken seriously by responsible historians. However, the charge of legalism continues to be leveled against Calvin, but not so much by Catholics, Jews, and liberals as by orthodox Lutherans. Characteristic is a comparison of Reformed and Lutheran theology by Reinhold Seeberg:

> God is, to pious minds in the Reformed Church, the Lord who rules omnipotently. The development of the universe is the product of his sovereign will; its goal his honor or glory. But the sovereignty of God is displayed above all through the "Law," which controls all life and all its ramifications. All that is done in the world, everything personal and natural, must subserve this end. Obedience is the whole content of life. Natural inclinations are bent and crushed beneath the pressure of the "law". . . . There is something "un-modern" in this magniloquent portrayal of the energy of obedience and that fanaticism of submission. . . . But the gospel, as it appears in Paul and John, we find in clearer and

brighter form in Luther than in Calvin. This God of Calvin is the omnipotent Will, ruling throughout the world; the God of Luther is the omnipotent energy of love manifest in Christ.[3]

This was originally written in 1898, only one year before the appearance of the first volume of Doumergue's monumental study of Calvin's life and work[4] in which Calvin is presented in a much more favorable light. But substantially the same analysis of Calvin's theology is repeated in the last (third) edition of Seeberg's *Dogmengeschichte* written in 1920.[5] Here we find repeated reference to "the legal (*gesetzlich*) tendency which is maintained in Calvin's doctrine of Scripture."[6] Similar phrases still appear in contemporary church histories written by German Lutheran theologians. Hans von Schubert, for example, avers that "the equation of the Old Testament with the New gives to this biblicistic moralism [of Calvin] the severe characteristic of Old Testament legality (*Gesetzlichkeit*)."[7] Earlier works, such as P. Lobstein's *Die Ethik Calvins* (1877), Ernst Troeltsch's *Social Teachings of the Christian Churches* (1911), and Paul Wernle's volume on Calvin in his trilogy, *Der evangelische Glaube* (1919), treated certain aspects of Calvin's concept of the law with some originality, but all of them were hindered by a sterile view of the Old Testament and an insufficient appreciation of the unity of the Bible. Because of the prevailing view of the law and the Old Testament prior to the rise of dialectical theology or the theology of the Word and the biblical theology movement, it is not surprising that Calvin's treatment of the law was viewed with little appreciation or understanding. Georgia Harkness wrote a fresh, interesting study in 1931, *John Calvin—The Man and his Ethics,* in which she corrects some of the misconceptions of Max Weber. But her understanding of Calvin's view of the law and the Old Testament is superficial and is burdened with the same old clichés:

> Calvin's system of doctrine is more Hebraic than Christian. It rests more upon the Old Testament than the New. His writings lack the note of warm, personal fellowship with Christ, and in his moral injunctions the Decalogue looms above the Sermon on the Mount. The place of Christ in Calvin's scheme of things is theological rather than personal and ethical.[8]

The same is true of the chapter on Calvin's theology and ethics in R. N. Hunt's *Calvin,* written two years later. He repeats Max Weber's judgment that both Luther and Calvin believed in "a double God": the gracious and loving God of the New Testament and "the autocratic deity of the old dispensation." With Luther, however, the God of the New Testament always prevailed. But with Calvin "the *deus absconditus* of the Old Testament was always in the foreground, for his scheme of redemption always had need of Him and could never be wholly brought into line with the teaching of the Gospel."[9]

On the continent this type of criticism was rarely heard after 1930, with the exception of the Lutheran historians cited earlier. But as late as 1943, the distinguished American scholar, Reinhold Niebuhr, was still charging that Calvin is guilty of biblicism in both theology and ethics, inclines toward legalism, thinks of sanctification as "a rigorous obedience to law," and has an ethical system which is "pretentious as well as obscurantist."[10]

Niebuhr's contemporary classic was an anachronism, however, as far as Calvin studies were concerned. For there had been a major shift in Calvin research in the 1930's, when a host of dissertations and studies concerning particular aspects of Calvin's theology appeared, many of them influenced by Karl Barth and Emil Brunner. Although these researches were characterized by a basic sympathy for Calvin's general position, they were sometimes marred by polemic interests. This was particularly true of the dispute about natural theology where Calvin was used to support the Brunnerian position by his student Gunter Gloede (*Theologia Naturalis bei Calvin,* 1935) and at the same time was claimed for the Barthian position by the brother of the great dogmatician, Peter Barth (*Das Problem der natürlichen Theologie bei Calvin,* 1935).

A major breakthrough came with the independent, exceedingly thorough work by Josef Bohatec, *Calvin und das Recht* (1934). Bohatec, however, is not a protagonist of any particular school of theology, although he is often sharply critical of the earlier studies of natural law and positive law by Troeltsch, Beyerhaus, and Lang. But Bohatec is primarily interested in the more general aspects of the question of law and its relation to civil law.[11] The first scholar in the modern period to recognize the christological nature of Calvin's concept of the law and its relationship to the covenant was Wilhelm Niesel. His *Die Theologie Calvins,* which first appeared in 1938, is a landmark in Calvin studies.[12] Most subsequent studies reflect his influence.

As a result, it is now possible to refer to Calvin as "a man of law"[13] without necessarily implying something ominous or opprobrious. It is being increasingly recognized—and in a constructive manner—that in order to understand the distinctiveness of Calvin's theology, one must see the role the law played in his thinking. Edward A. Dowey, for example, states that "Law is one of the basic concepts of Calvin's theology."[14]

Hence it is rather surprising that very few monographs or books have appeared in the last three decades which have dealt with this problem. François Wendel has a brief, balanced discussion of the law in his outstanding study of Calvin's thought,[15] and one or more aspects of Calvin's doctrine of the law are discussed in studies which are basically devoted to another subject.[16] But since the Second World War, only two books have been written about Calvin's concept of the law and both of these are limited to only one aspect of the problem. The one concerns the relationship between the Old and New Testaments, *Die Einheit des Bundes* (1958), by Hans H. Wolf. This is a rather brief and helpful study, but it concentrates on the nature of the covenant and thus only on the law as broadly conceived. The other work is the study by a Roman Catholic scholar, Jürgen Baur, *Gott, Recht und Weltliches Regiment im Werke Calvins* (1965). As the title indicates, the area of concern here is much the same as that of the works by Bohatec. Here again the chief questions dealt with are those of the relation between the righteousness of God and human justice, natural law, revealed law, and civil law, and the relation between church and state.

There are also a few fairly recent doctoral dissertations which deal with some aspect of Calvin's concept of the law. Three in particular are noteworthy: William C. Gentry, Jr.'s *A Study of John Calvin's Understanding of Moral Obligation and Moral Norms in Christian Ethics* (Southern Methodist University, 1970); Ralph R. Sundquist, Jr.'s *The Third Use of the Law in the Thought of John Calvin* (Columbia University, 1970); and Daniel Augsburger's *Calvin and the Mosaic Law* (University of Strasbourg, 1976). All three of these dissertations relate to the theme which is the particular concern of this study, viz., the third use of the law. But each one is more limited in its scope. Moreover they are not readily available to the scholarly world. Consequently, although many of the works cited make a distinctive and positive contribution to

Calvin's understanding of the law, a lacuna still exists. What is needed is a comprehensive treatment of this key issue. Toward that end the present study is offered.

NOTES

1. Friedrich Brunstad, *Theologie der lutherischen Bekenntnisschriften* (Gutersloh: C. Bertelsmann, 1951), 79, 80.

2. For documentation see especially two works which deal specifically with the questions of Calvin's personality and his activities in Geneva: Ernst Pfisterer, *Calvins Wirken in Genf* (Neukirchen Kreis Moers: Neukirchener Verlag, 1957); and Richard Stauffer, *The Humanness of John Calvin* (Nashville: Abingdon, 1971).

3. *Textbook of the History of Doctrines*, Vol. II (Grand Rapids: Baker Book House, 1952), 416.

4. *Jean Calvin les hommes et les choses de son temps* (Paris, 1899-1927).

5. *Lehrbuch der Dogmengeschichte* IV, 2, 5. Auflage (Basel: Benno Schwabe and Co., 1950), 560-566.

6. Ibid., 565, 613, 631.

7. Elfte Auflage (Tübingen: J.C.B. Mohr, 1950) p. 207. Karl Dietrich Schmidt refers to Calvin's "legal conception of Scripture which has become an earmark of Reformed Protestantism," *Grundriss der Kirchengeschichte*, 4. Auflage (Göttingen: Vandenhoeck und Ruprecht, 1953), 363.

8. Op. cit. (Nashville: Abingdon Press, 1958), 72. In a review of this paperback edition, the English Calvin scholar, T.H. L. Parker, complains that this book was out of date already at the time it appeared. It "starts out from the wrong premises, pursues an erring course and reaches largely mistaken conclusions . . . . It is a dismal hangover from the nineteenth century," *Scottish Journal of Theology*, Sept. 1961, 299.

9. (London: Centenary Press, 1933) 122.

10. *The Nature and Destiny of Man*, Vol. II (New York: Charles Scribner's Sons, 1947), 202, 203.

11. Cf. his later works: *Calvins Lehre von Staat und Kirche* (1936), and *Budé und Calvin* (1950).

12. The English translation, published in 1956, is unfortunately based on the first edition. In 1957, a revised edition appeared which contains some

significant modifications.
13. J. S. Whale, *The Protestant Tradition* (Cambridge: The University Press, 1955), 164.
14. *The Knowledge of God in Calvin's Theology* (New York: Columbia University Press, 1952), 222. In the final chapter of his book concerning the relation between the knowledge of God the Creator and the knowledge of God the Redeemer, Dowey uses the law as his chief illustration and comes to some very interesting conclusions which will be discussed in Chapter I.
15. *Calvin—Origins and Development of his Religious Thought* (New York: Harper and Row, 1963. Original, 1950).
16. In addition to the works cited already some of the more significant are: Erwin Mülhaupt, *Die Predigt Calvins* (1931); A. Göhler, *Calvins Lehre von der Heiligung* (1934); S. van der Linde, *De Leer van den Heiligen Geest bij Calvin* (1943); D. Wilhelm Kolfhaus, *Vom christlichen Leben nach Johannes Calvin* (1949); Fritz Büsser, *Calvins Urteil uber sich selbst* (1950); Ronald S. Wallace, *Calvin's Doctrine of the Word and Sacrament* (1953); and *Calvin's Doctrine of the Christian Life* (1959); Werner Krusche, *Das Wirken des Heiligen Geistes nach Calvin* (1957); Andre Biéler, *La Pensée Économique et Sociale de Calvin* (1959).

I

PROLEGOMENA

I. THE PLACE OF THE LAW IN CALVIN'S THEOLOGY

Some estimate of the role the law plays in Calvin's theology can be determined by where and in what manner he deals with the law in his writings. A mere perusal of the formal structure of the *Institutes* and his commentary on the Pentateuch reveals how greatly Calvin was concerned with this question. More important, such an examination offers important clues as to his method of interpreting the law.

A. *The Institutes*

It is significant that the basic treatment of the law in the final (1559) edition of the *Institutes* is found in Book II, which is about the knowledge of God the Redeemer. This was not the original pattern, for in the first edition of 1536, which contained only six chapters, the first chapter dealt with the law. This was followed by chapters on the creed (faith), the Lord's Prayer, the two evangelical sacraments, the false sacraments of the Catholic Church, and finally a chapter on Christian liberty (including the offices of the church and civil government). The opening sentence of chapter one is strikingly similar to the famous statement with which the final edition begins: "Nearly the whole of sacred doctrine consists in these two parts: the knowledge of God and of our ourselves."[1]

In the 1536 edition this reciprocal knowledge of God and humanity is not yet a major theme but is touched on only very briefly. Almost immediately Calvin begins discussing the law. First he considers its purpose, after which he gives a brief exposition of the decalog followed by a longer discourse on the meaning and the purpose of the law which he describes in a threefold manner: 1) the awakening of the knowledge of sin; 2) the restriction of the godless through fear of punishment; 3) its use for the Christian. Thus, already in the first edition Calvin taught the threefold use of the law (*triplex usus legis*).[2]

In all of the succeeding editions of the *Institutes*, however, the law is treated separately and follows the chapters on the knowledge of God and of ourselves. Although there is a remarkable consistency throughout the various editions of the *Institutes*—especially when one considers that the first edition, a slight compendium written by the 26-year-old Calvin, eventually became a tome of 80 chapters written when Calvin was 50—the 1539 edition represents a decisive break. This is particularly evident in the treatment of the law.

In the first edition, Calvin was still influenced considerably by Luther and followed closely the ordering of Luther's *Small Catechism*.[3] But in the second edition of 1539, Calvin comes into his own and shows a new mastery of his material. Here the theological significance of the place of the law in his theology is first discernible. The law is now related more closely to sin and redemption, thus anticipating the eventual placement in Book II of the final edition. In addition, an important chapter was added in the 1539 edition on the similarity and difference between the Old and New Testaments.

Wernle suggests two other ways in which Calvin develops his own position regarding the law in this second edition. He replaces the Lutheran exposition of the ten commandments with his own; and he stresses the unity of the Old Testament law with the spirit of the requirements of Jesus and that of the Mosaic law with Christian norms by "christianizing" the former and showing the origins of the latter in the Old Testament.[4]

If these facts were more widely known or were taken more seriously by those who are so quick to condemn Calvin as a legalist, much of the odium of this charge might have been eliminated. As Kolfhaus points out, "Treating the whole doctrine of the law under the title, 'Concerning God the Redeemer' . . . is completely Pauline and should prohibit, as P. Wernle says, attempts to dismiss his religion with the slogan 'law-religion'."[5] For Calvin in the *Institutes* develops his concept of the law within the framework of *Heilsgeschichte*. As we shall see later, he constantly warns his readers against separating the law from Jesus Christ (and the Holy Spirit) who is its substance, goal, and fulfillment.

Nevertheless, from one standpoint it is surprising that Calvin's chief treatment of the law is in Book II rather than in Book III of the *Institutes*, for he designated the third use of the law, the use as a norm and guide for the Christian, as the principal one. Consequently, one might expect the major treatment of the law to appear in the third Book, which deals with the application of the benefits of Christ by the believer in the context of the work of the Holy Spirit. But the law receives no separate treatment in Book III and is discussed only briefly in different contexts here, even though the essence of the law is love and its main requirement the obedience of faith, both characteristics of the life in the Spirit, which is the subject of this book.

One school of Calvin scholars, however, submits that the logical place for the treatment of the law, particularly the decalog, is in Book I, which deals with the knowledge of God the Creator. Since Calvin sometimes equates the moral law—which finds expression in the second table of the decalog—with the law of nature, the exposition of the decalog could possibly be envisioned in Book I.

One of the exponents of this viewpoint is E. A. Dowey, Jr., who maintains that the location of the analysis of the moral law and the decalog in Book II of the final edition of the *Institutes* is not a reliable index to Calvin's total evaluation of the law.[6] He warns against finding too much theological significance in the mere placement of any particular subject in the *Institutes*. Following Köstlin, he expresses dissatisfaction with the division of the 1559 edition into four books and asserts that "the really significant ordering principle of the Institutes in the 1559 edition is the duplex cognitio Domini, not the Apostles' Creed." Thus the *Institutes* is divided into two parts, not four: Book I on the revelation and knowledge of God the Creator, and Books II-IV on the revelation and knowledge of God the Redeemer.[7]

The merits or demerits of this thesis cannot be discussed here.[8] The way in which Dowey applies the law in relation to his thesis, however, does relate to our present theme. Having divided the *Institutes* into basically two rather than four books, he seeks for some concept which will relate the knowledge of God the Creator to that of God the Redeemer. He finds one possibility in the idea of the law, which "spans the two orders of the knowledge of God."[9] In order to support this thesis, Dowey proceeds to argue that the discussion of the moral law and the decalog in Book II is theologically misleading. "It is not the chief theological significance of the moral law or its content that determines

the placing of the decalog analysis in the *Institutes* of 1559 but rather
its accidental or historical link to the 'ceremonial supplements' . . . . The
content relates to God the Creator, the special act of giving it in this
form refers to the covenant . . . . Thus before 1559 the moral law does
not appear as a part of Calvin's soteriology . . . . "[10]

Dowey is correct in observing that the concept of law spans
the orders of creation and redemption. As we shall see later in this
chapter (Section II), the law did not originate with the revelation given
to Moses, for this was only a particular historical form of the law. And
as Calvin himself points out, the decalog is in a sense only a confirmation and clarification of the law of nature which has become obscured
by sin.[11] The law ultimately must be traced to God's orderly will in
creation.

Nevertheless, the "historical link" of the moral law (decalog)
and the Israelite cultus ("ceremonial supplements") is hardly "accidental" and is therefore not merely a formal relationship. The decalog is
not simply a collection of commands about how to live well, but is an
integral part of the covenant of grace which God concluded with his
chosen people Israel. Even Calvin recognized that some of these commands were not absolutely unique and had parallels in other legal
codes, but what gave them special significance and authority was their
incorporation into God's revelation on Sinai. The determining factor is
not so much their content as the context in which they were given. Not
the law as such but the Lawgiver, the Holy One, the Redeemer of Israel, was Calvin's concern.

There is no denying that for Calvin the content of the moral
law is essentially the same as that inscribed on the hearts of humans
"by nature." But Dowey, in reacting against some of the Barthian-
inspired Calvin research which passed over this fact too quickly, tends
to overestimate the significance of this correspondence and thus under-
plays the fact that in the decalog the moral law is radically reoriented
and thus put in an entirely new perspective. Now the law no longer
merely gives a dim apprehension of right and wrong and a sense of obligation toward God. As the law of the covenant, the response which it
calls for is sincere worship and grateful service, and a love which is a
spontaneous response to the redemptive love of God. The righteousness
which the revealed law requires points to Christ himself, the end of the
law. In a specific reference to the ten commandments, Calvin makes it
clear that Christ is the end of the law (Romans 10:4) and that the Spirit

gives life to the letter which by itself is lethal (II Corinthians 3: 6ff., 17). We will misunderstand and misuse the law if we fail to see that it was "clothed (*vestita*) with the covenant of free adoption."[12]

Consequently, it would appear that the treatment of the law in Book II of the *Institutes* is a factor of considerable importance. As suggested earlier, this precludes on the one hand a legalistic understanding of the law and on the other a one-sided "naturalistic" interpretation of the law. Positively expressed, this concentration on the law within the discussion of the work of God the Redeemer points to one of Calvin's themes, namely, that Jesus Christ is the substance and soul of the law.

This becomes apparent already in some of the chapter headings of Book II, which is divided into three parts: 1. the sin and corruption of humanity (chapters 1-5); 2. the revelation of the Mediator to the people of the old covenant (chapters 6-11); 3. the incarnation of the redeemer and his saving work on earth (chapters 6-11). The chapter titles of chapters 6-11, in which the discussion of the law occurs, are especially suggestive. Chapter six, for example, has the title, "Fallen man ought to seek redemption in Christ." The actual content of this chapter, however, is the reality of Christ in the Old Testament, i.e., under the law, and the Old Testament witness to Christ. The theme of chapter seven is "The law was given, not to restrain the people of the old covenant under itself, but to foster the hope of salvation in Christ until his coming." Chapter eight is simply, "An exposition of the moral law," but the title of the ninth chapter is again of special interest: "Christ, although he was known to the Jews under the law, was at length clearly revealed only in the gospel." The similarity and differences between the Old and New Testaments are then taken up in chapters ten and eleven.

By these chapter headings we can see that the moral law or decalog is viewed from the perspective of the Mosaic covenant and the revelation given to Israel, and this in turn within the wider context of the history of salvation. This is expressed succinctly in the superscription for the whole of Book II: "The knowledge of God the Redeemer in Christ, first disclosed to the fathers under the law, and then to us in the gospel." Calvin is thus concerned in Book II—especially in chapters 6-11—with the question of law and gospel. However, in contrast to the usual Lutheran understanding of law and gospel, for Calvin these two terms do not first of all connote two kinds of righteousness or ways of salvation–that of works and that of grace—but rather two modes of God's redemptive activity or *Heilsgeschichte*. Calvin also recognizes the narrower meaning of these terms and gives due attention to the Pauline antithesis of law and gospel, as we shall see later. But he is concerned first of all about the nature and unity of revelation. Consequently, in Book II the law is discussed as a form of God's economy of salvation under the old dispensation.

It should not be overlooked, however, that certain aspects of the law are discussed elsewhere in the *Institutes*. The second commandment also receives attention in chapters 11 and 12 of Book I; and even in the first five chapters, where Calvin has not yet come to the revelation of God in Scripture, he introduces the law at several crucial points.[13]

In Book IV, the law often enters into the discussion of the sacraments, especially where the sacraments of the New Testament are contrasted with those of the Old.[14] In the last chapter of Book IV, which deals with civil government, the second use of the law (*usus politicus*) is presupposed, although its formal treatment is found in Book II. Nevertheless, three important sections (14-16) in this chapter are concerned with the relation of natural, ceremonial, and moral law to civil laws.

At this juncture it is good to recall Dowey's point that the formal structure of the *Institutes* does not necessarily provide the best index to the theological significance of the law. This is particularly true in reference to Book III. Granted, one chapter deals directly with the law, namely, chapter 17: "The agreement of the promises of the law and of the gospel." But apart from this, there is no formal discussion of the law in Book III, even though much of this Book deals with the Christian life. There are numerous allusions to the law,[15] some of which are very significant, but this in no way indicates the significance of Book III in relation to Calvin's concept of the law. For as Paul Jacobs has pointed out, "The discussion of the doctrine of sanctification, the so-called ethic of Calvin (which is one of the main themes of Book III), is the expansion (*Entfaltung*) of the doctrine of the *tertius usus legis*."[16]

Calvin indicates as much himself, for he begins both chapters six and seven about the Christian life with references to the law. What is particularly noteworthy, however, is that in both cases he suggests that the law, even though it "contains in itself the newness by which his image may be restored in us"[17] and "provides the finest and best disposed method of ordering a man's life (*constituendae vitae*),"[18] can profitably be supplemented with other passages of Scripture. In short, Calvin bases the Christian life on the foundation (*fundamentum*) of Christ who "has been set before us as an example whose pattern (*forma*) we ought to express in our life."[19] The "more explicit plan" by which God wishes to shape his people therefore is found in such passages as Romans 12:1, 2: "I appeal to you therefore, brethren, by the mercies of God, to present your bodies as a living sacrifice . . . . Do not be conformed to this world but be transformed by the renewal of your mind . . . ."[20] This is how the "legalistic" Calvin develops the third use of the law![21] Moreover, here we have the basis, motive, and goal of the Christian life.

B. *The Catechisms*

This function of the law can be seen more clearly in the structure of Calvin's two Catechisms than in the *Institutes*. The earlier catechism of 1537, *Instruction in Faith,* appeared only a year later than the first edition of the *Institutes*, but already the structure of the later editions of the *Institutes* is presaged in several ways.[22] Sections 1-3—"All men are born in order to know God," "What difference there is between true and false religion," and "What we must know of God"— correspond to Book I of the 1559 *Institutes*. Sections 4-11 correspond to Book II. Here Calvin discusses the fall of humanity and the doctrine of sin. In section seven he introduces the law for the first time: "How we are delivered and restored to life." Here the accent is on the first use of the law, the *usus elenchticus*, whereby the law "exercises (*exerce*) us in . . . the knowledge of our sin and a consequent fear of the Lord."[23] The exposition of the decalog follows in the next section. The next three sections (9-11) also deal with the law, after which follows the discussion of faith. The transition is provided by section 11, "The law is a preparation to come to Christ." Sections 12 ff. describe various aspects of faith and correspond to Book III of the *Institutes*.

In section 17, however, Calvin returns to the law and relates it to sanctification. The title reads: "We are sanctified through faith in order to obey the law." In the *Institutes*, as we have seen, this is alluded to in Book III, but the formal explanation of the third use of the law comes in Book II, because this is where he discusses the three uses of the law.

The Geneva Catechism (French edition, 1542; Latin, 1545), like the final edition of the *Institutes*, represents a decisive change in structure, for it too is divided into four parts. But here the correspondence ceases, for in the 1559 *Institutes* the four parts correspond to the four parts of the Apostles' Creed. In the Geneva Catechism, the whole Creed is subjoined under one major division, namely, faith. This is the first part. The second concerns the law, after which Calvin takes up prayer and the sacraments.

Karl Barth, in his commentary on this Catechism, suggests that these four parts of the Catechism are in effect the content of the answer to question seven: "What is the right way of honoring God?" For Calvin answers the question thus: "To put all our *trust* in him; to study to serve him all our life by *obeying* his will; to *call upon* him . . . and lastly, to *acknowledge* him with both heart and mouth to be the author of all good things."[24] Barth concludes that the four parts given in this answer correspond to the four parts of the Catechism and constitute its foundation, namely, 1. trust (faith), 2. obedience (law), 3. request (prayer), and 4. praise (sacraments).[25]

Thus the structure of the Geneva Catechism expresses a more characteristic emphasis than the 1559 *Institutes*, for here the third use of the law is more prominent. In the *Institutes*, judged only by its formal structure, one might conclude that the second use was the principal one. But in the Geneva Catechism the accent is on the role the law is to play in the life of the believer.

Calvin's transition in this Catechism from the section on faith to that of the law is especially interesting because it reveals in capsule form the essence of his thinking about the law in relation to his theology as a whole. Moreover, in this transition are woven together many of the key elements which form the mosaic against which Calvin's concept of the law should be viewed. He concludes his discussion of faith by saying that the whole doctrine of the gospel is comprehended in two points: faith and repentance. Then the question, "What is repentance?" Answer: "Dissatisfaction with and hatred of sin, and love of righteousness, arising out of the fear of God; for these two things lead us to denial of self and the mortification of the flesh, so that we yield ourselves to be ruled by the Spirit of God, and bring all the actions of our life into obedience to the divine will."[26]

This is ostensibly a description of "the whole doctrine of the *gospel*," but this could just as well apply to the law, for Calvin usually explains the law in the framework of one or more of these concepts, i.e., hatred of sin, love of righteousness, the fear of God, self-mortification, being ruled by the Holy Spirit, and obedience to the will of God. A key notion, however, is that of a rule or norm (*regula* or *norma*). For Calvin conceives of the law primarily as a rule, and it is precisely this concept which occurs next in this transition from faith to the law. In the next to last question in the section of faith Calvin states that "the true rule for worshipping God is to obey his will." In the first question in the section on the law Calvin asks, "What rule of life has he given to us?" Answer: "His law."[27] In Part III of this chapter we shall see how this idea of a "rule" is one of the key expressions in Calvin's thinking about the idea of law.

C. *The Commentaries*

Normally we would not expect to discover any guidelines in something so unsystematic as a commentary; yet even here a valuable clue is provided. For Calvin did something rather unique—he arranged the last four books of Moses in a harmony and wrote a great commentary based on it.[28] This is remarkable enough, but the important thing to observe is the manner in which he organized his material.

In the preface to this Harmony Calvin explains that these four books contain two different types of material: historical narrative and doctrine or teaching (*doctrina*). In the former we have reflected, "as in a bright mirror, the incomparable power as well as the boundless mercy of God in raising up, and, as it were, giving birth (*gigenda*) to his church." In the doctrinal parts of these four books we are taught how "the church is instructed in true piety (including faith and prayer) as well as in the fear and worship of God; and thus the rule of a just and holy life is laid down, and individuals are exhorted to perform their various duties."[29]

Calvin divides the "doctrine" further into four major divisions: 1. a preface which contains various commendations of the dignity and authority of the law by Moses; 2. the *ten commandments* "in which God has comprehended briefly, indeed, completely, the rule of a just and holy life (*pie iusteque vivendi regulam*); yet not so as to separate

them from those scattered interpretations which the Lawgiver added";
3. the third division (*caput*) of doctrine consisting of *supplements* (*appendices*) which include ceremonial and judicial laws; 4. the end and use of the law, which Calvin describes here particularly in terms of *usus elenchticus*. "When God allures us so gently and kindly (*tam blande et suavitur*) by his promises, and then follows with the thunders of his curse, it is partly to render us inexcusable and partly to shut us up, deprived of all confidence in our own righteousness, so that we may flee to Christ who is the end of the law."[30]

The most distinctive feature of the Harmony, however, consists in the way everything except the historical narratives, which are combined in a separate section, is subsumed under an exposition of the decalog. All of the minute regulations, ordinances, ceremonies, and moral precepts found in Exodus-Deuteronomy are—whenever possible—attached to one of the ten commandments! Those of a more general nature are used either in the preface or appendix (which deals with the promises and threats) to this exposition of the decalog.

In some ways this is a greater monument to Calvin's systematizing genius than the *Institutes*. For to comprehend almost all of the legislation and detail of the Pentateuch within the framework of the decalog must have been a formidable challenge even for the genius of Calvin. However, some have found this effort more a cause for reproach than for admiration, suggesting that Calvin was not content to abide by the God-given order.[31] But such a criticism is captious and fails to understand Calvin's motive in attempting this Harmony.

Calvin was aware of the fact that he was exposing himself to criticism by making this rather novel attempt. No one would be more sensitive than he to the criticism that he had (in his own words) "inconsiderately and therefore unnecessarily altered the order which the Holy Spirit himself has prescribed to us." He explains further, "What Moses delivered in four books I have so attempted to collect and arrange that at first sight, and prior to a complete examination of the subject, it might seem that I was trying to improve upon it, which would be an audacious sacrilege." Fully conscious of all these hazards, Calvin, motivated by a pedagogical concern, nevertheless proceeded. "My purpose," he explains, "has been none other than this, namely, to provide some guidance for those readers who are insufficiently trained in order that they may meditate upon (*versentur*) the books of Moses more easily, conveniently and profitably."[32]

More important, from a theological standpoint, is the presupposition underlying and making possible this Harmony. We have already noted that Calvin subsumes almost all regulations, laws, and ceremonies under one of the ten commandments. This was possible for him—though not always easy[33]—because of his firm conviction that the decalog contains a perfect and complete rule for all true worship (the first table of the law) and justice and morality (the second table). This "spiritual worship . . . consists of faith, repentance (*poenitentia*), calling upon God (*Dei invocatio*), and praises which demonstrate our gratitude, yea even bearing the cross." From this spiritual worship follows "the promotion of justice towards men."[34]

For Calvin, the fundamental principles of revealed religion are contained in the Pentateuch, and the core of the Pentateuch is the decalog. In the ten commandments—or "ten words" as Calvin, following Hebrew tradition, puts it[35]—are found everything that we need for a rule for living well and uprightly. Hence all other laws, particularly the supplements (*appendices*) and political and judicial regulations, are only aids (*adminicula*) in the observance of the law and have no value when separated from the ten commandments. "Hence the wisdom of joining each precept to its proper commandment so that the law may be arranged as a whole."[36]

This relating the bulk of the Pentateuch to the ten commandments may appear to be a severe restriction, but we must keep in mind that Calvin never views the decalog in abstraction but always in the light of the fuller revelation given in Jesus Christ. Moreover, Calvin concludes his exposition of the ten commandments in the Harmony with a special section on "the sum of the law." He collates such passages as Deuteronomy 6:5, 10:12, 13; and Leviticus 19:18, and notes that Christ declares that ultimately nothing is required of us by the law except love: love of God and love of neighbor. Therefore, it can be said that Calvin's high esteem for the law, as summarized in the two tables of the decalog, is nothing other than an attempt to give meaning and content to that which lies at the heart of the Christian ethic, namely, love.

D. *The Liturgy*

In concluding this section, it is of interest to note how Calvin uses the law in his Strasbourg Liturgy. When Calvin came to Strasbourg in 1538, having been banished from Geneva, he became the minister of a small group of French exiles. He adopted the German liturgy of Bucer and had it translated into French. He made a few minor changes, however, one of which was to introduce the singing of the decalog in meter. Calvin was not the first to have done this, for in Bucer's description of the worship at Strasbourg between 1526 and 1539, he explains that after the confession of sins, the absolution, the singing of some psalms or hymns and a New Testament Lesson, "then the congregation sing again, this time the Ten Commandments, or something else."[37]

Nevertheless, in Bucer's German Liturgy of 1537, which Calvin copied, the decalog was not included. It is significant that in Calvin's liturgy the decalog is sung, not recited, and that it is introduced after the confession of sins and absolution, thus stressing the third use. This is brought out again in the fact that the two tables were divided by a short collect for grace to keep God's law. In his Genevan liturgy this practice, along with several others, disappeared, but this was due to "the extreme opinions that prevailed there among the magistry," not to a change of mind by Calvin. Consequently, "we may take the Strasbourg rites as being a better indication of Calvin's own."[38]

This survey of the place of the law in Calvin's systematic, catechetical, exegetical, and liturgical works provides us with a provisional indication of the importance and function of the law in his thought and practice. On the other hand, it has become apparent in the scattered references from Calvin's works that his use of the word law varies considerably depending on the context of the reference. Consequently, an introductory sketch concerning the variegated meanings of the law in Calvin's theology may prove helpful before beginning the main investigation. Prior to that, however, it is necessary to examine the implications of a passing reference in the Geneva Catechism, already noted, to obeying the will of God. For here Calvin substitutes "will" for "law," thus implying that the law, being an expression of the will of God, finds its origin or ground in that will.

II. THE ULTIMATE NORM: THE WILL OF GOD

The law of God is revealed to us in various ways and in various forms. Hence we can speak of natural, moral, ceremonial, and civil or positive law. But all of these forms are only variants of God's orderly will for humanity. Calvin places special emphasis on the moral law because of its permanent significance. This law, in its specially revealed form, has been mediated to us through Israel. As such it is linked to the old dispensation which has been superseded by the coming of Christ and the gospel.

The law, however, is not a passing phenomenon to be identified with a temporal aspect of the religion of Israel. Nor is it an afterthought on the part of God in view of the rebellion of humanity. Rather, for Calvin, the law is something primary, basic, and permanent in the wisdom and plan of God. More specifically, Calvin sees in the law a direct revelation and expression of the eternal will of God. The will of God is the origin and foundation of the law. Hence to regard the law lightly is to refuse to take God seriously.

A. *The Law as an Expression of God's Will*

In one of his earliest writings, the correlation of the law with the will of God is stated succinctly: "In the law of God a perfect rule (*reigle*) of all righteousness is presented to us which with good reason can be called the eternal will of God."[39] Similarly, in the final edition of the *Institutes:* "The precepts of the law . . . comprehend the will of God."[40] "God has revealed his will in the law."[41] Not that God's will is exhausted in the revelation of the law; but "the Lord, in giving us the rule of perfect righteousness, has referred all parts of it to his own will."[42]

The commentaries abound with similar statements. The important thing to note here is the certainty, clarity, and familiarity with which God's will is made known to us through the law. Concerning Deuteronomy 29:29 Calvin comments: "Moses exhorts us to embrace the doctrine of the law, in which God's will is declared to us, as if he were openly speaking to us."[43] In the "book of the law" are found "the oracles of heaven, that is, the declaration of the will of God."[44] And this will "is first made known (*monstratur*) to us in the law."[45]

One of the chief advantages we derive from the law is that "God reveals himself to us in the law and declares what kind of God he wishes to be toward us (*qualis erga nos esse velit*), lays down what he demands from us, and, in short, everything necesasary to be known."[46] For in the law God has delineated his own character;[47] here his will is, so to speak, "set before our face."[48] The Apostle Paul, even when arguing against the Jews' misuse and misunderstanding of the law, "concedes to them the knowledge of the divine will . . . which they had attained from the teaching of the law."[49] This is why deviation from the law is such a serious offence. For to depart from the law is to depart from the will of God, i.e., from the Lord himself.[50]

This relating of the law to the will of God as its origin and foundation is in itself neither unusual nor peculiarly Calvinistic.[51] Nevertheless, whenever emphasis is laid on the primacy of the will in the doctrine of God, there is frequently the suspicion of the alleged nominalist notion of an unconditioned, arbitrary will.[52] Since Calvin's doctrine of God and the divine will is often identified with that of two of the leading nominalist theologians, Duns Scotus and William of Occam, this question has a direct bearing on his concept of the law.

B. *God's Will Arbitrary?*

Those who accuse Calvin of having been overly influenced by the nominalist notion of the priority of God's will interpret Scotus and Occam as teaching that God's sovereign will alone determines what is good. Seeberg maintains that with these nominalists God is almost identified with free will which he exercises arbitrarily as omnipotent power. Laws are just and good not because of their intrinsic moral quality and worth, but simply because God has arbitrarily so decreed.

Duns Scotus, for example, taught that natural law depends wholly on the will of God and not, as Thomas Aquinas taught, on his mind, and that it is therefore not absolutely immutable. Since God is sheer free will, no reason can be found for his willing or not willing, since all willing is without ground or reason. Occam was more extreme in promulgating this Scotist emphasis. He maintained that God did not will things because they were good, but that they were good because God willed them. "Nothing is of itself good or evil, the free will of God being the sovereign arbiter of what is so."[53] This God, this irresponsible almighty will, whose mere whim, as it seemed, had arbitrarily determined what should be counted good or evil had also arbitrarily decreed certain means of salvation and just as arbitrarily predestined some to be saved and others not.[54]

Both Luther and Calvin were influenced by these nominalist theologians and their disciples, Luther even more directly than Calvin since one of his mentors was the last great nominalist theologian, Gabriel Biel.[55] But at the Collège de Montaigu in Paris the young Calvin was also introduced to the thought of the leading nominalist theologians. While this does not mean that he was uncritical of this philosophy, it is safe to state that "these (nominalist) views in a modified form constitute part of the furniture of Calvin's mind."[56] Karl Reuter, the German Calvin scholar, concludes on a similar note: "Calvin has gained a reformed knowledge of salvation, but his doctrine of God exhibits displays of nominalistic disturbances (*Störungen*).[57] However, to draw the following conclusion is another matter! According to Hunter, for Calvin

> the sovereign will of God was governed by no considerations but its good pleasure. He found refuge in these principles from difficulties which frequently confronted him in his exposition of Scripture. If it plainly laid the responsibility upon God for acts that were offensive to our moral sense, he fell back upon the postulate that that is good which God wills to be so. Just as he could have made a man an ass or a dog (*Inst.* III.22.1) and might have given any property to the stars, so his good pleasure was limited neither by physical laws nor even on occasion by moral.[58]

Hunter here is only echoing in a more cautious form the allegation of Albrecht Ritschl that Calvin, after the manner of the Scotists, reduced God to the bare notion of arbitrary will, without ethical content. This was repeated by Seeberg, Williston Walker, and others.[59] There is no denying that Calvin makes certain statements that resemble those of Scotus in particular, but it does not necessarily follow that their presuppositions are the same. Moreover, recent research has shown that many of these charges are based on a misunderstanding of what Scotus actually taught. For example, it is not true to say that he identified God's absolute power with the purely arbitrary.[60] Nor should we assume that anything which can be shown to have some affinity to nominalism is therefore ipso facto to be condemned as false!

Calvin, it is true, does not hesitate to affirm that God is a law unto himself, is above all laws, and is bound by no laws. In defense of his doctrine of predestination, for example, Calvin argues that "it is very wicked merely to investigate the causes of God's will. For his will is, and rightly ought to be, the cause of all things that are . . . . For

God's will is so much the highest rule of righteousness that whatever he wills, by the very fact that he wills it, must be considered righteous. When, therefore, one asks why God has so done, we must reply: because he has willed it."[61] Likewise in his commentary on Exodus 33:19: "God's will is superior to all causes, so as to be the reason of reasons, the law of laws and the rule of rules."[62]

Thus far Calvin is unquestionably closer to the nominalist approach to God and ethics than to Thomism. However, in order to do justice to Calvin, it is necessary to note the context of remarks like the above and the cautionary statements which often follow such seemingly "voluntaristic" passages. For example, shortly after asserting that "There is no need of weighing the judgment of God by ordinary rules"—which might be taken as the basis for an arbitrary ethics— Calvin cautions, "Nevertheless I do not suppose him to be without law (*ex lex*); for although his power is above all laws, still because his will is the most certain rule of perfect equity, whatever he does must be perfectly right; and therefore he is free from laws (*legibus solutus*) because he is a law to himself and to all."[63]

Again it would be easy to misinterpret Calvin and take freedom from all human conventions and laws to mean lawlessness. But what Calvin is fighting for here is the freedom of God. This is why he insists that "we must not suppose the existence of any superior law which binds God (*Deum adstringit*); he is a law to himself and his will is the rule of all justice." But Calvin hastens to add that "God does not reign as a tyrant over the world. In the perfection of his equity he may perform some things which seem to us absurd, but this is only because our minds cannot ascend high enough to embrace a reason only partially apparent and almost entirely hidden and incomprehensible in the judgments of God."[64] Consequently, when we cannot fathom God's ways, we should suspend our limited judgments, refrain from murmuring and recognize that God alone is the Judge who is far above us.[65]

Calvin concedes that this freedom of God, though always consistent with his character, allows him to modify or temporarily suspend his own laws or normal mode of operation. "God is a law to himself (*eum sibi esse legem*) .... He has not bound himself by an inflexible rule so as not to be free, if it so pleases him, to depart from the law." Again, however, this does not imply a groundless arbitrariness in God's actions. "He would have us acquiesce in his own admirable wisdom, which is the fountain from which all laws proceed."[66] Thus, while God is not determined in any of his actions by anything lying outside of himself, he does act by virtue of an inner necessity in accord with his own nature. And by nature he tends towards mercy and generosity.

Consequently, under the old covenant God purposely deviated from his own law occasionally because of the hardness of heart or intractability of his chosen people. The result was a leniency and clemency which they never could have experienced had God acted impartially according to his law.[67] God exercises his freedom for our good. Another illustration of this is when he "departs from his own law and turns to mercy" in order to "approve our imperfect works."[68]

Calvin not only often safeguards himself against the charge of a capricious God whose absolute power (*potentia absoluta*) knows no bounds; he specifically repudiates this idea. In the same section in the *Institutes* where he says that "Whatever God wills, by the very fact that he wills it, must be considered righteous," he later states flatly: "And we do not advocate the fiction of 'absolute might' (*absoluta potentia*); because this is profane, it ought rightly to be hateful (*detestabile*) to us. We fancy no lawless god (*non Deum exlegem*) who is a law unto himself . . . . But the will of God is not only free of all fault but is the highest rule of perfection, and even the law of all laws."[69] "This invention which the Schoolmen have introduced about the absolute power of God is shocking blasphemy! It is the same as if they said that God is a tyrant who resolves to do what he pleases, not by justice, but through caprice (*pro libidine*)."[70]

Calvin finds this doctrine of an arbitrary absolute might a "shocking" and "diabolical blasphemy" because he is convinced that "it is easier to dissever the light of the sun from its heat, or for that matter its heat from fire, than to separate God's power from his righteousness." Moreover, he also rejects the "monstrous speculations" of those papal theologians who suggest that

> God should be able to do more than is proper to him or to act without rule or reason . . . . For to make God beyond law is to rob him of the greatest part of his glory, for it destroys his rectitude and his righteousness. Not that God is subject to law, except inso far as he himself is law. For such is the agreement between his power and his righteousness, that nothing proceeds from him that is not considered, legitimate and regular . . . . His power . . . is tempered with righteousness and equity.[71]

The last two sentences in the above quotation also negate the claim that Calvin substantially held the Scotist view of a divine will that could operate amorally even though he explicitly rejected the nominalistic formula *ex lex*.[72] Calvin refuses to subject or limit God in any way to some higher order or necessity—and he certainly will not have God judged by ordinary human canons of what is just and right. But this does not mean that God's power is arbitrary or his will independent of his attributes of holiness and righteousness. "Nothing can be more preposterous than to imagine that there is in God a power so supreme and absolute (as it is called) that it deprives him of his righteousness."[73] Calvin therefore unites the power, equity and mercy (*clementia*) of God,[74] and declares that his "power ought to be joined with his gracious purpose (*potentia cum beneplacito*)."[75] Consequently, although God's will is the ultimate norm for our behavior, this will is constant and expresses the very heart and character of God. The reason "God is not answerable to law" is not because he "delights in uncontrollable power" but "rather because in the perfection of his infinite justice there is no need for law."[76] Hence there is nothing capricious in the law which expresses God's will, for the author is just, holy, and good and is true to himself. God, being infinitely kind, wise, and righteous, is incapable of evil. "God's goodness is so connected with his divinity that it is no more necessary for him to be God than for him to be good."[77] Thus there can be no dichotomy between God's power and his attributes. The sovereign Lord is free, but he always acts in accordance with his own character.[78]

C. *The Character of God*

However, even if it is conceded that God, according to Calvin, is consistent with his character, this raises the further problem of "the 'so-called' God of Calvin." This God, according to popular legend, is the God of the Old Testament, a stern, all-powerful Judge and Lawgiver who is inscrutable, unapproachable, and "utterly remote from sinful humanity."[79] If this is indeed Calvin's picture of God, his doctrine of the law will inevitably bear this imprint, for the law, being an expression of the will of God, necessarily reflects his character.

The nature of this study precludes any exhaustive study of Calvin's concept of God,[80] but a brief analysis should suffice to show

how inaccurate the old image is.[81] One of the difficulties in any such attempt, however, is that unlike most dogmatics, the *Institutes* does not provide us with a self-contained systematic exposition of the doctrine of God. This may seem strange, but it is entirely consistent with Calvin's purpose in writing the *Institutes,* which was not so much dogmatic as practical and edifying.[82] He hated "frigid speculation" and consequently devotes only one chapter (I.13, concerning the Trinity) to the doctrine of God. There is no formal discussion of the nature and attributes of God in this classic Protestant *Summa!*[83] Instead, Calvin concentrates on the more existential question of the *knowledge* of God the Creator and Redeemer.

Where much older Calvin research went astray was in assuming that the doctrine of predestination (or the sovereignty of God) was the central doctrine in Calvin's theology.[84] Calvin's doctrine of God was then deduced from references to God's will and decrees in the *Institutes* which dealt with predestination.[85] A more correct procedure would be to evaluate Calvin's doctrine of predestination in the light of his doctrine of God. The two are of course closely related, but Calvin's concept of God—or the law—should not be prejudged by one's evaluation of his doctrine of predestination.[86]

In the *Institutes* the real locus of Calvin's discussion of the nature of God and his attributes is in his discussion of faith in Book III rather than in Book I.[87] Nevertheless, because Calvin does distinguish between the knowledge of God the Creator and God the Redeemer, we should first examine some of the scattered references in Book I concerning the character of God.

1. God the Creator

In keeping with his general purpose, Calvin warns several times against speculation about God's essence (*essentia*) and divinity (*numen*).[88] His concern is not with what God is in himself but in his relationship toward us (*erga nos*). When he speaks of God's nature and attributes, it should be noted that even in Book I Calvin does not stress the sovereignty, majesty, and glory of God as exclusively and coldly as we have been led to believe. To be sure, he would never have us forget that God is the Holy One who cannot tolerate evil. Because the pious mind sees God to be "a righteous judge, armed with severity to punish wickedness, it ever holds his judgment seat before its gaze, and through fear of him restrains itself from provoking his anger."[89]

But this type of emphasis is not the primary one, even in the discussion of God the Creator, where we would expect to hear particularly about God's power and majesty. Rather, the accent is on God's goodness and grace. Contemplation of God's gifts should lead us back to God, the infinite source of all blessings.[90] Moreover, this recognition should move us to reverence and love him, since he alone is the author of all blessings. Hence our complete happiness is to be found in God.[91]

This knowledge and happiness, however, is contingent upon our being content with God's self-revelation. According to this self-revelation, God is represented as our guide and protector, the author of every good, the one who is kind and merciful. Therefore, we can repose in God with perfect trust and have no doubt that in his loving-kindness we will find a remedy for all our ills. For this reason we should be motivated to fear, reverence, and love God as father and honor and worship him as Lord.[92] Because he is this kind of God "the final goal of the blessed life (*ultimus beatae vitae finis*)" rests in the knowledge of him.[93]

God's glory, wisdom, power, and eternity are manifest in the world and in its maintenance as well as in the structure of the human body.[94] In his providential administration of society we see him as kindly (*beneficus*) and beneficent (*benignus*) toward all, although his clemency is particularly manifest toward the godly and his severity toward the wicked.[95]

We will not be attracted to God and motivated to serve him unless we have experienced his paternal love.[96] But the revelation of God the Creator in the world, in history, and in the being and experience of humanity, though clear and unmistakable, does not suffice, due to the darkness of our sinful minds. At best, human beings, apart from the revelation of Christ, have only a vague, uncertain conception of divinity (*intelligentia numinis*) and an awareness of the Divine (*sensus divinitatis*).[97] However, such a so-called knowledge of God, which is merely a vague and erroneous notion of divinity, is actually ignorance of God.[98] The net result of such "knowledge" is pride and ingratitude,[99] false religions, and gross idolatry.[100] In the light of the clear revelation of God in his works, our perverse ignorance and rebellion lead to only one conclusion . . . inexcusable![101] The charge, "without excuse," is written large over all of human existence. The fault is entirely our own, for the Lord has sought with the most zealous and manifold kindness (*plurima et varia benignitate*) to draw us sweetly (*suavitur*) to a knowledge of himself.[102] This is essentially the picture of God that emerges from the first five chapters of the *Institutes*, where Calvin has not yet come to the discussion of Scripture. Elsewhere in Book I, particularly in the chapters dealing with idolatry, he has occasion to refer to God's eternity, wisdom, power, and righteousness.[103] The most important discussion of the attributes of God occurs in this connection. In a brief depiction of the scriptural doctrine of God the Creator, Calvin indicates what godly minds should particularly look for in Scripture concerning God. But again he reminds his readers that he has not yet come to the covenant of grace and Christ the Mediator. Hence he abstains temporarily from citing any New Testament passages. "At present," he says, "let it be enough to grasp how God, the Maker of heaven and earth, governs the universe founded by him. Indeed, both his fatherly goodness and his beneficently inclined will (*voluntas ad beneficentiam proclivis*) are repeatedly extolled; and examples of his severity are given, which show him to be the righteous avenger of evil deeds, especially where his forbearance toward the obstinate is of no effect."[104]

Calvin then chooses a few select passages from the Old Testament in which God's "true appearance is exhibited . . . as in an image." Considering how many possibilities were available to Calvin, his particular choice is highly significant. His key text is Exodus 34:6, 7, where the mercy, grace, patience, compassion, and faithfulness of God are extolled.[105] Calvin also appeals to Psalm 145, in which "the sum of all his powers (*virtutes*)" is set forth. Here we read not only of the majesty and greatness of God but also of his abundant goodness and paternal care, plus the same attributes found in Exodus 34:6, 7, namely, that "the Lord is gracious and merciful, slow to anger and abounding in steadfast love . . . ."[106]

In Jeremiah 9:24 Calvin finds a less complete but very adequate dsecription of God: "I am the Lord who exercises mercy, judgment and justice in the earth." It is essential for us to know these three things, says Calvin: "mercy, on which alone the salvation of all of us rests; judgment, which is daily exercised against wrongdoers, and in even greater severity awaits them to their everlasting ruin; justice, whereby believers are preserved, and are most tenderly nourished." He hastens to add that God's truth, power, holiness, and goodness are not overlooked here, and in conclusion points to Psalm 25:8-10.[107]

This is Calvin's concept of God the Creator! How far it differs

from the popular caricature of "the God of Calvin" is self-evident. Yet
it is in the knowledge of God the Redeemer that we really see the heart
of God. To pass from death to life, we must by faith know God not only
as our Creator but also as our Redeemer. Such knowledge is obtained
only in the Mediator as he is known through the Word;[108] for there can
be no saving knowledge of God apart from Christ.[109]

2. God the Redeemer

Consequently, we must turn to chapter two of Book III of the
Institutes, where Calvin discusses faith. We are not thereby leaving the
category of knowledge under which Calvin treats the doctrine of God in
the first two books of the *Institutes*. For "faith rests not on ignorance,
but on knowledge. And this is, indeed, knowledge not only of God but
of the divine will."[110] Note that in considering faith, Calvin would also
have us keep in mind the divine will.

Here again the essentially personal, practical, and religious nature of Calvin's theology is prominent. He spurns speculation,especially
concerning the nature of God. "In understanding faith, it is not merely a
question of knowing that God exists, but also—and this especially—of
knowing what is his will toward us (*erga nos*). For it is not so much our
concern to know who he is in himself (*quis in se sit*), as what (*qualis*)
he wills to be toward us. [111] Faith is then defined as "a firm and certain
knowledge of God's benevolence toward us, founded upon the truth of
the freely given promise in Christ, both revealed to our minds and
sealed upon our hearts through the Holy Spirit."[112] The knowledge of
faith is received through the Word of God. For faith, however, it is not
enough to know the Word in general. Calvin is concerned that faith
may find in the divine Word something specific upon which to place its
dependence and confidence. Faith is not produced by every part of the
Word of God, for the warnings, admonitions and threatened judgments
will not instill the confidence and peace requisite for true faith. Nor can
faith find a firm basis in only a general knowledge of God. Faith must
pierce to the very heart and nature of God.

> But what if we were to substitute his benevolence or mercy in
> place of his will, the things of which are often sad and the procla-
> mation frightening? Thus, surely, we shall more closely approach
> the nature of faith; for it is after we have learned that our salva-

tion rests with God that we are attracted to seek him. This fact is confirmed for us when he declares that our salvation is his care and concern. Accordingly, we need the promise of grace which can testify to us that the Father is merciful, since we can approach him in no other way. Upon grace alone can the heart of man rest.[113]

Although the doctrine of faith is the subject under discussion in these passages, the references to the character of God are most illuminating. Calvin, in seeking to find a secure and certain basis for faith, places it in the benevolent goodness of God as a merciful, loving Father. This follows from his understanding of the proper object of faith as being Jesus Christ or the promise of mercy revealed in him. Calvin thus repeatedly stresses the goodness and mercy of God in his discussion of faith. "He alone is truly a believer, who, convinced by a firm conviction that God is a kindly and well-disposed Father (*propitium benevolumque patrem*) toward him promises himself all things on the basis of his generosity; who relying on the promises of divine benevolence toward him, lays hold on an undoubted expectation of salvation."[114]

These freely given promises of divine benevolence and mercy, which are the foundation of faith, find their yea and amen in Jesus Christ. "The reason for this fact is at hand: for if God promises anything, by it he witnesses to his benevolence, so that there is no promise which is not a testimony of his love."[115] The wicked, in rejecting these promises, bring upon themselves a heavier judgment. "Yet the force and peculiar nature of the promises are never extinguished by our unfaithfulness and ingratitude." Therefore the Lord, by his promises, invites us to receive "the fruits of his kindness" and "at the same time declares his love to man." However, since "no one is loved by God apart from Christ . . . it follows that we should turn our eyes to him as often as any promise is offered to us."[116]

In his discussion of repentance, Calvin stresses the same qualities in God. Although God's wrath rests on hypocrites, he is always ready to pardon and extend his mercy toward any who show dissatisfaction with self, and by his "kindly gentleness (*amica facilitate*)" wills to bring them to a genuine conversion or render them inexcusable.[117]

Elsewhere in Book III similar characteristics of God are prominent: his fatherly gentleness, kindness, goodness and generosity;[118] his boundless love and favor, fatherly compassion and mercy.[119]

The same picture of God is equally prominent in the commentaries and sermons. In his exegesis of Exodus 34:5, 6, Calvin notes that God's eternity, boundless power, clemency, and mercy are here expressed. Then he adds, "After having called himself 'merciful,' he claims the praise of clemency inasmuch as he has no more peculiar attribute than his goodness and gratuitous beneficence."[120] "Since God can never deny himself, he will always be merciful. This attribute is inseparable from his eternal essence."[121] God is "the Lord of mercy, who not only loves but is himself love and kindness . . . ."[122] "Though the treachery of men constrains God to use severity, yet he never forgets his own nature, and kindly invites to repentance those who are not wholly beyond remedy and offers to them the hope of pardon and salvation."[123]

Likewise in his homilies on I Samuel, Calvin refers to God's singular love toward us and his fatherly solicitude and goodness.[124] In a sermon on Job 36:1f. many of these qualities are drawn together. "It is not enough for us to conceive of God as the maker of the world, and to grant all power to him; but we must know him to be our father because he draws us to him with such gentle and loving care as if we were his own children. . . . To know God rightly we must taste of his goodness which he has uttered to us."[125]

Erwin Mülhaupt, after a thorough investigation of Calvin's sermons, concludes that for Calvin the chief characteristic of God's free will is its goodness or kindness (*bonte*). For God to be free means to be good. This is "an indication how God is portrayed according to the gospel." The evangelical, not the legal, character of Calvin's concept of God is what stands in the foreground.[126] Calvin also speaks frequently of God's majesty, but this is closely bound up with God's love. Hence Mülhaupt speaks of "the majesty of God's love united with his righteousness" as Calvin's most characteristic description of God's nature.[127]

Much the same conclusion has been reached by those who have investigated other writings of Calvin's. There is, in fact, a striking unanimity in the newer research concerning Calvin's doctrine of God. The present consensus completely overturns the older characterization of Calvin's God as being essentially almighty, deterministic, cold, and aloof, a God who was conspicuously lacking in the qualities of love, mercy, and compassion.

Years ago, B. B. Warfield, in an essay on Calvin's doctrine of

God, had already pointed out that Calvin laid at least as much stress on God's benevolent fatherhood as on his sovereign majesty, but Warfield was not read much beyond conservative Calvinist circles. Warfield's thesis, however, has stood the test of later research: "The sense of the divine Fatherhood is as fundamental to Calvin's conception of God as the sense of his sovereignty. . . . The distinguishing feature of Calvin's doctrine of God is, in a word, precisely the prevailing stress he casts on this aspect of the conception of God. . . . With all his emphasis on the sovereignty of God, Calvin throws an even stronger emphasis on his love."[128]

Josef Bohatec, who spent a lifetime studying Calvin's thought, has an illuminating section on the authority of God in his study of Calvin and French humanism. He asserts that Troeltsch, Ritschl, and Dorner err in asserting that with Calvin the love of God recedes before the sovereignty and righteousness of God and that there is a dualism between God's love and righteousness.[129] Bohatec produces impressive evidence to show that to the contrary Calvin speaks of the fatherly and amicable love and grace of God precisely in connection with his righteousness and authority. Calvin speaks indeed of the majesty of God, but not of an abstract majesty. It is rather a gentle majesty, imprinted with his mercy and love, which is the nature of God—in short, the majesty of love![130] Bohatec concludes that for Calvin "God's majesty is love, since it is grace; his love is majesty, since it is holy."[131]

According to Edward Dowey, "Gratuitous-goodness, gratuitous-mercy, or gratuitous-love—any one of these is the appropriate epithet for God the Redeemer in Calvin's theology . . . . For Calvin, God is never merely sovereign. He is sovereignly good, sovereignly just, sovereignly merciful and gracious."[132] Dowey further maintains that even "the doctrine of double predestination does not in any way change the picture of the God of gratuitous love. Rather it emphasizes it." Calvin can justly be labeled "a theologian of love."[133] J. T. McNeill agrees that Calvin's doctrine of predestination does not lead, as many have concluded, to a concept of God where the chief stress is on the demands of God's justice, with God's mercy playing a secondary role. "On the contrary," says McNeill, the theme of God's mercy "is constantly recurring and is given very great emphasis."[134] The Dutch historian, W. F. Dankbaar, gives a similar judgment: "Calvin placed no less emphasis on God's love and grace as on his holiness and righteousness. He was a rigorous prophet of the glory of God, but no less was he a comforter of hearts with a witness to God's faithfulness and forbearance."[135]

It may be fitting to conclude with the views of A. Mitchell Hunter, whose question about Scotism in Calvin's doctrine of God precipitated this discussion. He feels that Calvin's doctrine of predestination poses some serious questions, but he still concurs with the majority view concerning the God of Calvin.

> No one has ever spoken or written with more warmth of genuine feeling about the Fatherhood of God and all that it implies of love and care and compassion. An unwonted tenderness of tone steals into his voice when he pours out his heart on that theme. There is no greater error than to think that that great doctrine was alien to his mind and heart . . . . To Calvin the true knowledge of God was summed up in the knowledge of his fatherly love ratified by the experience of it . . . . Calvin had a vivid and profound sense of the divine majesty, but, while seeking to communicate it to others, he would not set it before them as the supreme object of their contemplation; that would be to plunge them into an awe that was mingled with terror. The principal thing was to be sure of his paternal goodness.[136]

Calvin's description of God the Creator and God the Redeemer is thus remarkably consistent. Were it possible to discover a dichotomy between the two, Calvin would be open to the charge of positing a hidden God, whose sovereign and inscrutable will is not essentially related to the gracious God revealed in Jesus Christ. It must be conceded that there is a real difficulty here, for in his treatment of reprobation Calvin sometimes seems to speak of a God who operates apart from Jesus Christ. This is an extremely complicated problem which falls outside the scope of this inquiry.[137] However, whatever problems arise in connection with Calvin's doctrine of the decrees, these must be viewed in the light of his doctrine of God and not vice versa. Moreover, as the remainder of this study will show, Calvin's concept of the law is viewed by him in direct connection with the revealed will of the Creator-Redeemer God, the God of the gospel.

D. *The Implications of this Identification*

This brief analysis of Calvin's concept of God has been a sort of detour, but it was necessary in order to determine what kind of God it is whose will is revealed in the law. An indissoluble connection binds Calvin's concept of God and his concept of the law. Hence a dark cloud would hang over his whole concept of the law as long as his understanding of the will of God was viewed as arbitrary and the nature of God as essentially non-gracious.

Now it is possible to take up Calvin's positive intention in identifying the law so closely with the will of God. Although the references are often casual and seemingly incidental, Calvin nevertheless reveals here a religious and ethical concern. This is the strongest argument of all against the contention that Calvin's stress on the law in conjunction with the will of God is symptomatic of an arid, speculative and impersonal juridical theology. To the contrary, the frequent combination of law-will reflects rather Calvin's pastoral concern for the ordinary believer. To the seeking soul who cries in anguish: How can I know the will of God? How shall I respond to that God? Where can I find a true and certain guide in life? Calvin answers: in the law, because in it we have a direct, unmistakable revelation of God's character and will for us.

This practical motive regarding the origin of the law in the will of God is seen first of all in the fact that through the law God's will is made plain to us. Nothing is worse than to wander in a labyrinth of uncertainty and doubt.[138] That person is to be pitied who is anxious and uncertain about the will of God. But "in the law his will is truly expressed."[139] Hence there is no excuse for those who stray into error and falsehood. For in the law we have a brightly burning torch to lighten our way in the darkness of moral uncertainty.[140]

Many things about God and his wisdom are beyond our comprehension. We should not trouble ourselves about these things, however, but rather "leave God to his own secrets, and exercise ourselves as far as we can in the law, in which God's will is made plain to us and our children."[141]

Such a view should be a source of comfort and encouragement to us, viz., that God's will is not ambiguous or doubtful since what is right has been prescribed in his law.[142] Axiomatically, of course, God's will can only be learned in his Word,[143] but the law in particular "leads us with straight, firm steps to the will of God."[144] No one is so wise "as to be unable from the daily instruction of the law, to make fresh progress toward a purer knowledge of the divine will."[145] Compliance with this will alone can be accounted real obedience; hence knowledge of the law is indispensable for the life of obedience.[146]

Then comes a second benefit provided by the law as an expression of the will of God. Not only does the law remove anxiety by making plain God's will for us, but it also reveals to us the rule of a holy life. "The rule of a holy life is contained in the law . . . it is the will of God that in his word we should consider not only his commandments and laws but also his covenant."[147] "It is God's will that all should be in subjection to his word and should seek the law for the regulation of their lives . . . ."[148] Law and will—these two are inseparable; without the former we are unable to know the latter. Without a knowledge of the latter, i.e., the will of God, the most sincere and serious attempts to please God will be fruitless. Therefore, "the law is often compared to a way; for except God prescribe to us what his will is and regulates (formet) all the actions of our life according to a certain rule, we should perpetually be going astray . . . . " [149]

Thus the law, by virtue of the fact that it originates in the will of God, gives us both a clear revelation of that will plus a certain rule for the life of faith. Finally, it is "the only rule of true religion."[150] The primary element in religion is the worship of God, and it is precisely here where the law is an invaluable aid. For "God cannot be truly worshipped, except when he himself teaches his people and prescribes to them what is necessary to be done. Hence when the will of God is revealed to us, then we can truly worship him."[151] Legitimate worship is only possible according to the rule of the law "whereby God is to be duly honored according to his own will."[152]

In conclusion, two points must be clarified which heretofore have come up only incidentally. Both are of the utmost theological significance. The one concerns the nature of the law in view of its origin in the will of God. The other concerns the nature of God in view of his revealed will in the law. In the former case a static concept of the law is guarded against and opposed. In the latter case a dualistic concept of God and his will is precluded.

1. The Dynamic Character of the Law

The law is an expression of the will of God. God's will, however, is not only the source or origin of the law in a formal sense, but is also its basis and content. Therefore, the question of the character and meaning of the law finds its primary answer here.

The law is first of all not a set of rules or group of statutes which have been promulgated once and then left to operate in isolation. If this were the case, the law might be a faithful expression of the will of God, but would be only indirectly and formally related to that will. It is true that what took place on Mt. Sinai was in a sense a once-for-all act. God revealed his will to his chosen people in the law. There, in this history which was the climax of God's great redemptive deed under the old covenant, the will of God was declared and set down in precepts. The law was formulated and reduced to ten commandments. This must always be kept in mind.

Yet, what was revealed at Sinai was not the first nor the final revelation of the will of God for his people in its more formal aspect, i.e., as law. Here we have the quintessence of the law, the eternal will of God in paradigmatic form. But the law is not only an expression of the will of God, it is the will of God. Hence the law, like the will of God, is a dynamic thing, meaningless apart from the living Lord and the redemptive history of which it is a part. As we shall see in the next chapter, from the beginning, i.e., prior to the fall, the law was imposed on Adam. For the relationship between God and humanity has always been one where law was necessary and desirable to determine the nature and limits of that relationship. The law is an aspect of the good creation. The form of the law varies because of the broken relationship brought about by sin, but the original purpose remains the ultimate one, viz., to govern the relationship between God and humanity. The law expreseses the orderly side of God's will for his creation.

A further consequence of this fundamental thesis of Calvin is that the law has a historical aspect. The form of the law is relative to time and circumstance, but the truth of the law ever remains the same. The law finds permanent expression in the decalog, but the decalog is only meaningful as a part of the covenant. The promulgation of the covenant in turn was a historical act. The law, moreover, requires interpretation. This was the role of the psalmists, prophets, and apostles, and above all our Lord himself. In Christ alone is the true meaning of the law revealed, for he is the personal and final expression of the will of God. Therefore, believers are directed by the law to Christ that they may know the will of God. But Christ refers believers back to the law which he (i.e., Christ) came to fulfill. Not only that, the law, and its true meaning, which is revealed in the life and ministry of Christ, can only be appropriated and understood by the assistance of the Holy Spirit. The will of the Lord—and thus the law of the Lord—and what that will requires is only accessible and possible to the one who, possessing the Spirit of regeneration, is led and empowered by that Spirit. The law, therefore, because it is an expression of the will of God, is a living, dynamic thing. It is spiritual. It is not a static norm but the living will of God. This becomes even more evident when one speaks of the Christian life. For that which is required by the law, namely, the obedience of faith, is directed ultimately not to the law but to the living will of God which lies behind and is expressed in the law. This, and not an incipient legalism, is the reason why Calvin appeals to Christians to let their lives and thinking be led by the law or by the will of God. The two concepts are for him almost interchangeable in this context.

This is the first important truth that is implied in Calvin's stress on the origin of the law in the will of God. In the following chapters this truth will be developed and illustrated.

2. The Unity of God's Will and Word

The second truth is equally fundamental, viz., the law is an expression of the one will of God which will is good and gracious as well as holy and righteous. A contrast with the Lutheran approach to the law emerges at this juncture. The law, for Calvin, is a revelation of the revealed, not the hidden will of God. The law represents his "proper work"; it is not a "foreign work" (*opus alienum*). It comes from his right hand, not his left; it expresses the love of God, not his wrath .

The above terminology is Luther's, not Calvin's, but therein is revealed a crucial difference between the Lutheran and Calvinistic approach to the law. This emphasis on the law as the revelation of the one, gracious will of God is the presupposition for Calvin's view of the essential unity of law and gospel. For both express the one will and Word of God .

The judgment of F. Loofs that "Calvin does not distinguish, as Luther does, between a revealed will of God and a hidden will (*voluntas abscondita*) of God,"[153] may not be altogether fair to Luther, but it is apropos to certain strands of Lutheranism. Nevertheless, there is a dualistic tendency in Luther's theology which has been taken up and developed both in Lutheran orthodoxy and by several contemporary Lutheran theologians.[154] The antithesis between law and gospel, according to this approach, is grounded in two wills of God, two words of God, and two modes of God's activity. [155]

This emphasis on an "original paradox" (*Ur-paradoxie*) and "a basic antimony" *(Grundantinomie)* in God's will and activity is a current theme of the theological triumverate of H. Thielicke, R. Bring, and E. Kinder. All three are scandalized by the Reformed accent on the unity of God and his work. In direct contrast to this unified concept of God they revel in the Lutheran "insight" which distinguishes Lutheran theology from all other theologies. According to this "insight," it is illegitimate to seek for an underlying unity behind the "competing (*konkurrierende*) duplicity of the will and work of God." A genuine Christian proclamation, according to this view, will speak of "a basic and thoroughly irreparable and unresolvable double aspect of God's government in the world." In reference to our redemption, one can even speak of "God against God," i.e., the gracious God against the wrathful God for our sake and our salvation. These insoluble paradoxes and antinomies lie at the heart of the Christian faith![156]

Calvin's concept of the law of God as originating in and as the expression of the one will of God stands in the sharpest possible opposition to this point of view.[157] In all of the references from Calvin cited in this chapter, not one of them so much as hinted at the kind of dualism which has become the hallmark of this type of German-Scandinavian Lutheranism. Calvin does distinguish between the secret will of God and his revealed will,[158] a hidden righteousness and a revealed righteousness,[159] but he never suggests that there is any discrepancy between the two. The will of God is one although we know only part of it. But that which we know is sufficient for us and reflects truly that part of the will of God which is not revealed to us.[160] Were God to reveal the whole of his righteousness to us, we would be overwhelmed and annihilated by it.[161] God has therefore revealed only that which is necessary and good for our welfare. Even the angels, in their service of God, regulate themselves according to his revealed will in the law, not the ineffable will which is too high for them.[162]

This distinction between the hidden and revealed will of God and a hidden and revealed righteousness seems to be very similar to the Lutheran distinction between God hidden and revealed. But the similarity is only a superficial one. A tension, if not a dualism in the Lutheran view, is carried over into the doctrine of the law and gospel. Calvin knows no such tension, much less a dualism. In no uncertain terms he rejects absolutely any notion of a double will of God. God's will may appear manifold to us, but "in him it is one and simple."[163] "Nothing agrees less with God's nature than that he should be of a double will."[164]

The believer, therefore, can confidently rejoice in the revelation of God's will in his law. The law should be his delight and the object of his constant meditation (Psalm 19:2). "For God has so depicted his character in the law that if any man carries out in deeds whatever is enjoined there, he will express the image of God, as it were, in his own life."[165] Accordingly, let us "embrace the doctrine of the law, in which God's will is declared to us, as if he were openly speaking to us."[166]

NOTES

1. "Summa fere sacrae doctrinae duabus his partibus constat: Cognitione Dei ac nostri," O. S. I., 37. Cf. the opening sentence of the 1559 edition: "Tota fere sapientiae nostrae summa, quae vera demum ac solida sapientia censeri debeat, duabus partibus constat, Dei cognitione et nostri," *Inst.* I.1.1. The latter represents only an amplification of the former with one exception: "sacred doctrine" is replaced by "wisdom." We are fortunate in having an excellent new translation in English of the first (1536) edition of the *Institutes*: *Institutes of the Christian Religion: 1536 Edition.* Trans. and annotated by Ford Lewis Battles (Grand Rapids: H. H. Meeter Center for Calvin Studies/Eerdmans, 1986).

2. The origin of the doctrine of the *triplex usus legis* is problematic. It is generally considered to have originated with Melanchthon, but the evidence is not conclusive. According to Wendel, both Melanchthon and Bucer recognized three uses of the law as early as 1530, op. cit., 198, but there is no explicit mention of three uses until the 1535 edition of the *Loci Communes*. Gerhard Ebeling, in an essay, "On the Doctrine of the *Triplex Usus Legis* in the Theology of the Reformation," in *Word and Faith* (Philadelphia: Fortress, 1963), 62-5, maintains that whereas the substance of this doctrine is expounded in the 1535 edition of the *Loci Communes*, the expression *usus triplex legis* is not yet used there. Ebeling finds this expression used as a technicus terminus for the first time in Melanchthon's *Catechesis puerilis* of 1540. Luther, he insists, did not teach the *triplex usus legis*. Battles also points out that Zwingli, in his *Exposition of the Christian Faith* (1531), "approaches Calvin's three uses" . . . (*Inst.* 1536), 250.

In the 1536 *Institutes* (which was written before Melanchthon's

1535 Loci appeared) Calvin does not yet use this expression but begins his discussion: "From this we can gather what is the function (*officium*) and use of the law. It is comprised of three parts," O.S.I., 61 (cf. Battles tr., 35.). Here, as elsewhere, Calvin borrows, adapts, and then often gives classic expression to a notion or motif which in earlier writers was only occasional and undeveloped.

    3. So D. J. Köstlin, "Calvin's *Institutio* nach Form und Inhalt," in *Theologische Studien und Kritiken,* 1868, 21. The sequence of topics in Luther's Catechism, however, was basically the same as that in numerous medieval books for the instruction of laity, J. T. McNeill, *The History and Character of Calvinism* (New York: Oxford Press, 1954), 124. On the sources and development of the *Institutes* see Wendel, op. cit., 112ff.

    4. Op. cit., 24, 25.

    5. Op. cit., 115.

    6. Op. cit., 232.

    7. Ibid., 42.

    8. A sharp critique of Dowey's thesis is given in the American edition of T. H. L. Parker's book, *Calvin's Doctrine of the Knowledge of God* (Grand Rapids: Eerdmans, 1959), 117 ff. Wendel's discussion would tend to support Dowey's position, for he writes: "Appearances notwithstanding, the relation between the last edition of the *Institutes* and the traditional plan of the Apostle's Creed remains rather external and formal. In fact, the dogmatic exposition in its new aspect consists of two main parts," op. cit., 121.

    9. Op. cit., 222.

    10. Ibid., 2 3 2

    11. *Inst.* II.8.1.

    12. *Inst.* II.7.2.

    13. See I.2.2.; I.4.4; I.5.13.

    14. See IV.14.18-26.

    15. See III.2.1, 6; III.3.16; III.6.1-3; III.7.1-3,5; III.11.17-20; III.12.1; III.13.3; III.14.8-11; III.19.2-6; III.23.2, 4.

    16. *Prädestination und Verantwortlichkeit bei Calvin,* 103. Quoted in Dowey, op. cit., 235.

    17. III.6.1.

    18. III.7.1.

    19. III.6.3. Cf. Comm. 1 Cor. 9:21 (CO 49, 448).

    20. III.7.1.

    21. This thesis will be developed further in the concluding chapter.

    22. The following year (1538) Calvin published a Latin version of this catechism, now using simply the title *Catechism* or *Institution of the Christian Religion.* This was translated into English and published privately by Ford Lewis Battles in 1972 and revised several times up to his death in 1979.

    23. O. S. I., 382. There is an English translation of this version by

Paul T. Fuhrman (Philadelphia: Westminster, 1949; Reprint, 1992)
    24. CO 6, 10 (emphasis mine).
    25. *The Faith of the Church* (New York: Meridian Books, Inc., 1958), 39. Barth feels this ordering is extremely important. "You realize how fitting it is to be cautious when one asserts the stiffness and severity of Calvin. Precisely it is Calvin who begins with the Creed, and now with God's demands upon us, as revealed in the law. Calvin does not begin by saying to us: This is what you should be! He begins by saying: We are enabled to put our whole life in God's hands through Jesus Christ. And this life has been put there by the same Jesus Christ. We have this 'trust'."
    26. Q. 128 (CO 6, 50).
    27. Qs. 129, 131 (CO 6, 52).
    28. This commentary on the Harmony of the Last Four Books of Moses takes up all of Vol. 24 and most of Vol. 25 of the *Calvini Opera*. The English translation is divided into four volumes totaling almost 2,000 pages.
        The translator of the English version of this commentary notes that J. B. Lightfoot attempted to harmonize the whole Old Testament by arranging texts in series. He also refers to an account of various harmonies of the Old Testament in a work by a Dr. Townsend. But no one apparently has tried to write a commentary on a harmony of the Pentateuch, *The Last Four Books of Moses Arranged in the Form of a Harmony*, Vol . I, vii, viii.
    29. CO 24, 5, 6.
    30. CO 24, 6-8.
    31. Georgia Harkness, op. cit., 65, finds "a homely example" in the application of the seventh commandment to the prohibition in Deut. 22:5.
    32. CO 24, 5, 6.
    33. Occasionally Calvin gives some indication of the struggle involved in trying to classify certain passages. He also admits that there is an inevitable arbitrariness in certain cases. For example, in the strictures against idolatry in Ex. 23:24; 24:13; Deut. 12:1-3 etc., he concedes that these "supplements" in some respects agree with and are applicable to the first commandment. But because of the express mention of idols, he finally concluded that they more properly fall under the second commandment, CO 24, 546.
    34. Preface to the Harmony (CO 24, 7, 8). Note how similar this definition of spiritual worship is to Q. 7 of the Geneva Catechism.
    35. Calvin also refers to the ten commandments as the "ten words" in the *Institutes* II.8.12. Cf. Geneva Catechism, Q. 133.
    36. Preface to the Harmony (CO 24, 7, 8). Commenting on some of these supplementary commandments such as Ex. 22:28; Lev. 19:32; Deut. 16:18 Calvin says, "It was not the design of God to add to the two tables, as if something better and more perfect had afterwards come into his mind—a shocking thought! He was therefore content with the rule once for all laid down

(semel tradita), although he spoke afterwards in a more ordered manner *(explicatius),*" CO 24, 609. Cf. Comm. Ex. 12:20 (CO 24, 135); Comm. Ex. 23:24 (CO 24, 546).

37. From his *Grund und Ursach ausz gotlicher schrift der newerungen an dem nachtmal des Herren,* quoted in William D. Maxwell, *An Outline of Christian Worship* (London: Oxford U. Press, 1939), 101. I am indebted to this book for most of the above information.

38. Maxwell, op. cit., 115.

39. *Instruction in Faith* (1537), (OS I., 383), ET., 24.

40. I.17.2.

41. II.8.59.

42. II.8.5. God is "the governor of heaven and earth, and we should esteem his will as the source of law and reason and the final appeal of justice," Comm. Dan. 4:34 (CO 40, 685).

43. Comm. Deut. 29:29 (CO 24, 256).

44. Comm. Ps. 73:16 (CO 31, 682).

45. Comm. 1 John 2:17 (CO 55, 320).

46. Comm. Isa. 8:20 (CO 36, 184).

47. *Inst.* II.8.51.

48. Comm. Jer. 9:15 (CO 38, 41). "The prophet [Jeremiah] affirms that the law has been set before the eyes of the Jews that they might know with certainty what is acceptable to God," Comm. Jer. 44:10 (CO 39, 257). "The will of God is no longer hidden or remotely isolated from them (the Jews), but is placed before their eyes" (i.e., in the law), Comm. Rom. 10:6 (CO 49, 198).

49. Comm. Rom. 2:18 (CO 49, 41).

50. Comm. Hosea 17:7 (CO 42, 463).

51. Luther also makes a veritable identification between the law and the will of God. "For Luther, the Law . . . in itself is an expression of the will of God, it is divine . . . . Resistance to the law, moreover, means resistance to the divine will of which it is an expression," Philip S. Watson, *Let God be God!* (London: The Epworth Press, 1947), 153, 109. Moreover, Old Testament theologians also remind us that this is a genuine biblical insight. "God is the lawgiver. In the law he reveals his will and gives form and purpose to the life of man . . . . In the law God reveals himself decisively," Ludwig Koehler, *Old Testament Theology* (London: S.C.M. Press, 1957), 109, 110. Cf. Walther Eichrodt, *Theology of the Old Testament,* Vol. I. (Philadelphia: Westminster, 1961), 38.

52. I use the word "alleged" advisedly, because the studies of E. Gilson *(The Spirit of Medieval Philosophy,* 1936), P. A. Vignaux *(William Ockham, 1950), and* M. Carré *(Realists and Nominalists,* 1946/67) have modified considerably the picture given of late medieval theology in both Protestant and Catholic text books. Of particular value in this connection is the weighty study of Gabriel Biel and late medieval nominalism by Heiko A. Oberman, *The Har-*

vest of Medieval Theology (Cambridge, Mass.: Harvard U. Press, 1963). In any case, in view of recent researches, one should be very cautious about calling Scotus a nominalist. Occam himself criticized Scotus' view of knowledge as a variety of extreme realism. See Carré, op. cit., 106. T. F. Torrance also maintains that Scotus is closer to realism than nominalism in his *Theology in Reconstruction* (Grand Rapids: Eerdmans, 1965), 78 ff., 188 ff.; and his *Space, Time, and Incarnation* (New York: Oxford U. Press, 1969), 27 ff., 64 f., 86 f.

53. Quoted in A. Mitchell Hunter, *The Teaching of Calvin* (London: James Clarke & Co., 1950), 54.

54. Seeberg, op. cit., Vol. II., 147 f., 185f.; and the articles on Scotus and Occam in *The Oxford Dictionary of the Christian Church,* edited by F. L. Cross (London: Oxford U. Press, 1958), 426 f. and 1462 f. For quite another estimate of the positions of Scotus and Occam, cf. Oberman, op. cit., 90 f.; and T. F. Torrance, *The Hermeneutics of John Calvin,* Part I, "The Parisian Background of Calvin's Thought" (Edinburgh: Scottish Academic Press, 1988). Seeberg also, in a later edition (4th) of his *Dogmengeschichte*, revises his previous estimate of Scotus. Cf. Vol. III., 652 ff.

55. Cf. Gordon Rupp, *The Righteousness of God–Luther Studies* (London: Hodder and Stoughton, 1953), 87 ff.; and Oberman, op. cit., 1 ff. One of Luther's principal instructors at Erfurt was Johann Nathin, a student of Biel's. On Luther's views of Occam see B. A. Gerrish, *Grace and Reason. A Study in the Theology of Luther* (Oxford: Clarendon Press, 1962), Chapter III, "Luther and Scholasticism."

56. Hunter, op. cit., 55.

57. *Das Grundverständnis der Theologie Calvins* (Neukirchen: Neukirchener Verlag, 1963), 154.

58. Ibid. Georgia Harkness also affirms: "With Duns Scotus, Calvin held that the will of God is wholly unconditioned," op. cit., 69. From one standpoint, however, we must insist that God is unconditioned, i.e., by any other factor or force outside of himself. But Harkness is equating unconditioned with arbitrary.

59. For references and a brief but solid discussion of Calvin's doctrire of God see B. B. Warfield, *Calvin and Augustine* (Philadelphia: The Presbyterian and Reformed Publishing Co., 1956), 151 ff.

60. See the balanced discussion of Wendel, op. cit., 127 ff. Even where there are clear echoes of Scotus, what Thomas McDonough says of Luther applies equally well to Calvin: "A close comparison of Luther's views with those of his nominalist masters usually reveals that we are dealing with two entirely different approaches to theology, despite verbal resemblances," *The Law and Gospel in Luther* (London: Oxford U. Press, 1963), 43.

61. *Inst.* III.23.2. Despite the nominalist ring of certain phrases in this passage, the editors of the LCC version of the *Institutes* note that similar state-

ments are also frequently found in Augustine, 949, n. 5.

62. CO 25, 110. Similar statements can also be found in Luther, such as the following from *The Bondage of the Will* (WA 18, 712): "God is that being for whose will no cause or reason is to be assigned as a rule or standard (*mensura*) by which it acts, seeing that nothing is superior or equal to it, but it is itself the rule of all things (*regula omnium*)." The comments on this passage by the late Princeton historian, E. Harris Harbison, could also be applied to Calvin: "Luther's study of Paul, together with his own personal experience of God's grace and power, persuaded him that no bounds whatever can be set to the will of God, no channel dug by man which God's will may not overflow, no law envisaged by man which exhausts the possibilities of divine action," "History and Destiny," in *Theology Today*, Jan. 1965, 399. For a more critical view of Luther's alleged "extreme voluntarism," especially in *The Bondage of the Will*, see Thomas M. Mc Donough, *The Law and the Gospel in Luther*, 40 ff.

63. Comm. Ex. 3:22 (CO 24, 49).

64. Comm. Dan. 9:14 (CO 41, 152). "Although the rectitude by which God regulates his judgments is not always apparent or made visible to us, still it is never lawful to separate his wisdom and justice from his power," Comm. Isa. 23:9, (CO 36, 391).

65. Comm. Jonah 1:13 (CO 43, 226). Cf. *Inst.* III.23.4.

66. Comm. Deut. 24:16 (CO 24, 631).

67. Comm. Ex. 21:18, 19 (CO 24, 624) and Comm. Deut. 20:12 (CO 24, 632).

68. Comm. Mal. 3:7 (CO 44, 485). Cf. Comm. Dan. 4:35 (CO 40, 688).

69. *Inst.* III.23.2. Cf. Inst. I.17.2.

70. Comm. Isa. 23:9 (CO 36, 391). "What the Sorbonne doctors say, that God has an absolute power, is a diabolical blasphemy invented in hell," Sermon on Job 23:1-7 (CO 34, 339).

71. *Concerning the Eternal Predestination of God* 179 (CO 8, 361). The will of God is "the supreme justice" (*summa iustitiae*), ibid., 59 (CO 8, 263). Cf. Comm. Rom. 9:19 (CO 49, 185).

72. So Jürgen Baur, op. cit., 181. For confirmation of this, he points to Calvin's explanation of God's command to Abraham to kill Isaac and the command for Hosea to marry a prostitute, Ibid., note 166. But if God wishes in unusual cases to overrule a commandment, such a decision need not be regarded as the arbitrary exercise of absolute power. Cf. Oberman, op. cit., 101.

73. Comm. Ps. 38:3 (CO 31, 387).

74. Comm. Ps. 40:3 (CO 31, 406).

75. Comm. Gen. 25:29 (CO 23, 354).

76. Comm. Ex. 11:2 (CO 24, 131). Cf. *Inst.* I.17.2.

77. *Inst.* II.3.5. Cf. *Inst.* I.16.3; II.8.5; IV.17.24.

78. Hunter, who was cited earlier (cf. note #55) in a critical context, eventually comes to a similar conclusion, op. cit., 32. Otto Weber also, after examining considerable evidence, concludes: "If one surveys his whole train of thought, it turns out that Calvin is truly no nominalist," *Foundations of Dogmatics*, Vol. I (Grand Rapids: Eerdmans, 1981), 407. This is confirmed by the investigations of A. Lecerf, *Etudes Calvinistes* (Neuchatel: Delachaux & Niestle, 1949), 19-24; G. C. Berkouwer, *Divine Election* (Grand Rapids: Eerdmans, 1960) 53-60, F. Wendel, op. cit., 126 ff., and above all the recent study by Alister E. McGrath, "John Calvin and Late Medieval Thought" *Archiv für Reformationsgeschichte* 77 (1986), 58 ff.

79. R. N. Carew Hunt, *Calvin* (London, 1933), 119. Cf. Harkness, op. cit., 63. One of the most extreme expressions of this viewpoint is found in Will Durant's volume on the Reformation in his series, "The Story of Civilization," Vol. VI. Speaking of Calvin he says, "We shall always find it hard to love the man who darkened the human soul with the most absurd and blasphemous conception of God in all the long and honored history of nonsense," *The Reformation* (New York: Simon and Schuster, 1957), 490. The force of this fantastic statement is abated considerably by noting that Calvin's "chief reliance was on St. Augustine, who drew predestinarianism out of St. Paul, who did not know Christ," ibid., 465.

80. On this subject see Garret A. Wilterdink, *Tyrant or Father? A Study of Calvin's Doctrine of God* (Bristol, Indiana: Wyndham Hall Press, 1985).

81. The revised and more positive estimate of Calvin the man—which has always colored judgments about Calvin's God—owes much to the great work of Doumergue. This is not readily accessible, but "the new Calvin" can be seen in almost all the recent studies of his life and work. Cf. Emanuel Stickelberger (Swiss), *Calvin* (E. T., 1959); Jean Cadier (French), *The Man God Mastered* (E. T., 1960); T. H. L. Parker (English), *A Portrait of Calvin* (1955); John T. McNeill (American), *The History and Character of Calvinism* (1954), Willem F. Dankbaar (Dutch), *Calvin. sein Weg und sein Werk (German Tr., 1959),* and Richard Stauffer *(French), The Humanness of Calvin* (E. T., 1971); Alexandre Ganoczy (Hungarian/German) *The Young Calvin* (Philadelphia: Westminster, 1987; original French ed. 1966); and William J. Bouwsma, (American), *John Calvin. A Sixteenth Century Portrait* (New York: Oxford U. Press, 1988).

82. Cf. my article, "The Development and Purpose of Calvin's Institutes," in *The Reformed Theological Review*, Oct. 1965, 65-72.

83. "It is a superficial judgment that regards him as a resolute systematizer whose ideas are wholly unambiguous and consistent and set in a mold of flawless logic," McNeill, op. cit., 201.

84. For a refutation of this thesis see Chapter I in Niesel's *Theology of*

Calvin, and Walter Kreck, "Die Eigenart der Theologie Calvins" in *Calvin Studien 1959* (Neukirchen Kreis Moers: Neukirchener Verlag, 1960), 26 ff.

85. Wernle rightly protests against this procedure and insists that we should look for Calvin's doctrine of God in his discussion of the first article of the Creed, not in his doctrine of predestination, op. cit., 39.

86. Karl Barth is the foremost example of one who is greatly indebted to Calvin and is generally sympathetic to his theology but who feels that the doctrine of predestination casts a shadow over Calvin's whole theology. For Barth, Calvin's doctrine of double predestination, "though not the root, is nevertheless the dark background of the answers which Calvin gives to all theological questions," "Calvin als Theologe," in *Reformatio,* VIII. Jahrgang, 516, 317. Barth's viewpoint finds expression in an essay by Henry Kuizenga,"The Relation of God's Grace to his Glory in John Calvin," in *Reformation Studies,* edited by Franklin H. Littell (Ricxhmond: John Knox Press, 1962). Without denying the difficulties posed by the doctrine of double predestination, Calvin's concept of the law can and should be judged on its own merits.

87. Dowey, op. cit., 148-153, has pointed out that the problem of the knowledge of God comes to the fore in the treatment of faith in Book III. He maintains, further, that failure to recognize this in previous studies on the knowledge of God has resulted in an unbalanced or faulty presentation of this question.

88. *Inst.* I.2.2; I.5.1,9.

89. *Inst.* I.2.2

90. *Inst.* I.1.1.

91. *Inst.* I.2.1. "Every blessing which can be conceived or desired is obtained and flows from this source [God]. God is not only the ultimate (*supremum*) of all our blessings, but also contains in himself the sum of all the parts of these blessings; and he is made ours through Christ," Comm. Rom. 5:11 (CO 49, 94).

92. *Inst.* I.2.2.

93. *Inst.* I.5.1.

94. *Inst.* I.5.1, 2, 4, 6.

95. *Inst.* I.5.7.

96. *Inst.* I.5.3.

97. *Inst.* I.3.1.

98. *Inst.* I.4.3.

99. *Inst.* I.5.4.

100. *Inst.* I.4.4; I.5.12.

101. *Inst.* I.5.14, 15. Cf. I.10.3 and Argument to Gen. Comm. (CO 23, 9, 10).

102. *Inst.* I.5.14.

103. *Inst.* I.14.3.

104. *Inst.* I.10.1.
105. "God in his revelation, as the God *erga nos,* is love. It is characteristic that Calvin, in his description of the nature of God (*erga nos*!) appeals to Exodus 34:6f . . . . To this correspond countless other expressions of Calvin,"O. Weber, op. cit., 405.
106. *Inst.* I.10.2.
107. Ibid.
108. *Inst.* I.6.1.
109. *Inst.* II.6. 4.
110. *Inst.* III.2.2.
111. *Inst.* III.2.6. Cf. I.2.2; I.10.2.
112. *Inst.* III.2.7. Cf. III.2.1; Comm. Eph. 3:12 (CO 51, 183)
113. Ibid. Apart from faith, however, God is not experienced in this way. Since "Christ is the only pledge (*pignus*) of his love;" apart from him we see only "tokens (*signa*) of God's hatred and wrath," Ibid.
114. *Inst.* III.2.16.
115. *Inst* III.2 32.
116. Ibid.
117. *Inst.* III.3.25.
118. *Inst.* III.18.7; III.19.5,8.
119. *Inst.* III.20.34-37.
120. Comm. Ex. 34:5 (CO 25, 114).
121. Comm. Dan. 9:9 (CO 41, 142).
122. Preface to Olivétan's New Testament (CO 9, 713).
123. Comm. Jer. 1:10 (CO 37, 482).
124. For references, see Mülhaupt, *Die Predigt Calvins,* 170.
125. Quoted in Torrance, *Calvin's Doctrine of Man,* 76.
126. Op cit., 161, 162.
127. Ibid., 170. In an introductory essay to a translation of some previously unpublishd sermons of Calvin on the Psalms, Mülhaupt reaffirms his previous position, namely, that one of the central themes of Calvin's sermons on the Psalms is "the majesty of our loving God. This expression," continues Mülhaupt, "is overall characteristic for Calvin. The legends to the effect that for Calvin the essence of his concept of God was law and power, but not the gospel, are gradually disappearing . . . . Calvin proclaims the God of the gospel, who wills the salvation of humanity; but at the same time he stands on guard to maintain the incomprehensible, mysterious character of this love of God," *Der Psalter auf der Kanzel Calvins,* 22.
128. Op. cit., 175-6.
129. *Budé und Calvin,* 333.
130. Ibid., 335-339.
131. Ibid., 341. For a more critical analysis of the relation of predesti-

nation and faith in Calvin's theology, see Chapter 4 in Victor A. Shepherd's thorough study, *The Nature and Function of Faith in the Theology of John Calvin* (Macon, Ga.: Mercer University Press, 1983).

132. *The Knowledge of God in Calvin's Theology*, 208, 210.

133. Ibid., 211f.

134. *The History and Character of Calvinism*, 211, 212.

135. *Calvin - sein Weg und sein Werk*, 212.

136. *The Teaching of Calvin*, 49, 50. This rather recent "consensus" concerning Calvin's doctrine of God also includes Calvin scholars like Niesel, Wendel, Torrance, Stuermann (*Calvin's Concept of Faith*, 1952), Jacobs, Berkouwer and others. The chief demurrer is Karl Barth, although he does not agree with the very one-sided views of scholars of a past generation such as Otto Ritschl and R. Seeberg. Two of Roland Bainton's former students echo Barth's objections: Henry Kuizenga, "The Relation of God's Grace to his Glory in John Calvin," and John Leith, "Calvin's Theological Method and the Ambiguity in his Theology"; both essays appear in *Reformation Studies*.

137. Cf. the admirable treatments of Paul Jacobs, *Prädestination und Verantwortlichkeit bei Calvin* (1937), and G. C. Berkouwer's *Divine Election* (1960), 56-61, 104-110, 139-143, et al.

138. One of my major reservations about William J. Bouwsma's brilliant study of Calvin is his thesis that Calvin's frequent use of the image of a labyrinth (along with abyss) refers to Calvin's deep-seated anxiety, *John Calvin*, 45ff. Rather, Calvin rejoices in the fact that God, thanks to his clear revelation in both the law and the gospel, and above all in Jesus Christ, has rescued us from the labyrinth of uncertainty.

139. "Brief Reply in refutation of the calumnies of certain worthless person" (CO 9, 259). "When he says [in Hosea 7:10] 'their God,' he expresses a strong condemnation, for God had manifested himself to them; yea, he had become familiarly known to them through his law," Comm. Hos. 7:10 (CO 42, 350).

140. "This folly is opposed to the knowledge which God had offered to them in his law: for God had ever exhibited to them the torch of his word (*facem verbi*); but when God thus gave them light, Israel was so credulous as to give heed to the delusions of Satan and the world," Comm. Hosea 7:11 (CO 42, 350).

141. Comm. Ezekiel 18:32 (CO 40, 459). "There is a certain rule contained in the law . . . Since then the will of God is known and made plain, why should we now dispute with men . . . ," Comm. Hosea 8 :12 (CO 42, 376).

142. Comm. Jer. 26:4 (CO 38, 517).

143. *Inst.* I.17.5.

144. *Inst.* II.18.8. "The law is set before our face that the will of God may be made known to us, " Comm. Jer. 9:13 (CO 38, 41).

145. *Inst.* II.7.12.
146. "No one obeys God except the man who knows his will. There-fore, obedience depends on the knowledge of God's will. Moreover, God has revealed his will to us in the law; hence only those men obey God who do what is agreeable to the law of God, " Comm. Acts 2: 23 (CO 48, 40).
147. Comm. Isaiah 24:5 (CO 36, 401, 2).
148. Comm. Gen. 12: 4 (CO 23, 179)
149. Comm. Jeremiah 32: 33 (CO 39, 20).
150. Comm. Malachi 1:11 (CO 44, 420). "The divine will is the uni-versal rule to which all religion ought to be conformed, " *Inst.* I. 4.3.
151. Comm. Micah 4:1, 2 (CO 43, 343).
152. *Inst.* I.12.1. Calvin concedes that God may reveal his will even to unbelievers, e.g., Nebuchadnezzar. But this revelation results in no clear and permanent comprehension of the will of God. In the case of Nebuchadnezzar there was some appreciation of the power and majesty of God. But the chief point he missed, namely, genuine worship and piety. This is possible only where there is a revelation of God's will in the law, Comm. Daniel 2:2 and 3:29 (CO 40, 560, 645).
153. *Dogmengeschichte* IV (1906), 887. Otto Weber, however, comes to a different conclusion concerning Luther: "It is true that some of his statements, particularly in *De Servo Arbitrio*, sometimes give the impression that Luther speaks of two Gods or of a double will of God. But later he avoided this, and in his lectures on Genesis it becomes clear that he actually is thinking of the one God and the one divine will in his revelation, " op. cit., 405.
154. "It is characteristic of Luther and Lutheran theology . . . that both wills (the divine or providential will and the divine salvific will) stand side by side without any relationship to each other, so that one is tempted to speak of a double Subject. That Luther thought dualistically in regard to the ruling ac-tivity of God requires no further proof. This dualism, moreover, has also be-come a principal theme of the newer Lutheran research," F. Flückiger, "Vorse-hung and Erwählung in der Reformierten und in der Lutherischen Theologie," in *Antwort* (1956), 521-2.
155. "God's revelation is divided (*zwiespaltig*): To the revelation of the wrath of God in the law is joined the gospel as the speech of God which is completely contrary to his law. Here we have to do with 'a duality (*Doppelheit*) which is incapable of being abrogated or rent in two: a duality of his demand-ing and judging will on the one hand, and his giving and creative will on the other.' Thus there is 'diverse working of God'," Wolfgang Berge, *Gesetz und Evangelium in der Neueren Theologie* (Berlin: Evangelische Verlagsanstalt, 1985), 9. The quotations are from W. Elert, *Der Christliche Glaube*, and H. As-mussen, *Gesetz und Evangelium*.
156. The previous paragraph is a summary of a section in Berge, op.

cit., 44. The quotations are from H. Thielicke, *Theologische Ethik* I.; E. Kinder, *Gottes Gebot und Gottes Gnade*; R. Bring, *Gesetz und Evangelium und der dritte Gebrauch.*

157. Hendrik Van Oyen, speaking from a Reformed standpoint, observes: "Instead of supposing that there is an inner cleavage in God himself between the revealed and hidden God, as is particularly common in Lutheran interpretations, we may presume the inner consistence of his rule in view of the faithfulness of God in history, and may assume the grounding of the law in this rule," *Evangelische Ethik* I (Basel: Friedrich Reinhardt, 1952), 101.

158. "Since Moses proclaims that the will of God is to be sought not far off in the clouds or in the abysses, because it has been set forth familiarly in the law (Deut. 30:14), it follows that he has another hidden will which may be compared to a deep abyss; concerning which Paul also says . . . ." (then follows a citation from Rom. 11:33, 34), *Inst.* I.17.2. Cf. III.20.43; Comm. Deut. 5:30 (CO 24, 208).

159. "There is a twofold righteousness of God. The one is revealed in the law . . . . There is another righteousness which transcends all the understanding (*sens*) and comprehension of his creatures," Sermon on Job 9:29-35 (CO 33, 496). The sermons on Job abound with references to this twofold righteousness of God. For further illustrations see R. S. Wallace, *Calvin's Doctrine of the Christian Life*, 112-13, and A. Göhler, *Calvins Lehre von der Heiligung*, 62ff.

160. "Though the justice of the law reflects only dimly the glory of the higher justice in the being of God which must remain hidden so long as men remain in the flesh, it nevertheless is a true revelation of the righteousness that dwells ineffably in the being of God," Wallace, *op.cit.,* 113, based on Sermon, Job 9:29-35 (CO 33, 459).

161. Sermon, Job 9:29-35 (CO 33, 459).

162. Sermon, Job 10:16, 17 (CO 33, 496). Cf. *Inst.* III.14.16.

163. *Inst.* I.18.3.

164. *Inst.* III.24.17. "There is also an unknown righteousness of God . . . but this righteousness, which is still hidden from us, is not traced back to a will of God which is contrary to that will revealed in the law. There is no double will in God," O. Weber, op. cit., 406-7. "Calvin does not delineate two wills in God, but thinks of the inaccessible abyss of God's inner being (cf. I.13.1, 2) and the mysteries of revelation itself," LCC Tr. of the *Inst.*, 212, n. 4.

165. *Inst.* II.8.51.

166. Comm. Deut. 29:29 (CO 24, 256).

II

CREATION AND LAW

I. NATURAL LAW AND THE LAW OF MOSES

Although the focus of this study is on the third use of the law—the law as a norm and guide for the Christian—one cannot ignore the concept of natural law and a cluster of related concepts which constitute the background and presupposition for Calvin's understanding of the revealed law of God. This becomes apparent in the opening section of the treatment of the moral law (ten commandments) in Book II, Chapter VIII: "Now that inward law (*lex interior*), which we have described as written, even engraved, upon the hearts of all, in a sense (*quodammodo*) asserts the very same things that are to be learned from the two Tables."[1]

Calvin then specifies that this "interior law" involves both the conscience and what is commonly called "natural law." He proceeds to explain briefly the relationship of natural law and revealed law in terms that appear to dispose of the continuing relevance and significance of natural law rather quickly. He prefaces his conclusion by pointing out that because sinful humanity is "so shrouded in the darkness of errors" and "puffed up with haughtiness and ambition," it does not begin to "grasp through this natural law what worship is acceptable to God." Accordingly, because of our dullness and arrogance, "the Lord has provided us with a written law to give us a clearer witness of what was too obscure in the natural law . . . . [2]

This position is only a variant of that taken earlier by Thomas Aquinas and Martin Luther, among others. Both of them saw the revealed law as given in the ten commandments as a specially accommodated restatement of the law of nature for the Jews. There are differences, especially in the case of Aquinas for whom natural law plays a more significant role, but both of them, along with Calvin, recognized the insufficiency of natural law and the need for divine law when it comes to the Christian life.[3] This does not mean, however, that this is the end of the matter as far as natural law is concerned. The concept plays a significant role throughout Calvin's theology and not simply in a negative way. References in the *Institutes* are rather rare, but the commentaries abound in references to "the law of nature" (*lex naturae*) or "natural law" (*lex naturalis*), "the law engraven on all by nature" (*legem naturaliter omnibus insitam*), "the voice of nature" (*vox naturae*), "the rule of equity" (*regula aequitatis*), etc.[4]

Two references in the *Institutes*, however, are extremely interesting. The first occurs in the context of a discussion of laws in the final chapter of the *Institutes*," Civil Government."

> It is a fact that the law of God which we call the moral law is nothing else than a testimony of the natural law and of that conscience which God has engraved upon the minds of men . Consequently, the entire scheme of this equity (*aequitatis ratio*) of which we are now speaking has been prescribed in it Hence, this equity alone must be the goal and rule and end (*scopus et regula et terminus*) of all laws.[5]

Two key notions here, conscience and equity, will be dealt with later, but before proceeding further it is necessary to understand how Calvin views the law prior to and apart from sin.

II. THE ORIGINAL NATURE OF LAW

Closely related to the idea that the law originates in the will of God is Calvin's view of the law prior to and apart from sin. These two presuppositions are fundamental to an understanding of the positive role Calvin assigns to the law. As we saw in the last chapter, the law is first of all the expression of the orderly will of God for his creation. Before the fall and rebellion of humanity which introduced sin and chaos into the universe, the law existed as the "constitution" of the universe. "Nature" was not then opposed to God and hence the "law of nature" was merely one way of expressing God's orderly will for both his creatures and his creation. The question of legalism does not yet enter the picture because the realities of sin and salvation are not yet factors. The law, thus understood, is primarily and essentially personal and positive, natural (in the God-created sense) and good, an expression of God's love for his creatures and the means by which they can respond in love. It is something basic and permanent in the wisdom and plan of God, not incidental or "accidental" and related only to sin and therefore negative.

In the creation of the world, especially in God's blessing and setting apart of the seventh day, we have an illustration of this fact. Calvin sees in Genesis 2:3 not only an example which God sets for all people but also an implicit command.

> God therefore sanctifies the seventh day, when he renders it illustrious that by a special law (*singulari iure*) it may be distinguished from the rest . . . . That benediction is nothing else than a solemn consecration, by which God claims for himself the meditations and employment of men on the seventh day . . . . First, therefore, God rested; then he blessed this rest, that in all ages it might be held sacred among men; or he dedicated every seventh day to rest, that his own example might be a perpetual rule.

Calvin proceeds to explain that this day of rest is not given to us to foster laziness and sloth but rather that we might have a special time to concentrate on God. This day should be for us a "sacred rest" (so the French) when we can withdraw from the hindrances (*impedimentis*) of daily life and dedicate ourselves entirely to God. However, because of our natural inclination to fail to give God his due and manifest the proper gratitude for what he is and his benefits toward us, the precept (*praeceptum*) is made amiable (*amabile*) by his example.[6]

Then follows a significant passage in which we see the relationship between the law which was given to the Jews, viz., the commandment concerning the Sabbath in the decalog, and this original, universal law upon which it is founded, which remains perpetually valid, even though the specific command in the decalog has been superseded by the advent of Christ.

> We must know that this [the observance of a day of rest] is to be the common practice (*commune exercitium*) not of one age or people only, but of the whole human race. Afterwards, in the law, a new precept concerning the Sabbath was given, which should be peculiar to the Jews for a certain time (*quidem ad tempus*), be-

cause it was a legal ceremony shadowing forth a spiritual rest, the
truth of which was manifested in Christ. Therefore, the Lord often testifies that he had given a symbol of sanctification to his ancient people in the Sabbath. Hence when we hear that the Sabbath
was abrogated by the coming of Christ, we must distinguish between what belongs to the perpetual government of human life
(*ad perpetuum humanae vitae regimen*) and what properly belongs to ancient figures, the use of which was abolished when the
truth was fulfilled . . . . Insofar as the Sabbath was a figure of this
rest, it was limited to a specific period. However, in that it was
commanded to men from the beginning (*ab initio*) that they might
exercise themselves in the worship of God, it is important that it
should continue to the end of the world.[7]

Here we have a concrete example of the way in which God's
orderly will for the creation takes on a normative character. Law in this
sense is an essential ingredient of life and has nothing to do with diso-
bedience or sin. Even more explicit for Calvin, however, is Genesis
2:16. His exegesis of this passage gives us an important clue to his
whole doctrine of the law.

Moses now teaches that man was the overseer of the earth, with
this exception, that he should still be subject to God. A law (*lex*)
is imposed upon him as a sign of his subjection (*signum subiec-
tionis*), for it would have made no difference to God if he had eat-
en indiscriminately of whatsoever fruit he pleased. Therefore, the
prohibition of one tree was a test of obedience.[8] In this way God
willed that from the beginning the whole human race should be
accustomed to reverence his deity (*numen*). It was certainly necessary that man, who had been adorned and enriched with so
many excellent gifts, should be held under restraint lest he break
forth into wantonness . . . . Therefore, abstinence from the fruit of
one tree was a sort of first trial (*quoddam rudimentum*) in obedience, that man might know that he had a ruler and lord of his life
on whose will he ought to depend and in whose commands he
ought to acquiesce. This, indeed, is the only rule of living well
and reasonably (*unica est bene et cum ratione vivendi regula*),
that men should exercise themselves in obeying God.[9]

Calvin then foresees possible objections from those who, re-
calling certain Pauline statements about the negative, secondary charac-

ter of the law, may object that there is an inconsistency here. Therefore, he adds immediately:

> It seems, however, to some as if this did not accord with the judgment of Paul when he teaches that "the law was not made for the righteous" (1Tim 1:9). If that is the case, when Adam was still innocent and upright, he had no need of a law. But the solution is ready at hand. For Paul is not there writing controversially but declares from the common practice of life (*ex cummuni vitae usu*) that they who freely run do not require to be compelled by the necessity of the law. As the well-known proverb states it, "Good laws spring from bad morals." However, he does not deny that God imposed a law on man from the beginning for the purpose of maintaining the right due to himself. Should anyone object by citing another statement from Paul, viz., that "the law is the dispensation of death" (2 Cor. 3:7), my answer is that this is accidental (*accidentale*) and results from the corruption of our nature. But at that time a precept (*praeceptum*) was given to man whence he might know that God ruled over him.[10]

It is important to note here that the killing, terrorizing work of the law is the consequence of sin and hence "accidental." "Had the pure integrity of our nature remained, the law would not have brought death on us; nor is it in itself opposed to men who are endowed with a sound mind which abhors sin."[11]

As Edward Dowey rightly observes,

> The concept of law here is seen to belong to the revelation of God the creator and to carry no hint of sin or disharmony. It is not something that comes in between God and man, destructive of a personal relation, but is the mode of that relation. This pure, or positive, or essential idea of the law is always distinguished clearly in Calvin's mind from the second conception, which does stand between God and man.[12]

It is possible to make a second distinction before proceeding to that knowledge of the law which is common to all people, even after the fall and apart from the law revealed to Israel. For the question arises, did the patriarchs, prior to the promulgation of the law on Sinai, have any special knowledge (i.e., in contrast to that which was common to all people) of the will of God in its normative character, i.e., as law?[13] No unequivocal answer can be given, but the possibility must be acknowledged on the basis of the following passages. Concerning Deuteronomy 31:10:

> Moses says that "he wrote" the law. Prior to this the doctrine of religion had only been expressed by word of mouth, for their fathers had handed down traditionally to their children whatever had been declared to them from heaven. Thus the religion and faith of the people in Egypt was founded only on the ancient oracles and traditions of their fathers. But since nothing is easier than for men's minds, in their vanity, quickly to forget true doctrine and to become involved in manifold errors, God, willing to provide against this evil, consigned the rule of piety to public records so that there might be no pretence of ignorance . . . .[14]

Since Calvin commonly refers to the law as "the doctrine of religion" and "the rule of piety," there is good reason to believe that he is here referring to God's law—or laws—prior to the Mosaic law, but yet distinct from natural law. This law was passed down from generation to generation among the faithful by oral tradition. This view is expressed more clearly in his comments on Genesis 26:5: "because Abraham obeyed my voice and kept my charge, my commandments, my statutes, and my laws." Calvin notes that commandments, statutes, and laws had not yet been written, but the answer, he feels, is this:

> Moses used these terms that he might show more clearly how diligently Abraham regulated his life according to the will of God alone . . . for the Lord often honors his own law with these titles for the sake of restraining our excesses; as if he should say that it lacked nothing for constituting it a perfect rule, but embraced everything pertaining to absolute holiness. The meaning, then, is that Abraham, having formed his life in entire accordance with the will of God, walked uprightly in his service (*in puro eius cultu*).[15]

III. NATURAL LAW

This brings us to the third aspect of the revelation of the law, apart from the law which was specially revealed to Israel through Moses, viz., natural law. This so-called natural law or law of nature is also divinely given, but it is common to all people and is engraved by God on the minds or consciences of all human beings. As was pointed out earlier, Calvin uses many different expressions (the law of nature, voice of nature, rule of equity, etc.) to express this one idea.[16] The basic question, however, is this: what is the function and purpose of the law of nature? Does the concept of natural law (along with a universal knowledge of God) play a significant *positive* role in Calvin's theology? If not, is this an essentially negative concept for Calvin? Concerning these questions, most modern interpreters of Calvin divide sharply.

A. *The Lineup*

Those who view the role of natural law in Calvin's theology in a largely negative light include W. Niesel, P. Barth, P. Brunner, M-E Chenevière, F. Wendel, T. F. Torrance, H. H. Wolf, Werner Krusche, T. H. L. Parker, A. Cochrane, and H. Hopfl. Taking a mediating position, i.e., giving more recognition to the positive possibilities and results of natural law, but in no way countenancing anything approaching a natural theology, are such Calvin scholars as G. Beyerhaus, E. Doumergue, J. Bohatec, W. Kolfhaus, E. A. Dowey, R. S. Wallace, D. Little, B. Milner, and W. Klempa.[17] H. Engelland, G. Gloede and J. T. McNeill go the farthest toward attributing a "natural theology" to Calvin, but even they do not suggest that Calvin is a proponent of natural theology as it is commonly understood.

The negative position has been expressed concisely by Niesel: "The law of nature has only one purpose: namely, to make men inexcusable before God. Since it becomes manifest in the dictates of the conscience, the latter too has no other object but that of depriving man of the pretext of ignorance and making clear his responsibility before God."[18] Niesel, and those who have been influenced by him and Karl Barth, are quite right in asserting that one of Calvin's primary concerns—both in the first five chapters of the *Institutes* and in his references to conscience and natural law—is to establish the fact that without exception human beings stand before God responsible for what they are and what they have done. A key statement in this regard is found in the discussion of sin in the *Institutes*: "The end of natural law, therefore, is that man may be rendered inexcusable."[19] "Without excuse" hangs like a huge banner over all of human existence. T. H. L. Parker accordingly concludes: "The revelation in the creation has only a negative function apart from the self-revelation of God as the Creator in the Scriptures."[20]

One can agree with Niesel, Parker, and others in this camp that this is the ultimate purpose of natural law. The question remains, however, whether this is the only function and possibility of the law of nature. The answer, as we shall see, is no.

This is only one side of the coin. Calvin presents both sides in Book II, chapter two of the *Institutes,* but Niesel and Parker have ignored the evidence which would force them to modify this one-sided claim. In II.2.12-17 Calvin describes those capacities which human beings still possess after the fall, particularly those of reason (*ratio*) and understanding (*intelligentia*). These natural gifts have been corrupted, but unlike the supernatural ones, they have not been obliterated by sin (II.2.12). Concerning celestial things (*res coelestes*), such as the pure knowledge of God, the nature (*ratio*) of true righteousness and the mysteries of the heavenly kingdom (II.2.13), the human mind doesn't even begin to comprehend the nature and character of God and his will toward us (II.2.18). But there is another realm, *viz.,* terrestrial things (*res terrenas*), which concerns this world and the present life. Here even sinful human beings are not destitute of the light of reason (*lux rationis*) but exhibit "a universal apprehension of reason and understanding (*universalem rationis et intelligentiae comprehensionem*) (II.2.13, 14).

In this context Calvin discusses natural law, general morality, the preservation of society, etc. First, he points out that the liberal arts, natural sciences, culture, government, the universal consent to certain fundamental laws, all law and right (*ius et fas*) (II.2.13) are only possible because God in his beneficence has left to humanity many excellent gifts. To reject or despise these gifts, abilities, insights, and accomplishments of "natural man," even though they may be pagan writers and philosophers, is to insult the Spirit of God! (II.2.15). Calvin proceeds to give specific illustrations of these accomplishments. At best, however, they are at the same time illustrations of the debility and perverseness of the human mind. "Lest anyone think a man truly blessed when he is credited with possessing great power to comprehend truth under the elements of this world, we should at once add that all his capacity to understand, with the understanding that follows upon it, is an unstable and transitory thing in God's sight, when a solid foundation of truth does not underlie it" (II.2.16).

When we come to the realm of spiritual things, i.e., the Kingdom of God, the prospects are dim indeed. Calvin says that spiritual wisdom (*spiritualem perspicientiam*) consists chiefly in three things: 1. knowing God; 2. knowing his paternal favor toward us (in which our salvation consists); and 3. knowing how to frame our life according to the rule of his law. In the first two points--and especially in the second-- "the greatest geniuses are blinder than moles" (II.2.18).

Yet it is noteworthy that precisely in this third area, that of the law, something more positive can be said, even though this pertains to the heavenly realm. In this third realm which is related to "the rule for the proper regulation of life" and which Calvin designates as "the knowledge of the works of righteousness," the human mind exhibits considerably (*aliquanto*) more acumen than in the other two areas relating to the Kingdom. Then Calvin quotes Romans 2:14, 15, a passage of no little significance in this connection. He observes: "If the Gentiles by nature have the righteousness of the law engraven upon their minds, we surely cannot say they are utterly blind as to the conduct of life. There is nothing more commonly recognized than that man is sufficiently instructed in a right rule of life by natural law (concerning which the apostle speaks here)" (II.2.22).[21] Calvin then describes the limitations of this knowledge and points out that finally it only renders us inexcusable. Nevertheless, however faulty it may be, the sinner still possesses "the knowledge of good and evil imprinted on his mind" (*Ibid.*).[22]

Therefore, although the law of nature ultimately places sinful humanity under the verdict, "inexcusable," it is nevertheless important to recognize the positive elements in this concept.

One area where the law of nature and the closely allied notion of equity play a prominent and positive role is in the realm of civil law and government. Calvin believes they are possible only because some knowledge of the law is common to all people.

> We observe that there exist in all men's minds universal impressions of a certain civic honesty and order (*ideoque civilis cuiusdam et honestatis et ordinis*). Since no man is to be found who does not understand that every sort of human organization must be regulated by laws, and who does not comprehend the principles of those laws. Hence arises that unvarying consent (*perpe-*

tuus consensus) of all nations and of individual mortals with regard to laws. For their seeds (*semina*) have, without teacher or lawgiver, been implanted in all men.[23]

Calvin uses similar language in commenting on the phrase in Romans 2:15: "In that they [Gentiles] show the law written on their hearts." "We cannot conclude from this passage," Calvin observes, "that there is in men a full knowledge of the law, but that there are some seeds of justice (*semina iustitiae*) implanted in their nature."[24]

The fact that there is a law of nature inscribed on the hearts of all people is also a bulwark against the breakdown of social life. Because of this common bond, people have some feeling and sense of responsibility toward each other;[25] chastity in marriage is held honorable and incest abhorred;[26] obedience of children to their parents is esteemed;[27] cruelty and brutality are regarded with disfavor, and death is feared.[28]

B. *The Appeal to Nature*

In close conjunction with the law of nature and natural law Calvin uses expressions such as: the "order of nature"[29] (*ordo naturae - ordre de nature*); the "sense of nature" (*sensus naturae*); the "voice of nature itself" (*vox ipsius naturae*); "nature itself dictates" (*ipsa natura dictat*); and simply "by nature" (*naturaliter*), or variant forms such as "the law engraven (or implanted) on all by nature"(*legem naturaliter omnibus insitam*).[30] Here again Calvin frequently speaks positively and makes an appeal to, or uses as a basis for comparison, the order of nature, the feeling of nature, or something similar. In the following passage this is amply illustrated. Speaking of tyrants Calvin says:

> Since some principles (*aliqua principia*) of equity and justice remain in the hearts of men, the consent of all nations is, as it were, the voice of nature itself or the testimony of that equity which is engraven on the hearts of men and which they can never obliterate . . . . Habakkuk, by introducing the people as speakers, sets before them, as it were, the common law of nature (*communem naturae legem*) in which all agree . . . . If any one of us will consider his own heart, he will find that this has been, as it were, engraven on us from nature (*quasi a natura nobis insculptum*) . . . . Then follow the words "how long?" This also is dictated to us

from nature (*dictatur nobis a natura*), i.e., that eventually there
will be an end to unjust plunders . . . . And, when the innocent are
oppressed, everyone cries out, "How long?" This cry which results from the feeling of nature (*nascitur ex naturae sensu*) and
the rule of equity (*regula aequitatis*) is at length heard by the
Lord . . . . Is not this feeling (*sensus*) implanted *(inditis est)* in us
by the Lord?

In his exposition of the seventh commandment, Calvin again
appeals to nature, the law of nature, etc., as a norm for proper behaviour.

If anyone objects that what has been disobeyed in many countries
is not to be accounted the law of the Gentiles the reply is easy,
viz., that that barbarism which prevailed in the East, does not nullify that chastity which is opposed to the abominations of the
Gentiles, since what is natural cannot be abrogated by any consent or custom. The prohibition of incests which is here given . . .
flows from the fountain of nature itself (*ipso naturae fonte*) and is
founded on the general principle of all laws (*generalo omnium le-
gum principio*) which is perpetual and inviolable . . . . Nature itself (*natura ipsa*) repudiates and abhors filthiness, although approved by the consent (*suffragio*) of men . . . . If this instruction
were founded on the utility of a single people, or in the custom of
a particular time, or on the immediate necessity, or on any other
circumstances, the laws deduced from it might be abrogated for
new reasons, or their observance might be dispensed with in regard to particular persons by special privilege; but since in their
enactment the perpetual virtue of nature (*perpetua naturae hones-
tas*) alone was regarded, not even a dispensation of them would
be permissible. It may indeed be decreed that it should be lawful
and unpunished, since it is in the power of princes to remit penal-
ties; yet that which nature declares (*natura dictat*) to be morally
corrupt cannot be made by a legislator into something morally acceptable. If anyone with a tyranical pride should dare to attempt
it, the light of nature (*lumen naturae*) which has been smothered
will shine forth and prevail . . . . Hence just and reasonable men
(*aequi et moderati homines*) will acknowledge that even among
the heathen nations this law (*ius*) was considered incontrovertible
(*insolubile*), just as if it had been imprinted and engraved (*fixum
et inscultum*) on the hearts of men.[32]

It should be obvious—and the illustrations could be multi-plied—that the God-created and ruled realm of the "natural," including natural law, plays an important positive role in Calvin's thinking.[33] To limit this concept of the "natural" to the ordering of the physical world[34] fails to do justice to Calvin's emphasis on the moral, social, and political realms which are included. Moreover, in the social as well as in the physical world, the "order of nature" or "law of nature" are never impersonal principles, but are always related to the personal, active will of the living God. This distinguishes Calvin from all philosophical and general ethical systems.[35] At the same time, the limitations and inade-quacies of natural law must be kept in mind. The existence of a written law is in itself a testimony to the inadequacy of natural law, even though the latter corresponds in essence to the second table of the de-calog.

IV. NATURAL THEOLOGY?

The question was raised earlier whether the concept of natural law plays a significant positive role in Calvin's theology. The answer, as we have seen, is an unequivocal yes. But a further question was raised as to whether we then also have present the elements of a natural theology. As the expression "natural theology" is usually understood, the answer must be a definite no. This is the other side of the picture.[36] It may seem to contradict the side already presented, for Calvin in this context speaks very negatively about "natural man." The explanation is that he operates with two concepts of nature. Nature in the positive sense refers to created perfection and humanity as an expression of the image of God. But "natural" and "nature" more often refer to fallen na-ture and all that is opposed to God and the law of our creation.[37]
Recall that Calvin said (*Inst.* II.2.18) that concerning a true knowledge of God, his kingdom, and his fatherly grace toward us, all people "are blinder than moles." In this realm of divine things (*in rebus divinis*) we are "totally blind and stupid" ((II.2.19). The mysteries of God are apprehended only by the revelation of the Holy Spirit. Wherev-er God does not shine by his Spirit, all is darkness. We can understand the mysteries of God only to the extent that we have been illuminated by divine grace (II.2.20, 21).
But what about this knowledge of good and evil imprinted on

our minds and our consciences which convict us of sin? To this Calvin replies, "When you hear of a universal judgment (*iudicium universale*) discriminating between good and evil, do not consider it to be sound and whole in every respect" (II.2.24). "If we want to measure our reason by God's law, the pattern (*exemplar*) of perfect righteousness, we shall find in how many respects it is blind" (II.2.24). In any case, it (our reason), fails almost completely in respect to the first table of the law, although in relation to the second table we have "a little clearer understanding."[38]

However, even this understanding is often deficient. Not only that—and this is crucial—"the natural man cannot be brought to acknowledge the diseased nature of his desires. The light of nature is smothered before he even enters upon this abyss" (II.2.24).

> Besides this, he is so puffed up with haughtiness and ambition, and so blinded by self-love, that he is as yet unable to look upon himself and, as it were, to descend within himself, that he may abase himself and confess his own miserable condition. Accordingly (because it is necessary both for our dullness and for our arrogance), the Lord has provided us with a written law to give us a clearer witness of what was too obscure in the natural law . . . (II.8.1).

Even though all people have the law engraven on their hearts and by nature have some idea of right and wrong, Calvin can still speak of human beings as being in reality ignorant of the true law.[39] Everyone requires the assistance of the written law "since all that is sound in our understanding is corrupted; we cannot perceive what is right unless we are taught from some other source . . . . What I have said before must be recalled, *viz.*, that whenever (the prophet) prays for understanding to be given to him for discerning the divine commandments (*praecepta Dei*), he condemns both himself and all mankind as blind for which the only remedy is the illumination of the Holy Spirit."[40] True, the voice of God (*vox Dei*), including the law, "resounds throughout the whole world," but it penetrates into the hearts of the godly alone. As for the rest of mankind, by their failure to submit to it, i.e., the voice of God, they are only rendered inexcusable.[41] The natural knowledge of the law, "the light of reason," "the feeling of nature" (*sensus naturae*), etc., for all practical purposes, leave humanity ignorant. Yet this "ignorance is no excuse before God; those who are without the law (of Moses) must perish."[42]

The clue to distinguishing Calvin's meaning as he speaks first positively of the knowledge and convictions of all people concerning God and his law and then negatively of their ignorance, errors, and complete failure, is this: the knowledge which humanity by nature possesses of the law, and their observance to a certain extent of what the second table of the law declares, though not unimportant, is nevertheless external, superficial, and thus finally worthless as far as in any way gaining God's approval. Whatever these positive assets and accomplishments of humanity, they in no way give a true apprehension or understanding of either God or his law. The law is a personal expression of the will of God; the law is spiritual and its requirements are spiritual. The correlate of the law is obedience, and the only obedience which deserves the name is that which honors God, the obedience of faith, and it is precisely this of which natural humanity is totally incapable. They are capable of a certain civil virtue, but this in no way assists them in recognizing the origin and Lord of the law who has touched their conscience. The opposite, in fact, is the case. The higher the morality, the greater the tendency toward self-sufficiency and pride, which separate them from God and involve them more seriously in sin. Therefore, whatever natural humanity knows or does apart from the grace or Spirit of God only increases their responsibility and deepens their guilt.

> There is no one, indeed, whose conscience doesn't reprove him, since God's law is written on the hearts of all; so we naturally distinguish between good and evil. But if we think of how great our stupidity is by concealing our faults, we shall not be surprised about this command of the prophets for us to expose our abomination to ourselves. For not only is that self knowledge of which I have spoken frigid, but it is also involved in much darkness so that he who is but partially conscious grows willingly hardened while he indulges himself.[43]

When one understands the real nature of the law and what it requires, it will readily be understood why all natural morality fails to correspond in any way to the intent of the law. Even the most scrupulous observance of the divine law by God's people fails utterly if the spiritual disposition of these people does not correspond to the spiritual requirements of the law.

> Human laws, then, are satisfied when a man merely keeps his hand from wrongdoing. On the contrary, because the heavenly law has been given for our souls, they must at the outset be constrained, that it may be justly observed. Yet the common folk, even when they strongly conceal their contempt of the law, compose their eyes, feet, hands, and all parts of the body to some observance of the law. Meanwhile, they keep the heart utterly aloof from all obedience, and think themselves well acquitted if they virtuously hide from men what they do in the sight of God . . . . They are now lacking in the chief point of the law. Whence, I ask, comes such gross stupidity, unless, disregarding the Lawgiver, they accommodate righteousness rather to their own predilection? Against them Paul strongly protests, affirming that "the law is spiritual" (Rom. 7:14). By this he means that it not only demands obedience of soul, mind, and will, but requires an angelic purity, which, cleansed of every pollution of the flesh, savors nothing but the spirit.[44]

We noted earlier that Calvin has two concepts of nature. By virtue of the fact that the image of God has not been totally destroyed, Calvin can still appeal to what "nature declares" and the law of nature. Because even fallen humanity reflects something of that nature which was originally theirs, this can still be a norm. Over against this essential nature of humanity, however, stands their fallen nature. It is this nature, which is actually reflected in our thinking and behaviour. The actual state of humanity is this: they are not only ignorant of the perfect rule of righteousness, viz., the law of God, and are incapable of refraining from doing that which they may sense to be wrong. That is bad enough, but they even hate the law of God and refuse to fear and love the Lawgiver. The law of God expresses the antithesis of all that fallen humanity by nature now is.

"The confused inventions (*tortuosa figmenta*) of the human heart and whatever is imagined by the perverted minds of the godless stand in opposition to the law of God which alone is right. It is certain that whoever would truly embrace the law of God must of necessity first of all rid himself of all wicked thoughts, yea rather break away from his own nature" (*a proprio ingenio discedat*).[45]

This is, of course, impossible. Hence without God's help sinful humanity rebels against the law whenever they are confronted with it. When the Psalmists and Solomon pray for God's assistance that they may keep his commands, we have in such cases evidence of "the stubbornness of our hearts, which *by nature* glory in rebellion against God's law unless they be bent" *(flectatur)*.[46] Not only are the hearts of human beings stubborn and rebellious. They "hate the law itself and curse God the Lawgiver."[47] This is to be expected, for human beings are *by nature* "so puffed up with arrogance and ambition and so blinded by self-love,"[48] that all they know "by nature"—whether natural law, conscience, common sense, a feeling of right and wrong, a sense of obligation to God—as far as God is concerned, is worthless. These gifts of God's condescension, patience, and grace are indispensable to human life. Before God, however, they are not only worthless; they only serve to condemn humanity and increase their guilt. Nature and law have thus become antithetical entities, just as spirit and flesh. The law is spiritual; natural humanity is carnal. Hence there can be no agreement between natural humanity and the law. They can no more be reconciled than darkness and light.[49] It should be clear that "men's hearts are hard as stone and stubbornly opposed to the law."[50]

In the light of this dark, pessimistic description of natural humanity, it might well be questioned whether Calvin's appeal to "the rectitude engraven on men's hearts," their consciousness not only of right and wrong but also of an eternal judge, has any real significance. Is his recognition of these positive elements, is this appeal to a primal nature and natural order merely a "hangover" of Stoic philosophy? Has Calvin unwittingly paved the way for a natural ethic, divorced from the revelation of God in Christ?[51]

The modern theologian may not be completely satisfied with Calvin's treatment of this subject, for problems which are now acute and are hotly debated (e.g., the relation of nature and grace), were then viewed from quite a different standpoint. Nevertheless, this much is clear. Calvin does not hesitate to affirm that all people are endowed with a sense of natural justice and equity. This knowledge and consciousness is seriously impaired, but yet not completely obliterated by sin. The result is that human beings, though capable of a degree of civil morality, are in the last analysis rendered inexcusable for their failure to measure up to what they ought to know and do. But all of this, i.e., their imperfect knowledge and external morality, does nothing for their eternal salvation. The revealed law, the law of Moses, coincides with and confirms this law of nature, but not vice versa.[52] We truly come to recognize the law of nature after we have been reconciled to God and illuminated by his Spirit, who writes the law (of Moses) on our hearts.[53]

V. INHERITOR OR INNOVATOR?

That the concepts of natural law, the order of nature, conscience, common sense, etc., assume an important place in Calvin's theology is incontrovertible. That Calvin does not attempt to build anything approaching a natural ethic, much less a natural theology, on the basis of these concepts, is equally sure. What is not so easy to determine, however, is the extent to which Calvin was an inheritor or an innovator in his use of these concepts. As is commonly recognized, the majority of these expressions are of pagan, not Christian origin. The notions of law, nature, and conscience in particular were central to Stoic thought. These concepts were then appropriated by the church fathers who to some extent "Christianized" them.[54] But as their thinking was often more Greek than Hebraic, they were usually far too uncritical in their appreciation of Greek thought. Consequently, it is questionable whether they were really successful in their "Christianization" of these Stoic ideas. They adopted them without sufficiently adapting them.[55]

The same judgment can be made of the scholastic use of the same notions. The scholastics, for the most part, were essentially optimistic about the capability of reason. Hence they assumed, as a matter of course, that "the law of nature," being perceived by the light of reason, was a matter of obligation for all human beings who enjoyed the use of their rational faculties. Thomas Aquinas in particular made great use of the concept of natural law. For him it is that part of the eternal law which pertains to humanity's behavior and is apprehended by their reason.[56]

The question arises, however, as to whether the Reformation represents a continuation of this modified (or Christianized) Stoic tradition or a break with it. According to the judgment of John T. McNeill, one-time dean of American Calvin scholars, there is no question but that the former is the case.

> There is no real discontinuity between the teaching of the Re-
> formers and that of their predecessors with respect to natural law.
> Not one of the leaders of the Reformation assails this principle. . .
> Natural law is not one of the issues on which they bring the Scho-
> lastics under criticism. With safeguards of their primary doctrines
> but without conscious resistance on their part, natural law enters
> into the framework of their thought and is an assumption of their
> political and social teaching.[57]

McNeill has few supporters, however. Paul Lehmann, for example, asserts just the opposite: "The Reformation really broke, in principle, with the whole tradition of natural law."[58] And despite the fact
that Luther's concessions to natural law were greater than Calvin's, Karl
Holl has demonstrated successfully (in my opinion) against Troeltsch
and Max Weber, that the natural law concept did not have a determining influence on his views.[59] He goes too far, however, in his assertion
that "Luther totally rejected the natural law concept."[60] Yet, his main
contention still stands, viz., that "The Reformation everywhere plays
down natural law and replaces the proofs derived therefrom with argu-
ments that are taken from Christian morality."[61]

The radically antithetical judgments of McNeill and Holl are
due in part to a different understanding of the term "natural law." There
was continuity in the sense that the Reformers did not hesitate to take
over the concept of the law of nature, even though they recognized that
the concept was of pre-Christian origin. There was discontinuity in that
they conceived of God and the world in a radically different way from
the Stoics, Cicero, and the whole classical tradition. They had a new
understanding of "divine justice" which was determined by the conception of God's order of creation. Behind nature they saw no independent,
abstract concept of eternal law and order but the living will of God the
Creator.

> It was this connection between nature and the will of God, firmly
> rooted in the faith in creation which enabled Christian theolo-
> gians and jurists to appropriate the conceptions of *lex naturae* and
> *ius naturae* . . . . By "the law of nature" Christians meant simply
> and solely the order of creation. They did not reject it as an idea
> derived from classical tradition, although they knew perfectly
> well that their theological interpretation of this divine primal or-
> der was not the same thing for them as it was for a Stoic philoso-

pher or for Aristotle. They did not reject it because, although it stood in a different theological connection, it seemed to express the heart of the matter: the right which proceeds from the God-created nature of man. Even the Reformers, who laid far greater stress on the depravation of human nature by sin than the scholastic theologians, were not afraid of using the concept of "the law of nature" because in their opinion sin does not destroy the constants of creation or alienate them from their original significance. They regarded it even as a proof of God's goodness that he had preserved these constants of creation in spite of the sinfulness of man.[62]

The Reformers' doctrines of the absoluteness of God's grace, on the one hand, and humanity's sin, on the other, profoundly distinguish them from the whole Stoic-classical tradition. Consequently, although in many respects Calvin and Cicero speak of natural law in the same way, the former's concept of depravity makes an all-important difference.[63] To a lesser extent, this emphasis on the radical nature of sin, including its impact on human cognitive faculties, separates Calvin (and the Reformers) from the scholastic conception of natural law.

The difference between the Roman Catholic and Reformation view of the law of nature, however, is not limited to their doctrines of sin and grace. They differ also in their understanding of the law itself. In medieval and scholastic thought a very important distinction is made between natural law and eternal law. The result is that natural law assumes a semi-autonomous status similar to that in the Stoic conception. In Thomas Aquinas, for example,

The eternal law consists of two realms: *natural law*, the source of which is reason, and *divine law* (*lex divina*), the source of which is revelation. Natural law partakes of the eternal law. But it is different from the divine law because it has been put into the rational nature of man itself . . . . It is not placed above man but coincides with him.[64]

The differences are there—and they are undeniable. A simple identification of Calvin's view of natural law with that of the Stoics or Thomas Aquinas is completely unjustified. It is equally unjustified, however, to assume that thereby the whole problem is eliminated. Calvin and the other Reformers broke, *in principle*, with the whole tradition of natural law. It is questionable, however, whether they did so *in practice*.[65] As François Wendel has pointed out, Calvin expended much skill in presenting a coherent doctrine of natural law, trying to reconcile the Pauline contributions and the definitions of the Roman jurists. Wendel further concedes that Calvin at least partially succeeded in distinguishing between the natural law in the political realm and in the human conscience. Yet he (Wendel) sees the persistence of this notion in Calvin's thought as a "foreign body" (*corps étranger*) which is difficult to assimilate and whose existence is only imperfectly justified when viewed next to the divine law expressed in the decalog.[66]

Calvin lived in a period when, despite the upheaval of the times, it was still assumed by all classical scholars that certain standards, values, and virtues were common to all humanity. In our time the humanist assumptions about morality and humanity are no longer so easily maintained. The rise of totalitarian states capable of bestial brutality, and the ensuing nihilism, has made these optimistic assumptions extremely suspect. Hence we should not be too hard on Calvin for accepting the assumptions of his time rather uncritically.

Nevertheless, Calvin's apparently unsuccessful synthesis of the humanist tradition with biblical revelation cannot be overlooked. For Calvin, who is the theologian par excellence of total depravity, is surprisingly optimistic concerning human possibilities in the realm of "natural" morality on the social and civic levels.[67] Without any hesitancy he can identify the "universal" sense of humanity, loyalty, and brotherliness with the biblical concepts of love and righteousness.[68] Here it could be asserted that Calvin the theologian and Calvin the humanist scholar stand side by side, "co-operating, but unreconciled in principle."[69]

However, one should not conclude from this that there is a serious tension between Calvin's doctrine of sin and his high evaluation of natural law and human potential in certain areas. In the first place, Calvin's recognition of human possibilities in the terrestrial realm has nothing to do with a liberal optimism about human nature and an ability to know anything or do anything which is true or good as far as God is concerned. There is no half-way point.[70] In the light of God's grace, natural humanity is totally and helplessly lost and condemned. From this perspective, nothing good can be said about them. Their only hope is to flee to Christ.

Secondly, Calvin's high evaluation of natural law and his acknowledgment of natural human achievement in several significant areas is not based on humanity's inherent goodness or worth but on God's grace. Calvin is thereby seeking to glorify not the creature but the Creator! Calvin can be very generous at times in his appraisal of natural humanity:

> In every age there have been persons who, guided by nature (*natura duce*), have striven toward virtue throughout life. I have nothing to say against them even if many lapses can be noted in their moral conduct. For they have by the very zeal of their honesty given proof that there was some purity in their nature . . . . These examples, accordingly, seem to warn us against adjudging man's nature wholly corrupted, because some men have by its prompting not only excelled in remarkable deeds, but conducted themselves most honorably throughout life.[71]

It would be a gross error, however, to see in this sympathetic appraisal a faint praise of the goodness of humanity. For Calvin immediately adds:

> But here it ought to occur to us that amid this corruption of nature there is some place for God's grace (*nonullum gratiae Dei locum*); not such grace as to cleanse it, but to restrain it inwardly. . . Thus God by his providence bridles perversity of nature, that it may not break forth into action; but he does not purge it within.[72]

What human beings know, sense, or do "by nature" is therefore for Calvin a continual testimony to God's good creation. Even the fall and humanity's thoroughgoing sin cannot eradicate the witness, however imperfect and dim, of the creation to the Creator. This lost world is still God's world. Depraved human beings are still God's, for they are creatures created in the image of God. Calvin thus wishes to affirm the amazing patience, grace, and faithfulness of God when he speaks of nature and the natural in a positive sense. It is only by God's grace that humanity's sin and rebellion have not wreaked their full consequences. Had human beings been left to themselves, utter chaos would have been the result; no culture or civilization would have been possible. Accordingly, natural law, as well as sinful humanity, to the extent that anything positive can be said about them, witness not to the capabilities of humanity but to the grace of God.[73]

Sinful humanity rebels against God's holy will as expressed in his law. The fact that sinful human beings nevertheless sporadically seek for truth and justice and cultivate social and civil amenities does not witness to their innate goodness, but rather to the superior power of God's law which is triumphant even "over man who cannot submit himself to the law. He isolates laws and norms from the Lawgiver and in his apostasy uses them as though they were his material and property. He does not do so in obedience, but still in his actions, in his conscience, in his judging others, and in his protest against complete anarchy, he manifests the superior power of God's work and law."[74]

John 1:3-5 is a key text for Calvin in this connection. Concerning the phrase, "in him was life," he comments: "God now likewise attributes to him [Christ] the preservation of what had been created; as if he were saying that in the creation of the world his power did not suddenly appear only to pass away, but that it is visible in the permanence of the stable and settled order of nature—just as Hebrews 1:3 says that he upholds all things by the Word or command of his power."[75]

Then follows: "The light shines in the darkness, and the darkness has not overcome it." According to Calvin, the Evangelist here maintains "that in the midst of the darkness certain remnants yet exist which show in some degree Christ's divine power." Note well! Whatever wisdom human beings may manifest is a witness to Christ's power, not their own. As Calvin adds a few lines later, "His [the Evangelist's] statement that the light shines in the darkness is not at all meant as praise of corrupt nature but rather to deprive ignorance of excuse."[76]

> There are two main parts in that light which yet remains in corrupt nature. Some seed of religion is sown in all: and also, the distinction between good and evil is engraven in their consciences. But what is the fruition at last, save that religion comes to monstrous birth in a thousand superstitions, and conscience corrupts all judgment, confounding vice with virtue? In short, natural reason will never direct men to Christ. The fact that they are furnished with wisdom for ruling their lives and are formed for the humanities and sciences disappears without effect.[77]

The law of nature thus testifies to the goodness of God, the restraining power of the Spirit, and the grace of Christ. But this law, which is implanted in all human beings by nature, is utterly inadequate to fulfill the true purpose of God's revealed will. For "the world, beguiled by the wiles of Satan," has permitted the law of nature "to become obsolete."[78] Hence the goodness and grace of God, which was first manifest in the law of creation, is now revealed in the law of the covenant. God's grace is evidenced even more fully in the fact that he did not leave us to grope in uncertainty and doubt concerning his will for human life. Rather, because of our dullness and arrogance, God has "provided us with a written law to give us a clearer witness of what was too obscure in the natural law, shake off our listlessness, and strike more vigorously our mind and memory."[79]

NOTES

1. *Inst*. II.8.1.
2. Ibid.
3. For Aquinas, see *Summa Theologiae* (New York: MacGraw Book Co., 1966) la2ae, 91.4: "Although through natural law the Eternal Law is shared in according to the capacity of human nature, nevertheless in order to be directed to their ultimate supernatural end men have to be lifted up, and through the divine grant of an additional law which heightens their sharing in the Eternal Law," p. 31. The page reference is to the Blackfriars edition which contains both the Latin text and an English translation. Cf. 91.5, p. 33.

"Why does one then keep and teach the Ten Commandments? Answer: Because the natural laws were never so orderly and well written as by Moses." "Against the Heavenly Prophets" in *Luther's Works* (American Edition), Vol. 40 (henceforth cited as LW) (Philadelphia: Muhlenberg Press, 1958), 98.
4. Specific references will be given later.
5. *Inst*. IV.20.16
6. Comm. Gen. 2:3 (CO 23, 33).
7. Ibid. (translation modified)
8. Compare *Inst*. II.1.4: "Adam was denied the tree of knowledge of good and evil to test his obedience and prove that he was willingly under God's command."
9. Comm. Gen. Gen. 2:16 (CO 23, 44).

10. Ibid.

11. Comm. Rom. 7:19 (CO 49, 133).

12. *The Knowledge of God in Calvin's Theology,* 225. This same passage (Comm. Rom. 2:16) moved M. Simon to make the profound observation that "For Calvin there is a relation between God and man which does not find expression in a law of God," "Die Beziehung zwischen Altem und Neuem Testament in der Schriftauslegung Calvins," in *Reformierte Kirchenzeitung* (Jan. 24, 1932), 26.

13. Lobstein, *Die Ethik Calvins,* raised a similar question over 90 years ago, but no one, to my knowledge, has attempted to answer it. He thought he found in a sermon on Job (Concio 116 on Job 31) the only case where Calvin recognizes a direct, special revelation of the law inscribed on the hearts of believers before the revelation of the law to Israel through Moses.

"We do not know," says Calvin, "whether Job lived before Moses; but since he could not have learned it first from Mosaic law he will have come to learn it [Here follows the Latin text of Calvin's exposition] from the law inscribed in the hearts of the faithful. Did not God to some extent (*aliquid*) include in those two tables of the law anything other than that which he has always inscribed in the hearts of his children?"

However, this remark, which has momentous consequences, is never further developed or utilized by Calvin. For here, without doubt, we have neither the so-called law-giving (*gesetzgebenden*) conscience nor a natural inborn gift of distinguishing between good and evil. No, Calvin says that the law has been inscribed in the hearts of his faithful, his children, through the Holy Spirit. However, one should not erroneously conclude from this that Calvin does not attribute to natural man a certain knowledge (*gewisse Erkenntnis*) of good and evil, 59-60.

14. Comm. Dt. 31:10 (CO 24, 230).

15. Comm. Gen. 26:5 (CO 23, 359).

16. It is possible to distinguish between the various nuances of these expressions and related ones such as "sense of nature" (*sensus naturae*) and conscience. This is not possible here, nor particularly fruitful for our concern. The interested reader can turn to Joseph Bohatec, *Calvin und das Recht,* 3-20; Gloede, *Theologia Naturalis bei Calvin,* 110-113; and Dowey, *The Knowledge of God in Calvin's Theology,* 56-72, and 245-6.

17. A brief survey of the views of all these authors, with the exception of T. H. L. Parker and Benjamin Milner, is given by William Klempa, "Calvin and Natural Law," in *Calvin Studies* IV, edited by John H. Leith and W. Stacey Johnson. Lectures given at a Colloquium on Calvin Studies at Davidson College and Davidson College Presbyterian Church, Davidson, North Carolina, 1988, 1-5.

18. Niesel, *The Theology of Calvin,* 102. In fairness to Niesel, it

should be pointed out that this quotation is from the English translation (1956) of the first German edition (1938). The second, revised edition (1957) is in many places a word-for-word replica of the first edition. This is true, e.g., of the first four sections of chapter six on the law. But the fifth and final section on the question of the law of nature has been considerably revised and enlarged. He omits the statement just quoted although the substance of the argument remains the same.

19. *Inst.* II.2.22: "Finis ergo legis naturalis est, ut reddatur homo inexcusabilis." A similar passage is found in a sermon on Eph. 4:17-19 (CO 51:598): "All the understanding and discernment that is in us, and all the judgment it is possible for us to have, serve no other purpose than to render us inexcusable." The conscience plays a similar role. Speaking of the possibility of knowing God the Creator apart from special revelation, Calvin writes: "But although we lack the natural ability to mount up unto the pure and clear knowledge of God, all excuse is cut off because the fault of dullness (*hebetudinis vitium*) is within us. And indeed, we are not allowed thus to pretend ignorance without our conscience itself always convicting us of both baseness and ingratitude . . . . Therefore we are justly denied every excuse . . .," *Inst.* I.5.15.

20. *The Doctrine of the Knowledge of God*, revised American edition (Grand Rapids: Eerdmans, 1959), 123.

21. "Et nihil est vulgatius, quam lege naturali (de qua istic Apostolus loquitur) hominem sufficienter ad rectam vitae norman institui." In his commentary on this same passage Calvin writes in a similar manner: "It is not legitimate to conclude from this passage that men have a full knowledge of the law, but only that there are some seeds of justice (*quaedam duntaxat iustitiae semina*) implanted in their nature; e.g., all nations have instituted similar religious observances, they have made laws for the punishment of adultery, theft, and murder, and have commended good faith (*bonam fidem*) in business negotiations and contracts . . . . There is, therefore, a certain natural knowledge of the law which says, 'This is good and desirable, but that is to be abhorred'" Comm. Rom. 2:15 (CO 49, 38). Recall also the passage cited from *Inst.* II.8.1 cited at the beginning of this chapter.

22. "Though they have no written law, the Gentiles are nevertheless by no means devoid of the knowledge of what is right and just. Otherwise they could not discern between vice and virtue, the first of which they restrain by punishment. The latter they commend and show their approval of it by honoring it with rewards. Over against nature he (Paul) places the written law, meaning that the Gentiles had the natural light of righteousness (*naturalem iustitiae fulgorem*), which supplied the place of that law by which the Jews were instructed, so that they were a law to themselves," Comm. Rom. 2:14 (CO 49, 38). Cf. Comm. Rom. 5:14 (CO 49, 97).

In this context Calvin defines natural law as "that apprehension of the conscience which distinguishes sufficiently (*sufficienter*) between just and unjust, and which deprives men of the excuse of ignorance, while it proves them guilty by their own testimony," *Inst.* II.ii.22. Cf. II.viii.1; III.xix.15. The role of the conscience in Calvin's theology has been treated briefly by Bohatec, *Calvin und das Recht*, 5-8; and very extensively by Gloede, *Theologia Natural- is bei Calvin*, 102-134. Dowey's treatment in *The Knowledge of God in Calvin's Theology*, pp. 56-72, 228-230, is the finest available and provides a necessary corrective to T. F. Torrance's almost complete neglect of this subject in *Calvin's Doctrine of Man*. Nevertheless, I feel that Dowey has gone too far in two re- spects: a. He gives the impression that conscience assumes more importance in Calvin's theology than it actually does; and b. like Gloede, he tends to make Calvin's position too optimistic. Although Dowey recognizes finally that with the *sensus divinitatis* and conscience Calvin is finally only interested in the ver- dict "inexcusable," (p. 72), this hardly compensates for his extremely positive evaluation of the powers of the conscience. Krusche, on the other hand, in *Das Wirken des Heiligen Geistes nach Calvin*, 85-89, is much too abrupt on his treatment of Calvin's concept of conscience. Yet his critique of Gloede (and thus indirectly of Dowey) is well taken. The testimony of conscience, which the Gentiles possess in place of a knowledge of the law, is indeed "sufficient," but only in the sense that it deprives them of the excuse of ignorance. It is "suffi- cient" to accuse them and present them guilty before the judgment seat of God (86, 88).

Klempa gives a brief, balanced summary of the nature of conscience according to Calvin:

> 1. "He speaks of conscience as the natural know- ledge of the law; that is, it is not itself the law but is- the knowledge of the law. A distinctive of conscience is its noetic character . . . ."
>
> 2. "Calvin associates conscience with the understand- ing rather than the will," and cites Comm. Rom. 2:15 in support of this.
>
> 3. "The knowledge which reason or conscience has of the law of nature is not a full knowledge." Again see Comm. Rom. 2:15 cited in note 24.
>
> 4. "For Calvin, conscience is a knowledge of general principles. In the *Institutes* II.2.23 he says that the intel- lect is very rarely deceived in general definitions; but it is illusory when it 'applies the principle to particular cases,'" "Calvin and Natural Law," 10-11.

Milner also makes the interesting observation that there is a close connection between conscience and the *sensus divinitatis*, both of which are as- pects of reason. Calvin, in fact, occasionally uses the terms interchangeably (e.g., in *Inst.* I.3.2-3). See his *Calvin's Doctrine of the Church,* (Leiden: E. J. Brill, 1970), 21. Cf. 33-4.

    23. *Inst.* II.2.13.

    24. Comm. Rom. 2 :15 (CO 49: 38). "The *seeds* of law are given with human reason and with the exercise thereof political order emerges," Milner, op. cit., 32.

    25. "Every man does not live nor is he born for himself; mankind is rather knit together with a holy knot *(sacro nexu)*. Therefore, unless we are disposed to overthrow the laws of nature, let us remember that we must not live for ourselves but for our neighbors," Comm. Acts 13:35 (CO 48, 3 03).

    26. Comm. Lev. 18:6 (CO 24, 663).

    27. Comm. Eph . 6 :1 (CO 51, 228).

    28. Comm. John. 1:14 (CO 43, 227, 8).

    29. In a sermon on 1 Tim. 5:4, 5 he explicitly relates the law of God to the order of nature: "Voire, comme s'il disoit qu'il y a une conformite, entre *la Loy de Dieu et l'ordre de nature* qui est engrave en tous hommes" (CO 53, 456). Similarly in his Comm. on Jonah 1:14: "We see that though these men had never known the *teaching of the law (doctriniam legis),* they were nevertheless so taught by nature *(naturaliter ita fuisse edoctos)* that they knew that the blood of man is dear and precious in the sight of God."(CO 43, 227). When Calvin uses "nature" in this sense, he is speaking of the norm which is created nature. The "order of nature" *(ordo naturae)* also refers to "the orderliness or constancy of God's will within nature." Human society is, of course, an essential part of the order of nature, but because of sin the "order of nature" in this connection is "less a description of nature as it is more a description of nature as it was originally and ought to be." Dowey, *The Knowledge of God in Calvin's Theology,* 67. Cf. R. S. Wallace, *Calvin's Doctrine of the Christian Life,* 141-47.

    30. Almost all of these expressions can be found in Calvin's expositions of Hab. 2:6 and Lev. 18:6 which contain at least ten variants using the word "nature" (CO 24, 661-663 and CO 43, 539). This list could be expanded by adding expressions which Calvin frequently uses as parallels such as: "conscience," "the light of reason" *(luce rationis),* "common sense" *(communis sensus)* and "experience teaches." In at least one instance Calvin uses one of these expressions along with law of nature in the same phrase: . . . "that *law of nature* which *common sense* declares to be inviolable," Comm. Gen. 1:28 (Co 23, 29). On the relationship of natural law, conscience, common sense, and experience cf. further Milner, op. cit., 33-5; and on the role of experience in Calvin's theology the essay by Willem Balke, "The Word of God and Experientia," in *Calvinus Ecclesiae Doctor,* hrsg. von W. H. Neuser (Kampen: J.H. Kok B.V., 1979), 19 ff.

    31. Comm. Hab. 2:6 (CO 43, 540, 1). Concerning Jer. 35:12-15,

"Here God shows the difference between his law and the precepts of Jonadab; for he simply required of the Jews what they ought willingly to have done. Had no law been written, natural light was enough to teach the Jews that it was their duty to obey God. For the law of piety (*lex pietatis*) is so written on our hearts as a testimony that no one can justly plead ignorance as an excuse. God then here declares that he required nothing but what nature itself indicated, even that the Jews should repent and form their life according to the rule of piety (*regula pietatis*). . . ." Cf. Comm. Gen. 12:5 (CO 23, 179); Comm. Ex. 22:1 (CO 24 689); Comm. Rom. 5:13 (CO 49, 96).

32. Comm. Lev. 18:6 (CO 24, 662).

33. "Calvin appeals to the 'order of nature' in many different ways. He, of course, admits that God never binds himself or us to act entirely according to the law of nature. But he frequently points out that God's dealings with men through the Gospel conform to the natural order of things, and calls men to respond to the grace of God with a like regard for the order of nature," Wallace, op. cit., 143.

34. So Peter Barth, *Das Problem der natürlichen Theologie*, 13 and 17, when defining the meaning of "order of nature." He also errs in asserting that *ordo naturae* and *lex naturae* are not almost interchangeable expressions, Ibid., 17. Cf. Beyerhaus, *Studien zur Staatsanschauung Calvins*, 67. Concerning the role of the conscience and law of nature as such, however, P. Barth acknowledges that "From this we see again and again, as the occasion calls for it, the manifold, rudimentary knowledge of good and evil in humanity, not as it is found in the light of the biblical revelation, but as it always was and is present after a certain fashion (*auf irgendeine Weise*). The focus is on the general human fact of the conscience. Calvin is aware of the fact that he is thereby utilizing a concept which has its origin in late classical moral philosophy. The same is true of the concept of the *lex naturalis*. Calvin is enough of a humanist to know the meaning the concept *lex naturae* possesses for Cicero from whom he borrows the idea. With this concept of the whole positive morality in its variety and questionableness, late classical philosophy points again to its origin in the implanted law of nature common to all men," ibid., 41.

35. "This constant reference to the highest lawgiver along with the natural as well as the written law and the living consciousness of the fact that man is incapable of basing the Christian life either on civil law, on reason, or on a detected or constructed order of nature distinguishes the reformer from all such attempts in his time or ours. . . . Just as it is impossible to make Calvin responsible for the identification of law as the order of nature with law as the manifestation of God's will, so it is also impossible to appeal to him when one would separate them. In both, God's Word goes to all who can hear; both are the uniform (*einheitliche*) Word of God," Kolfhaus, *Vom Christlichen Leben Nach Johannes Calvin*, 136.

36. Bohatec concludes his excellent analysis of such expressions as *lex naturae, ius naturae, ordo naturae,* and *conscientia* with a warning against saying too much or too little about the role these concepts play in Calvin's theology. He notes the inadequacy of natural law and then adds: "Nevertheless, one may not draw one-sided conclusions from the serious emphasis on these restrictions in view of Calvin's high estimation of the natural law. It is one-sided, on the one hand, to view Calvin as only occasionally taking into consideration the decline *(Abwandlung)* of the inborn moral law through the conditions of the state of sin (so Troeltsch); on the other hand, the opposite assertion that Calvin only attributes negligible value to the law of nature because of his strong conviction concerning sinful depravity (so Lang) is also erroneous. Against the first assumption is the fact that the various limitations of the natural law which were mentioned above stand together and this is of fundamental significance in the doctrine of the law *(Inst.* II.7.1), particularly in reference to the condition of the state of sin *(Inst.* II.2.22)," *Calvin und das Recht,* 20.

37. "There is a twofold nature: the one was produced by God, and the other is the corruption of it. This condemnation therefore which Paul mentions (in Eph. 2:3) does not proceed from God, but from a depraved nature. For we are not born such as Adam was at first created. . . . ," Comm. Eph. 2:3 (CO 51, 163; III.3.12). Cf. *Inst.* II.3.6; Comm. John 1:5 (CO 47,. 7). In paragraph four on natural man in the Geneva Confession, Calvin describes humanity's nature after the fall: "We acknowledge man by nature to be blind, darkened in understanding and full of corruption and perversity of heart so that of himself he has no power to be able to comprehend the true knowledge of God as is proper, nor to apply himself to good works. But on the contrary, if he is left by God to what he is by nature, he is only able to live in ignorance and to be abandoned to all iniquity." (O.S.I. 419). Cf. T. F. Torrance, *Calvin's Doctrine of Man,* chapter 8; and W. Krusche, *Das Wirken des Heiligen Geistes nach Calvin,* 65-67.

38. In Rom. 2:15 when Paul speaks of the law being written on our hearts "he speaks not of the power to fulfill the law, but of the knowledge of it," Comm. Rom. 2:15 (CO 49, 38). Thus, even if this understanding of God's will were tolerably clear, the important thing, viz., the will to act accordingly, would be totally lacking. "The man who is not yet regenerated by the Spirit of God will not be fit to start upon the smallest item of the law," Geneva Catechism, Q. 226 (CO 6, 79).

39. Speaking of the Romans before they had come in contact with the Jews, Calvin says: "They were ignorant of the law of God and had never heard the name of Moses," Comm. Dan. 11:36 (CO 41, 268). Granted, the reference here is to the revealed law, not natural law, but their ignorance of all that is truly good and just is implied. Without the divine rule of the law, "each of us follows what seems good in his own estimation, and we fall into a horrible labyrinth," Comm. Psalm 119:105 (CO 32, 259). A specific example is the

Sodomites, who were not under the law. For this reason Calvin concludes about them, "Hence it is no wonder if they wander and stumble in darkness." Comm. Ezekiel 16:50 (CO 40, 383). However, even though the ungodly walk in darkness, error, and vanity without life or light, *yet* this does not make it impossible for them to be conscious of doing wrong and know that their judge is in heaven," Comm. 1. Pet. 1:14 (CO 55, 222).

40. Comm. Psalm 119:73 (CO 32, 246). On the one hand, Calvin speaks of the heathen as being destitute of the law and the prophets. But he can quickly add, "Yet they were always endued with some taste of this doctrine." Here the reference is to "nature" and the law engraved on men's hearts. But there is no inconsistency here. For even of this natural apprehension of God's will and law Calvin explains that the heathen who had this "taste" (*gustus*) were "suffocated by many errors, "Comm. Ezekiel 18:23 (CO 40, 445). Cf. also Comm. Psalm 119: 27 (CO 32, 226).

41. Comm. Psalm 40:7 (CO 31, 412). Calvin even distinguishes between degrees of inexcusability, thus indicating that the knowledge of the law possessed by natural humanity is at best dim and confused. For example, when the Israelites practiced idolatry, this was absolutely inexcusable, for on them the light of the doctrine of the law had always shone. But the judgment, "absolutely inexcusable" (*prorsus inexcusabiles*), is not applied to the Idumeans, who also had "wholly departed from God, " because "all light had become extinct among them," Comm. Jer. 49 :12 (CO 39, 359).

42. Comm. Jer. 29 :19 (CO 38, 6601). The heathen, however, to whom no prophet had been sent and who had " no law" had somewhat more of an excuse" (*aliguanto plus excusiationis*), Comm. Jer. 16:11 (CO 38, 247).

43. Comm. Ezek. 16:1-3 (CO 40, 335). "They [ungodly men] do not desist from polluting themselves with every sort of vice, and from joining wickedness to wickedness, until in every respect they violate the holy law of the Lord and dissipate all his righteousness," *Inst.* I.4.4. Cf. Comm. on Hab. 1:16 (CO 43, 515).

44. *Inst.* II.8.6.

45. Comm. Psalm 119:113 (CO 32, 264). "In short, human reason, as well as human passions, are in disagreement (*dissidium*) with the law of God," Comm. Ps. 119:62 (CO 32, 241). "The whole of Scripture teaches that all of our affections, due to the corruption of our nature, are repugnant to the law . . . ," "End and Use of the Law" (CO 24, 726).

46. *Inst.* II.3.9. Referring to the fifth commandment, Calvin says: "Now this precept of subjection strongly conflicts with the depravity of human nature, which swollen with the longing for lofty position, bears subjection grudgingly," II.8.35.

47. *Inst.* II.7.10. Cf. Comm. Ps. 69:9 (CO 31, 641).

48. *Inst.* II.8.1.

49. Comm. Rom. 7:14 (CO 49, 128). ". . . men, who by nature were altogether opposed to the law," Comm. Luke 1:6 (CO 45, 11).

50. Comm. Deut. 30:11 (CO 24, 258). "We know how prone the minds of men are to loathe the law," Comm. Matt. 23:1 (CO 45, 619).

51. "Calvin is above all protected from the danger of building a natural ethic, despite the fact that he frequently appeals to the voice of nature which is clearly important for him. For his ethic, unlike all natural ethics, has as its final point of reference what humanity misses in the divine law. A natural ethic . . . does not engage the law as an objective power, which we only have to obey. It can only understand the law as an expression (*Ausdruck*) of our inner being or as an arrangement for the protection of the individual. With Calvin the law engages us from without, from its author, whether as *lex naturae* or *lex scripta*; it grasps us, takes residence within us, and is engraven on our conscience," Kolfhaus, *Vom Christlichen Leben*, 135. "It is a fact that the law of God, which we call the moral law, is nothing else than a testimony of natural law and of that conscience which God has engraved on the minds of men," *Inst*. IV.20.16.

52. "The assertion [of Gloede, *Theologia Naturalis bei Calvin*, 107] that the *lex naturalis* is identical with the *lex scripta* is false, or that "they cannot be separated from each other" (Gloede), is at best a half truth. For the capability of natural man to know the commandments of the first table is denied (II.8.24), even in the ideal case where the *lex interior* agrees with the content of the *lex scripta*. For one cannot really know the will of God in the commandments of the second table when they are separated from the first," Krusche, op. cit., 87.

53. "Submission to the natural order of things is not for Calvin a secondary or alien aspect of our duty which must be performed merely as a supplement or addition to the truly Christian part of the life of the believer, but is an essential part of Christian piety and an integral element in his new life in Christ. It is an expression of the restored 'imago Dei' in man," Wallace, op. cit., 144.

54. "Stoicism prepared the way for the Christian natural law. The great figures of Seneca and the emancipated slave as well as the appealing personality of Emperor Aurelius there adorned the Stoic school. Cicero, however, was its great popularizer, and the wealth of Stoic thought was handed down to the medieval world mainly in his writings." Whereas various fathers of the early church made use of the Stoic natural law, e.g., John Chrysostom, it was Augustine who first constructed a system of ethics in which natural law played a prominent role," Heinrich A. Rommen, *The Natural Law* (St. Louis: B. Herder, E.T., 1947, 6th printing, 1964), 21, 37.

55. See Felix Flückiger, *Geschichte des Naturrechts,* Band 1. *Altertum und Fruümittelalter* (Zollikon-Zürich: Evangelischer Verlag, 1954), 384ff.

56. The notion of an eternal law is found already in Augustine. As

Aquinas notes, "Augustine says that 'the Eternal Law is the supreme exemplar (*ratio*) to which we should always conform'," *Summa Theologiae*, la2ae.93,1,53. Aquinas elaborates in terms foreign to Calvin: "Now the divine will is intelligent since it is just, and the Eternal Law is the divine intelligence. Therefore the will of God is ruled by (*subditur*) the Eternal Law," ibid., 93, 4, 61. Further, "It is clear that natural law is nothing other than the sharing in (*participatio*) the Eternal Law by intelligent creatures," ibid., 91, 2, 21. On Aquinas' view of natural law see D. J. O'Connor, *Aquinas and Natural Law* (London: Macmillan, 1967). For Protestant perspectives cf. G. C. Berkouwer, *General Revelation* (Grand Rapids: Eerdmans, E.T. 1955), 192ff; and Emil Brunner, *Justice and the Social Order* (New York: Harper, E.T., 1945), chapter 12, "Justice and the Law of Nature." Brunner's warning is well taken, viz., that the modern discussion of the subject is vitiated by the ambiguity of the term. He feels that there are at least three different conceptions of the law of nature, the third of which he designates "the Christian law of nature," 85. Cf. David Little, "Calvin and the Prospects for a Christian Theory of Natural Law" in *Norm and Context in Christian Ethics*, edited by Gene H. Outka and Paul Ramsey (New York: Scribners, 1968), 175ff.

57. "Natural Law in the Teaching of the Reformers," in *The Journal of Religion* (July, 1946), 168. McNeill's viewpoint is carried over rather too prominently in the new English translation of the *Institutes* (Library of Christian Classics, Volumes XX and XXI) of which he is the editor. Cf. for example, note #5, p. 368: "Calvin's view of the commandments as a divinely authorized text expressing and clarifying the natural law engraved on all hearts is the traditional one."

58. "Law," in *A Handbook of Christian Theology* (New York: Meridian Living Age Books, 1958), 206. S. E. Stumpf, in the same volume, 246, also contradicts McNeill's asseveration that the Reformers did not criticize the Scholastics' view of the natural law: "The bold Christianization of the ancient doctrine, particularly in the Middle Ages by Thomas Aquinas, was criticized by the Reformers for reasons similar to those found in contemporary thought."

59. *The Cultural Significance of the Reformation* (New York: Meridian Living Age Books, E.T., 1959), 49f.

60. Ibid., 50.

61. Ibid., 51. Cf. Holl's critique of Troeltsch's article on natural law, *Religion in Geschichte und Gegenwart* 3. Auflage, IV. Band (Tübingen: J.C.B. Mohr, 1960), 697f.

62. Brunner, op. cit., 89, 90. "Christian faith in God as Creator is inseparably connected with the idea of God's law. In the combination, Creator-creation, there is implicit the idea of law and a definite order," G. Aulén, *The Faith of the Christian Church*, (Philadelphia: Muhlenberg, E. T., 1948), 188. Brunner has questioned whether the term "natural law," as it is now commonly

understood, is still serviceable in Christian theology. Aulén, sensing the same difficulty, distinguishes between the *lex creationis* and the *lex naturae*. The latter, he says, "could be described as a rationalized and secularized variety of *lex creationis*. The expression, "law of creation," is perhaps a happier solution than that of "Christian Law of nature," which Brunner employs in order to distinguish between the Christian and secular concepts of the law of nature. As Aulén observes, "The foundation of both is a universal law. The difference between them can be defined in this way, that *lex naturae* is a metaphysical conception while *lex creationis* is a religious concept, originating in the relation to God and inseparably connected with faith in God as Creator. The idea *lex naturae* or law of nature rests on the false assumption that in a purely rational way a reasonable system of law and justice could be deduced which would be both universally applicable and definite in content. In reality there is no such fixed natural law," op. cit., 189.

63. The radical difference between Calvin and Cicero is illustrated by Bohatec, *Calvin und das Recht*, 20-22.

64. Manser, *Das Naturrecht in Thomistischer Beleuchtung*, quoted in Berkouwer, op. cit., 196, 197. Cf. the essay by Allen Verhey in the festchrift for Henry Stob, *God and the Good*, edited by Clifton J. Orlebeke and Lewis B. Smedes: "Natural Law in Aquinas and Calvin" (Grand Rapids: Eerdmans, 1975) 80 ff., Verhey points out more parallels than most interpreters acknowledge, but fails to stress their major differences: 1. For Calvin, the law originates in the will of God, for Aquinas, in the divine reason. 2. Aquinas' view of the Eternal Law gives it an ontological basis and independence not found in Calvin. 3. Aquinas concedes far more ability to human reason than Calvin.Verhey makes the further point that although for both Thomas and Calvin the law leads to grace, "it does so in significantly different ways . . . . Thomas's natural law claims to lead to the fulness of the good life minus only the theological virtues. Calvin's natural law claims only to protect the boundaries of human nature, beyond which the image of God is lost entirely," 82.

65. So Lehmann, op. cit., 206.

66. *Calvin, Sources et Évolution de sa Pensée Religieuse*, 155.

67. Even Gloede, who otherwise is very sympathetic to Calvin's humanistic breadth, concedes that "Calvin is not completely uncritical of natural morality (*Sitte*)," op. cit., 110.

68. Cf. Bohatec, op. cit., 43-45, 61-65.

69. So Dowey in another connection, op. cit., 103. We see the same tendency in Bouwsma's *John Calvin*, viz., a positing of two Calvins—the humanist and the scholastic—who existed in tension with each other. Krusche, however, warns against trying to pit Calvin the rationalistic humanist against Calvin the theologian of revelation, op. cit., 84.

A possible way of resolving this tension or apparent inconsistencies and paradoxes in Calvin's theology is Mary Potter Engel's perspectival approach. She would account for these tensions by distinguishing between the perspective of humankind and the perspective of God. Seeming inconsistencies then can be accounted for by which perspective Calvin is utilizing in his view of any particular doctrine. In this case it would help to understand how Calvin can be so positive about humanity's natural gifts and possibilities, on the one hand, and so negative on the other. It all depends on which perspective or vantage point Calvin is employing at any given moment. See Potter's *John Calvin's Perspectival Anthropology* (Atlanta: Scholars Press, 1988), 1ff., 74ff., 198, n. 7.

70. The title of chapter three (Book II) of the *Institutes* depicts succinctly Calvin's position: "Only damnable things come forth from man's corrupt nature." "Fallen man lives in deliberate and constant rebellion. There can be no neutrality here: either men are rebels or they are sons. There can be no intermediate nature," T. F. Torrance, op. cit., 107. "The total corruption of man is, according to Calvin, indeed present, but that does not coincide, according to him, with the absence of all of God's gifts to human nature. Calvin is convinced that man with his gifts and in the functioning of these gifts can manifest his total corruption. In the background of Calvin's thinking is a deep sin-conception; we would call it a total-existential conception, which is religious in character and is governed by the question of man's heart towards God. The absence of true religious obedience of man to God does not exclude man's functioning with the gifts that are left to him in the world in which he yet receives his place," G. C. Berkouwer, *General Revelation,* 199.

71. *Inst.* II.3.3. The interpretation of this last phrase has been contested ("Exempla igitur ista monere nos videntur, ne hominis naturam in totum vitiosam putemus."). Bohatec takes it in a positive way. He feels that the crucial word "seem" (*videntur*) is not important, for he omits it in his quotation of this passage, op. cit., 22, n. 104. Niesel, however, considers this to be a deliberate omission which perverts the sense of the passage, *Die Theologie Calvins* (1957), 98, n. 98. Berkouwer, in his discussion of this subject, relies on Bohatec and is generally sympathetic with his interpretation, i.e., that human nature only seems to be not wholly corrupted. It may be significant that the key word *videntur* is missing in all the editions from 1539 to 1550! The French (1560) reads: "Ces exemples donc nous admonnestent, que nous ne deuons point reputer la nature de l'homme du tout vicieuse . . . ."

72. II.3.3.

73. One should view "the knowledge which the natural man has of God not as that which he has learned by his own autonomous reason, but rather as that which the Spirit of God has not allowed him to deny," E. P. Heideman, *The Relation of Revelation and Reason in E. Brunner and H. Bavinck* (Assen: Van Gorcum, 1959), 90.

74. Berkouwer, op. cit., 203. "The bond between God and man has

not, therefore, despite sin, been entirely severed. God does not leave man to himself, and man cannot get away from God. Instead, he remains lying within the pale of God's revelation, and under the bonds of his law," H. Bavinck, *Our Reasonable Faith* (Grand Rapids: Eerdmans, E.T., 1956), 408.

75. Comm. John 1:4 (CO 47, 5). "There are two distinct powers (*virtutes*) of the Son of God. The first appears in the architecture of the world and in the order of nature. By the second he renews and restores fallen nature . . . . What man naturally possesses from the grace of the Son of God is not entirely destroyed. But because by his dullness and perversity he darkens the light he still has, it remains for the Son of God to assume a new office, that of Mediator, and reform lost man by the Spirit of regeneration," Comm. John 1:5 (CO 47, 7). The commentary on the first verses of John's Gospel along with the Preface to the Commentary on Genesis should be read as commentaries on the first five chapters of the *Institutes*. When these three writings are viewed together, it will be clear that God the Creator, to whom Calvin restricts his argument in chapters 1-5 of the *Institutes*, is never any other than the one who is known in and works through the Spirit and the Son.

76. Comm. John 1:5 (CO 47, 6).

77. Ibid.

78. Comm. Gen. 38:24 (CO 23, 499).

79. *Inst.* II.8.1.

III

THE COVENANT AND THE DECALOG

I. THE COVENANT: THE CRADLE OF THE LAW

Calvin's concept of the law cannot be rightly understood and appreciated unless it is recognized that the law is essentially the law of the covenant. This does not negate but rather presupposes the revelation of God's orderly will in the creation and the knowledge of the law common to all people apart from any special revelation. But the latter, although the basis of a degree of morality and civic order, has been so vitiated by sin that it does not improve but rather intensifies the estranged relationship between God and fallen humanity. The revelation of God's will, either to Adam before the fall or to the patriarchs after the fall, had become so dim or corrupted that some new measure was required. This is why "the law was added about four hundred years after the death of Abraham. . . . This was not done to lead the chosen people away from Christ, but rather to hold their minds in readiness until his coming; even to kindle a desire for him, and to strengthen their expectation, in order that they might not grow faint by too long delay."[1]

A. *The Covenant: a Covenant of Grace*

It is indicative of Calvin's approach to the law that he begins his discussion of the law in the *Institutes* by relating it directly to Christ. This should not be surprising since the law is discussed under the general theme of "The Knowledge of God the Redeemer in Christ," which is the title of Book II. Law, however, in this context means more than the ten commandments or moral law but includes also "the form of religion handed down by God through Moses." This includes the sacrifices, ceremonies, and the whole cultus of the law, all of which point to

Christ and find their true meaning in him.[2]

Calvin can speak of the law in this way because he does not regard it abstractly and as an isolated entity but as an integral part of the covenant. He acknowledges that Paul did not always speak of the law in this sense, but this was because he often had to deal with Judaizers who taught that we can be justified by works of the law. In order "to refute their error he was sometimes compelled to take the bare law (*nudem legem*) in a narrow sense, even though it was otherwise clothed (*vestita*) with the covenant of free adoption."[3] The law for Calvin is thus the law of the covenant. There is, moreover, ultimately only one covenant and that covenant is the covenant of grace. In this regard, there is an important difference between Calvin and later Reformed theology which also taught a covenant of works.[4]

Calvin does occasionally refer to the Mosaic or Sinaitic covenant as the covenant of the law, but this does not mean that the Mosaic covenant was legalistic in contrast to the Abrahamic covenant of grace. Rather, this expression is merely another way of designating the Mosaic covenant, since it was ratified by the law. Calvin takes pains to avoid giving the impression that this covenant has any other substance than the Abrahamic covenant which preceded it or the subsequent "new covenant." Common to all three is the declaration, "I will be their God and they shall be my people" (Lev. 26:12; Jer. 31:33 et. al.).[5] In various ages, however, the historical form of the covenant varies. This is especially the case with the new covenant sealed by the blood of Christ.[6] But it would be a serious error to imagine that the Mosaic covenant in any way represents a retrogression from the Abrahamic covenant, which is clearly a covenant of grace.

For two reasons such thinking concerning the Abrahamic and Mosaic covenants is erroneous: 1. The Abrahamic covenant, similar to the Mosaic covenant, was not "free" in the sense that Abraham was now free to act as he pleased. God also lays his claim upon Abraham and requires from him the same obedience of faith which was required in the covenant given at Mt. Sinai. No formal law as such is involved, but the same basic principle is in operation. Calvin considers the command to Abraham, "Walk before me and be perfect" (Gen. 17:1), as essentially the same command which was given to the Israelites at Mt. Sinai. This "mutual stipulation," i.e., the requirement of faithful obedience on the part of the recipients of the covenant, is the "perpetual law" of all the covenants which God has made with people.[7] 2. The

Mosaic covenant, though distinguished by the fact that it is ratified by the law, is still a testimony of God's gratuitous adoption. It teaches that salvation is based on his mercy and invites people to call on God with confidence.[8]

However, this raises the question as to why the Mosaic covenant was necessary at all. The answer was partially given above (cf. quotation from the *Inst.* II.7.1), namely, to renew and intensify the desire of the chosen people for the promised deliverer. A fuller answer is given, however, when Calvin adds, "Moses was not made a lawgiver to wipe out the blessing promised to the race of Abraham. Rather, we see him repeatedly reminding the Jews of that freely given covenant made with their fathers of which they were the heirs. It was as if he were sent to renew it."[9] More importantly, "though God made his covenant with Abraham, Isaac and Jacob, yet he only formed for himself a church (*ecclesiam*) when the law was promulgated."[10]

The Mosaic covenant with its law is therefore not a step backwards but is rather an advance on the Abrahamic covenant. By the time of Moses the memory of the Abrahamic covenant had almost vanished. Hence the Mosaic covenant was not only necessary to refresh the memories of the Israelites; it was also more solid in that God now "bound the people to him by a fixed law and prescribed a fixed method of worship."[11] Due to the lapse of time and the indifference of humankind, it was necessary for God to engrave his covenant on tables of stone and have it written in a book "so that the unique grace which God bestowed upon Abraham might never again sink into oblivion."[12]

The nature of the covenant will be dealt with in more detail in Chapter IV, but the important thing to keep in mind here is that the Mosaic covenant which is the cradle, so to speak, of the law is characterized by the gratuitous or free adoption of the people of Israel. The foundations of Israel's relation to God in the Sinaitic covenant were grace and faith. In reference to this covenant Calvin says:

> God made a gratuitous covenant which flows from the fountain of his pity . . . . This covenant flows from God's mercy; it does not originate in either the worthiness or the merits of men. It has its cause, stability, execution, and completion solely in the grace of God. Whenever God's covenant is mentioned, his clemency, goodness, and inclination to love is also added . . . . God's covenant depends upon and flows from his grace.[13]

This point is crucial because Calvin's understanding of the Mosaic covenant determines his understanding of the law as an inseparable part of that covenant. For if the covenant promulgated at Mt. Sinai is a covenant of grace, then the law, which gives specific content to that covenant and confirms it, must also be viewed as an expression of God's grace.

B. *Relation of Covenant and Law*

Yet it is necessary to determine more precisely the relationship of the law to the covenant. This is not a simple matter because it is necessary to distinguish between the various nuances of the term law in a given context. For example, when by law Calvin means "not only the commandments but the whole grace of God on which the adoption of Israel depended,"[14] then law is a more comprehensive term than covenant. When it includes the covenant, it is simply the "form of religion" handed down by God through Moses.[15]

Although this comprehensive designation of the law is not uncommon, Calvin's usual practice is to refer to the law as a part of the covenant or as that which confirms and ratifies the Mosaic covenant. Here law means primarily the decalog or moral law but can also include the ceremonial, social, and civic laws contained in the Pentateuch. In such cases there is usually no doubt as to what Calvin means by the law since he refers explicitly to the precepts (*praecepta*) of the law. Concerning Jeremiah 11:10, for example, he notes that "the word 'covenant' indicates that God had not only delivered to them his precepts by Moses but had also adopted them as his own people and had at the same time pledged his faith to them ('I will be your God and you shall be my people.')."[16] He distinguishes further by noting that there are two parts in the covenant: 1. the declaration of doctrine and 2. its real (*realis*) confirmation.[17] The second part, the confirmation of the covenant, is the special office assigned to the law, taken in its narrower sense.

Thus the law, rather than undermining the gracious character of the covenant, establishes, confirms, and stabilizes it. "For nothing was better adapted to confirm the grace of God than the majesty which was displayed in the promulgation of the law."[18] For Calvin, law and grace originally do not stand in opposition to each other but instead are complementary. When God reconstituted his church at Sinai, having delivered his people from the bondage of Egypt, he confirmed this renewal of the covenant by the law and solemn rites so that his adoption could never fail. In this redemption from Egypt, "God did not act the part of a kind father for merely a day, but in the promulgation of the law he also established his grace so that the hope of eternal life might continue forever in the church." When Calvin speaks of the law in this way, he makes it clear that he is not speaking of the commandments abstractly conceived, the *nuda praecepta*, for the Holy Spirit in this passage "refers especially to the promises which are in Christ, by which God, in gathering his chosen people to himself, begot them again to eternal life."[19]

This distinction between the law as an integral part of the covenant and the law abstracted from the promises of the covenant is extremely important. The latter is the bare law *(nuda lex),* which, by itself, only threatens and condemns. It is the law in this restricted sense about which Paul speaks frequently in his Epistles. Calvin makes this clear in commenting on Romans 8:15: "Although the covenant of grace is contained in the law, yet Paul removes it from there; for in opposing the gospel to the law he regards only what was peculiar to the law itself, namely, command and prohibition, and the restraining of transgressors by the threat of death."[20]

Law in this sense connotes something more limited than "the rule of living well," Calvin's favorite phrase for describing the moral law. It signifies the form of the covenant peculiar to the law which stands in contrast to the substance of the covenant which is promise. Although faith and obedience are its corollaries, the promise remains even when the corresponding faith and obedience are lacking. This is not true of the law when it is separated from the promise and the Holy Spirit. This law is antithetical to the promise. However, the "law and the gospel are not at variance except that, in regard to justification, either the law justifies a man by merit of works or the promise bestows righteousness freely."[21] And even in the matter of justification this is only an apparent contradiction.

> The law and the promises have both come from God. Therefore, whoever alleges any contradiction between them blasphemes against him. . . . The law would be opposed to the promises if it had the power of justifying. For then there would be two oppos-

ing methods of justifying a man and, as it were, two contrary roads towards the attainment of righteousness. But Paul removes this from the law and therefore the contradiction is removed.[22]

Nevertheless, on the basis of this distinction it is possible for Calvin to say on the one hand that the law is a testimony of God's gratuitous adoption which teaches that salvation is based on his mercy, and then add that the covenant covenants conditionally (*sub conditione paciscitur*). In the latter case he is referring to that "special characteristic" (*proprium peculiare*) of the law, to the particular command which Moses received, in contrast to the "general doctrine" which he delivered.[23]

Calvin prefers, however, to think of the law and the covenant as different aspects of the same reality. The law for him is fundamentally *torah*, God's revelation to Israel, not *nomos* (although both are translated as "law" in English). Hence Calvin, in the manner of the Old Testament writers, sometimes uses the term law and covenant almost interchangeably.[24] He recognizes that the covenant in certain contexts has become a synonym for the law or commandments. An illustration of this is Hosea 8:1: "They have broken my covenant and transgressed my law." Calvin observes that the prophet here is actually repeating the same thing, "for the covenant and the law are here synonymous; only the word 'law', as I see it, is added as an explanation, as if he had said that they had violated the covenant of the Lord which had been sanctioned or sealed by the law."[25]

In the light of contemporary biblical scholarship, particularly in the Old Testament field, Calvin's emphasis on the law as an integral part of the covenant no longer seems strange. But when one reflects on the popular views of the law—and of Calvin—that have persisted until recently, it is possible to appreciate anew the reformer who is sometimes regarded as merely an unoriginal systematician. As Wilhelm Niesel has finely written:

> Moses is not the founder of a so-called religion of law but the prophet of the covenant God, witnessing to God's mercy and loyalty. The same is to be said of that theologian among the reformers who is usually regarded as the exponent of the law . . . . The "legalistic" Calvin has taught us to see most clearly the biblical concept of the law. He has praised the glory of the law because he recognized it to be the covenantal law of the gracious and faithful God, and imparted by him to his church.[26]

C. *The Law as a Gift*

Because of this close connection between the law and the covenant Calvin sees the law as a gift of God's grace. This is true even of the law as God's command and the decalog itself. Again, Calvin's view cuts across much popular thought of the law as a terrible burden and an unbearable demand imposed upon people. How often biblical law is confused with Kant's categorical imperative.

For Calvin, however, the law is essentially a means of grace because it is a revelation of God's will for his people and hence not a burden but a privilege, not a restriction but an aid, not a means to attaining righteousness before God but a guide for a people already redeemed and sanctified. That God "condescended to deposit his law" with the children of Israel was in itself an "inestimable favor."[27] This was a "singular privilege" which God bestowed upon the Jews alone. "He has not dealt thus with any other nation; they do not know his ordinances" (Psalm 147:20). "The other nations had not been placed under such obligations as the Jews, to whom God had given the law as a peculiar treasure."[28]

To be sure, the law also threatened and condemned. The numerous warnings in the Pentateuch give ample evidence of that. But this was necessary because of the proud, hard, stubborn people with whom God had to deal. Nevertheless, this negative aspect was not the primary function of the law. Its original purpose was to provide "a rule of a godly and holy life and a testimony of God's paternal favor."[29]

The law, therefore, was not a harsh yoke placed upon the children of Israel, but the sine qua non of their existence. It was indispensable for their welfare, "the very life and safety of the people . . . . If God had not kept the people united to himself by the sacred bond of the law (*sacro legis vinculo*), the fruit of their redemption would have been very meager, and even that benefit would have been lost."[30] The Israelites had just been delivered from a frightful bondage. They were God's chosen people, but not much more could be said for them. In and of themselves they were a fickle, stiff-necked band of grumblers. Morally and spiritually they were totally unprepared for the challenge that confronted them. They were defenseless against the paganism and idolatry which threatened them on every side.

Consequently, God, after redeeming Israel, gave her a law to bind this helpless, wayward people to himself. That he did so was not an imposition or restriction for them but their only hope and safety. For by the law Israel was "bound to her liberator." Had the Lord only redeemed them and let them go their way, the result would have been disastrous. God, in his grace, however, "was unwilling to cast them away after redeeming them; but by his law he testified that he would be the guide (*ducem*) of their whole life."[31]

They were like lambs going out into the midst of wolves. Hence God mercifully provided a fortification for them against the assaults of Satan. By giving them the law he placed fences (*claustra*) around them in order to protect them from all kinds of error.[32] The law was also "like a wall" (*instar maceriae*) between Israel and her pagan neighbors.[33]

Hence the terrible ingratitude and the great tragedy of their eventual rejection of this law, since God had given it as a banner (*instar signi*) by which he would preserve them.[34] In forsaking the law they prepared the way for their destruction as a nation and their dissolution as God's people. For the law had been given to them to provide a goal toward which they might direct their lives, lest they wander about aimlessly without a set course.[35]

For this reason the law—including the commandments—was a unique gift which called for obedience springing from faith in the covenant promises and also a profound gratitude. In the words of the prophets, God had married Israel. This alone was a singular honor and evidence of divine condescension. More than that, however, he lavishly adorned her with extraordinary gifts, the chief of which was the law. "By his law God entered into a new covenant with his people so that he did not leave them naked and bare, but adorned them with remarkable gifts."[36] Contrary to all other laws which bind and restrict, the law of God was a sign of his concern for the welfare of his people. For it was a "true and real happiness when God prescribed a certain rule" for his people. Otherwise they would have wandered in confusion. They had served a bitter bondage under the Egyptians; now they were to serve under a new lord, "under the government of God." And "this subjection is preferable to all the ruling powers of the world, i.e., when God is pleased to rule over us and assumes concern for our safety and performs the office of a governor."[37]

Closely related to this idea of the law as a protecting wall and a preserving rampart is the figure of the law as a bright light. In contrast to the moral and spiritual darkness into which the Israelites were going, the law was a brilliant light of revealed truth. It was like "a lamp shining before them amidst the general darkness of the world. Consequently, it was monstrous that the nation should refuse to follow the way which had been pointed out to them and do just the opposite, i.e., shut their eyes and plunge to destruction."[38] "God by his law so shone before them" that they should have reached the goal toward which he was directing them.[39] "They had been illuminated by his law and instruction just as by a very bright torch."[40] And yet they turned away from God, flaunted his commands, and gave their allegiance to the idols of the Gentiles. This made them totally inexcusable, for they alone possessed the light of the law. Even worse, this perfidy exposed their terrible ingratitude, which for Calvin is one of the most heinous sins of all. As he observes in relation to Hosea 4:6:

> The Lord also reproaches the Israelites for their ingratitude; for he had kindled among them the light of celestial wisdom in that the law, as is well known, was sufficient to guide men in the right way. It was as if God himself had shone forth from heaven when he gave them his law. How then did the Israelites perish through ignorance? Precisely because they closed their eyes against the celestial light . . . . They had maliciously suppressed the teaching of the law, and the law was capable of guiding them.[41]

It could be objected that the expression law, as Calvin uses it in the above passages, is practically a synonym for revelation or the word of God. For the law in this context is clearly more than the decalog or even the whole legal corpus. It comprehends the Mosaic revelation and thus is *torah* in the root meaning of that word. Calvin is not thereby denaturing the law of its true meaning, but on the contrary is remarkably sensitive to the various nuances contained in the Hebrew concept of *torah*.

According to Calvin, the act of Israel's redemption was not completed in the deliverance from Egypt. This was only the beginning. The climax of that redemption took place at Mt. Sinai where the promise was given content. Here the redeeming God gave his people a rule and bound them to himself. It was a gracious rule in that it was given to Israel to provide the guidance of the Savior God. The law was given not to deny but to confirm the grace of God.

This is why Calvin is so lavish in his use of encomiums to describe the law. Like the Psalmists he revels in its sufficiency and majesty, simplicity and beauty, profundity and power. The law of God is "everlasting righteousness and truth . . . the school of perfect wisdom."[42] "For God delivered the sum of all truth in his law . . . the whole sum of wisdom."[43] "It comprehends complete and perfect justice and prescribes a true and complete rule of living justly."[44] Here we have nothing less than "the oracles of heaven," for through the law we enter into "the school of God."[45] To be brought up in the school of God is to exercise oneself in the law, and this in turn is the equivalent of knowing "true religion."[46]

Calvin speaks frequently of the majesty of the law.[47] Yet he places particular emphasis on the fact that in the law God speaks intimately or in a familiar manner (*familiariter*) with us. In the doctrine of the law God not only revealed himself, but also "approached men familiarly lest they wander astray."[48] It was a "special grace" (*peculiari gratia*) when God gave his law to the children of Abraham, thereby "granting them a more certain and intimate (*propinqua*) knowledge of himself."[49]

In the law, therefore, there is both a revelation of God's majesty and his familiarity. Combined with these two facets of the law is that of certainty. In the condescension of making himself familiarly known to his chosen people God also gave them "a certain rule of religion."[50] Even to that primitive people in the wilderness "God's will was not ambiguous, for in his law he has declared what is right. If he should descend from heaven a hundred times, he would reveal nothing we need to know in addition to what he has said [in his law]. For his law is perfect wisdom."[51]

Presupposed in all these encomiums is the accompanying gift of the Spirit. Separated from the Holy Spirit, the law has either a negative effect—rebellion, hardness of heart, greater guilt—or none at all.[52] Not only the law but the whole of Scripture is a dead letter unless it is vivified by the Spirit.[53] Accordingly, the praise of the law by the Psalmists presupposes "the secret illumination of the Holy Spirit."[54] "If God does not enlighten us with the spirit of discernment, we are not competent to behold the light which shines forth in his law, even though it is constantly before us."[55] But if we sincerely love the law, this is "a sure sign of our adoption because it is the work of the Spirit."[56]

D. *Christ the Heart and Goal of the Law*

What is true of the Holy Spirit also applies to Christ. If the law is separated from Christ and does not lead to him, it is horribly perverted. Granted, there has been little mention of Christ thus far, although the many references to God's mercy and grace could be taken to imply the work of a Mediator. We need not rely on inferences, however, for Calvin lays great emphasis on the truth that Christ is the foundation, substance, life, spirit, fulfillment, perfection, and end of the law. Here we are at the heart of Calvin's doctrine of the law. To misunderstand him here is to misunderstand his whole concept of the law.

In view of the place of the law in Calvin's theology,[57] the centrality of Christ in Calvin's concept of the law should not be surprising. Yet the misunderstanding persists that Calvin, because of his esteem for the law, thereby minimized the grace of Christ. But we must remember that for Calvin, the law is the law of the covenant, and both are founded in Jesus Christ. Hence, as H.H. Wolf has observed, "The special esteem for the law by Calvin . . . has nothing to do with any legalism in a moral sense. Rather, what led Calvin to this emphasis on the law was its relation to its *anima* (Christ) and its being included in the covenant of grace."[58]

Note first of all that even where Calvin makes no explicit reference to Christ, when discussing the covenant or God's revelation prior to the coming of Christ, he presupposes that there was never any genuine knowledge of God and his law except through the Mediator. "We must hold to this principle," affirms Calvin in a statement of hermeneutical significance, that "from the beginning (*ab initio*) Christ was the true Jehovah."[59] At first glance, this might not seem to be a comment of any great import. In the context of this passage, however—the problem of the use of Zechariah 11:12 f. in Matthew 26:15—Calvin is making the important claim that what is said of God in the Old Testament can without any twisting or allegorizing be applied to Christ in the New Testament because the two can never be separated. Hence when Calvin discusses God's dealings with people, whether in creation, providence, redemption, or condemnation, Christ is presupposed. For "whatever is said of God applies to him (*in eum competat*)."[60]

Axiomatic for Calvin is the truth that Christ is "the perpetual Mediator" between God and humanity. "He was always the bond of union (*vinculum coniunctionis*) between God and man; nor did God ever reveal himself otherwise than through him . . . . For the distance between God and man has always been too great for any communication to be possible without a mediator."[61] "Therefore let us establish in the first place that from the beginning (*ab initio*) God made no communication with men except by Christ."[62] Moreover, "we must hold that the name of God is nothing but an empty imagination (*inane figmentum*) when it is separated from Christ . . . . He who conceives of God without Christ cuts away half of him (*dimidia sui parte eum mutilat*)."[63]

These unequivocal affirmations show that Calvin refuses to consider God in abstraction apart from Jesus Christ—and the same is true of his view of the law. Calvin clearly believes that God cannot be known otherwise than in Christ. Not only that, everything that we enjoy should not be thought of apart from him who is the eternal image of the Father. "For it is Christ alone who connects (*coniungit*) heaven and earth. He is the only Mediator who reaches from heaven down to earth. The fullness of all celestial blessings flow to us through him and we in turn ascend to God through him."[64] Every spiritual gift, everything that is holy and good, is mediated to us through him.[65] "We know that God's goodness is so exhibited to us in Christ that we should not seek for a particle of it anywhere else; for from this fountain we must draw whatever refers to our salvation and a happy life."[66] "Therefore, we shall find angels and men dry, heavens empty, the earth barren and all things worthless, if we want to partake of God's gifts otherwise than through Christ."[67]

Since one of the greatest gifts of God to Israel was the covenant and its confirmation, the law, it follows that both the covenant and the law are based upon and founded in him. Whether it is the covenant as such or "the gospel promised in the law," both were "settled (*constitisse*) in the free mercy of God and confirmed by the mediation of Christ."[68] "The main point (*praecipuum caput*) of the law and the foundation (*fundamentum*) of the covenant is that the Jews may have Christ as Leader and Governor. . . ."[69] As we have seen, Calvin sometimes distinguishes between two parts of the covenant, the promulgation of doctrine and its actual confirmation (by the law). "But the substantial perfection (*solida perfectio*) of the covenant in Christ would not be established (*constaret*) unless the authority of both did not belong to him."[70]

The law in its totality, or the Old Testament, comprises one consistent witness to Christ. It not only witnesses to him but includes him and leads us to him.[71] Moses and the prophets were ministers of Christ![72] Calvin even maintains that "if one were to sift thoroughly the law and the prophets, he would not find a single word which would not draw and bring us to him."[73] This latter statement is from one of Calvin's first writings after his conversion. In this "Preface to Olivétan's New Testament," written in 1535, he also explains that:

> God has confined his people in every possible way during their long waiting for the great Messiah by providing them with his written law, containing numerous ceremonies, purifications, and sacrifices, which were but figures and shadows of the great blessings to come with Christ, who alone was the embodiment and truth of them. For the law was incapable of bringing anyone to perfection; it only presented (*demonstroit*) Christ, and like a teacher spoke of and led to him, who was, as was said by St. Paul, the end and fulfillment (*la fin et accomplissement*) of the law.[74]

Calvin consistently held to this position. Twenty-five years later (only four years before his death) he writes in a similar vein: "We know that the most important thing in the whole doctrine of the law was that a Redeemer was to come, to reconcile the church of God and to rule it."[75] A year earlier, in the final edition of the *Institutes*, he again comments concerning Romans 10:4: "It is true that there was not such common knowledge as there ought to have been of the principle taught by the law that 'Christ is the end of the law,' but the truth and certainty of this appears from the law itself and the prophets."[76] In the Mosaic revelation "are included the gratuitous promises and indeed Christ himself."[77]

When Calvin thus thinks of Christ as the goal and fulfillment of the law, he often has in mind Romans 10:4, which has been alluded to twice in the above quotations. This is a crucial passage for understanding Paul's view of the law, but the key word in this text, "*telos*," like the Latin "*finis*," can mean either "end" in the sense of finish or termination, or "end" in the sense of goal or fulfillment. The question of the proper translation is still being debated by biblical scholars and theologians.[78]

However it is interpreted, this text is not crucial for Calvin's understanding of the law. He cites with approval Erasmus' rendering, "*perfectio*," concedes that "*complementum*" is also possible, but settles on the usual Latin rendering, "*finis*." Moreover, his interpretation of Christ's relation to the law corresponds to the twofold meaning of *telos* and *finis*, for Christ is both the fulfillment and goal of the whole law and is at the same time the end of the dispensation of the law. That is, he abolishes and supercedes those aspects of the law which were peculiar to the Jews and their cultus. According to Calvin, Paul shows us in this passage that:

> those who seek to be justified by their own works are false inter-
> preters of the law, because the law has been given to lead us by
> the hand to another righteousness. Indeed, every doctrine of the
> law, every command, every promise, always points to Christ. We
> are therefore to apply all its parts to him . . . . This remarkable
> passage declares that the law in all its parts has reference to
> Christ, and therefore no one will be able to understand it correctly
> who does not constantly strive to attain this mark.[79]

The obverse of this is that if the law is devoid of Christ and the Holy Spirit, it will not only be unprofitable; it will prove deadly to its adherents. All that then remains are bare commands (*nuda praecepta*) and inexorable sternness.[80] Without Christ the law is nothing but a shadow, lacking both substance and power;[81] it is empty, dark,[82] and useless.[83]

Christ is therefore not only the end but also the soul (*anima*) of the law. Calvin often speaks of Christ as both the soul and the end of the law in the same passage.[84] He prefers this to speaking of Christ as the spirit of the law, which he also does on occasion.[85] In either case he is only trying to point out that Christ alone gives life to the law which otherwise would have been dead.[86]

Before considering Calvin's exposition of the decalog, it should be noted that the ceremonies and sacrificial system of the law also find their meaning and fulfillment in Christ. This witness is actually more direct than that of the moral law. The whole priesthood of the law was in reality nothing but his image (*effigiem*).[87] All the minute regulations which pertained to the priests must be evaluated according to their end (*finis*). They were only shadows; yet "their chief purpose was to set forth the image (*imaginem*) of perfect holiness which was eventually beheld in Christ."[88]

Calvin warns that it would be "utterly ridiculous" to take this cultus of the law literally rather than as "shadows and figures corresponding to the truth."[89] If Christ had not been the substance and reality underlying the whole sacrificial system, these "shadows of the law" would have been a vain show and farce. For all the sacrifices and types of the law derived their power and effect from him. Their true and eternal stability depended on the grace of Christ.[90]

> From the law, therefore, we can rightly learn Christ if we consider that the covenant which God made with the fathers was founded on the Mediator; that the sanctuary, by which God manifested the presence of his grace, was consecrated by his blood; that the law itself, with its promises, was ratified by the shedding of blood; that a single priest was chosen out of the whole people to appear in the presence of God in the name of all, not as an ordinary mortal but clothed in sacred garments; and that no hope of reconciliation with God was held out to men but through the offering of sacrifice . . . . Hence there are good reasons why Christ is called the end of the law. [91]

The law in all of its aspects thus points to and finds its meaning in Jesus Christ who is its soul, spirit, life, substance, end, and fulfillment. Paul Wernle, however, calls this "a christianizing of the Old Testament and its history."[92] He expresses a grudging admiration for Calvin's "exegetical artistry" in this portrayal of the Old Testament in such a "decidedly Christian light", but feels that Calvin is "naive and unhistorical" in his approach.[93]

Calvin, however, has proven to have a sounder approach to the Old Testament than many of his critics of a past generation. He saw that the Old Testament, including the law, points beyond itself. It is an eschatological book. Therefore he insists that we interpret it in the light of its center and goal. It was Jesus himself who said, "Think not that I have come to abolish the law and the prophets; I have not come to abolish them but to fulfill them" (Matthew 5:17). He did this, explains Calvin, "by making alive the dead letter with his Spirit and then exhibiting in reality what had previously appeared only in figures."[94]

II. THE DECALOG

In addition to the moral law and the ceremonial law or sacrificial cultus, Calvin also refers to judicial laws.[95] In this threefold division he is following a tradition going back to Aquinas. The ceremonial and judicial laws, however, depend on and are grounded in the moral law. The ceremonial laws are joined to the first table of the moral law, the judicial laws to the second.[96] They are supplements (*appendices*), for their ultimate purpose is to aid in the observance of the moral law. They "are only helps which lead us by the hand to the required worship of God and the promotion of justice toward men . . . . Hence all external rites are useless nonsense if any worth at all is assigned to them apart from the commandments."[97]

This should not be understood as a devaluation of the importance of the cultic legislation and rites or of the social and civic legislation of Israel. Calvin sees all laws as a unified, inseparable whole. Just as the life of the covenant community could not be divided into moral, cultic and, civil departments, so the various laws must be seen in their unity. The stress on the moral law as the foundation for all other laws finds a parallel in Calvin's doctrine of Word and sacrament. The sacraments are only efficacious and meaningful when they are related to the Word. Similarly, the sacrifices were only efficacious when accompanied by the Word and ultimately only in that they pointed to "the" Word.[98]

A. *The Importance of the Decalog*

Yet it is only the moral law which is immutable and eternal.[99] Calvin therefore devotes most of two rather long chapters in the *Institutes* (II.7.8) to the moral law which is summarized in the decalog. This is not surprising in view of his definition of the moral law as "a perfect standard of all righteousness . . . which with good reason can be called the eternal will of the Lord."[100]

Calvin is not alone in his high evaluation of the decalog. Most of the reformers, particularly Luther, assigned a special place in their works to an exposition of the decalog. The majority of Reformation and subsequent Protestant catechisms also devote a special section to the decalog. The traditional topics in most catechisms are the Apostles'

Creed, Ten Commandments, Lord's Prayer and the sacraments. Calvin
was no innovator in this respect.

Yet Lobstein alleges that "of all the reformers Calvin is the
one whose ethic is most rigorously tied to the decalog."[101] And Kolfhaus maintains that for Calvin "absolutely valid principles—and indeed
valid for all men in all times—were provided for him in the law of God,
the decalog."[102] Calvin himself expresses the matter very strongly. It is
"detestable," he says when our morality or piety is based on "any other
rule of living than the common one given by God to the universal
church" (i.e., the decalog).[103]

On the other hand, Calvin does not surpass Luther in his eulo-
gies of the ten commandments. Their approach to the law differs considerably in emphasis, but they are in complete accord concerning the
worth and significance of the decalog. Lobstein's remark concerning
Calvin and the decalog is almost repeated by Karl Holl—but with reference to Luther. According to Holl, Luther's ethic is not based on any
doctrine of virtues or goods, but is one of obligation (*Pflichtenlehre*)
whose point of departure is the decalog.[104] Moreover, in a study of Luther's preaching of law and gospel, it is concluded that Luther, despite
the formal structure of his catechisms, actually treats the decalog from
the standpoint of faith. That is, the evangelical promise, not the law of
nature, is the background against which he interprets the commandments.[105]

Various statements of Luther's could be cited in support of
these contentions, but it should suffice to quote his glowing testimoni-
als in his Large Catechism. In the Preface he writes: "Anyone who
knows the ten commandments perfectly knows the entire Scriptures . . .
What is the whole Psalter but meditations and exercises based on the
first commandment?" He is even more eloquent in the conclusion to his
exposition of the ten commandments:

> Here, then, we have the ten commandments, a summary of divine
> teachings on what we are to do to make our whole life pleasing to
> God. They are the true fountain from which all good works must
> spring, the true channel through which all good works must flow.
> Apart from these ten commandments no deed, no conduct can be
> good or pleasing to God, no matter how great or precious it may
> be in the eyes of the world.[106]

B. *The Preface*

Calvin's use of the decalog cannot be fully appreciated if due attention is not paid to the significance he attaches to its preface: "I am the Lord your God, who brought you out of the land of Egypt, out of the house of bondage" (Exodus 20:2). He refuses to quibble about whether this preface is properly a part of the first commandment or is to be taken separately. The important thing is to recognize that these words form a preface to the whole law.[107] Some indication of how significant this preface is for Calvin is the space he devotes to it in the *Institutes* and especially in his *Harmony of the Last Four Books of Moses*. Here he collates various passages of similar import under the heading, "The Preface to the Law," a section which takes up 79 pages in the English translation![108] Nevertheless, the majority of Calvin interpreters —even those who devote at least a chapter to the subject of the law— strangely overlook this fact.[109]

Here again Calvin and Luther are basically one, although there is a difference. Luther, instead of emphasizing the preface, placed the accent on the theological significance of the first commandment which he calls "the fountainhead of all the commandments" (*fons omnium praeceptorum*).[110] It is "the chief commandment, from which all others proceed.[111] But he did not always include the preface in his exposition of the first commandment. In the original text of both his Small and Large Catechisms he omits the words, "I am the Lord . . ." and begins simply with "You shall have no other gods."

Various attempts have been made to explain this omission. Edmund Schlink suggests that the omission of these words does not mean that Luther thereby disregards their content. The reason they are missing is because in the Catechisms the ten commandments are followed by the three articles of the Creed which must be considered in the closest conjunction with the law. Therefore, Schlink submits that "in the place of the words 'I am the Lord your God' we should read the Credo. For in the Credo the 'your' is expanded and the triune God is confessed as the Lord of the ten commandments. But if the triune God is recognized in the gospel, then the decalog itself can be praised as a gift of God."[112]

This is rather tenuous reasoning. Somewhat more convincing is Heintze's proposal that Luther substitutes the first commandment for the "evangelically understood preface," but means the same thing. "This is the real reason why Luther gives such a prominent place to the first commandment in his exposition of the commandments."[113] Heinrich Bornkamm, on the other hand, insists that Luther's emphasis on the first commandment does not alter his general position concerning the natural character of the law.[114] Heintze, however, writing later, rejects this interpretation of Bornkamm's and assures us that nothing other than the "full, clear evangelical promise" forms the real background for the law.[115]

With Calvin also there is some question as to the relative importance of natural law over against the redemptive—covenant context of the decalog. As we saw in Chapter Two,[116] the formal content of the moral law is essentially the same, whether in its obscure, imperfect manifestation in the consciences of all people or in its written form as delivered to Moses. Calvin himself acknowledges the parallels between the decalog and the laws and customs of pagan cultures. He also notes that the same holds true for much of the cultic ritual of Israel. It varied little from the ceremonies and practices of the Gentiles. In themselves the ceremonies and the ten commandments are of little significance from a redemptive standpoint. "At first glance they appear trifling and of no importance, but their strength (*vis*) consists in the command and promise of God."[117]

Herein lies the special significance of the preface, although by virtue of the decalog's relation to the covenant, it also has a special place in the divine economy of salvation. The particular role of the preface, however, is to state more explicitly what the relationship is between the law and God's election and redemption of Israel. The preface does this by pointing God's people on the one hand to the authority and majesty of the Lawgiver and on the other to his gracious redemptive action in the past and in the present. In the preface, God "especially provides that the majesty of the law which he is about to give may never fall into contempt. To secure this he uses a threefold proof. 1. He claims for himself the power and right of authority in order to constrain the chosen people by the necessity of obeying him. 2. He holds out the promise of grace to draw them by its sweetness to a zeal for holiness. 3. He recounts his benefits to the Jews that he may convict them of ingratitude if they should not respond to his kindness."[118]

This "threefold proof," however, is basically a twofold appeal based on the two main parts of the preface.[119] The first consists of the words, "I am the Lord your God." "Here God shows himself to be the one who has the right to command and to whom obedience is due." Interestingly, Calvin does not dwell on God's right; even in this first phrase, where the accent is clearly on God's authority, he stresses God's fatherly kindness and covenant promise.[120] Hence he adds immediately, "Then in order not to seem to constrain men of necessity alone, he also attracts them with sweetness by declaring himself God of the church. For underlying this expression is a mutual relation contained in the promise: 'I will be their God and they shall be my people' (Jer. 31:33)."[121]

The second part of the preface contains a recital of the Lord's mercy and grace: "who brought you out of the land of Egypt, out of the house of bondage." Calvin's exposition of this phrase is particularly eloquent.

> The Lord means that they have been freed from miserable bondage that they may worship him as the author of their freedom in obedience and readiness to serve . . . . Deliverance is mentioned in order that the Jews may give themselves over more eagerly to God, who by right claims them for himself. But in order that it may not seem that this has nothing to do with us, we must regard the Egyptian bondage of Israel as a type of the spiritual captivity in which all of us are bound, until our heavenly Deliverer (*vindex*), having freed us by the power of his arm, leads us into the kingdom of freedom. . . .
>
> There is no one, I say, who ought not to be captivated to embrace the Lawgiver, in the observance of whose commandments he is taught to take special delight; from whose kindness he expects both an abundance of all good things and the glory of immortal life; by whose marvelous power and mercy he knows himself freed from the jaws of death.[122]

C. *God's Claim and God's Grace*

These two themes—God's claim and God's goodness dominate Calvin's whole discussion of the decalog. God claims us by virtue of his being both our Creator and Redeemer. As Calvin loves to repeat in the seventh chapter of Book III of the *Institutes,* "We are not our own . . . . we are God's." God's majesty and the correlate notion of the authority of the law are inseparable from his love and grace. The Israelites

were bound to him not only by the right of creation but also on account
of their redemption. "Therefore, they were no more their own masters
since God had purchased them for himself."[123]

God's claim is absolute; he requires the totality of ourselves.
Calvin does not hesitate to remind his readers of God's high demands.
But preceding the imperative, "thou shalt," is the indicative, "I am."
The grace of God does not render superfluous but rather makes possible
the imperative. God gives before he commands. And in his covenant he
gives nothing less than himself.

> Of course God desires that each one of us should be consecrated
> to him, that we should renounce all self will, that we should be
> subject to him and surrender to his guidance; but before he re-
> quires that of us, he bestows himself upon us . . . . This must sof-
> ten our hearts, even though they were harder than stone. Who are
> we that the Lord should condescend so low in order to make a
> covenant with us, and to promise us that he will be our Father and
> Saviour, so that he comes before us as one who has concluded
> with us a contract that is a gift? . . . . This should so delight us as
> to cause us to yield ourselves to God without hesitation since he
> persuades and invites us to do so by his example.[124]

Because the law functionally rests on the foundation of grace
and is an expression of grace, it has nothing to do with compulsion.
Calvin's "ethic" is an ethic of gratitude.[125] To obey the law means to
testify gratefully to God's salvation. The only obedience acceptable to
him is that which issues spontaneously and cheerfully from a new
heart. We should delight to do his will and yield ourselves willingly to
him.

In reference to Deuteronomy 6:20ff. Calvin comments, "The
only thing that Moses is saying in these verses is that the people should
give evidence of their gratitude by obeying the law . . . . The sum is that
there was good reason why they should observe all the precepts of the
law by which God intended that his people, after their redemption,
should praise his benefits."[126] Likewise Moses in Deuteronomy 29:2ff.
declares that "they were under obligation to keep the law, and he exhorts them to show their gratitude by faithful and sincere obedience."[127]

It is no coincidence that most of these parallels which Calvin
subsumes under the general heading, "Preface to the Law," in his commentary on the Pentateuch come from Deuteronomy. Calvin's under-

standing of the law might well be called Deuteronomic, for here above
all love and the law are so often coupled together. Neither for Calvin
nor the author of Deuteronomy is there any problem here. Law and love
are corollaries, not contraries. "Since God dealt with the Israelites so
generously, it would be gross perverseness on their part if such kindness did not attract them to love the law." Moreover, "by placing the
promised land, as it were, before their eyes he prepares their dispositions for submission and renders the reign (*imperium*) of so kind a father pleasant and delightful."[128]

The words of Deuteronomy 11:1 in particular moved Calvin
to compose one of the most beautiful passages in this section in his
commentary. This text must be read together, however, with Deuteronomy 10:21 which Calvin joins with it: "He is your praise; he is your
God, who has done for you these great and terrible things which your
eyes have seen . . . . You shall therefore love the Lord your God, and
keep his charge, his statutes, his ordinances, and his commandments always."

Calvin then adds:

> The point of this whole address is this, that the people should
> bear witness to their gratitude by their obedience, and thus being
> attracted by God's favors, should reverently embrace the law. For
> this reason also he requires them to love God before he exhorts
> them to obey the law itself. For although God might have com-
> manded them tyrannically and threateningly, he preferred to lead
> them gently to obedience by displaying before them the sweet-
> ness of his grace. In short, he exhorts them to respond with a cor-
> responding love. Meanwhile, we should note that free affection
> (*liberalem affectum*) is the foundation and beginning of rightly
> obeying the law, for what is elicited by constraint or slavish fear
> cannot please God.[129]

D. *The Sanctions of the Law*

It might be objected that this is a very one-sided presentation
of the law. It is true that the decalog itself is set in the framework of the
preface which speaks of God's great redemptive act. But the Pentateuch
is also full of warning and threats.[130] Is it justified to view the law so

positively in view of this negative aspect which is by no means incidental? Calvin's response to this question is provided in his Harmony of the Pentateuch where he has a long section titled, "The Sanctions of the Law Contained in the Promises and Threats."[131] (This follows the exposition of the ten commandments and two brief sections on the sum of the law.) He also discusses in this section some of the Pauline strictures against the law, but this topic will be taken up later. The most interesting point he makes here, however, is that where promises and threats and the mercy and wrath of God are related in the same context, the order is important; for first comes the promise, then the threat, first the mention of God's mercy, and then his wrath. Since this point ties in closely with Calvin's interpretation of the preface to the decalog, it may best be considered here.

A typical passage in this category is Deuteronomy 7:9f. Calvin notes that "The promise stands first because God chooses rather to invite his people by kindness than to compel them to obedience from terror. . . . Therefore, it is required of believers that they should love (*diligant*) God before they keep his commandments. We are taught here that the source and cause of obedience is the love with which we embrace God as our Father."[132]

This has a familiar ring, but in his commentary on Hosea he relates the promise-threat dialectic to repentance and shows considerable insight into the nature of discipline.

> We see that in the Scriptures promises and threats are mingled together and rightly so. For if the Lord were to spend a whole month reproving sinners, it would be possible for them to fall away a hundred times during that period. Hence after God shows men their sins, he adds some consolation and tempers his severity lest they should naturally lose courage. Afterwards he reverts again to threats. This was necessary because men, although they may be terrified with the fear of punishment, do not yet really repent.[133]

Calvin's understanding of repentance[134] in relation to its motive and stimulus comes out more clearly in his exegesis of Hosea 3:5: "Afterward the children of Israel shall return and seek the Lord their God and David their king; and they shall come in fear to the Lord and to his goodness in the latter days." Calvin takes the phrase "and to his goodness" to mean that "by this God does not wish to be dreaded by them but would rather sweetly attract them to himself, that they might obey him spontaneously, freely, and even joyfully." For "God only truly evokes reverence for himself in us when he gives us a taste of his goodness."

This is, so to speak, the preferred method. For when we are only confronted by God's majesty, we are struck with terror and want to hide from him. But this, says Calvin, is not true worship. A genuine reverence of God is only produced by a sense of his goodness; "for unless men perceive that God is inclined toward forgiveness (*placabilem*) toward them and are assuredly convinced that he will be propitious to them, no one will seek him, no one will fear him . . . . But everyone who has tasted of God's goodness sets his life in order that he may obey God." This goodness, Calvin concludes, is exhibited to us in Christ; "not a particle of it is to be sought for anywhere else.."[135]

A key text for Calvin in his discussions of this subject is Psalm 130:4 "There is forgiveness with thee, that thou mayest be feared." This, according to Calvin, is God's approach to the sinner, not that of threats of judgment and doom. It is commonly thought that repentance is largely negative and results from a fear of God's wrath. Calvin, however, believes just the opposite. It is rather a turning toward God who draws the trembling sinner to himself by manifesting his mercy and goodness. "The beginning of repentance," he declares, "is a sense of God's mercy."[136]

This all sounds rather uncharacteristic of Calvin and does not seem to fit the image of the Genevan reformer. Although many judgments of Calvin's activities in Geneva are superficial, it is incontrovertible that he was a strict disciplinarian. Many of his sermons, particularly on certain books of the Old Testament, abound with concrete denunciations of sins.[137] For Calvin, however, there was no inconsistency in this, for in Geneva he was dealing with many who professed Christ but whose lives denied him. He felt he had many precedents for this is Scripture, especially in the prophets who also dealt with a smug, pleasure-seeking, wayward people. Those who did not respond to the gracious entreaties and forbearance of the Lord were severely denounced and threatened with punishment.

Hosea, for example, denounces the Jews of his time for their faithlessness which manifests itself in swearing, lying and killing (Hosea 4:1, 2). Calvin concludes that:

It was necessary, therefore, for the prophet to speak so sharply with such blockheads, for a gentle and kind warning proves effective only to the meek and teachable. When the world, however, becomes hardened against God, it is necessary to resort to this severity which we see in the words of the prophet. Hence let those to whom the office of teaching is entrusted see to it that they do not warn gently those who are hardened in their vices but let them imitate the passion of the prophet.[138]

There is a time to be firm and a time to be gentle! To the non-Christian or child of God who comes sincerely and humbly, bring the good news of reconciliation and hope. But for hypocrites, the hardened and perverse, the only alternative is a message of warning and judgment. Calvin warns, however, that the latter approach may only be used as a last recourse. In Daniel nine he discerns the following pattern:

This passage teaches us how the Lord exercises his judgments, not by utterly destroying man, but by holding his final judgment, as it were, in suspense, since by these means he wishes to impel men to come to their senses. First, he gently and mercifully invites both bad and good by his word; he also adds promises in order to entice them, and then, when he sees that they are either dull (*tardos*) or stubborn (*refractarios*), he adds threats in order to rouse them. When even threats fail to awaken them, he takes up arms and chastens the dullness of mankind. When these scourges in turn prove to be of no avail whatsoever, then it becomes apparent how utterly hopeless these people really are.[139]

Note that Calvin does not relate this threatening, punitive work of God to the law as such. The idea of the law, of course, is never absent. Nevertheless, for Calvin the law is to be used in a manner quite different from the traditional Lutheran approach. He cites Jeremiah's warning to the people, "Cursed be the man who does not heed the words of this covenant" (Jeremiah 11:3). But this, says Calvin, is not the approach God uses in the law! The prophet had to threaten with a curse because of the inflexibility of the people. However,

if the Jews had been more teachable (*dociles*) and submissive, God would have begun to be more gentle and would have attracted them by words of kindness and love. But since he was dealing with perverse characters, he had to address them in this manner in

order to strike terror in their hearts and thus make them more at-
tentive . . . . We see, therefore, why he began with a curse. In the
law, however, God followed another order (*sequutus est diversum
ordinem*); for he first embraced them (*complexus est*) with a rule
of living well and even added promises which were to induce the
people to have willing dispositions. Finally he appended the curses.[140]

It would be false to conclude that Calvin therefore operates
with a gospel-law schema. The matter is far more complex than that;
nor does the dynamic of Calvin's thought warrant any such neat reduction. Calvin was extremely flexible in this regard and clearly knew neither a dogmatic law-gospel or gospel-law schematization.[141] What is
important to note at this juncture is that for him the law is not a preliminary, albeit necessary word. The law functions in different ways according to time and circumstances. But for God's people it is not only
an instrument of the gospel; it is presupposed by the gospel and eventually acts in the service of the gospel. For the law, as we have seen, is
not a correlate of sin; nor is its principal function that of revealing the
wrath and curse of God. The hatred of sin comes rather from a confrontation with God's goodness and grace. The reason for this is that the law
is founded in the saving will of God, the redeemer of Israel.[142]

E. *Principles of Interpretation*

In order to understand the place of the decalog in Calvin's
thought, his three principles or rules of interpretation are no less important than the significance he attaches to the preface. Again, how much
misunderstanding could have been avoided if these principles had been
given adequate recognition.[143] Calvin is very careful to state these before he undertakes an exposition of the individual commandments.
First, the principles briefly stated:

1. The law is spiritual and therefore requires not only outward
observance but also inner, spiritual righteousness. Our obedience must
be directed primarily to God, who is a spiritual Lawgiver, rather than to
the letter of the law. We learn how to do this from the law's best interpreter, Christ, who adds nothing to the law of Moses but only restores it
to its original purity.[144]

2. "The commandments and prohibitions always contain more than is expressed in words." Each of the commandments is to be taken as a synecdoche, i.e., as a part which expresses the whole.[145] The commandments only set forth by way of example the most frightful and heinous cases of each kind of transgression. The partial or incomplete expression of God's will was necessary in order to shock people into the realization of the gravity of their sins. This accounts for the negative form of the commandments.[146]

In order, therefore, to discern God's true will and intention in the commandments, one must go beyond the mere words. To confine one's understanding of the law to the bare, literal commandments is ridiculous. This does not mean, however, that people are free to give their own interpretations of the commandments. They are no wax nose!

A proper understanding of the true import and design of each commandment can be acquired by applying the following rules. First, determine the subject or concern of each commandment, then its end or purpose, and finally its scope by applying the other side of the commandment or prohibition. In other words, if the command is negative, also consider the positive implications and vice versa.[147]

3. God has divided the commandments into two tables which "contain the whole of righteousness." The first is concerned with the worship of God, the second with our duties of love toward our neighbor. Jesus confirms this in his summary of the commandments. The two tables are inseparable, but the second is dependent on the first since the worship of God is "the beginning and foundation of righteousness."[148] The essence of the law is thus love.[149]

F. *Exposition of the Individual Commandments*

Calvin's interpretation of the ten commandments in the *Institutes,* his Catechisms, Commentaries, and sermons provides numerous illustrations of his application of these three principles. Prior to his discussion of the individual commandments, however, he briefly defends his numbering of the commandments, since it differed from the division of the Roman Catholic and Lutheran Churches. On the one hand, he urges that "each man ought to have a free judgment and ought not to strive in a contentious spirit with one who differs from him" on this matter. On the other hand, he obviously feels quite strongly about the merits of placing four commandments in the first table and six in the second.[150]

1. The First Table

Calvin is not concerned about whether the preface to the decalog is considered a part of the first commandment or not. But since he devotes considerable attention to its significance, his explanation of the first commandment, "You shall have no other gods before me," is relatively brief. Like most of the commandments, its form is negative, and if interpreted literally, is limited in scope. But as Calvin universalizes it and interprets it positively, it assumes tremendous breadth and depth. For "the purpose of this commandment is that the Lord wills alone to be preeminent among his people and to exercise great authority over them."[151] This rather formal statement is directed primarily against impiety, superstition, and apostasy.[152]

Positively, however, these words comprehend "the true piety of the heart,"[153] or the "inner worship of God . . . . God, therefore, calls for the affections of the heart that he alone may be spiritually worshiped."[154] "Inner" or "spiritual worship" means "to worship and adore him with true and zealous godliness (*studio pietatis*)."[155] This true worship can be further subsumed under four headings: 1. adoration, 2. trust, 3. invocation, and 4. thanksgiving. All four should direct our minds to the living God and his glory. "Thus, steeped in the knowledge of God, they may aspire to contemplate, fear, and worship his majesty; to participate in his blessings; to seek his help at all times; to recognize, and by praises to celebrate, the greatness of his works—as the only goal of all the activities of this life."[156]

In view of this approach to the first commandment, it is no wonder that for the reformers it was a maxim that everything depends on a correct understanding of the first commandment. For what is required here is a knowledge of the true God based on his Word combined with faith.[157]

The second commandment, prohibiting the worship of images, which in the Catholic and Lutheran churches is included with the first, receives special emphasis in the Reformed tradition. Zwingli in his little guide to the Christian faith, *Christliche Anleitung*, has a special section, "Concerning Images," even though he does not give an exposition of the various commandments.[158] Calvin also devotes two chapters to this subject in Book One of the *Institutes* in addition to his treatment in the decalog exposition. John Leith accordingly maintains that "Calvin's protest against idolatry is one of the dominating themes of his theology and churchmanship."[159]

For Calvin, it is not simply a concern about visible representations such as pictures, images, or crucifixes. These are only creations of the hand, but they indicate an idolatrous heart which is not content with God as he has revealed himself in his Word and in his Son. This craving for some visible symbol shows that "man's nature, so to speak, is a perpetual factory *(fabricam)* of idols."[160]

The sum of the second commandment is that "the worship of God must be spiritual in order that it may correspond with his nature."[161] Consequently, in this commandment God "wholly calls us back and withdraws us from petty observances, which our stupid minds, crassly conceiving of God, are prone to invent."[162] It is not that Calvin is opposed to sculpture and painting. They are gifts of God, which, when used properly, can be used for God's glory and our good. But to try to portray the majesty of God in some visible form is a "perverse misuse" of these arts.[163] For Calvin, as for other reformers, idolatry in all its forms is ultimately an attempt to "confine the absolute in relative forms."[164]

Calvin also comments at length on "the threatening words" ("for I the Lord your God am a jealous God . . .") and the promise ("but showing steadfast love to thousands . . . ") attached to the second commandment. He seeks to show that there is no injustice in the former type of punishment,[165] and that God manifests his mercy not merely "unto thousands" (the traditional English translation), but "unto a thousand generations."[166] Calvin often uses this phrase to emphasize the vastness of God's mercy, and finds it particularly helpful in supporting the doctrine of infant baptism. After quoting this phrase, he writes: "God's boundless generosity, in showing itself there, first gives men ample occasion to proclaim his glory, then floods godly hearts with uncommon *(non vulgari)* happiness, which quickens men to a deeper love of their kind Father, as they see his concern on their behalf for their posterity."[167]

In the third commandment the positive implication is that "God wills that we hallow the majesty of his name." Here "he vindicates his own right and protects the holiness of his name." This means not only that our thought as well as our words should serve to glorify God; we must also take care lest we in any way abuse or defame his Holy Word, the sacraments, or his works.[168] Calvin feels that this commandment has particular reference to oaths and hence devotes special attention to this question.[169] Since this commandment is clearly a "synecdoche," the positive significance of this particular prohibition is that "every oath should be a testimony of true piety, whereby the majesty of God himself should receive its proper glory."[170]

The exposition of the fourth commandment commands special interest because of the Sabbatarian tendency in Reformed churches. It is usually assumed that the legalistic application of the fourth commandment to Sunday in Puritanism and Reformed churches is a direct consequence of Calvin's position. Otto Ritschl, for example, holds that Calvin, as well as Bucer, regards the Sabbath commandment as a "strict ordinance of God" whose Christian observance is absolutely necessary for the maintenance of the church. "In this legalistic interpretation of the fourth commandment there comes to the fore Calvin's slavish subjection to Old Testament regulations and standards which is characteristic of the Reformed churches which follow Bucer and him."[171]

This is patent nonsense and makes one wonder whether Ritschl actually read Calvin. In order to appreciate the breadth of Calvin's position, however, it is necessary to understand something of the historical background. Most of the early church fathers were of the opinion that the Jewish Sabbath had been abrogated but that in its place the Lord's Day, Sunday, had been given to the church. This view prevailed until the sixth century, when the position was occasionally taken that the glory of the Jewish Sabbath had been transferred to Sunday; but this view was never universally accepted. The Protestant reformers, like the church fathers, distinguished between the two days and insisted that the ceremonial aspects of the Sabbath had been abrogated.[172]

However, the early fathers, according to Calvin, only went half way. "We must go deeper," he says, and then suggests three purposes for which this commandment was given. 1. By the rest of the seventh day God meant to represent to the Israelites spiritual rest. It follows that "believers ought to lay aside their own works to allow God to work in them." 2. By this commandment God intended that a specific day should be set aside for worship, meditation, and the strengthening of piety. 3. This day was also given as a day of rest for servants and those under authority.[173] In short, it was given "to symbolize spiritual rest, for the preservation of ecclesiastical polity, and for the relief of servants."[174]

Calvin thus holds at the same time that the fourth commandment has been abrogated insofar as it is a ceremonial and legal ordinance of the Jews, but that the deeper significance of the commandment still has relevance for us.[175] This is due to the coming of Christ who abolishes the ceremonial aspect of the commandment but embodies and fulfills its original purpose. Christ is the truth behind the figure (*figura*).[176] "For he himself is the truth, with whose presence all figures vanish; he is the body, at whose appearance the shadows are left behind. He is, I say, the true fulfillment of the Sabbath." (After this Calvin quotes Romans 6:4, 5 and Colossians 2:16, 17.)[177]

On this basis, Calvin sees the continuing relevance of this commandment. Two of the three purposes for which it was given, viz., worship and rest, "are equally valid for all ages."[178] The first purpose, when spiritually or symbolically understood, is for Calvin the basic one. The third, he concedes, is "an inferred, not a principle reason" for giving the commandments.[179]

Calvin stressed the importance of worship (the second purpose), but not on a legalistic basis. Christ is the fulfillment of the Sabbath, not the day Sunday. Hence we worship on Sunday, not because this is required by the fourth commandment, but simply because this accords with the primitive and traditional Christian practice. This is in turn based on the fact that Sunday is the day of resurrection, but this removes the observance from the legal or ceremonial aspects of the Sabbath commandment. The chief point, as far as both worship and rest are concerned, is that a settled day or days be set set aside "for the hearing of the Word, the breaking of the mystical bread *(mystici panis)* and for public prayers."[180]

Calvin's reasoning at this juncture is surprisingly liberal and pragmatic, so much so, in fact, that Paul Jewett, following Karl Barth, complains about the "expedient" approach of the Reformers in failing to see the biblical-theological relation of Sunday and the Sabbath.[181]

Calvin, in any case, first points to the practice of the Jews, and then concludes that since this (worship and rest from ordinary labor) was beneficial for them, why not also for us? If God granted them this much, would he give us anything less? Calvin's main argument, however, is that this kind of arrangement is necessary in order to avoid confusion and chaos. He takes Paul's words as his motto, namely, that "all things should be done decently and in order" (1 Corinthians 14:40). Regular worship services and a stated day of rest are a means toward keeping order in the church. Ideally—at least for Calvin—we would set aside a certain time each day for public worship and prayers, but he concedes that this is not always practicable. Consequently, one day in particular is set aside for this purpose.[182]

Calvin was admittedly overzealous in promoting this order (attendance at Sunday services in Geneva was required), but he would probably reply that this was a necessary expedient and was not done in a spirit of "rigid scrupulousness" but for the sake of order in the church and "the peace of the Christian fellowship."[183] He does not object if churches wish to set aside other "solemn days (*solemnes dies*) for their meetings, provided there be no superstition."[184]

One may object to Calvin's emphasis on Sunday worship, but it is clearly not legalistically grounded. More than once he warns about "superstition" and "rigid scrupulousness" in this matter. Moreover, in his discussion of Paul's rejection of the Jewish observance of certain days (Galatians 4:10, 11; Romans 14:5; Colossians 2:17) he says that "because it was expedient to overthrow superstition, the day sacred to the Jews [the Sabbath] was set aside; because it was necessary to maintain decorum, order and peace in the church, another was appointed for that purpose."[185]

"It is clear" from these two passages "that for Calvin the Christian Sunday is not, as in the Westminster Confession XXI.8, a simple continuation of the Jewish Sabbath 'changed into the first day of the week,' but a distinctively Christian institution adopted on the abrogation of the former one, as a means of church order and spiritual health . . . . Calvin's position is consciously anti-Sabbatarian."[186] Sunday, for Calvin, was not a day to be wasted with frivolous activities. But neither was it a day to be regulated by countless religious scruples which would make it into a grim experience of negations. It is the day of re-creation, the day of our Lord's resurrection. "Therefore that day is a reminder to us of our Christian freedom."[187]

However, Calvin does not stop here. It is not true that he (and the other reformers) "gave little attention to the positive significance of the day."[188] Formal worship was exceedingly important for him, but he saw in this commandment far more than that. Many of his references to "worship" do not mean simply attending church services, but refer to a spiritual rest which is "nothing else than the truly desirable and blessed death of man which contains in it the life of God . . . ."[189] This is another way of expressing the first and foremost purpose of this commandment.

The commandment thus has an eschatological orientation in that it points to the eternal rest of God; but it is also rooted in the order of creation. When God rested on the seventh day of creation and blessed it, this was evidence of his special concern for humanity's welfare. "That benediction is nothing else than a solemn consecration by which God claims for himself the endeavors and employments (*studia et occupationes*) of men on the seventh day."[190] He established this "perpetual rule" that we might be gently and lovingly attracted by his own example and thus dedicate ourselves entirely to him.[191] What an inestimable privilege is granted to human beings who are invited to imitate the Creator! This should be no small incentive in observing this "sacred rest."[192] This spiritual rest, as was noted above, means a resting from our works that God may work in us. Thus we will come to be formed in his image.[193]

But the memory of this order of creation was almost obliterated among the heathen, and practically obsolete with the patriarchs.[194] Hence the renewing of this ordinance in the giving of the law added another feature. The Sabbath was now to the Jews also a sign that God had sanctified them, i.e., separated them from the Gentiles (Exodus 31:13, 14; Exekiel 31:12, 13 etc.). The Sabbath was given as a sign or symbol to remind Israel that God was her sanctifier.[195] It was in effect a sacrament, "an outward sign of an inner reality," i.e., their sanctification.[196]

The implication of this for us is "the death of the flesh, when men deny themselves and renounce their earthly nature, so that they may be ruled and guided by the Spirit of God."[197] This, of course, is a life-time process. Thus in this one commandment we see the goal of the whole law, as well as of the Christian life, namely, the restoration of the image of God in us. The beginning and end of this new life is in Christ who is the substance and fulfillment of this commandment. In him we realize more and more the reality of our having died to the old life by being buried with him in baptism. The whole Christian life is therefore a "mortification," "until completely dead to ourselves, we are filled with the life of God."[198]

This commandment, however, not only points back to the or-

der of creation and the sanctification of the church, but also points forward to the eternal Sabbath and the fulfillment of the whole meaning of
that day. Quite apart from Mosaic law, the Sabbath concept has three
focal points: the creation ordinance, the new creation in Jesus Christ,
and the consummation in him at the end of time. He is the purpose and
fulfillment of that true rest referred to in Hebrews 4:3-10. To enter into
God's rest (Hebrews 4:10), of which the promised land was only a symbol, is to experience "God's perpetual Sabbath, in which the highest human happiness consists, in which there is a likeness between men and
God, in which they are united with him."[199] This perfection is symbol-
ized already in the fact that the Sabbath was the seventh day, for in
Scripture the number seven denotes perfection. "It would seem, therefore, that the Lord through the seventh day has sketched for his people
the coming perfection of the Sabbath in the Last Day, to make them aspire to this perfection by unceasing meditation on the Sabbath throughout life."[200]

The fourth commandment, as interpreted by Calvin, thus
comes to express the basic pattern of the Christian life. Its scope is extended far beyond stated times of rest and worship to include a continual meditation on God's great work of restoring creation to its rightful
destination. This meditation is not a passive thing, however, but involves the whole person throughout one's life. Calvin expresses this el-
oquently in a dialectic fashion: We must rest from our works that God
may work in us; we must yield our hearts, wills and selfish desires to
him that he may rule in us; we must rest from our activities that we may
find rest in him; we must die to self that he may live in us. This process
must continue until we are filled with the life of God. All this comes
about by virtue of being grafted into the body of Christ and through the
reign of his Spirit in us.[201]

2. The Second Table

In keeping with his rules of interpretation, Calvin avers that
the fifth commandment is concerned not only with the relationship of
parents and children, but with all stations and ranks in life. "Though the
words refer only to father and mother, we must understand all who are
over us. . . . For there is no authority, either of parents, or princes, or
governors of any kind, no empire and no honor, except by God's de-
cree; for so it pleases him to order the world."[202] The literal meaning is

that children should be humble and obedient toward their parents. But "the chief point of the commandment" is that "it is right and pleasing to God for us to honor those on whom he has bestowed some excellence; and that he abhors contempt and stubbornness against them."[203] Moreover, honoring our superiors means not only being reverent and obedient but even that we be grateful.[204]

Thus far, according to Troeltsch, "this looks as though it were the same as the patriarchalism of Lutheranism developed from the ideal of the family. Only the continuation shows that this is meant somewhat differently."[205] The reference here is to a later section in the *Institutes* discussing the implications of the fifth commandment:

> But we also ought to note in passing that we are to obey our parents only 'in the Lord' (Ephesians 6:1). . . . For they sit in that place to which they have been advanced by the Lord, who shares with them a part of his honor. Therefore, the submission paid to them ought to be a step toward honoring the highest Father. Hence if they spur us to transgress the law, we have a perfect right to regard them not as parents, but as strangers who are trying to lead us away from obedience to our true Father. So should we act toward princes, lords, and every kind of superiors. It is unworthy and absurd for their eminence (*eminentia*) so to prevail as to pull down (*deprimendam*) the loftiness of God, upon which it depends, and to which it ought to lead us.[206]

The words of the sixth commandment, "You shall not kill," also have essentially a positive significance. The purpose of this commandment is: "The Lord has bound mankind together by a certain unity; hence each man ought to concern himself with the safety of all. . . . By this rule (*regulam*) God wills to guide your soul."[207] This concern means far more than just looking out for the general welfare of our neighbors. Calvin, interpreting the commandment again from the perspective of the Sermon on the Mount, notes that the Lord here condemns anger and hatred of every kind. It follows, then, that he requires us "at the same time to love all men from the heart and apply ourselves to their maintenance and care." For he "wills that the brother's life be dear and precious to us."[209]

There was a reference above to the unity of humanity. Calvin finds a twofold basis in Scripture. In the first place, humanity is created in the image of God; secondly, we share the same flesh. Hence "if we do not wish to violate the image of God, we ought to hold our neighbor sacred. And if we do not wish to renounce all humanity, we ought to cherish his as our own flesh." This exhortation, Calvin adds, is "derived from the redemption and grace of Christ."[210] Calvin explains in several other contexts what he means by this and reveals at the same time both his catholicity and social concern. In his chapter on the sum of the Christian life he points out that the gifts which we have received from the Lord have been entrusted to us on the condition that they be applied to the common good of the church (cf. 1 Peter 4:10). We are all members of one body (1 Corinthians 12:12f.) and therefore must apply all our powers to the common advantage of the whole body. All our gifts from God as well must be dedicated to him or else they will be abused.[211]

Calvin recognizes that there are people who are not easy to love and whom we might not be inclined to help. But he continually comes back to the thesis that however unlovely they may be, they are created in God's image. This image is seen more clearly in members of the household of faith, but it exists in all people. Therefore, we are not allowed to regard any person as a stranger or despise some one as contemptible or worthless. For "the Lord shows him to be one of whom he has deigned to give the beauty of his image. . . . God, as it were, has put him in his own place in order that you may recognize toward him the many and great benefits with which God has bound you to himself." Even when people hate and curse us and treat us unjustly, we must not consider their evil intention, but "look upon the image of God in them which cancels and effaces their transgressions, and with its beauty and dignity allures us to love and embrace them."[212]

Although this love must embrace "all men who dwell on earth," there is of course a special bond between those who are members of the body of Christ. This unity and the concomitant obligations of mutual love are particularly impressed on us in the sacrament of the Lord's Supper. In this sacrament we are not only "made completely" one with Christ and he with us, but we are all made one body by such participation.

> We shall benefit very much from the Sacrament if this thought is impressed and engraved upon our minds: that none of the brethren can be injured, despised, rejected, abused or in any way offended by us, without at the same time injuring, despising and

> abusing Christ by the wrongs we do; that we cannot disagree with
> our brethren without at the same time disagreeing with Christ;
> that we cannot love Christ without loving him in the brethren;
> that we ought to take the same care of our brethren's bodies as we
> take of our own; for they are members of our body; and that, as
> no part of our body is touched by any feeling of pain which is not
> spread among all the rest, so we ought not to allow a brother to be
> affected by any evil, without being touched by compassion for
> him . . . . For Christ, inasmuch as he makes himself common to
> all, also makes all of us one in himself.[213]

The purpose of the seventh commandment is: "Because God
loves modesty and purity, all uncleanness must be far from us." The
positive meaning of the commandment is "that we chastely and conti-
nently regulate all parts of our life."[214] Characteristic of Calvin is his
conclusion that "God is here commending modesty" and thereby condemns whatever opposes it.[215]

From a modern standpoint, Calvin's interpretation of this commandment is probably the least satisfying, for he views marriage rather
negatively. Basically it appears to be "a necessary remedy to keep us
from plunging into unbridled lust."[216] Calvin here is only following
Paul, but he does not use in this connection the beautiful analogy of the
church as the bride of Christ in Ephesians five.

A somewhat amusing illustration of Calvin's medieval outlook
is his exposition of Deuteronomy 24:5 where there is a regulation that a
newly married man cannot go into the army or any business which will
take him away from his bride. He is to be left "free at home one year, to
be happy with his wife whom he has taken." As Calvin points out, if the
husband leaves his wife immediately after their marriage, there is the
danger that she may fall in love with some one else while he is gone—
or that he may fall into the same temptation. There is some practical
wisdom in this observation, but Calvin's next comments are singularly
revealing:

> But that God should permit a bride to enjoy herself with her hus-
> band affords no small proof of his indulgence. Inevitably the lust
> of the flesh must affect the relation of husband and wife with
> some sin; yet God not only pardons it, but covers it with the veil
> of holy matrimony, lest that which is sinful in itself should be so

imputed. Nay, he spontaneously allows them to enjoy themselves.[217]

Note, however, that in the *Institutes* Calvin again admonishes
his readers to consider primarily not the commandment as such but the
Lawgiver behind the commandment. "It is he who, since he ought to
possess us completely in his own right, requires integrity of soul, spirit,
and body."[218]

The eighth commandment, like the sixth, is another paradigm
which comprehends almost the whole Christian life. As Calvin interprets this commandment, it takes on relevance for social and economic
life as well as for personal life and attitudes. As André Biéler observes
in his monumental work on Calvin's social and economic teaching, this
commandment, as Calvin explains it, shows how "the Christian order
(l'ordre chrétien) of ownership which prevails among the members of
the body of Christ in his church should inspire the juridical or political
order in its regulation of all the members of society."[219]

The seeds of an authentic social gospel and the twentieth century drive for economic justice can be found here.[220] However, in contrast to some Christian social action which hardly differs from its secular equivalent, Calvin again urges us to keep in mind the authority
behind all social concern, the Lawgiver himself.[221] The second table of
the law must be grounded in the first or our efforts will be fruitless.
Equally important, this commandment, like all the others, is ultimately
a command to love. Calvin, accordingly, begins his discussion of this
commandment in his Harmony of the Pentateuch with the words:
"Since love (*caritas*) is the end of the law, we must look for the definition of love there. This, then, is the rule of love, that everyone's rights
should be safely preserved, and that none should do to another what he
would not have done to himself."[222]

More specifically, by this commandment "we are forbidden to
regard longingly (*inhiare*) the possessions of others, and consequently
are commanded to strive faithfully to help every man to keep his own
possessions." This means that not only theft, but also fraud, deceit, and
any other illegal means used to acquire goods are forbidden. Moreover,
as Calvin understands the commandment, an employee who is careless
or guilty of waste also violates the spirit of the commandment, "for we
defraud our neighbors of their property if we repudiate the duties by
which we are obligated to them."[223]

The positive implication of the ninth commandment is that "we should faithfully help everyone as much as we can in affirming the truth, in order to protect the integrity of his name and possessions . . . Hence this commandment is lawfully observed when our tongue, in declaring the truth, serves both the good repute and the advantage of our neighbors."[224] What is condemned, moreover, is not merely an evil tongue but evil thoughts, false suspicions, and uncharitable judgments as well.[225] This commandment, according to Calvin, even forbids us "to affect a fawning politeness (*scurrilem urbanitatem*) barbed with bitter taunts under the guise of joking."[226] In sum, moved by the "true fear and love of God,"[227] and possessed with a spirit of "equity and humanity,"[228] we must do everything possible to protect and promote the cause of our neighbors.

Calvin attaches special importance to the tenth commandment.[229] For this commandment "forbids conceiving in the heart all that which the other commandments prohibit committing in act against the rule of love."[230] As we have seen, Calvin interiorizes all of the commandments, so that even where the words only refer to external acts, Calvin, following Jesus, applies them also to our thoughts and motives. Yet there is a difference here, for the primary purpose of the other commandments was that the Lord might moderate and rule our desires and affections, whereas this commandment goes even deeper and touches our thoughts even before they have become conscious desires. Here God "ascends to the fountain itself, and at the same time points out with the finger, as it were, the root from which all evil and corrupt fruits spring forth."[231] Calvin accordingly distinguishes between intent and coveting. The former involves "deliberate consent of the will where lust subjects the heart, but covetousness can exist without such deliberation or consent when the mind is only pricked or tickled by empty and perverse objects."[232]

The real point of this commandment—as of all the commandments—is simply love. "Since God wills that our whole soul be possessed with a disposition of love (*dilectionis affectu*), we must banish from our hearts all desire contrary to love."[233] In this commandment "God therefore commands a wonderful ardour of love (*mirabilem dilectionis ardorem*), which he does not allow one particle of covetousness to hinder."[234]

This completes the analysis of the ten commandments viewed particularly from the perspective of Calvin's first two principles of interpretation. The third, concerning the significance of the two tables of the law, is in a sense not a rule or principle of interpretation but rather a redefining of the essence and scope of all the commandments.

III. THE SUM OF THE LAW

In his catechisms, commentaries, and the *Institutes,* Calvin passes immediately from the analysis of the decalog to "the sum of the law."[235] This is a discussion of the meaning of the two tables of the law, taken as a unit, in the light of Christ's teaching about the law. When Calvin points to our Lord's summary of the law under two heads (Matthew 22:37-39; Luke 10:27), namely, the love of God and love of neighbor, he is only designating formally what he did in effect in his exposition of each individual commandment. His exposition of the commandments is nothing other than an application of the method employed by Christ himself as recorded in the Gospels. Thus complaints to the effect that the reformers ignored the Sermon on the Mount fall to the ground.[236] Calvin's exposition of the ten commandments is at the same time an exposition of the Sermon on the Mount. The result, as we have seen, is a penetrating, concentrated emphasis on the inner spiritual meaning of the law.

However, by specifically emphasizing the fact that the law is divided into two tables—which is not accidental but divinely ordained— Calvin wishes to indicate the crucial connection between faith and love, between religion and ethics. In general, God's purpose in all the commandments was simply "to instruct us in love" (*nos ad caritatem institueret*)."[237] But this love has two foci: the love of God and the love of neighbor. These two are not to be confused although they are interdependent and inseparable. This is what we learn from the division of the law into two tables.

Calvin finds the basis for this division in the two tables of stone on which the ten commandments were originally written.[238] But the actual significance of this division is not determined by the existence of the two tablets as much as by the importance attached to the two tables of the law by Moses, Christ, and Paul. Calvin cites Deuteronomy 10:12-16, 6:5, and Leviticus 19:18 to show that Moses reduced the law to loving God with all our hearts and our neighbor as ourselves. He recognizes that Moses did not unite these two commandments in one passage, but that "Christ by whose spirit he spoke" reveals the true intention of Moses by uniting them (in Matthew 22:37-40). Christ by doing this was virtually saying that "the whole perfection of righteousness, which is set before us in the law, consists in two parts . . . ."[239]

Love is the essence of both parts, but this love necessarily expresses itself differently when directed toward God as over against the neighbor. The love commanded in the first table (commandments 1-4) expresses itself in worship, whereas the love enjoined in the second table (commandments 5-10) is expressed in "the duties of love" toward our neighbors.[240] The term "worship," however, as Calvin conceives it, has, as we have seen, an extremely broad meaning. Similarly, the commandments of the second table comprehend the whole gamut of virtues by which the Bible describes the Christian life in all its horizontal relationships.

A. *The Love of God*

Under the worship or love of God, Calvin commonly includes piety or godliness (*pietas*),[241] faith, fear and reverence. In his Geneva Catechism (1545) he defines the love of God in the following way: "To love him as God should be loved. That is, that he be acknowledged as at once Lord and Father and Savior. So to the love of God is joined reverence to him, the will to obey him, and trust placed in him."[242]

Calvin's usual way of describing the obligations of the first table, however, is simply as *pietas,* for the first table of the law tells us that we should "serve God with true piety."[243] Yet this is only another way of describing faith which is also equated with the nature of the first table. This is significant, for if the word love is used in a more restricted sense, it means that for Calvin the sum of the law consists of faith (toward God) and love (toward the neighbor), which are commonly considered antithetical to the law. The latter, though indispensable, must always be subordinated to the former.[244] In other words, good works must be grounded in faith, or the proper order of law and gospel will be overturned.

The love of God, or pure worship, also includes fear and reverence.[245] For Calvin, fear and love are not contradictory but are rather complementary aspects of the same attitude. The fear of God, when understood in this positive sense, like love, "includes faith, and is in fact, properly speaking, produced by faith."[246] Consequently, Calvin can say on the one hand that "the first rule (*prima regula*) in the worship of God" is the free and spontaneous love of him,[247] and assert on the other hand that the beginning of genuine observance of the law is fear of God's name.[248] Fear is thus almost an equivalent for reverence.[249] There is, of course, a type of fear which is opposed to love, the servile fear or dread which is the experience of the wicked when they are confronted with God and his wrath. But this is completely different from the childlike fear or reverence which is characteristic of believers.[250]

An important text for Calvin in this connection is Deuteronomy 10:12: "And now, Israel, what does the Lord require of you, but to walk in all his ways, to love him, to serve the Lord your God with all your heart and with all your soul, and to keep the commandments and statutes of the Lord, which I command you this day for your good?" He cites this passage frequently, for he feels that Moses here describes the sum and end of the law. In his commentary on the Pentateuch he has a beautiful exposition of this passage in which almost all of the components of the true worship and love of God are drawn together along with the corollary of a voluntary and spontaneous obedience. Note how he begins this discussion—as in his discussion of the law in the *Institutes*—with a reference to what we should already know from nature and experience.

> Although he [Moses] commends the law again since it prescribes nothing but that which nature itself does not dictate to be most certain and just, and which experience demonstrates to be more profitable or more desirable than anything else, yet, at the same time he reminds us of the way of keeping it. Therefore he sets before us at the same time the fear and love of God. For, since God is the Lord, he rightly wishes to be feared by virtue of his dominion (*merito pro imperii*). However, since he is our Father, he asks (*postulat*) to be loved, as it is stated in Malachi 1:6. Let us learn, therefore, that if we wish to prepare ourselves for keeping the law, we must begin with the fear of God which is consequently "the beginning of wisdom" (Psalm 111:10; Proverbs 1:7 and 9:10). But since God has no pleasure in extorted or forced obedience, love (*dilectio*) is immediately added. This merits our serious consideration that since there is nothing more pleasant than to love (*diligere*) God, it is nevertheless of primary importance in his worship. Anyone who is not attracted by such kindness must

be made of iron since he invites and exhorts us to love him for no other reason than because he loves us. Yea, he had already anticipated us with his love (*dilectio*) as we read in I. John 4:10. Meanwhile, we can deduce at the same time that nothing is pleasing to God which is offered "reluctantly or under compulsion," for "God loves a cheerful giver" (2 Cor. 9:7). Granted, Paul is speaking here of almsgiving; but this voluntary and free zeal for obedience, such as we see in good and honorable children who take delight in subjection to their parents, ought to be extended to all the actions of their lives. Certainly the reverence which is offered to God flows from no other source than the tasting of his paternal love (*amor*) toward us by which we are drawn to love him in return. As it is written in Psalm 130:4, "There is forgiveness with thee that thou mayest be feared." Whenever we hear then what Scripture constantly impresses upon us, "Love the Lord, all of his gentle ones!" (Psalm 31:2, Calvin's reading), let it be a reminder to us that God represents himself to us as loving (*amabilem*) that we may willingly and with appropriate cheerfulness acquiesce in what he commands.[251]

From the first table of the law, then, we learn everything required of us in respect to God. The love of God is expressed in worship, and worship in turn is an expression of the total person in grateful and humble response to one's Creator, Redeemer, Father, and Lord.

Not everything has been said yet about worship, however, even when it is characterized as piety, faith, fear, and reverence, all of which make up our love to God. For all of this depends on the knowledge of God. Faith and piety are the main components of the legitimate spiritual worship of God, but "faith is not some cold and empty imagination (*figmentum*), but it comprehends much more; for when the will of God is made known to us and we embrace it so that we worship him as our Father, then we have faith. Hence the knowledge of God is a prerequisite for faith . . . . Where there is no certain knowledge of God, there is as yet no religion; piety is already extinct and faith is abolished."[252]

This is why the law is so important, why even the requirements and demands were Israel's greatest gift and treasure. For the true knowledge of God was revealed in the law. The first table, above all, revealed everything necessary for the true, spiritual worship of God which is in turn the source, motive, and power for all further expression of the life of faith, love, and hope. However, underlying and presupposing all true worship and the knowledge of faith is the recognition that God will only be worshiped and served according to his revealed Word. That is, no knowledge is possible, no love or obedience acceptable, unless it is characterized by one basic attitude, namely, sincere and humble submission to God's Word. If we have not learned this from the law, we have learned nothing at all. This motif runs through the whole of Calvin's thinking about the law like an endless variation on a theme. The sin of Israel—and to a lesser extent that of the pagan world—was an unwillingness to abide by and be content with the revelation of God. Like curious, restless children who have all they need or really want and still incessantly crave that which is not meant for them (or good for them), so all people are not content to take God at his word and follow humbly and gratefully. Instead they always seek to devise new means and cleverer and more satisfactory ways of worshiping and serving him.

The history of Israel and humanity is simply a history of repeated attempts to devise new forms of worship. By nature we seek to be more religious than we are required to be! But in so doing we only secretly substitute the creature for the Creator and usurp God's rightful authority. Call it idolatry or call it the ever sinister threat of a natural theology, it is at bottom the same—a refusal to accept God and follow him on his own terms, i.e., in his self-revelation. The contempt of God's word is the root of all error, a disgrace to his majesty, and the height of ingratitude.[253]

In a nutshell: "Here indeed is pure and real religion: faith so joined with an earnest fear of God that this fear also embraces willing reverence, and carries with it such legitimate worship as is prescribed in the law."[254]

This same thought is expressed in its most complete form in the commentary on the phrase from Micah 4:1, "And he will teach us his ways . . . ."

> Here in a few words the prophet defines the lawful (*legitimus*) worship of God. For it would not be enough for the nations to come together to one place to confess that they are worshipers of one God if they did not also show real obedience. True obedience depends on faith, as faith depends on the Word. It is, therefore, especially worthy of note that the prophet here sets God's Word

in the center to show us that religion *(pietas)* is founded on the obedience of faith, and that God can be worshiped only when he himself teaches his people and tells them what they ought to do. When God's will is revealed to us, we can truly adore him. When the Word is taken away, some form of worship remains, but there is no real *(solida)* religion which could please God.[255]

B. *The Love of Neighbor*

It has become apparent at several points that the first table of the law constitutes the foundation for the second. In several passages cited earlier we saw that obedience, if it is to be acceptable to God, must be the obedience of faith. This is another way of stating that true obedience issues from a genuine love and fear of God. The term "obedience" is one way of describing the duties of the second table. As over against the "duties of religion" or our relationship to God, we turn now to our duties in human society or the love of our neighbor. Whereas *pietas* was the general term used to comprehend the chief requirements of the first table, righteousness *(iustitia)* is its usual counterpart in the ethical sphere. "The declaration of Christ stands sure that nothing of us is required by the law except that we should love God together with our neighbors. From this a brief and clear definition may be laid down, namely, nothing is required for living well except piety and righteousness."[256] Again there is a broader and narrower sense of the term. Righteousness, like love, encompasses both tables,[257] but technically it "refers to all the duties of love *(caritas)*."[258]

Love, righteousness, and obedience, then, are all comprehensive terms which apply primarily to our conduct in society, i.e., the second table. But love of neighbor is no more a vague feeling or attitude devoid of content than the love of God. It entails the practice of right *(ius)* and equity *(aequitas)* toward people.[259] It requires that we "embrace men with a sincere affection,"[260] but that does not imply sentimentality. The accent is on sincerity, which, along with integrity, simplicity, and innocence comprise the main requirements of the second table regarding our dealings with our fellows.[261] Sham, deceit, and hypocrisy are to be shunned above all.

Before discussing the key text about loving our neighbors as ourselves, it is imperative that we have some appreciation of the great weight Calvin lays on the connection or relationship between the two tables. This was clearly a matter of great concern for him, for in many places he deals at length with this subject. His concern was threefold: 1. that the tables should not be confused and the distinction between love of God and neighbor thereby obliterated; 2. that they never be separated; and 3. that the second table be firmly rooted in the first—love must always issue from faith.

In the *Institutes,* after concluding his exposition of the tenth commandment, Calvin adds (before starting a new section), "Here, then, is the second table of the law, which amply teaches us what we owe men for the sake of God, upon the contemplation of whom the whole nature of love (*tota caritatis ratio*) depends. Hence, you will fruitlessly inculcate all those duties taught in this table, unless your teaching has fear and reverence toward God as its foundation."[262] In the next section he adds that first "our soul should be entirely filled with the love of God. From this will flow directly the love of neighbor."[263]

The Scriptures, however, often refer only to the second table of the law and seem to omit or disregard the first table. The prophets, for example, were constantly exhorting the Jews to repent and be honest, kind, merciful, and just, and seemingly neglected the love of God as such. And in the New Testament, Jesus himself spoke of "the weightier" matters of the law as being "justice and mercy and faith" (Matt. 23:23).[264] Some scholars in Calvin's time, feeling a difficulty here, solved the problem by applying the injunctions which properly relate to the second table to both tables.[265] This Calvin will not countenance, for he regards it as a dangerous confusion of the two.

His answer is that the second table is so often placed in the foreground in the Bible not because it is more important than the first nor because it is ever conceived of as independent of the first, but rather because of our innate tendency of hypocrisy. The Jews in the Old Testament, particularly in the time of the prophets, were extremely "religious", constantly affirmed their love for God, revered the temple, and reveled in worship and sacrifices. Their "heirs" in the New Testament, the Pharisees, were equally fond of prayers, fasting, and religious exercises. But much of this was a sham. Therefore, says Calvin, the duties of the second table were urged more frequently than those of the first. Righteousness depends on piety, but when the latter becomes hollow and formal, the former becomes a practical proof of the latter. In religious ceremonies and exercises the real intention of the heart, the genuineness of faith, is not revealed, whereas in the visible works of love we witness real righteousness. Hence when the prophets demanded mercy and justice, they did "not overlook the fear of God, but demanded earnest proof (*seriam probationem*) of it by its signs."[266]

Consequently, when the prophets stress social righteousness (Amos 5:24; Micah 6:8; Zechariah 7:9, 10), when Christ speaks of these things (justice, truth, mercy) as "the weightier matters of the law", and when Paul calls love "the fulfilling of the law" (Romans 13:8) and "the bond of perfection" (Col. 3:14), "nothing was further from their intention than to draw us away from the fear of God in order to devote ourselves to our duties toward men."[267]

> For Paul here [Rom. 13:8] does not refer to the whole of the law, but speaks only of what the law requires from us in regard to our neighbor. Without doubt it is true that the whole law is fulfilled when we love our neighbors; for true love towards man flows only from the love of God. It is its evidence (*testimonium*) and, as it were, its consequence (*effectus*).[268]

To the possible suggestion that this isolation of the second table in so many places in Scripture might be taken to imply that love (righteousness) is more important than piety (worship) Calvin reacts with horror.[269] As if people should be given the preference over God![270] No, piety toward God, Calvin affirms,

> ranks higher than the love of our brothers. Therefore the observance of the first table is more valuable in the sight of God than the observance of the second. But since God is invisible, piety is a thing which is hidden from the perception of men. Although ceremonies were instituted so that it [piety] might be manifested, they are not sure proofs (*certa argumenta*) of its existence. For it often happens that no one is more diligent and zealous in observing ceremonies than hypocrites. God, therefore, wants to test our love for him by exhorting us to love one another as brothers. For this reason love is called the fulfilling of the law . . . not because it is superior to the worship of God, but because it is the proof of it. I have said that we cannot see God; he therefore presents himself to us in our brothers, and in their persons demands of us what we owe to him. Consequently, the love of the brother is born only of the fear and love of God.[271]

It would be a terrible mistake to conclude that there is any hint in the Scriptures that love is possible without faith or can be expressed apart from it. They are united in declaring that faith and the worship of God come first. Love is always subordinate.[272] Love "flows from faith;" therefore we must begin with faith not love.[273] However, the dependence of the second table on the first, or love on faith, by no means implies that the latter is secondary or unimportant. Love is essentially one; only its form varies. In the second table we have the outer confirmation of the inner reality of the first table. On the other hand, even though the love of neighbor is a test of the sincerity and reality of our love towards God, Calvin never suggests that the former supplants or is the only means of expressing the latter. Love cannot be divided, Calvin insists in various ways, but this never means that the only way of loving God in practice is to practice love on the horizontal level with our fellows. There always remains a *pietas,* a communion with God in worship and devotion, which is never rendered irrelevant by an active life of service for Christ and his kingdom in the world.

The history of the church could almost be written in terms of the vacillation between these two poles. The proper balance has rarely been maintained. The pendulum has swung back and forth between a pietism devoid of active social expression and concern and a concern for social and civic righteousness divorced from piety which deteriorates into a sterile moralism. Luther said that the test of a good theologian was his ability to distinguish properly between law and gospel. For Calvin a variant of this test would be the maintenance of the proper relationship between the two tables of the law. This unity in diversity is the key to the whole of the Christian faith, for the two tables of the law correspond to the two parts in Christianity.[274] For "the whole perfection of the Christian man consists in two parts; faith towards Christ and love towards our neighbors. All the duties of our life are related to these two parts."[275]

Calvin has some strong words for those who would either confuse or separate these two parts of Christianity:

> He who separates the one from the other will have nothing left but something mutilated and mangled. Hence it is clear what sort of teachers they are who do not even mention faith and only urge honesty and integrity toward men. This, I say, is a pagan philosophy lurking beneath the mask of righteousness. If that even de-

serves to be called a philosophy which performs its duties so bad-
ly that it robs God who has the preeminence of his rights. Let us
remember therefore that the Christian life is complete in all its
parts only if we direct our energies both to faith and to love.[276]

One matter remains, namely, the meaning of the words, "You
shall love your neighbor as yourself." Again Calvin engages in a polemic, this time against the "Sophists" and doctors of the Sorbonne.
They commonly interpreted this verse as enjoining first of all self-love
and only secondly love of others. This may sound strange to the modern mind—a command to love one's self—but it was no isolated phenomenon in the church, even after the Reformation,[277] and has found
advocates in our own time in the apostles of self esteem. Calvin (and
Luther) took an unequivocal stand here. Axiomatic for him was the
principle that "our life shall best conform to God's will and the pre-
scription of the law when it is in every respect most fruitful for our
brethren." He goes on to assert that

in the entire law we do not read one syllable that lays a rule on
man as regards those things which he may or may not do, for the
advantage of his own flesh. Obviously, since men were born in
such a state that they are all too much inclined to self-love—and,
however much they deviate from truth, they still keep self-love—
there was no need of a law that would increase or rather enkindle
this already excessive love . . . .He lives the best and holiest life
who lives and strives for himself as little as he can . . . . Indeed, to
express how profoundly we must be inclined to love our neighbors, the Lord measured it by the love of ourselves because he
had at hand no more violent or stronger emotion than this.[278]

But who is our neighbor? Calvin takes his clue from the parable of the good Samaritan and concludes that we are under obligation to
show love and kindness toward the whole human race. The point of this
commandment is that "the whole human race is united by a sacred bond
of fellowship." The remotest stranger is our neighbor, "because God
has bound all men together for the purpose of helping each other."
Hence all that is required for some one to be considered our "neighbor"
is that they be human beings; for "we cannot obliterate our common nature."[279] Granted, the more closely a person is related to us "the more
intimate obligation we have to assist him." There are natural ties which

inevitably make for closer relationships and a consequent sense of particular responsibility. God does not object to this but has, rather, in his providence made this possible. However, "we ought to embrace the whole human race without exception in a single feeling of love (*uno caritatis affectu*)."[280] "Even those who are the most alienated from us should be cherished and aided just as our own flesh."[281]

This interpretation of "neighbor" has been criticized by both Barth and Brunner, but for different reasons. Barth objects rather strenuously to this appeal to our common nature as being "more Stoic than Christian."[282] His objection stems largely from his particular interpretation of the parable of the good Samaritan.[283] Brunner questions Barth's reasons for asserting that this is a Stoic view which has no basis in Scripture, but he too finds Calvin's understanding of the love of neighbor inadequate. He sees here a similarity to Kant's ethic of reason whereby we are to "acknowledge and reverence the same personal dignity in every man." According to Brunner, both Calvin and Zwingli were guilty of equating *agape* with this human rational love. Luther, on the other hand purportedly "clearly recognized the spontaneously individualizing nature of *agape*, its origin, its oneness with faith and its antagonism to all law."[284]

There is no doubt a similarity between the Stoic view and Calvin's reasoning that we should love our neighbor because we are all one flesh and share a common nature.[285] But the differences are not insignificant. Calvin does not say that we are to love our neighbors simply because they are members of the human race. Nor are we to love them in the last analysis because of what they are in themselves. Love for our fellow human beings is not based on their *character indelibilis*, a static quality of their own, nor on the capacities they possess which may be developed by instruction and education.[286]

Our co-humanity is a factor in Calvin's reasoning, but this is linked closely with the idea of the image of God in humanity which "especially (*praesertim*) ought to be a sacred bond of union."[287] The bond that unites the human race is thus not so much humanity as such as God himself. Even nature should teach us that "man was created for the sake of man;"[288] but the particular motivation of the believer is to be found elsewhere. For people "are to be contemplated not in themselves (*per se*) but in God. Therefore, if we rightly direct our love, we must first turn our eyes not to man . . . but to God, who bids us extend to all men the love we bear to him, that this may be an unchanging principle: whatever the character of man, we must yet love him because we love God."[289]

As we saw in Calvin's exposition of the sixth commandment, it is the presence and image of God in our brothers and sisters which makes them objects of our love. If God has deigned to grant his image to all people, we cannot despise them. For in our neighbors we are confronted by God. Moreover, it must be kept in mind that Calvin says that these exhortations are based not only on our sharing the image of God, but also on "the redemption and grace in Christ." Among Christians, moreover, there is the further bond of being one body in Christ.[290]

The christological basis of this commandment is seen in the pattern of love. Our love of the neighbor is not some natural possibility, but is a reflex action, an expression of gratitude for what God in Christ has done for us. "We love because he first loved us." It is only when our lives are "entirely filled with the love of God" that we will be able to love our neighbor.[291]

A prior redemption was also the basis for God's command to the Israelites to care for the stranger and sojourner in their midst.[292] In Deuteronomy 10:19, for example, the Israelites are exhorted to love the sojourner because they too were once sojourners in Egypt. They must be compassionate to others because God had first been compassionate toward them in delivering them from bondage in Egypt.[293]

This represents a fundamental difference from either a Stoic or Kantian ethic. Calvin does not hesitate to appeal to the order of creation, but he proceeds to develop this commandment on a distinctly Christian basis. He would remind us that in the last analysis the love of neighbor "seeks its cause in God, is rooted in him, and is directed toward him."[294]

The sum and purpose of the whole law then comes to this:

> the fulfillment of righteousness to form human life to the archetype (*exemplar*) of divine purity. For God has so depicted his character (*ingenium*) in the law that if any man carries out in deeds whatever is joined there, he will express the image of God, as it were, in his own life . . . . Here is the object of the teaching of the law: to join man by holiness of life to his God, and as Moses says, to make him cleave to God.[295]

The "perfection of this holiness" consists in the double commandment to love God "with all our heart, soul, and strength, and our neighbor as ourselves."[296] For "on these two commandments hang all the law and the prophets" (Matthew 22:40)—but not the gospel! Hence a distinction must be made here between the law and the gospel.

> In this passage Christ does not state in general (*generaliter*) what we ought to learn in the Word of God, but explains, according to the circumstances of the occasion, the end (*scopum*) to which the commandments are directed. But the free forgiveness of sins by which we are reconciled to God, confidence in calling on him, which is the pledge (*arrabon*) of our future inheritance—and all the other parts of faith, although they hold the first rank in the law, do not "depend on these two commandments." For it is one thing to demand what we owe and another thing to offer what we do not possess.[297]

The law serves the gospel, historically follows it, and is presupposed by it; but the distinction between the two must be maintained. It is also necessary to keep in mind that this law, the law of the covenant and a gift of God's grace, when misunderstood and perverted, can be turned into the law of sin and death, the law which offers a righteousness which is unalterably opposed to the righteousness which comes by faith. The clarification of this double meaning of the law and the relationship between law and gospel is the subject of the next chapter.

NOTES

1. *Inst.* II.7.1. In the written law God "sealed up his grace that the knowledge of it might never be obliterated," Comm. Ps. 78:5 (CO 31, 723).
2. Ibid.
3. *Inst.* II.7.2.
4. See Donald J. Bruggink, "Calvin and Federal Theology," in *The Reformed Review*, Sept., 1959; E.H. Emerson, "Calvin and Covenant Theology," in *Church History*, June, 1956; and James B. Torrance, "Calvin and Puritanism in England and Scotland: Some Basic Concepts in the Development of

'Federal Theology'." in *Calvinus Reformator: His Contributions to Theology, Church, and Society* (Potchefstrom, South Africa, 1982).

    5. Cf. *Inst.* II.8.14 and II.10.8.

    6. Comm. Ex. 12:14 (CO 24, 290); Ex. 31:13 (CO 24, 584); Jer. 31:31 (CO 38, 688). "The whole law belongs to the varying '*modus administrationis*' of the one covenant of grace," H.H. Wolf, *Die Einheit des Bundes. Das Verhältnis Vom Altem und Neuem Testament bei Calvin* (Neukirchen: Neukirchen Kreis Moers, 1958), 50.

    7. Comm. Gen. 17.1 (CO 23, 234); Comm. Jer. 18:1-6 (CO 38, 294). This "mutual stipulation", however, should not be taken to mean that God's covenant depends on our obedience. Calvin flatly denies this in his Comm. on Daniel 9:4 (CO 41, 133).

    8. Comm. Ex. 19:1 (CO 24, 192, 193).

    9. *Inst.* II.7.1. "God has never made any other covenant than that which he formerly made with Abraham and at length confirmed by the hand of Moses," Comm. Jer. 31:31 (CO 38, 688).

    10. Comm. Jer. 7:22 (CO 37, 691). Cf. *Inst.* IV.2.7.

    11. Comm. Ezek. 16:8 (CO 40, 342).

    12. Comm. Ex. 19:1 (CO 24, 192).

    13. Comm. Daniel 9:4 (CO 41, 133, 134).

    14. Comm. Ezek. 20:12 (CO 40, 483). Similarly in his Comm. on Ps. 119:17 (CO 32, 222): "By the term 'law' is included not only the ten commandments but also the covenant of eternal salvation, with all its provisions, which God has made."

    15. *Inst.* II.7.1. Cf. Comm. Isa. 24:5 (CO 36, 401); Heb. 7:12 (CO 55, 89).

    16. Comm. Jer. 11:10 (CO 38, 109). In Jer. 11:1-5, according to Calvin, "The prophet speaks indiscriminately (*promiscue*), sometimes of the covenant, at other times of the things it embraces, i.e., of all the precepts which it includes" (CO 38, 101).

    17. Comm. Heb. 3: 2 (CO 55, 36). Calvin adds that the "*solida perfectio*" of both parts appears in Christ.

    18. Comm. Deut. 33:2 (CO 25, 383). "The law was simply the renewal of the covenant, by which its remembrance (*memoriam*) might be fixed unalterably (*sanciret*)," Comm. Rom. 9:4 (CO 49, 173).

    19. Comm. Ps. 111:9 (CO 32, 170).

    20. Comm. Rom. 8:15 (CO 49, 149).

    21. Comm. Gal. 3:17 (CO 50, 213). Cf. Comm. Ps. 89:33 (CO 31, 824).

    22. Comm. Gal. 3:21 (CO 50, 218).

    23. Comm. Ex. 19:1 (CO 24, 193).

    24. Cf. Comm. Ex. 19:17 (CO 24, 202); Comm. Ps. 93:5 (CO 32, 18).

This parallelism of law and covenant so common in the Psalms is also found in the prophets. Cf. W. Eichrodt, *Theology of the Old Testament*, Vol. I. (Philadelphia: Westminster Press, 1961), 54.

25. Comm. Hosea 8:1 (CO 42, 362). Cf. Comm. Ps. 81:9 (CO 31, 763); Comm. Jer. 34:18, 19 (CO 39, 95).

26. *The Theology of Calvin*, 94. "The law would not be the law if it were not hidden and enclosed in the ark of the covenant," Karl Barth, "Gospel and Law," in *Community, State, and Church*, 71.

27. Comm. Deut. 30:15 (CO 25, 55). The law is a "singular benefit of God," Comm. Rom. 7:13 (CO 49, 127).

28. Comm. Mal. 4:4 (CO 44, 494). Cf. Comm. Ps. 93:5 (CO 32, 18).

29. Comm. Deut. 31:24-26 (CO 25, 355).

30. Comm. Ps. 111:7 (CO 32, 169). "This covenant with its provisions of commands and promises, is the charter of Israel's existence as the chosen people of God . . . and the important thing is that the commands, no less than the promises, are the gift of God to his people," T.W. Manson, *Ethics and the Gospel* (London: SCM Press, 1960), 18.

31. Comm. Ezek. 20:12 (CO 40, 483).

32. Comm. Ezek. 13:19 (CO 40, 294).

33. Comm. Ezek. 11:12 (CO 40, 234).

34. Comm. Hosea 8:12 (CO 42, 377).

35. Comm. Ezek. 20:7 (CO 40, 476).

36. Comm. Ezek. 16:9 (CO 40, 343).

37. Comm. Jer. 30:9 (CO 38, 619). This concept of the law as a gift and as the life, joy, and hope of God's people finds an echo in many statements of Barth: "Always when he wills and creates a people for himself, God also explains what he wants of man. He establishes his law . . . .It is the grace of God which is attested to us by the claim of God," *Church Dogmatics* II.2, 575. "For the children of God there is nothing bitter about the severity of the law from which there is no escape, the mercy which reveals our misery, the freedom and glory of God, which take from us all claim, the order which obtains here . . . . There is nothing shameful about it. They do not need to flee from it. It is all sweet. It is the greatest possible honor," *Church Dogmatics* I.2, 393.

38. Comm. Isa. 5:13 (CO 36, 111). Cf. Comm. Dan. 9:5 (CO 41, 137).

39. Comm. Ezek. 20:5 (40, 475).

40. Comm. Isa. 42:4 (CO 37, 74).

41. Comm. Hos. 4:6 (CO 42, 274). Cf. Comm. Hos. 7:11 (CO 42, 350).

42. Comm. Ps. 119:142 (CO 32, 279). Cf. Comm. Ps. 119:137 (CO 32, 277).

43. Comm. Ezek. 18:8 (CO 40, 430).

44. Comm. Jer. 23:22. Cf. *Inst.* II.2.21.

45. Comm. Ps. 73:16 (CO 31, 682). The law contains "a heavenly storehouse (*thesaurus*) of doctrine," Comm Deut. 33:19 (CO 25, 388).

46. Comm. Jer. 16:11 (CO 38, 247). Cf. Comm. Jer. 44:10 (CO 39, 257).

47. Comm. Ex. 25:8f. (CO 24, 405); Comm. Jer. 26:4, 5 (CO 38, 517); Comm. Matt. 15:1 (CO 45, 446); *Inst.* II.8.13.

48. Comm. Ps. 68:34 (CO 31, 636). Cf. Comm. Hosea 7:10 (CO 42, 350).

49. Comm. Ps. 19:7 (CO 31, 199).

50. Comm. Jer. (CO 39, 251).

51. Comm. Jer. 26:4 (CO 38, 517). Cf. Comm. Jer. 44:10 (CO 39, 257). This does not mean that the later revelation of God to the prophets is superfluous. The role of the prophets, however, is largely interpretive. The law remains, so to speak, the foundation or bed-rock of God's revelation. See Comm. Jer. 26:4f. (CO 38, 517, 518). The relation of the law and the gospel is discussed in detail in Chapter Four, Section II.

52. See *Inst.* II.2.21; III.2.33; Comm. Ps. 40:7 (CO 31, 412); Comm. Ps. 86:11 (CO 31, 795).

53. *Inst.* I.9.3. Comm. Ps. 119:133 (CO 32, 275). Cf. the discussion of this subject in Chapter Four, Section III, A.

54. Comm. Ps. 73:16 (CO 31, 682).

55. Comm. Ps. 119:12 (CO 32, 219). Cf. Comm. Ps. 119:27 (CO 32, 226).

56. Comm. Ps. 119:159 (CO 32, 286).

57. Cf. Chapter One, II.

58. *Die Einheit des Bundes*, 50-51. "What makes its [the law's] value unique is that it is wholly oriented towards Christ," 197. Cf. Niesel, op. cit., 95-98.

59. Comm. Zech. 11:14 (CO 44, 314).

60. Comm. Heb. 3:3 (CO 55, 37).

61. Comm. Gen. 48:16 (CO 23, 584, 585). Cf. Comm. Ex. 3:2 (CO 24, 35).

62. Comm. Acts 7:30 (CO 48, 144). "Since the beginning of the world God has had no communication with men but through the intervention (*intercedente*) of his eternal Wisdom or Son," Comm. Gal. 3:19 (CO 50, 216). Cf. *Inst.* IV.8.5.

63. Comm. John 5:23 (CO 47, 115).

64. Comm. Gen. 28:12 (CO 23, 391).

65. Comm. Acts 10:4, (CO 48, 227); Comm. Ex. 28:4 (CO 24, 430).

66. Comm. Hosea 3:5 (CO 42, 265).

67. Comm. John 1:16 (CO 47, 14).

68. *Inst.* II.10.4. Cf. Comm. Gen. 28:12 (CO 23, 391).
69. Comm. Acts 13:16 (CO 48, 289).
70. Comm. Heb. 3:2 (CO 55, 36). A whole paragraph here is inexplicably missing from the new English translation of Calvin's Commentary on Hebrews by W. B. Johnston (Torrance Edition).
71. This is the theme of Chapter 6 of Book II of the *Institutes*.
72. Comm. Matt. 17:6-8 (CO 45, 489).
73. Preface to Olivétan's New Testament (CO 9, 815). Cf. Comm. John 5:38 (CO 47, 127); Sermon on Eph. 2:19-22 (CO 51, 427).
74. CO 9, 801.
75. Comm. Mal. 3:1 (CO 44, 462). Cf. the title of Chapter 7, Book II of the *Institutes*.
76. II.6.4.
77. Comm. Acts 7:38 (CO 48, 51). This sentence is an exact parallel to one in the Commentary on Ps. 19:8 (CO 31, 201) except that there Calvin substitutes "gospel" for "gratuitous promises."
78. For recent surveys of how various commentators line up on this issue see Ernst Käsemann. *Commentary on Romans* (Grand Rapids: Eerdmans, 1980), 282f.; and Leon Morris, *Epistle to the Romans* (Grand Rapids: Eerdmans, 1988), 380f. Most recent expositions and translations (except C.E.B. Cranfield and the New Jerusalem Bible) interpret *telos* as suggesting an end of the Jewish way of attaining righteousness, but many of them also conclude that it is not a case of "a strict either or", i.e., end or goal. So, e.g., James G. Dunn, *Romans 9-16*. Word Biblical Commentary 38B (Dallas: Word, 1988), 589.
79. Comm. Rom. 10:4 (CO 49, 196). Further allusions to Rom. 10:4 are found in: Comm. Gen. 17:13 (CO 23, 242); Comm. Ps. 119:17 (CO 32, 222); Comm. Lk. 24:27 (CO 45, 807); Comm. Acts 7:52 (CO 48, 164); Comm. Eph. 2:20 (CO 51, 175); Comm. Heb. 4:10 (CO 55, 49); *Inst.* I.6.2; II.7.2.

Luther's comments on this passage in his *Lectures on Romans* (1515-16) are very similar. Here, he says, Paul "wanted to give us an impressive proof of the fact that the whole Scripture, if one contemplates it inwardly, deals everywhere with Christ . . . . Every word in the Bible points to Christ," Tr. by Wilhelm Pauck, Library of Christian Classics (LCC). Vol XV (Philadelphia: Westminster, 1961), 288. In his *Lectures on the Epistle to the Hebrews* (1517-18) Luther interprets the phrase "Christ is the end of the law" in the light of Matt . 5 :17, "I came not to destroy the law but to fulfill the law," Tr. by James Atkinson, LCC, Vol. XVI, *Luther: Early Theological Works* (Philadelphia:Westminster, 1962), 139. The accent is different, however, in the later *Lectures on Galatians* (1531). In regard to Luther one must be extremely cautious, for, as Heinrich Bornkamm points out, it would be easy to compose a list of antithetical statements where on the one hand Luther asserts that the law has been abolished, but then maintains that the law continues to be in force for the

Christian. His conclusion—which is strikingly reminiscent of Calvin—is that "as far as the matter of justification is at issue, the law is abrogated. But so far as we must fight with sin until our death, it remains in force until the end of the world," *Luther und das alte Testament* (Tübingen: J.C.B. Mohr, 1948), 116-117.

80. Comm. Ps. 19:8 (CO 31, 201).

81. Comm. John 1:17 (CO 47, 18); Comm. John 5:23 (CO 47, 124).

82. "Without Christ, the sun of righteousness, there is no light in the law and even in the whole Word of God," Comm. 2 Cor. 3:14 (CO 50, 44).

83. Comm. Heb. 7:18 (CO 55, 92).

84. Cf. Comm. Isa. 29:11 (CO 36, 492); Comm. Ezek. 16:61 (CO 40, 395); Comm. Lk. 24:46 (CO 45, 817); Comm. John 5:46 (CO 47, 128).

85. Comm. 2 Cor. 3:17 (CO 50, 45); *Inst.* II.7.1.

86. Comm. John 1:17 (CO 47, 18); Comm. John 5:39 (CO 47, 125); *Inst.* I.9.3.

87. Comm. Numbers 6.2 (CO 24, 303).

88. Comm. Lev. 21:1 (CO 24, 448).

89. *Inst.* II.7.1.

90. *Inst.* II.7.16; Comm. Ex. 25:8 (CO 24, 405); Comm. Lev. 6:1 (CO 24, 526); Comm. Heb. 7:18 (CO 55, 92).

91. Comm. Lk. 24:27 (CO 45, 806, 807).

92. *Calvin*, 397.

93. Ibid., 269.

94. Comm. Matt. 5:17 (CO 45, 171).

95. *Inst.* IV.20.14.

96. *Inst.* IV.20.15. Cf. "The Use of the Law" (CO 24, 728); Preface to Comm. on Isaiah (CO 36, 19).

97. Preface to the Harmony of the Last Four Books of Moses (CO 24, 7, 8).

98. Cf. Wallace, *Calvin's Doctrine of the Word and Sacraments*, 135-141.

99. Sermon on Deut. 23:18-20 (CO 28, 115).

100. *Instruction in Faith* (O.S.I., 383).

101. *Die Ethik Calvins*, 46.

102. *Vom christlichen Leben*, 115.

103. *Inst.* IV.13.12

104. *Gesammelte Aufsätze zur Kirchengeschichte*, Vol. I.(Tübingen: Mohr, 1932), 178. Cf. H. Bornkamm, *Luther und das Alte Testament*, 104-116

105. Gerhard Heintze, *Luthers Predigt von Gesetz und Evangelium* (München: Chr. Kaiser, 1958), 110f., 134f. Cf. Thomas M. McDonough, *The Law and Gospel in Luther. A Study of Martin Luther's Confessional Writings* (Oxford: Oxford U. Press, 1963), Chapter IV.

106. From *The Book of Concord* (Philadelphia: Fortress Press, 1959), 361, 407. The latter statements about the necessity of good works being done in accord with the law of God are repeated substantially in Calvin's Geneva Catechism, Q. 230 (CO 6, 82). Cf. the Heidelberg Catechism, Q. 91.

107. *Inst.* II.8.13. Cf. Comm. Ex. 20:1 (CO 24, 209).

108. In the *Corpus Reformatorum* 72 large columns are given to this theme (CO 209-261).

109. Doumergue notes this in passing but makes little of it, *Calvin* IV, 182. Kolfhaus (*Vom christlichen Leben*) and Wallace (*Calvin's Doctrine of the Christian Life*) both have excellent chapters on the law and deal briefly with its interpretation; but neither mentions the role the preface plays. The same is true of Lobstein, Wernle, Niesel, Göhler, Gloede, Bohatec, Wolf, and Dowey. Benjamin Farley alludes to the preface in the second of his eight principles for interpreting the decalog, but does not spell out its significance even though Calvin dwells on this theme in his second sermon on the ten commandments based on Gen. 5:4-7, *John Calvin's Sermons on the Ten Commandments*, 27.

110. Sermon on Deut. 1 (WA 28, 510), quoted in Heintze, op. cit.,

111. Cf. "Large Catechism," *Book of Concord*, 408-9.

111. "Large Catechism," op cit. 410.

112. *Theologie der lutherischen Bekenntnisscriften* (München: Chr. Kaiser Verlag, 1948), 189.

113. Op. cit., 113.

114. Op. cit., 115.

115. Op. cit., 115.

116. Section II.

117. Comm. Ezek. 4:3 (CO 40, 104-5).

118. *Inst.* II.8.13.

119. In both his 1537 and 1545 Catechisms he makes only a twofold distinction, O.S.I., 383 and CO 6, 54.

120. When God "speaks to us of his dominion [in Deut. 5.6-7] which is over us, and when he refers to himself as our God, that ought to make us aware of his paternal goodness," *Sermons on the Ten Commandments*, No. 2 on Deut. 5:4-7 (CO 26, 254).

121. *Inst.* II.8.14.

122. *Inst.* II.8.15.

123. Comm. Ex. 20:1, 2 (CO 24, 209, 210). Note the prominence of the ideas of freedom and voluntary obedience in these pas-sages. This comes out again in the commentary on the parallel text in Lev. 19:36: Moses "relates the favor of redemption that they may willingly submit themselves to his law and to him from whom they received their deliverance. For whenever God calls himself Jehovah, it ought to suggest his majesty, before which all men ought to be humbled. The mention of redemption, however, should automatically elicit

from us voluntary submission" (CO 24, 212). Cf. Comm. Deut. 11:5 (CO 24, 238).

124. Sermon on Deut. 29:9f. (CO 28, 513), quoted in Niesel, *Theology of Calvin*, 93.

125. This is also the case with the Heidelberg Catechism which treats the decalog not in Part I, which deals with guilt, but in Part III, which is on gratitude.

126. Comm. Deut. 6:20ff. (CO 24, 225).

127. Comm. Deut. 29:2ff. (CO 24, 243). Cf. Comm. Deut. 11:18 (CO 24, 229).

128. Comm. Deut. 6:1 (CO 24, 246). Cf. Comm. Deut. 8:1 (CO 24, 239).

129. Comm. Deut. 11:1 (CO 24, 237). "It is not enough that we fear God in a servile manner, as if we were being forced; rather, it is imperative that love be joined with it," *Sermons on the Ten Commandments*, No. 2, on Deut. 5:4.7 (CO 26, 255). "For what is gained if we obey God while gritting our teeth while our heart craves the opposite?" Ibid., Sermon No. 8 (CO 26, 322).

130. T. W. Manson points out that of the 613 specific commandments in the Pentateuch, 248 are positive and 365 prohibitive, op. cit., 20.

131. CO 24, 5-58.

132. Comm. Deut. 7:9f. (CO 25, 19, 20). Cf. Comm. Deut. 10:12f., (CO 24, 723).

133. Comm. Hosea 2:2 (CO 42, 223).

134. Calvin's view of repentance is dealt with more fully in Chapter V, Section I, C.

135. Comm. Hosea 3:5 (CO 42, 264, 265).

136. Comm. Hosea 6:1 (CO 42, 319). Cf. Comm. Jer. 9:24 (CO 38, 52).

137. Georges Barrois provides us with a vivid example in his summary of some unpublished sermons on Isaiah, "Calvin and the Genevans," in *Theology Today*, Jan., 1965, 458-465. Cf. Benjamin W. Farley's translation of *John Calvin on the Ten Commandments*, especially Sermons 9 (CO 25, 334 ff.) and 11 (CO 26, 359 ff.) which deal respectively with adultery and bearing false witness.

138. Comm. Hosea 4:1 (CO 42, 268).

139. Comm. Daniel 9:13 (CO 42, 148). Cf. Comm. Ezek. 20:15 (CO 40, 488).

140. Comm. Jer. 11:3 (CO 38, 99).

141. Cf. Chapter V, Section E.

142. Lobstein, op. cit., 56-7.

143. Dowey, op. cit., 226-7; Büsser, *Calvin's Urteil über sich selbst*, 37-8; and Farley, op. cit.; 26-8, are the only Calvin scholars who take note of

their significance. Farley not only lists these principles of interpretation in the introduction to his translation of Calvin's sermons on the Ten Commandments but also adds five others "inferred" from Calvin's approach in the sermons, viz,: 1 - "The sufficiency of God's will," 2 - "The God of the Decalog is both a righteous and a merciful God," 3 - "Calvin's role of opposites," 4 - "The strong language of the Law," 5 - The precept of love. "In addition," says Farley, "there are three other principles that appear in the sermons and exercise occasional control over Calvin's interpretation of the law: 1 - the image of God in man; 2 - a text's natural sense, and 3 - the principle of accommodation" (278). Some of these "principles" are so general that they apply more generally to Calvin's overall hermeneutic than to the law as such.

144. *Inst.* II.8.6, 7. For a refutation of the older view that Calvin's ethic "stands somewhere in the middle between Moses and Christ and that he brought them both to a compromise with each other," see the critique and careful exegetical study of Dieter Schellong, *Das evangelische Gesetz in der Auslegung Calvins* (München: Chr. Kaiser Verlag, 1968), 9. After examining Calvin's exposition of the Sermon on the Mount in detail, Schellong concludes: "Calvin's interpretation of the commands of Jesus in their absoluteness (*Unbedingtheit*) could hardly be conceived of more radically than they are," 71.

145. The French edition has "qu'une partie est mise pour le tout" instead of the Latin "synecdoche," *Inst.* II.8.8. In his commentary on the fifth commandment, Calvin explains further that in the commandments, "God by 'synecdoche' embraces under a specific rule a general principle" (CO 24, 605).

146. *Inst.* II.8.10.

147. *Inst.* II.8.8. Doumergue has summarized these three rules succinctly: The commandments "are at the same time particular and general, negative and positive, material and spiritual," *Calvin* IV, 182.

Luther approached the commandments in much the same way. "He expands the brief imperatives of the Mosaic law . . . and shows how they take in what he believes to be the full range of man's moral duties and Godpleasing works. He is obviously not content to limit the ten commandments to simple 'don'ts' and to stick slavishly and narrowly to the single sentence 'thou shalt not.' On practically every page of the decalog section of the [Large] Catechism, he exhorts us energetically to attend to our positive obligations . . .," McDonough, op. cit., 75. Cf. the similar treatment in Melanchthon, *Loci Communes Theologici* (1521), edited by Wilhelm Pauck, LCC Vol. XIX: *Melanchthon and Bucer* (Philadelphia: Westminster, 1969), 53-57.

148. *Inst.* II.8.11. Cf. II.8.50, 51. This point will be amplified in Section III on the sum of the law.

149. *Inst.* II.8.12. More specifically, the "honor, fear and love" of God, and "everything pertaining to the love toward men." In II.8.2 a similar phrase is used: We owe God "glory, reverence, love, and fear." The phrase

which prefaces each answer to the questions concerning the ten commandments in Luther's Small Catechism is: "We should fear and love God . . . " *Book of Concord*, 342, 344.

150. *Inst.* II.8.12. This division is generally accepted by biblical scholars today.

151. *Inst.* II.8-16.

152. Ibid.

153. Geneva Catechism (1545), Q. 142 (CO 6, 54).

154. Comm. Ex. 20:3 (CO 24, 262).

155. *Inst.* II.8.16. ". . . each one of us, from his mother's womb, is wonderfully adept at devising idols," Comm. Acts 28:6 (CO 48, 562).

156. Ibid. Büsser, op. cit., 38-47, deals at length with these four facets of worship in order to illustrate Calvin's judgment of himself. In his discussion of "thanksgiving," or prayer, he alludes to the exposition of the Lord's Prayer in the *Institutes* (III.20.34f.) and notes that Calvin sees ethical implications in each of the petitions and thus gives "concentrated guidance for the Christian life generally. Thereby prayer moves into the middle of the law," 45.

157. Comm. Deut. 12:32 (CO 24, 284).

158. See the modernized German version edited by Gerhard C. Muras (Hamburg: Furche Verlag, 1962), 45-51.

159. John H. Leith, "Calvin's Polemic Against Idolatry," in *Soli Deo Gloria. New Testament Studies in Honor of William Childs Robinson*, edited by J. McDowell Richards (Richmond, VA; John Knox, 1968), 111. Carlos Eire, who has written the definitive book on the subject, points out how the attack on idolatry usually led to iconoclasm in the early stages of the Reformation, and this, in turn, led to revolution. See especially Chapters 6 and 8 in his *War Against Idols. The Reformation of Worship from Erasmus to Calvin* (New York: Cambridge U. Press, 1986).

160. *Inst.* I.11.8.

161. Comm. Ex. 20:4 (CO 24, 376).

162. *Inst.* II.8.17.

163. *Inst.* I.11.12. Niesel warns that "We should be wary of the argument that nowadays people are immune to the danger of idolatry, at least insofar as this refers to objects of pictorial art" *The Gospel and the Churches*, 224. And John Leith concludes his essay on "Calvin's Polemic Against Idolatry" with this warning: "The idols of our time, to be sure, are not the idols of the sixteenth century. Yet the nature of man is still an idol factory. Men continue to substitute the figments of their imagination for God," Ibid., 123.

164. Wilhelm Pauck, *Heritage of the Reformation*. Revised edition (Glenco: Free Press, 1961), 171.

165. *Inst.* II.8.19, 20.

166. *Inst.* II.8.21. Cf. note #31 in LCC Translation. This phrase

shows that God "is inclined more to humanity and beneficence than to severity," 1545 Catechism, Q. 158 (CO 6, 60).

167. *Inst.* IV.16.9. Cf. IV.16.15.

168. *Inst.* II.8.22.

169. *Inst.* II.8.22-27.

170. Comm. Ex. 20:7 (CO 24, 559).

171. *Dogmengeschichte*, Vol. III, 193. Contrary to what might be expected, Georgia Harkness is quite happy about Calvin's approach to the fourth commandment. She distinguishes—as so many fail to do—between the views of Calvin and later English Puritans and concludes that "there is little here, except the imperative obligation to attend church, which savors of the Puritan sabbath," *Calvin—The Man and His Ethics*, 122.

172. Harkness, op. cit., 119. Cf. H. B. Porter, *The Day of Light —The Biblical and Liturgical Meaning of Sunday* (London: SCM Press, 1960), 19-24; and Paul K. Jewett, *The Lord's Day. A Theological Guide to the Christian Day of Worship* (Grand Rapids: Eerdmans, 1971).

173. *Inst.* II.8.29.

174. Geneva Catechism, Q. 171 (CO 6.64).

175. *Inst.* II.8.32; 1545 Catechism, Qs. 168, 181 (CO 6, 63, 66).

176. Geneva Catechism, Q. 184 (CO 6, 66).

177. *Inst.* II.8.31. "The annulment of it [the Jewish Sabbath] cannot be understood except by the recognition of its spiritual purpose," Comm. Heb. 4:10 (CO 55, 47).

178. *Instruction in Faith* (1537), (OS I, 385). Cf. *Inst.* II.8.32.

179. Ibid.

180. *Inst.* II.8.32.

181. "By making the Sabbath Commandment merely a type and shadow, by reducing it to an expedient custom, the Reformers erred on the side of Marcion; they failed to do justice to the church's inheritance in Israel . . . they failed to appreciate the unity of redemptive history, the continuation of sabbatical division of time in the New Testament Church," *The Lord's Day*, 105. For Barth, see *Church Dogmatics* III, 1 (Edinburgh: T & T Clark, 1958), 225ff., and *Church Dogmatics* III, 4 (Edinburgh: T & T Clark, 1961), 47ff.

182. *Inst.* II.8.32, 33.

183. *Inst.* II.8.33. "In order to prevent religion from either perishing or declining among us, we should diligently frequent the sacred meetings, and make use of the external aids which can promote the worship of God," *Inst.* II.8.34.

184. *Inst.* II.8.34.

185. *Inst.* II.8.33.

186. Notes 41 and 44, pp. 399, 400 in the LCC translation of the *Institutes*.

187. Comm. 1 Cor. 16:2 (CO 49, 567).

188. Porter, op. cit., 24.

189. Comm. Ex. 20:8 (CO 24, 578).

190. Comm. Gen. 2:3 (CO 23, 33).

191. Ibid.

192. *Inst.* II.8.30.

193. Geneva Catechism, Q. 177 (CO 6, 66).

194. Comm. Ex. 20:11 (CO 24, 580, 581); Comm. Ex. 16:5 (CO 24, 167).

195. Comm. Gen. 2:3 (CO 23, 33); Comm. Ex. 20:8 (CO 24, 577); Comm. Ezek. 20:12 (CO 40, 483).

196. *Inst.* II.8.29.

197. Comm. Ex. 20:8 (CO 24, 577). Cf. Geneva Catechism, Q. 173 (CO 6, 64).

198. *Inst.* II.8.31. Cf. the beautiful section in the chapter on "The Sum of the Christian Life, " III.8.1.

199. Comm. Heb. 4:10 (CO 55, 47).

200. *Inst.* II.8.30. For those, however, for whom this interpretation of the number seven is "too subtle," Calvin will not be adamant and hence also proposes simpler interpretations, *Inst.* II.8.31.

201. *Inst.* II.8.29; Comm. Heb. 4:10 (CO 55, 47); Geneva Catechism, Q. 184 (CO 6, 68). This note is missing in Luther's exposition in the Large Catechism. Instead he lays great emphasis on keeping the day holy by devoting it to "holy words, holy works, holy life." The closest he comes to Calvin's first purpose is to say that we "should make every day a holy day and give ourselves only to holy activities." On one point he sounds much more puritanical than Calvin: "We must realize that God insists upon a strict observance of this commandment and will punish all who despise his Word and refuse to hear and learn it, especially at the times appointed, " *Book of Concord,* 377-8.

202. Geneva Catechism, Qs. 194, 195 (CO 6, 70). "In this commandment, as in the others, God by 'synecdoche' comprehends, under a specific rule, a general principle, namely, that lawful commands should obtain due reverence from us," Comm. Ex. 20:12 (CO 24, 605).

203. *Inst.* II.8.8.

204. *Inst.* II.8.35, 36.

205. *Social Teachings,* Vol. II, 900.

206. *Inst.* II.8.38. This statement is very important for seeing in perspective Calvin's view of submission to the state. The obedience which is required toward higher authorities is limited and derivative because it is always subordinate to the only absolute authority, which is God. Cf. *Inst.* IV.20.32, and Comm. Eph. 6:1 (CO 51, 228).

207. *Inst.* II.8.39.

208. Geneva Catechism, Q. 199 (CO 6, 72).
209. *Inst.* II.8-9.
210. *Inst.* II.8.40.
211. *Inst* . III.7.5.
212. *Inst.* III.7.6. Cf. *Inst.* IV.20.38; Comm. Gal. 5:14 (CO 50, 251).
213. *Inst.* IV.17.38. Although most of this material has not come from the section in Book II where Calvin discusses the sixth commandment, it all ties in with his positive approach to the commandments. This is significant, for it shows how the decalog provides the basis for much of Calvin's doctrine of the Christian life, and that, rather than restricting his outlook, it allows for a great freedom and breadth of spirit.
214. *Inst.* II.8.41.
215. *Inst.* II.8.44.
216. *Inst.* II.8.40.
217. Comm. Deut. 24:5 (CO 24, 652).
218. *Inst.* II.8.44. "We must always keep in mind the nature of the Lawgiver, whom, we have said, observes not only the outward act but rather pays attention to the affections of the mind," Geneva Catechism, Q. 202 (CO 6, 72).
219. *La Pensée Économique et Sociale de Calvin,* 358.
220. See *Inst.* II.8.46; Comm. Ex. 22:25 (CO 24, 679); and references from sermons on this subject in Wallace, *Calvin's Doctrine of the Christian Life,* 119.
221. *Inst.* II.8.46.
222. Comm. Ex. 20:15 (CO 24, 669).
223. *Inst.* II.8.45.
224. *Inst.* II.8.47. Cf. Comm. Ex. 20:15 (CO 24, 713, 714).
225. Geneva Catechism, Q. 211, (CO 6, 74).
226. *Inst.* II.8.48.
227. Ibid. Here again Calvin says we should "turn our eyes to the Lawgiver, who must in his own right rule our ears and heart no less than our tongue . . . " Ibid.
228. Geneva Catechism, Q. 212 (CO 6, 76).
229. "It is clear that this commandment applies also to the preceding ones," Comm. Ex. 20:17 (CO 24, 717).
230. *Instruction in Faith* (OS I, 388).
231. Comm. Ex. 20:17 (CO 24, 719). Cf. Geneva Catechism, Q. 214 (CO 6, 76). Doumergue feels that it is precisely in this distinction that "the great struggle between the Roman Catholic and Calvinist" lies, *Calvin* IV, 188.
232. *Inst.* II.8.49.
233. Ibid.
234. *Inst.* II.8.50.

235. Comm. Deut. 10:12, 13 (CO 24, 721). In the Geneva Catechism, Q. 217, he refers to the two tables as "a brief compendium of the law (CO 6, 76).

236. So, for example, Hugo Röthlisberger, *Kirche am Sinai -Die Zehn Gebote in der Christlichen Unterweisung* (Zürich: Zwingli Verlag, 1965), who is critical of the whole tradition of giving a central place to an exposition of decalog in catechetical instruction. See pp. 130f., 143ff. However, cf. Schlink, *Theologie der lutherischen Bekenntnisschriften*, 190, who maintains that Luther's exposition of the ten commandments in the Large Catechism also is based on the Sermon on the Mount.

237. Comm. Rom. 13:9 (CO 49, 253).

238. *Inst.* II.8.11, 12, 51.

239. Comm. Deut. 10:12 f. (CO 24, 721). Cf. *Inst.* II.8.11. Calvin also sees in Titus 2:12 a Pauline illustration of these two parts of the law, ibid.

240. *Inst.* II.8.11.

241. No single English word expresses the richness of the term *pietas*, which means religion, piety (without the unfortunate connotation attached to the word since the rise of "pietism"), and godliness, and in medieval Latin love or goodness. The French equivalent, *piété*, also means godliness, but can refer to reverence and devotion toward parents or God. It is the latter idea which is prominent in Calvin's usage. A beautiful definition is given in the *Instruction in Faith:* "True piety consists in a pure and true zeal which loves God altogether as Father, reveres him truly as Lord, embraces his justice and dreads to offend him more than to die" (O.S. I., 379). More briefly in the *Institutes*: "I call 'piety' that reverence joined with the love of God which the knowledge of his benefits induces," I.2.1. Cf. Introduction to LCC Tr., li f.; and the fuller treatments of F.L. Battles, *The Piety of John Calvin: An Anthology Illustrative of the Spirituality of the Reformer* (Grand Rapids: Eerdmans, 1978); and Lucien Joseph Richard, *The Spirituality of John Calvin* (Atlanta: John Knox, 1974), especially Chapter III, "Devotio and Pietas," and pp. 116ff.

242. Q. 218 (CO 6, 78).

243. Comm. Deut. 10:12 f. (CO 24, 721). Cf. Comm. Ex. 20:12 (CO 24, 602); Comm. Lk. 2:25 (CO 45, 89); Comm. Gal 5:14 (CO 50, 251); *Inst.* IV.20.9.

244. *Inst.* II.8.53. Cf. IV.20.15, and Comm. Heb. 6:11 (CO 55, 76).

245. *Inst.* II.8.50. Cf. III.2.26.

246. Comm. Deut. 31:9 (CO 24, 452).

247. Comm. Dan. 9:4 (CO 41, 134, 135).

248. *Inst.* III.14.8. Calvin is thinking here of such texts as Ps. 111:10 and Proverbs 1:7. In a different context he says that "the proper worship of God (*legitimum Dei cultum*) begins with faith," Comm. Ps. 78:7 (CO 31, 724); and that "the principal part of 'worship' is faith, from which proceeds prayer,"

Comm. Hos. 12:6 (CO 42, 463).
249. "Legitimate honor and worship are comprehended under the name of fear", Comm. Deut. 6:20-25 (CO 24, 225).
250. *Inst.* III.2.27.
251. Comm. Deut. 10:12 (CO 24, 723). We have here the basis for the third use of the law. Obedience is required of the believer, but it is only acceptable when it is a grateful response to God's prior love and grace. "When it is required of believers that they should love (*diligo*) God before they keep his commandments, we are thus taught that the source and cause of obedience is the love with which we embrace God as our Father," Comm. Deut. 7:9 (CO 25, 20). Cf. Comm. Ps. 145:20 (CO 32, 420); Comm. Dan. 9:7 (CO 41, 135); *Inst.* III.7.2.
252. Comm. Hosea 6: 6 (CO 42, 331). A "sure knowledge of God" is "the basis of true religion," Comm. Jer. 7: 9 (CO 37, 688). On the other hand, piety is a prerequisite of any true knowledge of God (*Inst.* I.2.1,2), which is also "born of obedience," *Inst.* I.6.2. With these various accents and qualifications, Calvin is trying to guard against the error that the knowledge of God can be abstract, that faith is possible without knowledge, true worship apart from revelation, love without fear and reverence, and obedience without faith and gratitude. See Comm. 1. John 2:3 (CO 55, 3 10).
253. Comm. Ex. 19:12 (CO 24, 200); Comm. Deut. 5:32 (CO 24,214); Comm. Isa. 5:24 (CO 36, 119); Comm. Jer. 6:19 (CO 37, 661); Comm. Zeph. 1:5, 6 (CO 44, 10, 13); 1545 Catechism, Qs. 128-130 (CO 6, 50); *Inst.* I.3.3; I.12.1, 3; II.8.5; III.7.2 Ingratitude, for Calvin, is one of the most heinous of sins.
254. *Inst.* I.2.2.
255. CO 43, 342.
256. Comm. Deut. 10:12 f. (CO 24, 722). When Simeon is described as being "righteous and devout" in Luke 2:25, Calvin sees here a reference to the two tables of the law and concludes: "In these two parts consist integrity of life," Comm. Lk. 2:25 (CO 45, 89).
257. As in *Inst.* II.8.2. However, later in this same section, righteousness is contrasted with "religion," which is the first table of the law.
258. Comm. Lk. 1:75 (CO 45, 50).
259. *Inst.* II.8.53. Calvin elsewhere adds "uprightness (*rectitudo*), purity and holiness," Comm. Gen. 18:19 (CO 23, 259); *Inst.* II.8.2.
260. *Inst.* IV.20.15.
261. Comm. Ezek. 18:9 (CO 40, 433). Cf. *Inst.* II.8.52. The second table of the law requires us to "conduct ourselves innocently towards men according to the rule of love (*caritatis regulam*)," Comm. Deut. 10:12 f. (CO 24, 722). Cf. Comm. Gen. 18:19 (CO 23, 259).
262. II.8.50. Cf. II.8.11. "We fear God when we live justly with our

neighbors. For piety is the root (*radix*) of love . . . . No one ever loves his neighbor from his heart unless he fears and reverences God," Comm. Ezek. 18: 5 (CO 45, 632).

263. II.8.51. Cf 287. Comm. Mt. 22: 37 (CO 45, 611) .

264. Calvin understands "faith" in this passage as "truthfulness toward men," not faith towards God, *Inst.* II.8.52 .

265. So, for example, Melanchthon in his *Annotations in Evangelium Matthaei* (1523).

266. *Inst.* II.8.52.

267. Comm. Deut. 10:12 (CO 24, 722).

268. Comm. Rom. 13:9 (CO 49, 253).

269. *Inst.* II.8.53.

270. Comm. Matt. 23:23 (CO 45, 632). Cf. Comm. Zech. 7:9 (CO 44, 225).

271. Comm. Gal. 5:14 (CO 50, 251).

272. *Inst.* II.8.53.

273. Comm. 1 Tim. 1:5 (CO 52, 253). Calvin is particularly fond of this text, for here too he finds a clear reference to the *summa* of the law.

274. Comm. Heb. 5:11 (CO 55, 76).

275. Comm. Philemon 5 (CO 52, 442). The "sum of the law," therefore, and the "sum of the Christian life" are basically the same thing viewed from a different vantage point. Cf. *Inst.* II.8.51-55 (the sum of the law) and III.7.1-8 (the sum of the Christian life).

276. Comm. Heb. 6:11 (CO 55, 76). "This is the main difference between the gospel and philosophy. Although the philosophers speak on the subject of morals splendidly and with praiseworthy ability, yet all the embellishment which shines forth in their precepts is nothing more than a beautiful superstructure without a foundation, for by omitting the first principles, they propound a mutilated doctrine, like a body without a head," Comm. Rom. 12:1 (CO 49, 233).

277. See Barth, *Church Dogmatics* I., 2, 387-8, for illustrations of the pervasiveness of this error both in the early church and in the post-Reformation period.

278. *Inst.* II.8.54. Calvin can hardly restrain his contempt for this position. Such reasoning, he asserts, should "not be considered worth a hair," ibid. Those who argue in this manner "are asses and have not a spark of love," Comm. Gal. .5:14 (CO 50, 251).

279. Comm. Lk. 10:30 (CO 45, 613).

280. *Inst.* II.8.55.

281. Comm. Lev. 19:18 (CO 24, 724). For Calvin, Isa. 58:7, "You shall not despise your own flesh" [the Vulgate reading], signifies our neighbor. Thus Isaiah is saying here that "we are joined by a common nature," Comm.

Gal. 5:14 (CO 50, 251). This text is also cited in *Inst.* III.7.6 and explained there in a similar way.

282. *Church Dogmatics*, I, 2, 419 f.

283. Ibid., 417 f.

284. *The Christian Doctrine of the Church, Faith and the Consummation* (Dogmatics, Vol. III), 309, 310. Ironically, Brunner himself operates with a view of the law which is more Kantian than biblical and hence finds law and love contradictory notions.

285. On the impact of Stoicism on Calvin's thought see Quirinus Breen, *John Calvin: A Study in French Humanism*, second edition (Hamden, Conn.: Archon Books, 1968). He points out Calvin's early interest in Seneca and Calvin's admiration for Cicero and concludes: "We have evidence, therefore, that the revival of the classics, and with it of Stoicism, was one of the factors conditioning the Reformation," 73. For significant differences, however, between Calvin and the Stoics see Charles Partee, *Calvin and Classical Philosophy* (Leiden: E.J. Brill, 1977), 68ff., 122ff.

286. These are all characteristics of the Stoic conception of humanity according to Barth, op. cit., 423.

287. Comm. Gal. 5:14 (CO 50, 251). For Calvin the creation ordinance which binds humanity together and the claim of the divine image in the neighbor mean essentially the same, Göhler, *Calvins Lehre von der Heiligung*, 72. This is brought out clearly in the Comm. on John 13:34 (CO 47, 318), "Love is indeed extended to those outside, for we are all of the same flesh and are all created in the image of God." For a recent and comprehensive treatment of the much debated *imago Dei* question in Calvin's theology, see Mary Potter Engel, op. cit., Chapter II.

288. Comm. Lk. 10:30 (CO 45, 614).

289. *Inst.* II.8.55.

290. Cf. pp. 49f. (in this MS) (based on *Inst.* II.8.40).

291. *Inst.* II.8.51.

292. Comm. Lev. 19:18 (CO 24, 724).

293. Comm. Deut. 10:17-19 (CO 24, 674).

294. Comm. John 13:34 (CO 47, 318).

295. *Inst.* II.8.51.

296. Ibid.

297. Comm. Matt. 22:40 (CO 45, 614, 615). Cf. Comm. Lk. 10:26 (CO 45, 610).

IV

LAW AND GOSPEL[1]

I. INTRODUCTION

A. *A Hermeneutical Problem*

The question of the relation of law and gospel for Calvin is closely related to his understanding of Scripture and revelation. More specifically, it is a question of the relation of the Old and New Testaments. The real issue is the interpretation of the Old Testament. Since World War II this hermeneutical question has been in the forefront of biblical scholarship.[2]

Calvin's stress on the unity of the two Testaments is well known. For scholars of a past generation, when the accent was on the diversity of the Testaments, this was frequently a stumbling block. A rather common complaint was that Calvin so stressed the unity of the Testaments that their alleged differences were of no real significance. Seeberg, for example, maintains that "Calvin's legalism results in a tendency to blur the boundaries between the Old and New Testaments."[3] Wernle likewise alleges that "Calvin in his moral zeal actually denies the difference between the Old and New Testaments, closes his eyes to all of the new values (*Werten*) which Jesus brought into the world, and lowers him to the level of a correct interpreter of the old Moses. How much clearer the Anabaptists were on this point!"[4]

Doumergue, on the other hand, writing some ten years before the above works of Seeberg and Wernle appeared, concludes quite differently. After a brief analysis of Calvin's treatment of this subject in chapters 9-11 of Book II of the *Institutes*, he comments: "As you can see, it is remarkably inaccurate to repeat that Calvin has confused the

Old and the New Testaments. We should not emphasize (*approfondir*) too much the differences between the two covenants and thus deepen the chasm between them. Calvin does not do this. For him the differences do not destroy the unity. The differences refer to the diverse manner by which God has administered his doctrine, rather than to the substance of that doctrine."[5]

Almost all of the more recent Calvin studies substantiate Doumergue's judgment.[6] Yet certain contemporary Lutheran and Roman Catholic theologians continue to be critical of Calvin's handling of this problem.[7] In actuality, what they reject is not merely Calvin's particular interpretation, but the Reformed approach to the Scriptures. For Calvin's position in this regard is essentially that of Zwingli's; other reformers such as Bucer, Bullinger, and Peter Martyr, as well as the Reformed confessions, follow the same line. The same is true of Melanchthon.[8] Both Barth and Brunner basically approve of Calvin's stress on the unity of the Testaments. Barth, in fact, goes beyond Calvin in this respect. As far as the Lutheran theologian, Edmund Schlink, is concerned, however, both Calvin and Barth are at fault here in their emphasis on the unity of the covenants and in their understanding of the relationship of law and gospel.[9]

Brunner's approach to the law and gospel dialectic is more Lutheran than Reformed. But when it comes to Calvin's analysis of the unity and distinction of the covenants, he prefers Calvin to Luther. In an appendix in his *Dogmatics*, Vol. II, he has a critique of Wilhelm Vischer's controversial *Christuszeugnis des Alten Testaments*. In contrast to this approach, he writes,

> it does one good to read Calvin's commentaries, with the sobriety of their historical critical exposition . . . . The greatness of Calvin—we may indeed say his unparalleled greatness as an expositor—consists in the fact that he, who knew more about the actual connection (in revelation) of the two Testaments, kept so close to the historical "natural" sense and resisted the temptation to allegory, even in its typological form.[10]

The latter statement is not altogether accurate, for Calvin only opposed the kind of allegorizing indulged in by Origen. Luther also eschewed Origen's allegorizing but was not as consistent as Calvin in avoiding this approach. Both reformers employed a typological method of interpreting many Old Testament passages, but Calvin generally was more concerned about the literal historical meaning of a text than Luther.

B. *Terminological Distinctions*

Once again it is extremely important to note precisely what Calvin means by the expressions law and gospel in this context. For example, in his discussion of this subject in Book II, chapters 9-11 of the *Institutes*, law and gospel refer primarily to the Old and New Testaments or covenants. Thus in the title of Chapter 9, "Christ, although he was known to the Jews under the law, was at length clearly revealed only in the gospel," we could substitute Old Testament or old covenant for law, and New Testament or new covenant for gospel. In the broad sense of the word "gospel" for Calvin also "includes those testimonies of his mercy and fatherly favor which God gave to the patriarchs of old." But in a more technical sense the word "gospel" refers to "the proclamation of the grace manifested in Christ."[11] Similarly "law" in this case is a comprehensive term and covers the whole era or dispensation of the old covenant. "Law," therefore, does not mean primarily the decalog or a legal corpus in this context.

Accordingly, in chapters 10 and 11 Calvin no longer uses the law-gospel terminology but speaks instead of the similarity and the difference between the Old and New Testaments. When law and gospel are used in this sense, their substance is the same; only the form of administration differs. For "the covenant made with all the fathers is so much like ours in substance and reality that the two are actually one and the same. Yet they differ in the mode of administration."[12] As we saw earlier, there is fundamentally only one covenant, and that a covenant of grace. The distinction between the old and new covenants is largely a difference in the mode in which this one covenant was administered.

This is all very familiar to anyone who has read the chapters in the *Institutes* which consider this subject. What is not always recognized—particularly by the critics of Calvin's view of law and gospel—is that there is not only a difference of form between the law and the gospel (or the two covenants) but also an antithesis between them in so far as the law in a narrower sense is opposed to the gospel. A case in point is Galatians 3:19, where Paul sets the law given to Moses in opposition to the promise given to Abraham. In such cases Calvin does not hesitate to speak of the accusing, killing function of the law and its threats and curse. This aspect of the law in its narrower sense is taken up in Chapter 7 of Book II of the *Institutes* and is discussed even more fully in Calvin's exegetical writings on the Pauline Epistles and related texts. Here Calvin does not differ significantly from Luther, except in emphasis and discretion. Calvin often points out, for example, that when Paul and other biblical writers refer to the law in this narrow sense, that is, as opposed to the gospel, it is separated from the promises of grace and is considered only from the standpoint of its "peculiar office, power and end."[13]

This law, which is the antithesis of the gospel, is not the whole law, the *tota lex*, but the bare law, the *nuda lex*. It is the law abstracted from its real setting which is the covenant. Such a law is a bare letter without the vivifying Spirit of Christ. It has nothing but rigorous demands which place all human beings under a curse and the wrath of God.[14] The law, thus understood, can only be described as the antithesis of the gospel, for it implies a type of righteousness which is diametrically opposed to the righteousness of faith. Hence when Paul speaks of the law in passages like Romans 3:21-31 and Galatians 3:10, he "rightly makes opposites of the righteousness of the law and that of the gospel."[15]

The relation of law and gospel, therefore, can be described in a threefold manner: 1. a unity of substance; 2. a distinction in the form or mode of administration and instruction; 3. an antithesis of letter and Spirit. The important thing to keep in mind in these comparisons is that in the first two cases the word law is used in a comprehensive sense and is usually synonymous with the Old Testament or the covenant under the old dispensation. In the third case the law is used in a more popular sense, that is, in its negative, narrower connotation.

II. UNITY OF SUBSTANCE

It is impossible to discuss the unity of substance without entering into the second division concerning the difference of form. For Calvin invariably makes this contrast between substance and form in the same passage or context. Nevertheless, for the purpose of keeping these distinctions clear, insofar as possible, I shall try to separate them. This may at first create the false impression that Calvin places an inordinate emphasis on the unity of the law and the gospel, but it will become clear in the next section that he goes to even greater lengths to illustrate their differences.

A. *A Question of the Unity of Revelation.*

We noted earlier that the covenant made with the patriarchs and Old Testament fathers is basically the same as the new covenant in respect to its substance and reality. This statement (II.10.2) is the fundamental principle for the whole of chapter ten, "The Similarity of the Old and New Testaments." For this assertion immediately distinguishes Calvin from opponents on two sides: the Roman theologians (the "papists"), on the one hand, and Servetus, the Antinomians, and Anabaptists, on the other. Already in the 1539 edition of the *Institutes* a chapter on the similarity and the differences between the Testaments was inserted. In the final edition of 1559 this theme was further developed into three separate chapters.[16] In his commentaries and sermons also he frequently felt constrained to emphasize this truth. Yet Calvin was no innovator in this regard, for both Melanchthon and Bucer had already written concerning this theme in a similar fashion. And all three, in turn, were following Augustine's stress on the unity of the substance of the Testaments in his treatise against the Manichean, Faustus.[17] However, as is so characteristic of Calvin, he frequently gives a traditional doctrine or position a peculiar twist or stamp of his own.

The issue here for Calvin is not simply the unity of revelation, important as that is. Ultimately, it is a question of the unity of God himself. In those places where the law is depicted as opposed to faith or the gospel, Calvin does not minimize the antithesis. At the same time, however, he occasionally warns his readers that it would be completely false to conclude that God is "unlike"[18] or "inconsistent with himself."[19] A good illustration is Hebrews 1:1,2 where several contrasts are made: the Son with the prophets, we with the fathers, and the variety of means of revelation under the old covenant with the one final revelation given in Christ. Here we have various antitheses. Nevertheless, Calvin cautions, in this diversity the author of the Epistle "sets before us one God, in case anyone should think the law is in conflict with the gospel (*cum evangelio pugnare*), or that the author of the latter is different from that of the former. . . .The agreement between the law and the gospel is established, because God, who is always like himself, whose Word is unchanging, and whose truth is unshakable, spoke in both together."[20] Calvin will not countenance anything that resembles Marcion's view of two Gods, a Creator God or Demiurge, revealed in the Old Testament, who has nothing in common with the supreme God of love whom Jesus came to reveal. Consequently, whatever variations there may be between God's activity under the two covenants, "the doctrine of God is the same and always agrees with itself (*et sui perpetuo similem*), so that no one may accuse God of changeableness (*variationis*) as if he were inconsistent."[21] The necessity of a new covenant necessarily implies that the old covenant is somehow imperfect and will eventually become obsolete. But Calvin admonishes us again to remember that the new covenant is not contrary to the first covenant. Otherwise this would seem to signify that God is not true to himself and is in some way inconsistent.[22] Calvin's concern about the unity of law and gospel is thus ultimately a concern about the unity of God's holy will and saving purpose. God is one; therefore his revelation is fundamentally one.

B. *Basically Only One Covenant*

A problem, nevertheless, is posed by the fact that both Jeremiah and Ezekiel speak of a "new covenant." The author of the Epistle to the Hebrews reiterates this and goes further by saying that the new covenant, which is ratified by the blood of Christ, makes the old covenant obsolete (Hebrews 8:6-13). How then can Calvin maintain that there is essentially only one covenant, the covenant of grace, which is common to both the Old and the New Testaments? The answer, as far as Calvin is concerned, is that whatever the modifier "new" may mean as applied to the covenant, the newness applies only to its form. Thus when Jeremiah promises a "new covenant" to the Jews, this refers to the form or manner in which "Christ and the grace of the Holy Spirit" are received. "New" here means "the whole external manner of instruction (*docendi ratio externa*). But the substance (*substantia*) remains the same."[23]

In Isaiah 2:3, where we read, "Out of Zion shall go forth the law . . . ", Calvin does not hesitate to interpret "law" in this verse as referring to the doctrine of the gospel. He continues, "We conclude from this that it [the gospel] is not new or a recent innovation, but that it is the eternal truth of God which had been given in all ages before it was brought to light." Then he draws the corollary which is very similar to his explanation of the new covenant in Jeremiah. "We also gather," he adds, "that it was necessary that all the ancient ceremonies should be abolished and that a new form of instruction (*nova docendi forma*) should be introduced, although the substance of the doctrine continued to be the same. For the law formerly proceeded out of Mount Sinai (Ex. 19:1); but now it proceeded 'out of Zion', and therefore it took on a new form."[24]

Similarly, in Isaiah 42:4, when the prophet writes, "and the coastlands wait for his law," Calvin recognizes that the Hebrew word for law, *torah,* means teaching or doctrine. "Thus the prophets are accustomed to speak of the gospel, in order to show that it will not be new or contrary to what was taught by Moses."[25] The content of the covenant was always the same, for the Lord always covenanted with his servants thus: "I will be your God, and you shall be my people" (Lev. 26:12). With these words "God comprehends generally the substance of his covenant. For what is the design of the law except that the people should call upon him and that he should also exercise care over his people?"[26] When the prophets used this formula, they pointed out that "life and salvation and the whole of blessedness are comprehended in these words."[27] Therefore, for Calvin it is very important to keep in mind that "all men adopted by God into the company of his people since the beginning of the world were covenanted to him by the same law and by the bond of the same doctrine as obtains among us."[28]

C. *A Unity in Christ*

It remains to be seen just what this substance is which is common to the various covenants. Calvin, fortunately, is very explicit on this point. "By substance I understand the doctrine; for God in the gospel brings forth (*profert*) nothing but what the law contains." Not only that; "God has so spoken from the beginning that he has not changed, no not a syllable, with regard to the substance of the doctrine."[29] "The gospel was not given to add anything to the law or the prophets." In the New Testament "we shall not find one syllable added to either; it is only setting forth more plainly that which had been taught before . . . . There is an agreement in all the Holy Scripture: of the Old and the

New Testament."[30]

Granted, Calvin is overstating his case here, but this "doctrine" which comprises the unity of revelation is not some abstract teaching but Christ himself; or, to be more accurate, "Christ clothed in his own promises (*promissionibus suis vestitum*)."[31] Calvin finds the biblical basis for this position in the statements of Jesus (and the apostles) that the law and the prophets bear witness to him.[32] On the basis of such passages Calvin concludes: "We see now the agreement *(consensus)* there is between the Old and New Testaments to *establish faith in Christ (ad stabiliendam in Christo fidem)*."[33]

Moreover, this conclusion follows quite naturally from Calvin's oft-repeated assertions that Christ is the *fundamentum, anima, spiritus, scopus, finis* and *perfectio* of the law! Consequently, when discussing the difference between the Old and New Testaments in terms of substance and form, Calvin points out that the difference does not consist in the fact that Christ is absent in the one and present in the other. Christ, by being the heart and life of both Testaments, was always present with God's children, whether Abraham or Paul. The difference, rather, consists in the way by which he was known to them and in the nature of their knowledge of him.

"Jesus Christ is the same yesterday and today and forever" (Heb. 13:8). "Yesterday," says Calvin, "comprehends the whole period of the Old Testament." Moreover, the author of the Epistle is not discussing the eternal existence of Christ, in Calvin's opinion, but is speaking rather of "the knowledge of him which flourished among believers in every age and which was the enduring foundation of the Church." This text, therefore, refers primarily to the nature of our knowledge of Christ. But "the manifestation of Christ, as far as its external form and manner is concerned *(quantum ad externam speciem et modum)*, was different under the law from that which we have today."[34] Since Christ is one and unchangeable, there can be no opposition between the law and the gospel.[35]

This conviction makes it possible for Calvin to assert that the law is the foundation and core of Scripture, that the prophets, apostles, and even Christ himself are nothing but expounders and interpreters of the law,[36] that the prophets and the New Testament are not "additions or abridgements" *(addidamenta vel defectiones)* but rather "supplements *(complementa)* to the law."[37] This is why Calvin insists that

Christ was not a new law-giver, but rather an interpreter of the law. Christ adds nothing essential to the law, since the gospel was already present in a sense in the law. His role is thus simply that of a "faithful interpreter."[38] He did not add anything to the law; "he only restored it to its integrity."[39]

At first glance it would seem that Christ is here degraded to the status of a prophet or rabbi. But Calvin's intention—which is clear in the light of his overall treatment of this subject—is just the opposite. For if Christ is the substance and soul of the law, the eternal Mediator to whom the law and prophets bear witness, and apart from which his ministry is incomprehensible, then Christ's "faithful interpretation" of the law is nothing other than a self-witness. Only through Christ do we understand who the Christ (Messiah) is as witnessed to in the Scriptures. For "in order that Christ may be made known to us through the gospel, it is necessary that Moses and the prophets should go before as guides to show us the way . . . . From the law, therefore, we may properly learn Christ if we consider that the covenant which God made with the fathers was founded on the Mediator."[40] "For what is offered (*proponitur*) to us in Christ except what God has promised in the law?"[41]

The presupposition for this whole argument is Calvin's conviction that "Christ did not first begin to be manifested in the gospel."[42] As the eternal Son of God, one of the holy Trinity, he was continually present and at work in redemptive history. A corollary of this is the truth that Christ cannot be rightly understood apart from the Old Testament. Even after his advent, Moses and the prophets are not made superfluous. They continue to be witnesses to him. Apart from them we cannot understand who the Messiah of Israel is. "He did not come forward as one unknown, but the Father had long ago marked him out (*insignierat*) in the law and the prophets, so that he might bring his distinguishing marks (*notas*) with him and be recognized from them."[43] And now that he has come, he "is as truly heard in the present day in the law and the prophets as in the gospel."[44] The witness of the Old Testament to Christ is therefore not optional for the Christian Church. To refuse this witness is to court disaster, since to depend on the witness of the New Testament alone means uprooting Christ from his proper milieu. "In order that our faith may firmly rest in Christ, we must come to the law and the prophets."[45] Calvin seems to be arguing in a hermeneutical circle, but this conforms to the dialectical relationship of the Old and New Testaments. On the one hand, the Old Testament witnesses to

Christ. This witness, moreover, continues to be indispensable. On the other hand, as was noted above, Christ is the true interpreter of the Old Testament. From either standpoint the Old Testament remains a dead letter and an enigma apart from Christ. For Christ is the aim (*scopus*) and the end (*finis*) of the law.[46] If the Jews in Christ's time had only realized that Christ is the true end (purpose) of the law, they should have accepted the truth that the law refers them to Christ.

> When the Jews excluded Christ from the law, they turned it in a different direction. Thus in reading the law they wandered aimlessly, so the law has become to them a twisted thing, like a labyrinth, until it is referred to its proper end (*suum finem*), which is Christ. If, therefore, the Jews seek for Christ in the law, the truth of God will appear clearly to them, but as long as they wish to be wise without Christ, they will wander in darkness and never arrive at the true meaning of the law. And what is said of the law applies to the whole of Scripture; when it is not taken as referring to Christ, who is its sole aim (*unicum scopum*), it is distorted and perverted.[47]

Calvin felt so strongly about this that he sometimes made somewhat extravagant claims concerning the relation of Christ to the Old Testament. In his Preface to Olivétan's New Testament, for example, he maintains that "if one were to sift thoroughly the law and the prophets, he would not find a single word which would not draw and bring us to him."[48] Calvin does not intend, however, that we take him literally! His basic point, in any case, is that the whole of Scripture points to and finds its culmination in Jesus Christ. "We must hold that Christ cannot be properly known anywhere but in the Scriptures. And if that is so, it follows that the Scriptures should be read with the aim of finding Christ in them. Whoever turns aside from this object (*scopus*), even though he wears himself out all his life in learning, will never reach the knowledge of the truth."[49]

Since Christ is the substance of the two Testaments, they cannot be separated without irreparable damage. The form of the one surpasses and supersedes the form of the other. But the substance is not transferred from the one to the other. Hence neither Testament makes sense apart from the other. The gospel does not supplant the law but rather confirms it and gives actuality to its shadows.[50] Consequently, "Where the whole law is concerned, the gospel differs from it only in clarity of manifestation."[51]

D. *The Faith of the Old Testament Believers*

The question remains, however, as to what this substance of doctrine meant concretely for those living under the law. In what sense can it be said that the fathers of the Old Testament possessed Christ? If New Testament believers are joined with the Jews of the Old Testament in the unity of faith as far as substance is concerned,[52] wherein does this unity lie?

Chapter ten (of Book II) in the *Institutes* deals specifically with this subject, but again Calvin's exegetical writings provide a richer source of material. One reason is that much of the material in chapter ten is polemically motivated. That "rascal," Servetus, and certain "madmen of the Anabaptist sect regarded the Israelites as nothing but a herd of swine," for they held that the promises given to Israel were confined to this life and had nothing to do with the Christian hope.[53] For Calvin, this position has fatal consequences and undermines the very foundation of biblical revelation.

We need not concern ourselves with his counterarguments. It should be sufficient merely to mention the ten or more things which Calvin lists as being common to the Old Testament fathers and ourselves. But it must be kept in mind that when all this is claimed for believers under the law, it is eschatological in nature. That is, although they had "a sure participation (*certam communionem*)"[54] in the blessings of the new covenant, their experience of these blessings depended on the reconciliation eventually wrought by Christ and the consequent gift of the Holy Spirit.[55] In addition, because Christ had not appeared in the flesh and was therefore known to them in only a fragmentary, shadowy way, their experience of God's grace, though actual, was merely a slight taste of that which we enjoy in the gospel. The degree of difference between the quality of their knowledge and experience and ours is considerable. This will be seen in the next section. But for the moment note what the fathers possessed in principle:

"They participated in the same inheritance and hoped for a common salvation with us by the grace of the same Mediator."[56] They had the same "rule of reverence and piety,"[57] the same faith,[58] the same grace,[59] the same hope,[60] the same church[61] and the same spiritual worship.[62] This is all brought together in a discussion of Galatians 4:1 ff. Calvin raises the question: "Since the church of God is one, how is it that our condition differs from that of the Israelites?" Then he points out wherein they agree and differ. The points of agreement are these:

> We today have the hope of the same inheritance as the fathers un-
> der the the old covenant; for they were partakers of the same
> adoption . . . . In spite of their external slavery their consciences
> were free . . . . They so bore the yoke of the law on their shoul-
> ders that they worshiped God with a free spirit. More particularly,
> they had been taught about the free pardon of sins, and their con-
> sciences were delivered from the tyranny of sin and death. Hence
> we must conclude that they held the same doctrine as ourselves,
> were joined in the true unity of faith, placed reliance with us on
> the one Mediator, called on God as their Father, and were gov-
> erned by the same Spirit. All this leads to the conclusion that the
> difference between us and the ancient Fathers lies not in sub-
> stance but in accidents.[63]

In short, although the fathers under the law viewed these things only from a distance, they nevertheless had exhibited to them "the same Christ, the same justice, sanctification, and salvation."[64]

E. *The Sacraments of the Old Covenant*

Much of the above is Calvin's answer to Servetus, the Anabap-
tists, and similar "fanatics" who denied the spiritual character of the hope and inheritance of the fathers, thus excluding them from the hope of eternal salvation.[65] On a related but slightly different point Calvin came into conflict with the "papists". It was a scholastic dogma that the difference between the sacraments of the two dispensations consisted in this: those under the law only foreshadowed God's grace, whereas those under the gospel give it as a present reality.[66] They appealed to Augustine who had said, "The sacraments of the old law only promised the Saviour, but ours give salvation."[67] Calvin, however, proceeds to sup-
ply more quotations from Augustine to show that the Roman scholars have no right to claim him for their position.

It might appear at first glance that Calvin is just quibbling about words. The issue at stake, however, is at bottom the same as that involved in the question of the nature of the promises given to the fathers. The real issue is whether Christ and the reality of the gospel are essentially absent under the old dispensation and whether God's goodness and grace are only experienced after the incarnation of Christ. This Calvin will not concede.

Consequently, when scholastic theologians such as Lombard and Aquinas assert that the ceremonies and sacraments of the fathers are empty signs which are devoid of truth and substance, Calvin strongly demurs. When they point to texts like Rom. 2:29, Col. 2:17, Heb. 9:12-22, and Heb. 10, Calvin concedes that there is no question about the disparagement of the ceremonies under the old covenant. But he insists at the same time that the point of the argument of both Paul and the author of the Epistle to the Hebrews is that the ceremonies have been distorted and perverted. What is being challenged in these passages is not the ceremonies themselves, but their superstitious abuse. "What wonder, then," he exclaims, "if ceremonies, cut off from Christ, are divested of all force!"[68]

For Christians to hanker after such ceremonies is of course out of the question. But under the law these ceremonies were a real blessing to the Israelites, just as baptism and the Lord's supper are to us, for the substance is the same. "Therefore, whatever is shown to us today in the sacraments, the Jews of old received in their own—that is, Christ with his spiritual riches. They felt the same power in their sacraments as we do in ours; these were seals of divine good will toward them, looking to eternal salvation."[69]

In the last analysis, Calvin maintains, this is only what Augustine meant. The latter's statement, which seemed to support Calvin's opponents, must be interpreted in the light of other statements which Calvin cites: "The fathers drank the same spiritual drink, but not the same physical one, as ours. See, therefore, how faith remains while signs change . . . . In the mystery they had the same food and drink as we; but in signification, not in appearance (*sed significatione non specie*). For the same Christ represented to them in the rock (cf. I Cor. 10:4) has been manifested to us in the flesh."[70]

F. *Christ in the Old Testament*

Everything Calvin has asserted thus far about the fathers and their sacraments presupposes that Christ has always been present in some sense with the covenant people. Ignore Calvin's rather radical Christocentrism at this point, and everything falls to the ground. Hence, although he can speak of "the fullness of grace that the Jews tasted under the law,"[71] this was all contingent on the coming of Christ in the flesh and his death and resurrection. The real efficacy of his saving work was actually held in suspension until his incarnation. The ceremonies always "looked to Christ (*Christum resperisse*)". If these ceremonies and sacraments had not been directed to him, they would have been "a fleeting and worthless thing (*rem evinandem ac nihili*)."[72]

To imagine that God's goodness and grace were not really experienced until the advent of Jesus Christ is an affront to God. Titus 3:4 might seem to undercut this position, for Paul declares, "When the kindness of God our Saviour appeared . . . ." But Calvin comments:

> First it may be asked whether God's kindness began to be known in the world only at the time when Christ was manifested in the flesh, for it is certain that from the first the fathers knew and experienced God's kindness, mercy and favor towards them . . . . The answer is simple, that the fathers under the law tasted God's goodness only by looking towards Christ on whose advent all their faith depended (*in Christum respiciendo a cuius adventu pendebat tota eorum fides*). Thus God's kindness may be said to have appeared when he showed this sure pledge of it and gave actual proof that he had not so often promised salvation to men in vain.[73]

This experience of God's goodness and grace by the fathers was thus basically eschatological, for it pointed to and depended on the coming of Christ. But it was both a realized as well as a futuristic eschatology, in that their faith and hope were even in their day strengthened and nourished by a real experience of Christ. For his "power and grace, inasmuch as he is the redeemer of the world, were common to all ages."[74] Christ was "the true God who from the beginning did not fail to spread out the wings of his grace."[75] "For whence came light and day to the holy fathers in old times or to us now, but because the manifestation of Christ always sent forth its rays afar, so as to form one continual day?"[76] The substance of the law, which is its doctrine, consequently "accords with (*respondet*) the gospel and includes Christ within it."[77] Its principal part is the gratuitous covenant of salvation.[78] Therefore, Moses "directed his disciples to Christ in order to seek salvation from him

.... Since the same covenant is common to us and the ancient people, it is not to be doubted that they 'chose life' who of old embraced the doctrine of Moses."[79] Calvin can say this because he is convinced that in Moses, i.e., in the law, "faith is to be chiefly (*praecipue*) considered. It follows from this that all those who are not guided by the law to faith make little progress in it."[80]

The Old Testament, therefore, should not be regarded as essentially a law-book or as merely a primitive story of an ancient people. It is the book of the covenant, and the covenant promise which binds all God's children together is simply, "I will be your God and you shall be my people." In these words, as they are explained by the prophets, "are included life and salvation and the whole of blessedness."[81] So if the question is asked "whether under the law there was a sure and certain promise of salvation, whether the fathers had the gift of the Spirit, whether they enjoyed the remission of sins," the answer is affirmative. For "it is clear that they worshiped God with sincere heart and a pure conscience and that they walked in his commandments—which could not have been the case unless they had been inwardly taught by the Spirit. It is evident that whenever they thought of their sins, they were raised up again by their assurance of gratuitous pardon."[82]

In this first division on the unity of law and gospel it should be clear why Calvin evaluates the Old Testament revelation so highly. Not because of a legalistic spirit or an "Old Testament religion," but because of the strong conviction that both the law and the gospel are ultimately a single witness to the variegated and manifold but unchanging grace of the God and Father of our Lord Jesus Christ. The story of God's saving history, beginning with Adam and continuing until the last day, is an unfolding of the truth that the "holy catholic church" has been redeemed through the one saviour of the world, Jesus Christ, "the same yesterday and today and forever."

This truth finds classic expression in the Genesis Synopsis (*argumentum*):

> After Adam, by his own desperate fall, had ruined himself and all his posterity, this is the basis (*fundamentum*) of our salvation, this is the origin of the church, that we, being rescued out of profound darkness, have obtained new life by the sheer grace of God: that the fathers (according to the offer made to them through the Word of God) are by faith made partakers of this same life; that

this Word itself was founded on Christ; and that all the godly who have lived since that time were sustained by the very same promise of salvation by which Adam was raised from the first fall. Consequently, the perpetual succession of the church has flowed from this fountain, i.e., that the holy fathers, one after another, having by faith embraced the offered promise, were gathered together into the family of God in order that they might have a common life in Christ . . . . Moreover, since the foundation (*principium*) of faith is to know that there is only one true God whom we worship, it is no ordinary confirmation of this faith that we are comrades (*socios*) of the patriarchs. For since they possessed Christ as the pledge of their salvation when he had not yet appeared, so we hold fast to the God who formerly manifested himself to them.[83]

III. DISTINCTION IN FORM

A. *A Difference of Degree*

The differences between the law and the gospel, as we saw earlier, consist principally in the mode of dispensation or manner of instruction. Here also the *tota lex* is the object of inquiry. Hence the differences we shall observe in this section refer primarily to the form or manner of God's self-revelation and our apprehension and experience of it. It is a case of more or less; the substance remains the same. These differences, though only relative, are by no means inconsiderable. Calvin, considering the age in which he lived, was remarkably sensitive to the historical character of God's revelation. In this respect, it could be said that he saw the differences between the law and the gospel more clearly than Luther.

According to Calvin, the unity of the two Testaments consists basically in three points: 1. The hope of immortality was granted also to the Jews; 2. The old covenant as well was founded on God's mercy alone; 3. The Jews had Christ as their mediator and knew him as such, thus being united to God.[84] The differences, however, are five: 1. The Jews were given the hope of immortality under the figure of earthly blessings, but now this inferior method has been superseded; they required this inferior method because of their immaturity. 2. Truth is exhibited by types in the Old Testament, as the Epistle to the Hebrews indicates, but openly in the New; this also was necessary because the

Jews were in a state of tutelage. 3. The Old Testament has the character of a letter, the New of the Spirit; that is, the Old lacks the Spirit, the New is engraved on the heart, as Jeremiah points out. The Old Testament is deadly because it involves a curse, the New is an instrument of life. The Old is a shadow and must vanish away, the New will stand forever. 4. The Old Testament produces fear and trembling, except for the promises which properly belong to the New, whereas the New produces freedom and joy. 5. The revelation of the Old Testament was confined to the Jewish nation. In the New the Gentiles also are invited to share its blessings.[85]

The treatment of two of the above differences (#3 and #4) will be deferred to the next section on the antithesis between the law and the gospel; not because an absolute antithesis is implied, but because the difference between letter and spirit, works and faith, and bondage and freedom is of quite a different character from the more "evolutionary" type of difference depicted by the use of comparatives and superlatives. By "evolutionary" I mean only that in this section there is a development from grace to grace—although the actual manifestation of Christ marks a definite transition.[86] Where the word "antithesis" is used, a much sharper break is implied. Even here, however, the break or antithesis is not absolute, because the law, as such, is still adventitiously invested with certain qualities of the gospel. This distinction should become clear as illustrations are given.

A rather comprehensive, yet succinct, description of the difference between law and gospel in terms of the "more" of the gospel over against the "less" of the law is given in the *Institutes*, IV.14.26. The contrast here is actually between the sacraments of the Jews and those of Christians. But this applies also to the general distinction between law and gospel.

> Both [law and gospel] attest that God's fatherly kindness and the graces of the Holy Spirit are offered us in Christ, but ours is clearer and brighter. In both Christ is shown forth, but in ours more richly and fully, that is, in accordance with that difference between the Old and the New Testament, which we have discussed above. And this is what Augustine meant . . . in teaching that when Christ was revealed, sacraments were instituted, fewer in number, more majestic in signification, more excellent in power.

The substance is the same; the difference consists in the manner and character of the revelation we enjoy.[87] The fathers also enjoyed God's grace, but they were granted only a small portion, its complete perfection being deferred until the time of Christ.[88] God's self-manifestation to believers under the law was only partial (*in parte*). In the advent of his Son, however, God communicates himself to us wholly. He has, of course, manifested himself to us in other ways as well, "but in figures or by power (*virtute*) and grace. In Christ, however, he has appeared to us substantially (*essentialiter*)."[89] For in Christ "are hid all the treasures of wisdom and knowledge" (Col. 2:4). "All the promises of God find their yea and amen" in him (2 Cor. 1:20). Therefore, it was to be expected that there is "a more abundant (*plenior*) revelation" of God's will in Christ than under the law.[90] The fathers knew something of the divine goodness and spiritual kindness promised in Isaiah 55:1, but "it is poured out far more generously and abundantly" to those who are in Christ.[91]

We saw in the first section how insistent Calvin was on the reality of the experience of God's goodness and grace enjoyed by the fathers. However, he is equally concerned to show how superior the blessings of the gospel are compared to those of the law. In countless ways he seeks to show the superiority of the reality which is ours in Christ in contrast to the suspended grace which was theirs in the promises and ceremonies of the old covenant. By doing this Calvin does not intend to disparage the dispensation of the law. For in the law and the prophets God has, as it were, opened up his own heart to us and revealed his secrets.[92] Even so, what is promised and enjoyed in the gospel is "far better and more excellent than anything granted under the law," even during the golden days of David and Solomon.[93]

B. *Earthly Types—Spiritual Reality*

Calvin took great pains to refute Servetus' contention that the promises given to the Jews had no reference beyond their earthly and literal import. Nevertheless, he does not hesitate to point out that the promises of the law did differ in character from those of the gospel. The ultimate purpose of the Old Testament promises was to direct and elevate the minds of the Jews to the heavenly heritage. Yet, in order "to nourish them better in this hope, God displayed it for them to see and, so to speak, taste, under earthly benefits. But now that the gospel has more plainly and clearly revealed the grace of the future life, the Lord leads our minds to meditate upon it directly, laying aside the lower mode of training he used with the Israelites."[94]

The old covenant was in reality spiritual, but "it was annexed to earthly figures (*terrenis figuris*)."[95] "What was fulfilled in Christ by the hidden, heavenly power of the Spirit was in his case foreshadowed by oil, various vestments, the sprinkling of blood and other earthly ceremonies . . . . However spiritual the meaning of these shadows may have been, they were nevertheless simply shadows, and are properly called earthly because they consist of elements of this world."[96] The fathers under the law were partakers of the same life in Christ which we experience, but "they were confined (*fuisse conclusos*) under the hope that was to be revealed. It was necessary for them to seek life from Christ's death and resurrection. But this event was not only far distant from their eyes but also hidden from their minds. They therefore depended on the hope of revelation, which at last followed in due time. They could not have obtained life without its being in some way manifested to them; but between us and them there is this difference, that we, as it were, hold in our hands already revealed him whom they sought as he was obscurely promised to them in figures."[97]

This distinction between earthly types and temporal ceremonies, on the one hand, and spiritual, eternal reality, on the other, is one of the themes of the Epistle to the Hebrews. Calvin is at his best here. One only has to read his brief résumé of the argument in Hebrews 7-10 in the *Institutes* (II.11.4) to appreciate his sensitivity to the nuances of this difficult epistle. The contrast there between the external figures and types of the old covenant with the solid hope which is characteristic of the new is a theme which fascinated him. Because of this particular interest in the Christian hope, T. F. Torrance has labeled Calvin's eschatology as "the eschatology of hope."[98] This is related to his distinction between the transitory nature of the law (as a legal system) and the permanence of the gospel. His explanation of Hebrews 4:8 is characteristic:

> We see then that the land of Canaan was a rest, but a shadowy one, beyond which believers ought to progress. In this sense the apostle says that Joshua did not give them rest, because under his leadership the people entered the promised land in order to strive

on towards heaven with greater zeal. From this one can readily infer the sort of difference there is between them and us. Although
the same goal (*scopus*) is set before both, they have in addition
external types (*externi typi*) by which they were guided. We do
not have such types nor do we need them since the simple thing
itself (*res ipsa nuda*) is set before our eyes. Even if our salvation
is still placed in hope, yet in regard to the doctrine (*ad doctrinam
spectat*), it leads directly to heaven. Christ does not stretch out his
hand to lead us around by figures, but rather in order to take us
from this world and lead us to heaven. The apostle separates the
shadow from the reality, however, because he was dealing with
Jews who clung too much to external things.[99]

In short, the difference between the nature or quality of the
promises of both dispensations is simply this: "The gospel points out
with the finger what the law foreshadowed under types (*sub typis*)."[100]
The Law and the Prophets "gave a foretaste of that wisdom which was
one day to be clearly disclosed, and pointed to it twinkling afar off
(*procul emicantem*). But when Christ could be pointed out with the finger, the kingdom of God was opened."[101]

C. *Shadow—Substance*

Calvin uses a host of metaphors and similes to bring out more
clearly the nature of this difference between the two covenants. One he
employs very frequently is that of the shadow (*umbra*) which he contrasts with truth or reality (*veritas*) and body (*corpus*) or substance
(*substantia*). Christ is the reality of the shadows and ceremonies of the
law which are abolished when he appears.[102] "For the shadows immediately vanish at the appearance of the body."[103] In the Old Testament the
reality was absent; there was only an image and a shadow in its stead.
The New Testament, however, "reveals the very substance of truth as
present."[104] In one place the metaphors of shadows and reality, external
figures and the Spirit, are all combined. The occasion is the well known
text, John 4:23:

Here we must first ask why and in what sense the worship of God
may be called spiritual. To understand this we must note the antithesis between the Spirit and external figures, as between the

shadow and the reality (*veritas*). . . . But did not the fathers worship him spiritually under the law? I answer that since God is always true to himself, from the beginning of the world, he could not have approved any kind of worship except the spiritual, which alone is compatible with his nature. Moses himself bears abundant witness to this . . . . But although the worship under the law was spiritual, it was wrapped up in so many outward ceremonies that it had a flavor of carnality and earthliness . . . . Hence we may well say that the worship *(cultus)* of the law was spiritual in its substance, but with respect to its form somewhat carnal and earthly. For that whole economy *(ratio)* whose reality is now openly manifested to us was shadowy.[105]

This difference is also described commonly in terms of distance. The metaphor of a shadow is sometimes used there too, but in this case the idea is not so much that of insubstantiality as obscurity. That which was distant and obscure under the law is now near at hand. That which was concealed under the law becomes visible under the gospel. In a certain sense the shadows of the law even "hid the Spirit."[106]

The fathers were actually offered the forgiveness of sins through their ceremonies and sacrifices, but it was "obscure and shown to them at a distance." We, however, whose souls are sprinkled with the blood of Christ by the hidden power of the Spirit, have this absolution "set before our eyes and placed, as it were, in our hands."[107] Using the illustration of the temple, Calvin portrays the Jews as standing at a distance on the porch *(procul in atrio)*, whereas Christ by his blood has opened to us the heavenly sanctuary—we may even advance freely into the presence of God himself.[108]

Colossians 2:17 is particularly relevant in this connection: "These are only a shadow of what is to come; but the substance belongs to Christ." According to Calvin, the apostle here

contrasts shadows with revelation and absence with manifestation . . . . The substance of those things which the ceremonies formerly prefigured is now presented before our eyes in Christ. . . .Paul contrasts the bare appearance of the shadow *(nudum umbrae aspectum)* with the solidity of the body . . . . While our sacraments represent Christ as absent from sight and distant of place

but testify that he has been once manifested, they also offer him
to us to be enjoyed.[109]

D. *Other Similes and Analogies*

1. Eating: Satisfaction, Yet Longing

Another way Calvin likes to describe the difference between
the fathers' experience of God's grace and ours is in terms of eating a
meal. The fathers drew from the same fullness of Christ that we do but
"they had a more scanty taste of the benefits of God." When Christ appeared in the flesh, "the blessings were poured out, as it were, with a
full hand, even to satisfaction."[110] "God gave to them some taste of his
love in this life, as we taste him now. However, Christ, who is the substance of all good things and of eternal life, was only promised to them,
but he is given to us. They desired him, as being far off; we enjoy him
as being present."[111] In reference to 1 Peter 1:12, Calvin says that the
fathers "spread the tables, so that others might afterwards feed on the
provisions laid on it. They indeed by faith tasted those things which the
Lord has by their hands transmitted to us to enjoy. They also partook of
Christ as the real food of their souls. What is given now is the exhibition of this."[112]
          It would be a great mistake to conclude that this difference is
insignificant. True, they enjoyed the same food, but they were more
like servants who have done all the preparation. They enjoyed only a
slight taste of the sumptuous feast, but they had to stand off at a distance and wait in anticipation for a chance to enjoy fully what the more
favored guests at the table (those under the gospel) are now enjoying to
satiety. The figure fails, however, in that the fathers under the law did
not get even a clear glimpse of the heavenly food (Christ) which nourished their souls, whereas at an actual banquet servants get a very good
look at that which their guests are enjoying.
          The comparison, granted, is only of the less with the greater.
But how much greater! They had a taste, yes, but theirs was only a
"small portion of grace (*exigua gratiae portio*)" which pales into insig-
nificance in comparison with the "prominence (*eminentia*)" that is
ours.[113] In magnifying this difference, however, Calvin does not wish
to detract from the glory of God's revelation under the law. The fathers
had only a taste of that grace which has been so lavishly poured out on

us, even though they saw Christ dimly only through figures and types; "yet they were satisfied and never fell away from their faith."[114] They did not have much, by comparison, but they had as much as they were capable of taking. Like babies who can only digest milk and pablum, they were capable of receiving only a very simple and primitive diet. But to the extent that they were capable, God in his wisdom and goodness fed them. Thus they were just as satisfied as a baby who has eaten a simple but adequate meal.

However, again the parallel breaks down, for a baby who has eaten enough is completely satisfied and has no desire for anything more solid. The Old Testament saints, however, though satisfied, yet desired to see the things which we see and hear (see Luke 10:24; Matthew 13:17; I. Peter 1:10-12).

> Although the fathers were content with their lot and enjoyed a blessed peace in their own minds, yet this did not prevent their desires from extending further (cf. John 8:56; Luke 2:29) . . . . Due to the curse by which the human race is crushed, it was impossible that they should be anything but inflamed with the desire of the promised deliverance. Let us learn therefore that they longed for Christ like men who are famished and yet they possessed a serene faith, so that they did not murmur against God, but kept their minds in patient expectation until the proper time (*maturum tempus*) of revelation.[115]

But how can one reconcile this "longing" referred to in Luke 10:24 and 1 Peter 1:10-12 with the statement in John 8:56: "Your father Abraham rejoiced that he was to see my day; he saw it and was glad"? "How, even with the eyes of faith, did Abraham see the revelation of Christ?" Calvin, after quoting Luke 10:24, replies: "Faith has its degrees (*gradus*) of seeing Christ." He continues:

> The ancient prophets beheld Christ afar off, as he had been promised to them, and yet were not permitted to behold him as present since he made himself intimately and completely visible (only) when he came down from heaven . . . . Abraham's rejoicing testifies that he looked upon the knowledge of Christ's kingdom as an incomparable treasure; and we are told that he rejoiced to see the day of Christ so that we may know there was nothing he valued more. But all the godly receive from their faith the fruit

that they are satisfied with Christ alone and in him are fully and
completly blessed and happy, their conscience calm and cheerful.[116]

2. Pedagogy: Childhood—Maturity

The fact that the fathers experienced only a relatively small
portion of the grace of Christ was not due to God's parsimoniousness.
As we have seen, they were not capable at that childlike stage of development of receiving more. The era of the law was a period of infancy in
God's economy of salvation. Consequently, Calvin also portrays the
difference between the Testaments in terms of growth or education. He
calls the dispensation of the law the period of the infancy of the church;
that of the gospel the maturity of the church.[117]

Here Calvin employs his well known method of "accommodation." Moses, for example, had to "accommodate himself to the capacity of ignorant people and did not ascend higher than childish rudiments
(*puerilia rudimenta*)."[118] "Since they had not yet come to know Christ
intimately, they were like children whose weakness could not yet bear
the full knowledge of heavenly things."[119] Hence, although the law fundamentally contained the same teaching as the gospel, those who lived
under it were placed by God under a pedagogue. Perfection, however,
could only be obtained in the school of the gospel.[120]

It is necessary to make a distinction which also applies to
much of the preceding analysis. In these references to the childhood of
the church, two different things have been under discussion: doctrine or
teaching and the figures or ceremonies. The doctrine is incomplete and
does not measure up to the fullness and clarity of our instruction under
the gospel. The doctrine is nevertheless indispensable. We cannot ignore the promises of Moses and the prophets; it is necessary even for us
to turn to them. But the rudiments of the figures and ceremonies (in
contrast to the rudiments of doctrine) are another matter. Calvin refers
to this aspect of the *paedagogia* as an "antiquated tutelage" to which
the Christian is forbidden to return. For it is foolish and shameful to return to "a childish age that is past."[121]

In this connection, another problem emerges for Calvin. Is it
not very presumptuous to imagine that we who live in the glorious age
of the gospel are superior to eminent saints of old such as Abraham,
Moses, and David? In the light of Paul's admonitions to us in passages

like Eph. 4:2, 1 Cor. 3:2, and Gal. 4:19 to make progress lest we remain immature babes in the faith, how dare we refer to their meager understanding as "childhood"? After all, there is hardly a person in the Christian church whose faith begins to compare with that of Abraham. The prophets also "so excelled in the power of the Spirit as to illumine the whole world through it even today."[122] "How then can we dare to boast that we are superior to such men? Is it not much preferable to speak of them as the heroes and of us as the children?"[123]

One can almost feel the sense of awe with which Calvin raises such rhetorical questions. But he quickly submits an answer:

> Here we are not asking what grace the Lord has bestowed on a few, but what ordinary dispensation (*ordinariam dispensationem*) he has followed in teaching his people; such as is seen in the teaching of the prophets themselves, who were endowed with a peculiar insight above the others. For even their preaching is both obscure, like something far off, and is embodied in types. Besides, however remarkable the knowledge in which they excelled, inasmuch as they were forced to submit to the common tutelage of the people, they also are to be classed as children. Finally, no one then possessed discernment so clear as to be unaffected by the obscurity of the time.[124]

Some people (Anabaptists?) took offense at this variety of God's government of the church and charged God with inconsistency. Calvin replies that "God ought not to be considered changeable merely because he accommodated diverse forms to different ages, as he knew would be expedient for each . . . . If a householder instructs, rules and guides his children one way in infancy, another way in youth, and still another way in manhood we shall not on this account call him fickle and say that he abandons his purpose." It is not God but rather people who are changeable! Therefore God had to accommodate himself to the varied capacities of his people from age to age.[125] This is why God appeared to the fathers under the law "not as he was in himself (*non qualis in se erat*), but insofar as they could endure the rays of his infinite brightness."[126]

3. An Artist: Rough Sketch—Vivid Color

In the law God was continually coming to his people and preparing their minds and hearts for the advent of his only Son. This coming is marked by degrees of clarity. To bring this out more graphically Calvin also uses the analogy of an artist. He takes his cue from the reference in Hebrews 10:1 to the law as "having a shadow of the good things to come." In his commentary on this passage he observes that the word "shadow" here connotes something different from its use in Col. 2:17 where it is contrasted with solid substance. Here, he says, the ancient ceremonies are likened to "the rough outlines (*rudibus lineamentis*) which are the foreshadowing of the living picture. For artists, before they draw the vivid colors with paint, usually draw an outline in pencil of that which they intend to portray." The difference, then, which the author of Hebrews makes between the law and the gospel, is this: "The former has foreshadowed in an elementary and sketchy outline what today has been expressed in living and graphically printed color . . . . Although it [the law] had in it no image of heavenly things like the final masterpiece from the artist's hand, yet it gave some sort of indication which was of some use to the fathers, even though our condition is much preferable."[127]

Calvin uses the same metaphor in comparing the ceremonies of the fathers with our sacraments. The differences between them are considerable, he observes, for "as painters do not portray in the first draft a likeness (*imaginem*) in vivid colors, but first draw rough and imperfect lines in black and white, so the representation of Christ under the law was unpolished (*impolitam*) and was like a first sketch. But in our sacraments he is beheld distinctly and as alive."[128]

4. Light: Dawn—the Splendor of Midday

Any discussion of law and gospel in Calvin's theology would not be complete without reference to the text and simile he uses more frequently than any other. The text is Malachi 4:2, the simile that of sunlight. The particular emphasis here is on the gradual dawning of the time of salvation. Note, however, that the progress is not from darkness to light, but from a little light to full light. Moreover, the light at dawn is the same light we see at midday, namely, Jesus Christ, the Sun of Righteousness. Calvin does refer occasionally to the period of the law as a "dark cloud" and only a "lamp" in comparison with the splendor and open light of the gospel, but even here there is progress from the less to the greater. At the time of the law "things were very obscure and God governed his people under a dark cloud (*sub obscura nube*). . . . But now Christ the Sun of Righteousness has shone upon us. It is just as though we were in the brightness of midday. The law appears as no more than a lamp *(lucerna)* for the governing of our life, because Christ points out to us in full splendor the way of salvation."[129]

The Old Testament saints "had nothing more than little sparks of that light of life whose full brightness lightens us today."[130] Yet they had sufficient light to be able to stay on the road on which they ought to walk. "Though the brightness of dawn is not as great as that at midday, yet as it is sufficient for making a journey, travellers do not wait until the sun is fully risen. Their portion of light resembled the dawn, which was enough to preserve them from all error and guide them to eternal blessedness."[131]

There was nothing haphazard in all this: God was acting not only according to our capacity but also according to his divine plan.

> For the Lord held to this economy and this order (*hanc oeconomiam et hunc ordinem*) in administering the covenant of his mercy. As the day of its full exhibition approached with the passing of time, the more he increased each day the brightness of its manifestation. Accordingly, at the beginning, when the first promise of salvation was given to Adam (Gen. 3:15), only a few feeble sparks glowed. Then, as it was added to, the light grew in fullness, breaking forth increasingly and shedding its radiance more widely. At last—when all the clouds were dispersed—Christ the Sun of Righteousness fully illumined the whole earth (cf. Mal. 4).[132]

As Calvin makes these comparisons, he is always mindful of the truth that Christ came not to abolish the law and the prophets but to fulfill them. Nevertheless, he does not hesitate to assert that Christ, "by the brightness of his gospel, causes those sparks which shone in the Old Testament to disappear."[133] This might seem to undercut everything Calvin has said before about the continuing relevance and value of the Old Testament revelation. But the solution is that now the revelation of the old covenant is fully illumined by the advent of the Sun of Righteousness. No longer, in view of his advent, can the believer read the Old Testament as if Christ had never come. The dispensation of the law points toward him and has found its true meaning in him. Hence we are to seek him in the law as well as in the gospel. For "Christ is as truly heard in the present day in the law and the prophets as in his gospel."[134]

This does not exhaust the similes and metaphors Calvin uses to depict the law-gospel relationship. He also likens the gospel to an open book and the law to the enigmatic way in which God was known under the law.[135] Elsewhere he uses the metaphor of a race track. Moses and the prophets entered their disciples in the race but only got them started whereas the "proper office" of Christ is to bring his disciples to the finishing post.[136] Again, in accordance with his principle of accommodation, Calvin points out the simplicity of our sacraments and forms of worship in contrast to the more numerous and complicated means of the old dispensation.[137]

E. *The Fundamental Difference: a Suspended Grace* [138]

We have had more than enough evidence already to show that Calvin is not unaware of the historical character of revelation and the diversity of the two covenants. Even so, his exegesis of certain passages is no longer tenable by contemporary canons of scholarship. This allowed him to interpret the Old Testament more christologically than would be possible today. Nevertheless—particularly over against the prevailing hermeneutics of that day—he shows a remarkable reserve and sobriety.

But we have not yet come to the decisive difference in his distinction between the form of the law and the gospel. For all the grace which the fathers enjoyed was in a sense a "suspended (*suspensa*)" grace. It is not simply a matter of more or less. What they knew and experienced, even though it was relatively insignificant in comparison with that enjoyed by those living under the gospel, was real, not illusory. They had more than simply bare promises. The promises themselves, being the living word of God, contained life and offered a true hope. But whatever they had, whatever they received or experienced, was all contingent upon the manifestation of the Son of God in the flesh.[139] The revelation to the fathers was eschatological in that what they enjoyed was based on that which was not yet a visible, historical reality. The power of the cross (and resurrection) at the center of history illuminates and gives efficacy to all that precedes and follows. However, until the day when that reconciliation was actually effected there would be doubt and uncertainty, not from God's side, but on the part of those who had lived before the cross.[140]

Calvin takes this "suspension" so seriously that he can even say that "in a certain sense grace was suspended (*suspensa erat*) until the advent of Christ."[141] Consequently, under the law there was no true and real expiation to wash away sins. Old Testament believers therefore "embraced by faith the substance and the body of the shadows when they voluntarily offered themselves to keep the covenant of God."[142] True, in common with us "they were undoubtedly convinced (*certo persuasi erant*) that God was propitious toward them since he had pardoned their sins . . . . But we are superior to them not only in instruction (*doctrina*), but in effect or completeness (*effectu vel complemento*), since God today not only promises us the pardon of our sins, but also testifies and affirms their entire blotting out and becoming abolished through the sacrifice of his Son . . . . Since, therefore, expiation was suspended until the manifestation of Christ, there was never any true expiation under the law. All its ceremonies were only shadowy representations."[143]

"Suspension" means therefore that "the ceremonies imperfectly represent (*adumbrarent*) Christ as though (*tanquam*) he were absent! whereas today he is represented to us as actually present."[144] One should not conclude, however, that they therefore had no share at all in the grace of Christ. They "possessed him as one hidden, and, as it were, absent . . . absent not in power of grace, but because he was not yet manifested in the flesh."[145]

Consequently, when Paul and the author of Hebrews refer to the shadows of the law and the inadequacy of its cultus, this does not mean that they had no reality. "Their fulfillment had been, so to speak, held in suspense until the appearance of Christ . . . . This must be understood not of efficacy but rather of mode of signification. for until Christ was manifested in the flesh, all signs imperfectly represented (*adumbrabrant*) him as if absent, however much he might make the presence of his power and himself inwardly felt among believers."[146] Unless one goes "beyond" the ceremonies and sacrifices of the law there is "nothing substantial" in them. For the old covenant was "wrapped up *(fuisse)* in the shadowy and ineffectual observance of ceremonies and delivered to the Jews. It was temporary because it remained, as it were, in suspense until it might rest upon a firm and substantial confirmation. It became new and eternal only after it was consecrated and established by the blood of Christ."[147]

Another way of expressing this notion of a "suspended grace" is in terms of the Holy Spirit. For the true efficacy of this grace depended not only on the advent of Christ but also on Pentecost and the outpouring of the Spirit. Granted, he illuminated the godly under the old covenant as well, but the Spirit is "more bountifully and abundantly poured out in the Kingdom of Christ."[148] The fathers could neither have worshiped sincerely and with a pure conscience nor rightly obeyed God's commandments without having been "inwardly taught by the Spirit." But again the power of the Spirit and the concomitant realization of God's mercy were exhibited "much more abundantly in the reign of Christ."[149]

As we have seen above, everything promised to and shared in by the fathers looked forward to and depended on the kingdom of Christ. But this kingdom comes in power only after the ascension of Christ. Therefore, when John says that "the Spirit had not yet been given" (John 7:39), the meaning is not that the fathers had no share of the work of the Spirit. They did, in a sense, but this too, like their participation in the fullness of the grace of Christ, was in a state of suspension until Jesus was glorified. The Spirit is eternal, so the meaning of this text, according to Calvin, is that "so long as Christ dwelt in the world in the lowly form of a servant, that grace of the Spirit which was poured out on men after the resurrection of Christ, had not come forth openly." This is why the apostle speaks here as if the Spirit had not existed before. He "does not simply deny that the grace of the Spirit was revealed to believers before the death of Christ, but that it was not yet so bright and clear as it would be afterwards. For the chief glory of Christ's kingdom is that he governs the church by his Spirit."[150]

F. *The Nature of Promise and Fulfillment*

Before concluding this section, one more matter requires further clarification. For the difference between law and gospel is a relative one in two senses. It is relative in the first place because the substance is the same; the difference is largely one of form. But the difference is also relative in that we who live under the gospel have something else in common with the fathers. We share the same promises, which for us as well are still to a large extent not completely realized. The indicative is more prominent in our faith, but we still live under a "not yet." To be sure, the form and nature of our promises is far superior to theirs; but they remain promises nonetheless. Theirs were foreshadowed by types; in the gospel they are pointed out with the finger. Yet they are still promises. We still live by faith and hope. We too wait for "the full time of revelation."

Because of this, Calvin warns the readers of his *Institutes* that in this respect we are no different from the ancient fathers. We both live by faith in God's promises, for the gospel as well as the law consists of promises. The difference lies in the character of the promises and the degree of realization.[151]

This was a live issue at that time because Servetus maintained that the promises ended at the time of the law. His position was that by faith in Christ we share in the fulfillment of all the promises. Calvin reacts to this suggestion with horror: "As if there were no difference between us and Christ!" Then he explains: "I had just declared that Christ left unfinished nothing of the sum total of our salvation. But it is wrong to assume from this that we already possess the benefits imparted by him." He proceeds to quote Col. 3:3, Rom. 8:24, and 1 John 3:2 and adds: "Although, therefore, Christ offers us in the gospel a present fullness of spiritual benefits, the enjoyment thereof ever lies hidden under the guardianship of hope (*sub custodia spei*), until, having put off corruptible flesh, we be transfigured in the glory of him who goes before us. In the meantime, the Holy Spirit bids us rely on the promises . . . . We enjoy Christ only as we embrace him clad in his own promises (*promissionibus suis vestitum*)."[152]

How, then, are we to think of the relation between the Testaments? Is it adequate to describe the relation simply in terms of promise and fulfillment as is so often done today? Does the category of *Heilsgeschichte* sufficiently describe this relationship?[153]

Years ago M. Simon dealt with this question and came to the conclusion that a twofold division such as prophecy and fulfillment is not adequate to describe Calvin's thought. Based largely on an interpretation of Heb. 10:1 and Col. 2:16, he proposed that in Calvin there is rather a threefold arrangement: silhouette (i.e., the rough sketch in black and white), the finished portrait in vivid colors, and the reality it-self. From this he concluded that there is a threefold development in *Heilsgeschichte*: Old Testament, New Testament, and kingdom of God.[154]

At first glance this seems quite plausible, but as H. H. Wolf has pointed out, the difference between the covenants lies not in their substance but in the varying forms of administration. The real contrast (*Gegenüber*) is between the covenant and the kingdom of God.[155]

The important thing, in any case, is to note that there is within the one covenant a development, but not from promise to fulfillment, at least from our side. It is only justified to speak of promise and fulfill-ment from God's side, for, as Calvin points out, to say that the Christian under the gospel still lives by promises is no reflection on the complet-ed work of Christ. In his flesh Christ has accomplished the whole of our salvation. The Christian, by faith-union with Christ, shares all of that redemption which has been accomplished once and for all. "The promises offer Christ" to us that we may "enjoy a true participation (*communicatione*) in him."[156]

However, there is an eschatological tension between the con-firmation and manifestation of the Old Testament promises we have in the advent of Christ and the final revelation and redemption which will be experienced in the consummation of all things.[157] "The perfect ac-complishment (*solidum complementum*)" of the Old Testament promis-es (such as Isaiah 54:13 and Jer. 31:34) "does not appear in one day. It is enough that believers now obtain a taste of those blessings in order to cherish the hope of the full enjoyment of them at a future period." It is a serious error to imagine that within the commencement of the gospel we have "an immediate and perfect exhibition of those things which we see accomplished from day to day."[158]

Standing above and beyond—and working in—both the law and the gospel is the kingdom of Christ. There is a contrast between less and more in law and gospel, but both have in common an incom-pleteness which stands in contrast to the perfection of the kingdom of God. Hence whether one prefers to speak of a twofold or threefold de-velopment in the history of salvation depends on whether the emphasis is on the one covenant of grace or the two stages within that covenant.

Calvin's terminology in describing this relationship is very in-teresting. He speaks of promise and fulfillment, but "fulfillment" is not to be taken in an absolute sense. Note, moreover, that Calvin does not use the expression "promise and fulfillment" in a technical sense.[159] For the fulfillment of the Old Testament promises is the beginning of the kingdom of Christ (not that Christ first began to reign until after his ascension; yet, properly speaking, the kingdom of Christ begins at this point). Calvin warns against confusing the perfection of Christ's reign with its initiation (*exordium*).[160] Hence he speaks of the "the lowly beginnings of the gospel (*humilibus evangelii exordiis*)"[161] and describes the visible appearance of Christ's kingdom in the very language he formerly used to describe the inferiority of the law in comparison with the gospel.[162] The promises of the law and the prophets are fulfilled in a sense with the advent of Christ and begin to be realized no longer proleptically but actually in the kingdom of Christ. Christ was sent to the Jews "in order to accomplish the truth of God by performing the promises given to the fathers."[163] It is thus no small gain that Christ has appeared and has established the kingdom of God predicted by the prophets. But as they under the law waited and longed for its appearance, so we under the gospel wait and long for his coming in glory which will mark its consummation. We too live by hope, but it is a hope of a different quality since the "grace of God has shone on us through the gospel."[164]

Consequently, the promise-fulfillment category is only adequate and accurate if it is qualified. For "the relation is not that of simple promise and fulfillment, but promises of different degrees of clarity."[165] In the law we have dark, hidden promises in contrast to the clear, manifest promises of the gospel.[166] Because of the difficulty in depicting this difference in terms of promise and fulfillment, it may be better to use other categories of Calvin's. He refers, for example, to the gospel as "that which ratifies and confirms" what had been promised in the law.[167] The gospel is also the "exhibition"[168] or "manifestation"[169] of the promises of the law. Or the difference can be described as that of a hidden and manifest revelation.[170] And sometimes, instead of speaking of the law as "promise", Calvin calls it "a testimony (*testimonium*), the living image of which is set forth in the gospel."[171]

We have come to the end of the second aspect of the relationship between the law and the gospel. For Calvin, the relationship is not a simple one. The accent has been on unity, but at the same time Calvin has shown an appreciation for the nature of the historical unfolding of God's redemptive history. Thus the criticism that Calvin obliterates the distinction between the Old and New Testaments is clearly unwarranted. Nor is it possible to understand how the Dutch Roman Catholic theologian, Alting von Geusau, can claim that for Calvin it is not important whether the redemption contained in the promise lies in the past or the future since for him redemption as a historical event is merely a "sign of a message. This indicates," continues von Geusau, "a transcendent view of the plan of redemption which proceeds from the one unchangeable God. In this view lurks the danger that the historical form of revelation in the visible world is not fully brought to expression."[172]

Calvin, to the contrary, explicitly warns against confusing different ages *(confusio tempororum)*.[173] To insist on a more radical distinction is to approach the border-line beyond which it will be difficult to maintain the unity of God, the unity of revelation, and the unity of the church. As we proceed now to a difference in law and gospel of a more radical character, let us keep in mind that for all the diversity, variation, and modification of God's revelation in the law and gospel, God is always true to himself. The "constancy of God" is the first and the last word.[174]

IV. ANTITHESIS BETWEEN LETTER AND SPIRIT

At last we come to that aspect of the law which most Protestants take for the whole: the law that is opposed or contrary to the gospel, the law that is separated from Christ and the Holy Spirit. This is what Calvin calls the bare law *(nuda lex)* which accuses and troubles the conscience, the law in itself and as such which is isolated from the covenant and the promises. This law requires perfection; where that is lacking, it curses, condemns, and kills. It demands what only the gospel can give.

Does Calvin really recognize such a law? Or is this aspect of the law subordinated to a very minor role and passed off as an unimportant footnote? How can one who has praised the law so highly do justice to this doctrine which has been the touchstone of evangelical theology ever since Luther? In view of all that Calvin has said thus far about the law, can he escape a moralism which is a constant threat to a full-blown freedom in Christ? Is it true that Calvin "sometimes comes near to transforming the gospel into a new law?"[175] Or that "the gospel as it appears in Paul and John" is found "in clearer and brighter form in Luther than in Calvin"?[176]

A. *Exegesis of Key Passages*

The simplest and most direct way of answering these questions is to examine Calvin's exegesis of key texts in the New Testament, especially those in the Pauline Epistles. However, the antithesis between law and gospel is also stated with particular force in John 1:17: "For the law was given through Moses; grace and truth came through Jesus Christ."

Calvin begins by comparing the ministry of Moses with the reign of Christ and noting that the contribution of Moses "was extremely scanty compared to the grace of Christ." This is reminiscent of the comparisons in the last section. The sharpness of the contrast seems to have escaped Calvin. But then he immediately adds: "But we must notice the antithesis in his contrasting of law and truth; for he [the Evangelist] means that the law lacked both of these." By "truth and grace" Calvin understands "the spiritual fulfillment of those things of which the bare letter (*nuda littera*) was contained in the law." Thus "the truth consists in the grace which was finally exhibited in Christ. From this it follows that if you separate the law from Christ, nothing remains in it but empty forms (*inanes figures*)."

The fundamental question here, however, Calvin continues, is "the validity of the law in itself (*per se*) and apart from Christ. And the Evangelist denies that there is anything substantial in it until we come to Christ." Then in language reminiscent of Luther, "Moreover the truth consists in our obtaining through Christ the grace which the law could not give . . ." *viz.*, "the free forgiveness of sins and the renewal of the heart."[177]

One of the strongest texts of this sort in the Pauline corpus is Romans 4:15: "For the law brings wrath, but where there is no law there is no transgression." Calvin minces no words here and states unequivocally that "since the law produces nothing but vengeance, it cannot bring grace. The law would, it is true, point out the way of life to men of virtue and integrity, but since it orders the sinful and corrupt to do their duty without supplying them with the power to do it, it brings them in their guilt to the judgement seat of God."[178]

In any discussion of the law two texts of similar import are always brought forward: Romans 5:20 and Galatians 3:20. The former reads, "The law came in (intruded, N.E.B.) to increase the trespass . . . " Calvin begins his exegesis by making a characteristic distinction: Paul

"does not describe here the whole use and office of the law, but is dealing only with the one part which served his present purpose."[179] But after this word of caution, Calvin proceeds in a rather Lutheran fashion:

> In order to set forth the grace of God, he tells us that it was neces-
> sary that men's destruction should be more clearly revealed to
> them. Men were indeed shipwrecked before the law was given,
> but since they seemed to be surviving, even in their destruction,
> they were submerged into the deep, in order that their deliverance
> might appear more remarkable when, contrary to human expecta-
> tion, they emerge from the floods which overwhelm them. It was
> not unreasonable that the law should in part be given for the very
> reason that it might again condemn men who had once already
> been condemned.[180]

The other text which seems to imply an exclusively negative
and secondary role for the law is Gal. 3:19: "Why then the law? It was
added because of transgressions." Calvin again begins by noting that
"there are many uses of the law. But Paul confines himself," he continues,

> to that which bears on his present subject. He did not propose to
> inquire in how many ways the law is advantageous to men. It is
> necessary to put readers on their guard concerning this point, for I
> have found that many have fallen into the error of acknowledging
> no other use of the law except that which is expressed here . . . .
> This is therefore not a complete definition of the use of the law.
> Those who acknowledge nothing else in the law are in error.

Thus far we have only those distinctions which are so characteristic of Calvin. Now, however, he comes to the actual meaning of the
text:

> Paul means that the law was promulgated in order to make known
> transgressions and thus to compel men to acknowledge their guilt.
> As men are naturally too ready to excuse themselves unless they
> are aroused by the law, their consciences are drugged.

But now comes the crucial question: "Since the law is the rule
of a godly and upright life, why is it said to be added 'because of transgressions' rather than 'for the sake of obedience'?" The answer:

However much it may point out true righteousness, yet due to the
corruption of our nature, its instruction (*doctrina*) only increases
transgressions until the Spirit of regeneration comes and writes it
on the heart. This Spirit, however, is not given by the law but is
received by faith. I would have my readers remember that this
saying of Paul's is not of a philosophical or political character,
but expresses a purpose of the law which the world has never
known.[181]

Several phrases in the above citations deserve special mention,
but let us first turn to Calvin's comments on two more passages. The
one is Gal. 2:19: "For I through the law died to the law, that I might
live to God." Nowhere does Calvin sound more like Luther than in his
comments on this text.

We must not ascribe to Christ that work which is properly the
task of the law. It was not necessary for Christ to destroy the
righteousness of the law since the law itself slays its disciples . . .
It is the law which forces us to die to itself, for it threatens our destruction, leaving us nothing but despair, and in this way drives
us away from trusting in it . . . . As soon as the law begins to live
in us, it inflicts a fatal wound by which we die, and at the same
time breathes life into the man who is already dead to sin. Those
who live to the law, therefore, have never felt the power of the
law or even tasted what it is all about; for the law, when it is
rightly understood, makes us die to itself . . . . The law bears
within itself a curse which slays us. Hence it follows that the
death which is inflicted by the law is truly deadly. Another kind
of death is contrasted with this, *viz.*, the life-giving fellowship of
the cross of Christ . . . . This death is not mortal but is the cause
of a better life because God rescues us from the shipwreck of the
law and by his grace restores us to another life.[182]

The last illustration—and the most important one—is found in
Calvin's treatment of 2 Cor. 3:6f. "For the letter (written code, R.S.V.)
kills, but the Spirit gives life." Calvin's mentor, Augustine, had written
a special monograph on this theme,[183] and Calvin himself is especially
detailed in his commentary. He deals first of all with the occasion for
Paul's remarks and concludes that in contrast to those people who had
impressed the Corinthians with their brilliant oratory, Paul wishes to

show that the chief glory of the gospel and its ministers is the power of the Spirit.

"At any rate," he adds, "there is no doubt that by 'letter' he means the Old Testament and by the 'Spirit' the gospel." He vigorously rejects Origen's approach to this passage and the influence of this exegesis in subsequent centuries. Rather, by the word "letter" Paul simply means "an external preaching which does not reach the heart, and by the word 'Spirit' the life-giving teaching which, through the grace of the Spirit, is given effective operation in men's souls."[184]

Calvin rightly perceives the connection between this passage and the prophecy of Jeremiah 31:31. Paul, he maintains, had this verse in mind and was trying to show that it had been fulfilled in his preaching. Paul's opponents, on the other hand, lacked the power of the Spirit with all of their vain and pompous talk.

Then Calvin raises the question of the Old Testament fathers. Did God only speak to them externally without touching their hearts by his Spirit? This would seem to be the case if the old covenant was essentially a dead and external letter. Calvin's twofold answer is very important and must be quoted in full.

> My first answer is that Paul is here considering what belonged peculiarly to the law. For although God was at that time working through his Spirit, that did not come about through the ministry of Moses but through the grace of Christ, as is said in 1 John 1:17
> . . . . Certainly God's grace was not inactive all that time; but it is sufficient for this comparison that it was not the peculiar blessing of the law. For Moses had fulfilled his office when he had delivered the doctrine of life with its added promises and threats. That is why he calls the law the letter because it is in itself a dead preaching . . . .
>
> My second answer is that these things are not affirmed absolutely (*simpliciter*) of the law or of the gospel, but only in so far as (*quatenus*) the one is contrasted with the other, for even the gospel is not always Spirit. Yet when the two are being compared, it is true and proper to affirm that it is of the nature of the law to teach men literally so as not to penetrate beyond their ears, but it is of the nature of the gospel to teach them spiritually since it is the instrument of God's grace. This depends on God's appointment (*Dei ordinatione pendet*), for it has pleased him to manifest

the efficacy of the Spirit more in the gospel than in the law; for it is the work of the Spirit alone to teach men's minds effectively.[185]

Calvin sharpens this antithesis as he takes up the description of the law as a "ministry (or dispensation) of death" in verse seven. After analyzing various aspects of the comparison, he concludes by examining briefly the characteristics of the law and the gospel. He reminds us again that Paul is not speaking of the whole doctrine found in the Old Testament, nor of the ancient fathers' experience of God's goodness. Nevertheless,

> The law was engraved on stones and thus it was literal teaching. This defect had to corrected by the gospel since the law was bound to be transitory (*fragilis*) as long as it was consigned only to tablets of stone. Thus the gospel is a holy and inviolable covenant because it was promulgated under the guarantee of the Spirit of God. From this it follows that the law was a ministry of condemnation and death, for when men are taught of their duty and are told that all who do not satisfy God's righteousness are accursed, they are convicted and found guilty of sin and death. Thus from the law they receive nothing but this condemnation, for there God demands what is due to him, and yet gives no power to perform it. But by the gospel men are regenerated and reconciled to God by the free remission of sins, so that it is the ministration of righteousness and so of life.[186]

This is not the end of Calvin's discussion, for he dwells at some length on that which is common to both the law and the gospel as well as the sense in which Christ has put an end to all that is peculiar to the ministry of Moses. However, the main features of Calvin's understanding of the law, taken in a more restricted sense, should be evident.

On the basis of his exposition of these selected passages, at least one conclusion can be made: Calvin recognizes fully the negative function of the law. Moreover, he acknowledges that this is a proper function of the law *in so far as* the ministry of Moses is opposed to the ministry of Christ and the gospel. This is, of course, not the complete picture; only one aspect or part of the law is dealt with when the law is so portrayed. On the other hand, the origin of this concept of the law is not to be traced to a mere misunderstanding or misuse of the law; nor can these strong words of Paul be dismissed simply as a polemic against an abuse of the law.[187] The law as such has certain characteristics which not only differentiate it from the gospel but place it in a sense in opposition to the gospel.

This much is incontrovertible; and this is only a sampling. Countless references of a similar nature abound in his sermons, the *Institutes*, and elsewhere in the Commentaries.[188]

B. *The problem of a Unified Concept of the Law*

The real problem, however, is not that of showing that Calvin takes the accusing, condemning function of the law seriously. Rather, the difficulty is to integrate this concept of the law with his understanding of the law as a whole. (This difficulty is not peculiar to Calvin; contemporary scholars also have a hard time integrating Paul's diverse references to the law, let alone reconciling these references with the portrayal of the law in the Old Testament.) For it could be maintained that Calvin has not thoroughly integrated this aspect of the law into his system as a whole; and that he operates with two concepts of the law, with the more Pauline one playing a subordinate role. This is a very complex problem, for despite his numerous definitions, warnings, and qualifying phrases (the key one being "in so far as—*quatenus*"), no simple solution is readily apparent.

We saw in Chapter One, where a preliminary attempt was made to sketch the meaning of the law for Calvin, that he frequently reconciles the apparent contradictions between David (as in Psalm 119) and Paul concerning the law by replying: David is speaking of the whole law, the Word of God; Paul is speaking of the law in a limited sense. Thus David, when praising the law, is thinking not only of the precepts and commandments but also of the promises of salvation as well. He rejoices in the law of the covenant, God's gift to Israel. Presupposed in these encomiums of the law is the free adoption of the people of God; his grace has preceded his command. The revealed law rests on the foundation of the gospel.

Paul, on the other hand, was often dealing with Judaizers who perverted and abused the law. They separated it from the grace and Spirit of Christ. And when the Spirit of Christ does not give life to the law, it is not only unprofitable but deadly. Without Christ the law comes to us as sheer demand, rigorous, uncompromising, and inexorable. No one can meet these demands, and hence all people are sentenced to death and condemnation, an existence under the wrath of God. True, the law, even by itself, is the Word of God and serves a beneficial purpose; but it is experienced in this way only when Christ appears to us in it and enlightens us by his Spirit. But once Christ is taken away and the law is separated from the Holy Spirit, only a dead letter, an external sound, confronts us.[189]

Is this, then, the basic reason why the majority of Paul's references to the law are so negative while Deuteronomy and the Psalmists praise God for it? The answer for Calvin is no. To be sure, the limiting of the law only to its requirements and commands, and abstracting it from Christ and the efficacy of the Holy Spirit is no small factor. Nevertheless, it is not only the law, in a restricted sense, but the whole old covenant as such which is null and void. Apart from Christ and the Holy Spirit, the whole Word of God is merely a dead letter without life and light.[190] Moreover, the function of humbling sinners, subduing their pride, and stripping them of all their defenses does not belong exclusively to the law. This is common to the prophets and the gospel as well.[191] In both the law and the gospel we are confronted with the majesty of the holy God. Both, therefore, produce fear and awaken slumbering consciences.[192] When the gospel is preached aright, the whole world is summoned to the judgment seat of God. The gospel, like the law, can be a sword which slays.[193]

The opposition of Moses and Christ, law and gospel, therefore, does not depend solely on the absence of Christ or the Holy Spirit. Both can produce a negative reaction and both have ultimately the same doctrine and goal. The law contains the gospel and the gospel contains the law. There is a distinction in form which results in the not yet or the less of the law being taken up by the present and fuller realities and blessings of the gospel. But this does not explain how Calvin—and the Scriptures—can speak almost simultaneously both so positively and so negatively about the law. We have not yet come to the fundamental antithesis which distinguishes the law from the gospel.

C. *The Peculiar Office of the Law*

The crucial distinction for Calvin is this: the antithesis lies in the special or peculiar office, function, and ministry of the law. Something intrinsic and inherent in the law, something characteristic of its very nature, sets it over against the gospel in the sharpest possible way. (The reference now is neither to the substance nor even the form of the law as such.) For what separates the law from the gospel like fire and water is the matter of justification. There are two kinds of promises and two kinds of righteousness: legal promises and evangelical promises, the righteousness of works and the righteousness of faith. Here there is no more or less, no gradation. These are two opposing systems which are totally irreconcilable. In a very special way the law is a ministry of death and the gospel a ministry of life and salvation. When the law is separated from the promises and the gospel, where it is viewed according to its distinctive properties in contrast to those of the gospel, the antithesis is profound and radical.

But this only raises further questions. For if, as Calvin maintains, the law, including the commandments, was a marvelous gift of God's grace, the bulwark of Israel, her joy and her treasure, how is it that it only curses and kills? Were the offers of righteousness and life by Moses to the people of Israel a sham? The answer hinges again on a careful distinction of Calvin's. Moses, he explains, had two offices: one was universal (*in universum*), viz., "the instruction of the people in the true rule of piety." In this sense he was a minister of the whole law and accordingly preached repentance and faith. In this capacity Moses proclaimed the promises of the divine mercy; he was, in short, a preacher (*praeconem*) of the gospel! This task he performed faithfully and well.[194]

But Moses also had another office (*munus*) which, unlike his universal office, he did not have in common with Christ. "This office was particularly imposed upon him, to demand perfect righteousness of the people and to promise them a reward, as if by a compact, upon no other condition than that they should fulfill whatever was enjoined upon them; but also to threaten and declare judgment against them if they ever wandered from the way." Therefore, it is important to "distinguish between the general doctrine which was delivered by Moses and the special commission (*mandatum*) which he received."[195]

On the basis of this distinction Calvin is able to explain how Paul can speak of the same law as holy and good and also as the law of sin and death. Thus, according to Calvin, in Gal. 3:19, where Paul is discussing "the peculiar office, power and end of the law," he separates

it from the promises of grace. We should approach similar texts such as
Rom. 4:15 and 2 Cor. 3:6, 7 in the same way. Likewise, the antithesis
in Heb. 12:18-20 "proves that what was entrusted to Moses is separate
and distinct from the gospel."[196] It follows from this that insofar as Moses is distinguished from Christ, his ministry has ceased, although his
"official task (*legatio*)" was identical with that which Christ afterward
discharged. Paul, because of the situation in which he found himself,
often pointed to that which was peculiar to Moses and distinct from
Christ, even though they are in perfect agreement as far as the substance of their doctrine is concerned.[197] However, when Paul thus refers only to that office of the law peculiar to the ministry of Moses, he
is not referring to the ten commandments; "for the will of God must
stand forever."[198]

Moses' double office corresponds to the twofold meaning of
the law. Consequently, when Paul in Romans 10:5 speaks of "the righteousness of the law" in connection with Moses, this must not be applied to "the whole office (*functionem*) of Moses, but to that part of it
which was peculiarly entrusted to him." When the word law is used in
this restricted sense, "Moses is implicitly contrasted with Christ."[199]

D. *Five Differences Between Law and Gospel*

The law, taken in this restricted sense, differs from the gospel
in the following ways: 1. It covenants conditionally.[200] The usual procedure in the law is that God appears to act according to a strict agreement. If the people do their part, they will enjoy God's favor. But if
they fail to obey, there is no hope. "Thus the original covenant only
avails to man's condemnation."[201] 2. Related to this is the opposition
between the righteousness of the law and the righteousness of faith concerning the cause of justification. The law requires works, whereas
faith directs us to Christ. This is why Paul often opposes the law to
faith—not because of doctrine but because of the opposition of faith to
works.[202] Or, instead of speaking of two kinds of righteousness, the difference can be described in terms of promises: "The promises of the
law depend on the condition of works while the gospel promises are
free and dependent solely on God's mercy."[203] However, in the writings
of Moses many evangelical as well as legal promises stand side by side.
The promises of the law are technically only those which particularly

pertain to the ministry of the law.[204] 3. The special function of the law was not to incline people's hearts to the obedience of righteousness. The office (*officium*) of the law, rather, was to lead people step by step to Christ that they might seek pardon from him and the Spirit of regeneration.[205] 4. The law, by itself (*per se*), i.e., in contrast to the special characteristics of the gospel, is an external letter. The gospel is peculiarly spiritual in character for it teaches inwardly the heart and mind. The nature of the law is such that "in itself and separated from the gospel, it is dead and destitute of the Spirit of regeneration."[206] This was why a new covenant was required—that the law might be written and sealed on our hearts by the Holy Spirit.[207]

Finally, 5. due to the different dispensations, even the appearance of God is different in the law and in the gospel. Under the law God "was prompt to mete out stern and terrifying punishments for every human transgression." Now under the gospel God "seems to have laid aside his former wrathful mood and punishes more gently and rarely."[208] Under the law God took vengeance; under the gospel the strict conditions of the law are moderated, for God regards his children with kindness and pardons their faults.[209] "In the precepts of the law, God is but a rewarder of perfect righteousness, which all of us lack, and conversely, the judge of evil deeds. But in Christ his face shines, full of grace and gentleness, even upon us poor and unworthy sinners.[210] Under the law perfect obedience is required, but in the gospel, through the interposition of pardon, only the will to obedience is pleasing to God.[211] In the promulgation of the law there was nothing but sheer terror, whereas in the gospel God's invitation is full of love. Calvin even goes so far as to say that God takes on the form of a severe Judge in the law.[212] He appears as an avenger! But in the gospel "with fatherly kindness he gently invites us to salvation and soothes our troubled minds by offering us the forgiveness of sins."[213]

These comparisons are rather surprising, coming from Calvin. But they are further evidence that he does not reduce both Testaments to the same level. On the other hand, if one took these statements out of context and ignored the first two sections of this chapter, one might conclude that Calvin was dangerously close to being a Manichean heretic! Nothing, of course, could be further from Calvin's intention. In fact, in the context of the last two passages cited above he engages in a polemic against the "gross error" of imagining that the God of Israel was different from ours. To make this error is "to cut God in two"! This error originates in the failure to see: 1. that we have here different modes of God's dealing with people; God's essence is the same;[214] 2. that everything hinges on the different dispensations; 3. that there is no contradiction in this diversity because the Israelites were taught by the law to seek for salvation nowhere but in Christ;[215] and 4. that grace and truth in Jesus Christ were not absent in the Old Testament; but they were not a benefit of the law as such.[216]

E. *How God's Good Law Brings a Curse and Death*

The last point is an important one and requires further elaboration. Keep in mind that Calvin is not speaking here about the whole law or the Old Testament in its totality, but about what is peculiar to each dispensation. Consequently, when the law in 2 Cor. 3:6 f. (meaning the Old Testament here) is designated letter, and the gospel Spirit, Paul is not speaking "absolutely (*simpliciter*) of the law or of the gospel, but only in so far as they are opposed to one another; for even the gospel is not always Spirit."[217] In Jer. 31:31-34 and in 2 Cor. 3:6-11 Jeremiah and Paul, "because they are contrasting the Old and New Testaments, consider nothing in the law except what properly belongs to it. For example, the law contains here and there promises of mercy, but because they have been borrowed from elsewhere (*quia sunt aliunde ascitae*), they are not counted part of the law, when the simple nature (*pura natura*) is under discussion."[218] Moses, by himself, has nothing to offer us. Nevertheless, he was a minister of the gospel, for the law was not devoid of those benefits which we receive today through the gospel. But they were then, "as it were, adventitious (*quasi adventitium*); for all of those benefits were dependent on Christ and the promulgation of the gospel."[219]

Yet when it comes to a comparison of the two ministries, it must be maintained that each by nature possesses its own attributes. Despite all they have in common, the special function of the law is to fill sinner's minds with fear, and by setting forth its terrible curse, to cut off all hope of salvation. Whereas both the gospel and the law are empty and useless (even harmful to the reprobate) without the Spirit of regeneration, an inherent quality in the law makes it particularly deadening. The law is a less appropriate vessel for the Holy Spirit than the gospel. Therefore, Calvin approves of Augustine's statement: "If the Spirit of grace is absent, the law is present only to accuse and kill us."[220] The same could not be said of the gospel, for "it is of the nature of the gospel to teach spiritually because it is the instrument of Christ's grace. This depends on God's disposition (*ordinatione pendet*), for it has pleased him to manifest the efficacy of the Spirit more in the gospel than in the law; for it is the work of the Spirit alone to teach men's minds effectively."[221]

This does not yet solve our problem, for the question then arises as to whether the original purpose of the law, even taken in a restricted sense, was only to condemn and kill. If so, the only conclusion is that all of the offers in the Old Testament to walk in the commandments and be blessed, to obey God and live, etc. were not well-meant offers. God then would only be tantalizing his people with promises which were from the outset incapable of fulfillment.[222] A partial answer Calvin offers is that even this possibility served its purpose, which was for the good and not the hurt of God's people (i.e., it forced them to forsake their own righteousness and flee to Christ for refuge); but that does not really answer the first question. For if the original purpose of the law was to kill—even though its ultimate result was salutary—it would reflect both on the law and on God for having willed something which could only hurt and bring a curse.

Calvin's answer ultimately is that although Paul says the law is deadly to us, Calvin vindicates it against any possible objection when he shows that this evil is accidental (*accidentale*) and therefore must be imputed to ourselves.[223] Hence when Paul describes the law as a "minister of death" (2 Cor. 3:6), "it is accidental to it on account of the corrupt nature of man. The law itself does not produce sin, but finds sin in us. It offers life to us but we, because of our corruption, derive nothing but death from it. Therefore the law is only deadly in relation to men."[224] It is not the law that is defective, but the weakness of our flesh.[225] The fact that we can not be justified by works is not due to the imperfection of the law. The promise is made of no effect by our sin and corruption. It is possible to speak of the "defect" of the law, but that defect arises from our infirmity.[226] It was for this reason that the first covenant was made void[227] and only resulted in condemnation.[228]

Underlying this whole discussion is a great hypothetical "if". "God shows us in his law how we could and should arrive at life, if our nature were such that there was nothing to impede us."[229] "If the integrity of our nature had remained pure, the law would not bring death on us, nor oppose the man who is of a sound mind and who shrinks from sin."[230] "If our will were completely conformed and composed to obedience to the law, its knowledge alone would suffice to gain salvation."[231]

However, this is not our actual situation, and therefore the curse and deadly wound of the law is "not only accidental but perpetual and inseparable from its nature. The blessing which it offers us is excluded by our depravity, so that the curse alone remains."[232] "Since our carnal and corrupted nature contends violently against God's spiritual law and is in no way corrected by its discipline, it follows that the law which had been given for salvation, provided it met with suitable hearers (*auditores idoneos*), turns into an occasion for sin and death."[233]

All this may appear rather intricate and hypothetical, but it does not differ essentially from the dialectic expressed by the Apostle Paul in Romans chapter seven. "The very commandment which promised life proved to be death to me." Yet "the law is holy, and the commandment is holy, just and good . . . . We know that the law is spiritual; but I am carnal, sold under sin . . . . So then I of myself serve the law of God with my mind, but with my flesh I serve the law of sin" (Rom. 7:10, 12, 14, 25).[234]

The gospel is good news, however, because this "defection" of ours is "accidental" and cannot therefore "abolish the glory of God's goodness" in his generous promises. Our perfidy does not and cannot nullify the steadfast love of the God who condescended to covenant with his people. "God exhibited a remarkable proof of his goodness in promising life to all who kept his law—and this will always remain perfect (*integrum*)."[235] True, "the wickedness and condemnation of us all are sealed by the testimony of the law. Yet this is not done to cause us to fall down in despair or, completely discouraged, to rush headlong over the brink--provided we duly profit by the testimony of the law."[236]

Thus the law, even when it seems to oppose the gospel, is ultimately for our good—provided we duly profit from its testimony. Although we are prevented from enjoying the blessed life it promised because of our wickedness, yet in the providence of God it becomes a means toward our salvation. "Thereby the grace of God, which nourishes us without the support (*subsidio*) of the law, becomes sweeter, and his mercy, which bestows that grace upon us, becomes more lovely."[237]

Precisely how God uses this law which curses and kills for our salvation is one of the themes of the next chapter.

NOTES

1. A modified and condensed version of this chapter appeared in *Calviniana. Ideas and Influence of John Calvin*, edited by Robert B. Schnucker (Kirksville, MO.: Sixteenth Century Journal Publishers, 1988). See my essay, "Law and Gospel or Gospel and Law? Calvin's Understanding of the Relationship," 13-32.

2. In addition to the Old Testament theologies of Eichrodt, von Rad, Vriezen, etc., see especially two symposia: *Essays on Old Testament Hermeneutics*, edited by Claus Westermann (Richmond, Va: John Knox Press, 1963) and *The Old Testament and Christian Faith*, edited by Bernhard W. Anderson (New York: Harper and Row, 1963). Cf. the relevant discussion of Otto Weber, *Foundations of Dogmatics* I, 287ff.

3. *Dogmengeschichte* IV, 2, 566.

4. *Calvin*, 13.

5. *Calvin* IV, 199.

6. Besides Niesel's and Wendel's works on Calvin's theology see R. S. Wallace, *Calvin's Doctrine of Word and Sacraments*, chapters 1-4; H. Berger's *Calvin's Geschichts Auffassung*, chapter 9; and, above all, H. H. Wolf, *Die Einheit des Bundes: Das Verhältnis von Altem und Neuem Testament bei Calvin*.

7. For the latter see George H. Tavard, *Holy Writ or Holy Church* (London: Burns and Oates, 1959), 101;2; L. G. M. Alting von Geusau, *Die Lehre von der kindertaufe bei Calvin* (Bilthoven: Uitgeverij H. Nelissen, 1963) 171-173; 185-6.

8. For comparisons of Calvin and Bucer see Wendel, *Calvin*, pp. 209-213; for Peter Martyr, see J. C. McLelland, *The Visible Words of God*, 86-100.

9. See "Gesetz und Paraklese," in *Antwort*, 332.

10. The *Christian Doctrine of Creation and Redemption*, Dogmatics Vol. II, 211-12.

11. *Inst.* II.9.2.

12. *Inst.* II.10.2.

13. Comm. Ex. 19:1 (CO 24, 193).

14. Cf. Comm. Deut. 30:11 (CO 24, 258); Comm. Psalm 19:7, 8 (Co

199-201); Comm. Rom. 10:5 (CO 49, 197); Comm. 2. Cor. 3:6 (CO 50, 40); *Inst.* II.7.2; II.9.4.

    15. *Inst.* II.9.4.

    16. Cf. Wendel, *Calvin*, 208-9.

    17. Ibid., p. 211.

    18. "Certum est legem cum fide non pugnare: alioqui Deus ipse sibi esset dissimilis," Comm. Gal. 3:12 (CO 50, 209). Cf. Sermons on Gal. 2:15, 16 (CO 50, 420) and Gal. 3:11-14 (CO 50, 5°3)

    19. Comm. Hab. 2: 4 (CO 43, 530).

    20. Comm. Heb. 1:1,2 (CO 55, 9). The same can be said of the Holy Spirit: he is "everywhere equal and in conformity with himself . . . . he cannot vary and differ from himself," *Inst.* I.9.2. "It is certain that the Spirit is not in conflict with himself (*Spiritum secum non pugnare certum est*), " *Inst.* III.17.11.

    21. Comm. Isa. 2:3 (CO 36, 64).

    22. Comm. Jer. 31:31 (CO 38, 687). "He who once made a covenant with his chosen people has not changed his purpose as though he had forgotten his faithfulness," ibid.

    23. Comm. Jer. 31;32 (CO 38, 688). God "does not promise anything different [in Jer. 31:33] regarding the essence (*summam*) of the doctrine, but he makes the difference consist in the form only," Comm. Jer. 31:33 (CO 39, 691).

    24. Comm. Isa. 2:3 (CO 36, 64).

    25. Comm. Isa. 42:4 (CO 37, 63).

    26. Comm. Jer. 31:33 (CO 38, 692).

    27. *Inst.* II.10.8.

    28. *Inst.* II.10.1.

    29. Comm. Jer. 31:31 (CO 38, 688).

    30. Sermon 2 Tim. 3:16, 17 (CO 32 294. Cf. Comm. 2 Tim. 3:17 (CO 52, 384): "The writings of the Apostles contain nothing else than the true and genuine explanation (*meram et germanem explicationem*) of the law and the prophets together with a manifestation (*manifestatio*) of the things expressed in them."

    31. *Inst.* II.9.3. Cf. *Inst.* III.2.6: Christ "clothed with his gospel (*evangelio suo vestitum*)."

    32. Cf. Luke 24:27, 44; John 5:39, 46; Acts 28:23.

    33. Comm. Acts 28:23 (CO 48, 569).

    34. Comm. Heb. 13:8 (CO 55, 190).

    35. Sermon Gal. 3:19 (CO 50, 541).

    36. See *Inst.* IV.8.6-8.

    37. *Inst.* IV.10,17. Cf. I.6.2.

    38. Comm. Matt. 5:31 (CO 45, 175).

    39. *Inst.* II.8.7.

40. Comm. Luke 24:27 (CO 45, 175). Cf. Comm. Ex. 25:8 (CO 24, 405).

41. Comm. Ezek. 16:61 (CO 40, 395).

42. Comm. John 5:39 (CO 47, 125).

43. Comm. John 5:37 (CO 47, 124).

44. Comm. Matt. 17:5 (CO 45, 488).

45. "Quare ut solide fides nostra nitatur, veniendum est ad legem et prophetas," Comm. 1 Pet. 2:6 (CO 55, 236).

46. ". . . . non alium legi et prophetis scopum esse quam Christum," Comm. Matt. 17:3 (CO 45,486). "Et certe [Christus] solus est legis finis ac perfectio," Comm. James 1:25 (CO 55, 396). Cf. Comm. Rom. 10:4 (CO 49, 196); *Inst.* II.7.1.

47. Comm. 2 Cor. 3:15 (CO 50, 45). Barth argues cogently along these lines in his *Church Dogmatics* I, 2, 481-490.

48. Co 9, 815.

49. Comm. John 5:39 (CO 47, 125).

50. "The revelation of God comes to us in the Old Testament in what we might call lucid fragments. These fragments form parts of a mighty whole culminating in the advent of Christ . . . . Yet this incomparable and insurpassable reality does not place the Old Testament in the shadows; for owing to numerous coherences in which the Old Testament witnesses to the coming of Christ, it still illuminates the reality of salvation in Jesus Christ," G. C. Berkouwer, *The Person of Christ*, 137, 141.

51. *Inst.* II.9.4.

52. Comm. John 10:16 (CO 47.245).

53. *Inst.* II.10.1. Servetus had also affirmed that under the law faith, as well as remission of sins, was "earthly and carnal," *Christianismi Restitutio* (1553), 322, 324, quoted in the LCC Tr. of the *Inst.*, 429, n.2.

54. *Inst.* II.11.10.

55. See *Inst.* II.6.2.

56. *Inst.* II.10.1.

57. *Inst.* II.11.1. Cf. Comm. Heb. 7:12 (CO 55, 89): "It is common to both [Christ and Moses] to offer God's lovingkindness to us, to set down the rules for holy and godly living, to teach the true worship of God, and to encourage us to faith and patience and all the practice of holiness."

58. Comm. Heb. 11:13 (CO 55, 155). "All the fathers from the beginning of the world were approved by God in no other way than by being united to him by faith," Comm. Heb. 11:2 (CO 55, 144).

59. *Inst.* II.11.2.

60. Comm. Jer. 31:12 (CO 38, 661); *Inst.* II.10.7f.

61. *Inst.* II.11.2.

62. Comm. Ex. 25:8 (CO 24, 404). "The worship of the law was spiri-

tual in substance but carnal and earthly in its form," Comm. Jer. 4:23 (CO 47, 89).

63. Comm. Gal. 4:1 (CO 50, 224).

64. Comm. Heb. 10:1 (CO 55, 121). Cf. *Inst.* II.11.10.

65. Cf. Comm. 1 Peter 1:12 (CO 55, 218); *Inst.* II.10.2f.; II.11.1f.

66. *Inst.* IV.14.23. By "sacraments" in the Old Testament Calvin means principally circumcision and the various sacrifices, purifications, and other rites enjoined in the law of Moses, IV.14.20. The term "sacrament" in this broad sense "embraces generally all those signs which God has ever enjoined upon men to render them more certain and confident of the truth of his promises." These include everything from the tree in the Garden of Eden and the rainbow to certain miraculous signs manifested to Abraham and Gideon, IV.14.20.

67. Quoted in *Inst.* IV.14.26. Cf. II.11.10 where Calvin also discusses Augustine's view of the relation of law and gospel. In this instance Calvin is not completely satisfied with Augustine

68. *Inst.* IV.14.25.

69. *Inst.* IV.14.23.

70. Quoted in *Inst.* IV.14.26.

71. *Inst.* II.7.1. When comparing this grace with that experienced by believers under the gospel, however, Calvin repeatedly emphasizes its relative paucity.

72. IV.14.25.

73. CO 52, 428.

74. Comm. John 8:58 (CO 47, 215).

75. "Concerning the Secret Providence of God," CO 9, 305.

76. Comm. John 9:5 (CO 47, 220). Cf. "The Westminster Confession," VII.5.6. George Hendry's explanation of these articles also applies to Calvin's view: "Though the temporal mission of Christ is of eternal and decisive importance in the work of grace, it is not to be thought of as an isolated act, still less an act which signifies a change in the disposition of God toward sinful men; it is the expression of the eternal purpose of grace which forms the framework of all his dealings with men. The mission of Christ is an event in time, but it is the event that seals the covenant of grace, which is for all times. If we, who look back to it, can participate in it as a present reality, why should not the people of the Old Testament, who looked forward to it, do the same?", *The Westminster Confession for Today* (Richmond: John Knox Press, 1960), 93.

77. Comm. Ps. 19:8 (CO 31, 201).

78. Comm. Ps. 119:103 (CO 32, 258).

79. Comm. Deut. 20:19 (CO 25, 56, 57).

80. Comm. Heb. 11:24 (CO 55, 161).

81. *Inst.* II.10.8.

82. Comm. Heb. 8:11 (CO 55, 103).

83. CO 23, 11-12. Referring to Matt. 11:27, Calvin comments: "Therefore, holy men of old knew God only by beholding him in his Son as in a mirror (cf. II. Cor. 3:18) . . . . God has never manifested himself to men in any other way than through the Son, that is, his sole wisdom, light and truth. From this fountain Adam, Noah, Abraham, Isaac, Jacob and others drank all that they had of heavenly teaching. From the same fountain all the prophets have also drawn every heavenly oracle that they have declared," *Inst.* IV.8.5.

84. *Inst.* II.10.2.

85. This paragraph contains the main points of Chapter 11 (Book II.) of the *Institutes*. An even more succinct listing is provided in the L.C.C. Translation (based on O. Weber's German edition): 1 - The representation of spiritual blessings by temporal; 2 - Truth in the O.T. conveyed by images and ceremonies, typifying Christ; 3 - The O.T. is literal; the New spiritual; 4 - Bondage of the O.T. and freedom of the New; 5 - The O.T. has reference to one nation, the New to all nations.

86. "Where the whole law (*tota lex*) is concerned, the gospel differs from it only in clarity of manifestation," *Inst.* II.9.4.

87. Comm. Heb. 8:6 (CO 55, 100).

88. Comm. Heb. 11:39 (CO 55, 170). "The prophets had but a limited experience of the grace brought by Christ . . . ," Comm. 1 Peter 1:10 (CO 55, 216).

89. Comm. Col. 2:9 (CO 52, 104).90. Comm. Isa. 54:13 (CO 37, 277).

91. Comm. Isa. 55:1 (CO 37, 281, 282).

92. Comm. Daniel 9:22 (CO 41, 165). Yet "their instruction (*doctrina*) was not as excellent as ours, nor were their promises so full and firm," Comm. Daniel 9:25 (CO 41, 181).

93. Comm. Daniel 9:24 (CO 41, 171).

94. *Inst.* II.11.1. Cf. Comm. Isa. 1:19 (CO 36, 47, 48).

95. Comm. Rom. 15:8 (CO 49, 273). In most of the English translations of Calvin's Commentaries *figura* is often translated as "type" rather than "figure." Since Calvin uses the word *typus* also I have observed this distinction, although there is no significant difference in their use as applied to the cultus of the law. "Figures," "types," and "ceremonies" indicate almost the same thing in this context. See the note on "type" in the LCC Tr. of the *Inst.*, 349.

96. Comm. Heb. 7:15 (CO 55, 91). Cf. Comm. Matt. 27:51 (CO 45, 782); Comm. Eph. 1:3 (CO 51, 146).

97. Comm. 1 John 1:2 (CO 55, 302).

98. In his book, *Kingdom and Church—A Study of the Theology of the Reformation* (Edinburgh: Oliver & Boyd, 1956). He describes Luther's as "the eschatology of faith," and Bucer's as "the eschatology of love." But he

adds that all three were united in thinking of the kingdom of Christ in terms of faith, hope, and love.

    99. Comm. Heb. 4:8 (CO 55, 47, 48). Cf. Comm. Heb. 10:19 (CO 55, 128).

    100. *Inst.* II.9.3.

    101. *Inst.* II.11.5. Under the law Christ's kingdom "was as yet hid, as it were, under coverings (*sub involucris*). In descending to earth, he, so to speak, opened heaven to us, so that we might have a near view of those spiritual riches which were before exhibited under figures (*sub figuris*) at a distance. This enjoyment of the visible Christ (*Christi manifestati fruitio*) discloses the difference between us and the prophets," Comm. 1 Peter 1:12 (CO 55, 218). Cf. Comm. John 1:18 (CO 47, 19).

    102. Comm. Isa. 2:3 (CO 36, 64). Cf. Comm. Heb. 4:8, cited above (note #99).

    103. Comm. Heb. 4:10 (CO 55, 49). Calvin immediately adds: "Therefore our first concern must always be to teach that Christ is the end of the law."

    104. *Inst.* II.11.4. This very important passage reads in the original: "Alterum Veteris et Novi testamenti discrimen statuitur in figuris, quod illud absente veritate, imaginem tantum et pro corpore umbram ostentabat: hoc praesentem veritatem et corpus solidum exhibet." Cf. Comm. Heb. 8:5 (CO 55, 98, 99).

    105. Comm. John 4:23 (CO 47, 88, 89). Calvin also uses the simile of a mirror to describe the ceremonies in contrast with the reality which we have in Christ. In the ceremonies "the fathers had a mirror; we have the substance," Comm. Gal. 3:23 (CO 50, 220). Cf. *Inst.* II.11.1.

    106. Comm. John 4:23 (CO 47, 89).

    107. Comm. Zech. 13:1 (CO 44, 342).

    108. Comm. Matt. 27: 51 (CO 45, 51). The veil of the temple was also a symbol of distance which is done away with in the gospel. Hence Moses was veiled; but in Christ God presents himself with an open face, Comm. Ex. 24:29 (CO 25, 118). Cf. Comm. Lk. 10:24 (CO 45, 362); Comm. 1 Peter 1:10 (CO 55, 216).

    109. Comm. Col. 2:17 (CO 52, 110, 111). Cf. Comm. Heb. 10:1 (CO 55, 121); *Inst.* II.9.1.

    110. Comm. John 1:16 (CO 47, 17)

    111. Comm. Acts 13:32 (CO 48, 299). Cf. Comm. Isa. 1:19 (CO 36, 48); *Inst.* II.9.1.

    112. Comm. 1 Peter 1:12 (CO 55, 218). In his Comm. on John 4: 36 (CO 47, 96) Calvin uses a different figure, but one with similar import. There he compares the law and the gospel to sowing and reaping. The law and the prophets have sown, but the harvest comes only with the teaching of the gospel.

113. Comm. Heb. 8:10 (CO 55, 103).
114. Comm. Heb. 11:13 (CO 555, 155). Calvin is thinking here particularly of the "faithful" in Hebrews 11.
115. Comm. Lk. 10:24 (CO 45, 362). Cf. *Inst.* II.11.6.
116. Comm. John 8:56 (CO 47, 214, 215). Cf. Comm. Gal. 3:23 (CO 50, 219).
117. Comm. Gal. 4:1 (CO 50, 225). Cf. Inst. II.11.5. In IV.1.24 he refers to the earlier period as "the swaddling clothes (*incunabula*) of the church"!
118. Comm. Heb. 7:12. The "teaching (*doctrina*) of the law was not complete in every detail (*numeris omnibus*), but only rudiments were delivered in it," Comm. John 4:25 (CO 47, 90, 91). "They had been trained in rudiments only, thus remaining far beneath the height of the gospel teaching," *Inst.* II.9.4. Cf. II.7.16.
119. *Inst.* II.7.2. Cf. Comm. Jer. 33:15 (CO 39, 67).
120. Comm. Heb. 12:25 (CO 55, 185). Cf. *Inst.* II.11.2. Calvin often stresses the unity of the church. See Comm. Gal. 3:23 (CO 50, 219); Comm. Gal. 4:1 (CO 50, 224).
121. *Inst.* I.11.3.
122. *Inst.* II.11.6.
123. Comm. Gal. 4:1 (CO 50, 225).
124. *Inst.* II.11.6. In his Comm. on Gal. 4:1 (CO 60, 225) Calvin again distinguishes between individuals in the Old Testament who were endowed with extraordinary gifts and the general economy (*oeconomia*) by which they were governed.
125. *Inst.* II.11.13.
126. Comm. Matt. 17:2 (CO 45, 482). The context here is the account of the transfiguration. Calvin notes that the apostles also did not witness "a complete exhibition of the heavenly glory of Christ, but under symbols which were adapted to the capability of the flesh he enabled them to taste in part what could not be fully comprehended."
127. Comm. Heb. 10:1 (CO 55, 121).
128. Comm. Col. 2:17 (CO 52, 110, 111).
129. Comm. Dan. 9:25 (CO 41, 182). "Salvation was first revealed for certain (*certo*) when Christ was manifested in the flesh, so great was the obscurity in which all things were covered in the Old Testament, when compared with the clear light of the gospel," Comm. Rom. 8:15 (CO 49, 149). "The promises made then were shadowy and confused, so that they shone only like the moon and the stars compared with the clearness of the gospel which brightly shines on us," Comm. Heb. 8:10 (CO 55, 103).
130. Comm. John 1:18 (CO 47, 19).
131. Comm. Gal. 3:23 (CO 50, 220). The fathers may have possessed only "a small spark of light" but it was sufficient to lead them to heaven,

Comm. Heb. 11:38 (CO 55, 169).
    132. *Inst.* II.10.20. Cf. II.7.16; II.9.1; IV.8.7 and especially Comm. Mal. 4:2 (CO 44, 490, 491).
    133. Comm. Matt. 17:5 (CO 45, 488).
    134. Ibid. This brief statement provides a fundamental ground rule for Calvin's interpretation of the Old Testament.
    135. Comm. Dan. 7:10 (CO 41, 57).
    136. Comm. John 4:25 (CO 47, 91).
    137. Comm. Heb. 1:1 (CO 55:10); *Inst.* 4.14.26.
    138. I have developed the notion of "suspended grace" more fully in an essay for a festschrift for Oscar Cullmann's 65th birthday: "Calvin and Heilsgeschichte," in *Oikonomia, Heilsgeschichte als Thema der Theologie,* hrsg. von Felix Christ (Hamburg-Bergstedt: Herbert Reich, 1967), 163-170.
    139. "Whatever God at that time conferred (upon the fathers), it was, as it were, adventitious *(quasi adventitum)*, for all those benefits were dependent on Christ and the promulgation of the gospel," Comm. Jer. 31:34 (CO 38, 697, 698). Cf. Comm. 1 John 1:2 (CO 55, 301).
    140. "Those who lived under the law, even though they were hindered by the distance, were nevertheless partakers of the promise; there was a participation *(societas)* in the same grace." But "their faith stood, so to speak, in suspension, until Christ appeared in whom all the promises of God are yea and amen," Comm. Acts 13:32 (CO 48, 299). By his advent Christ has given us a "certainty" by showing us the Father (John 14:9) which the fathers could not experience to the same extent, Comm. Isa. 25:9 (CO 36, 420). Cf. Comm. Dan. 9:25 (CO 41, 180). Note that the Latin adjective *suspensus* means not only suspended, but also doubtful and uncertain.
    141. Comm. Col. 2:14 (CO 52, 108). Cf. Comm. Rom. 16:23f (CO 49, 290).
    142. Comm. Ex. 24:4 (CO 25, 76). Cf. Comm. Ex. 25:8 (CO 24, 405); Comm. Lev. 6:1 (CO 24, 526).
    143. Comm. Dan. 9: 25 (CO 41. 180, 181) .
    144. Comm. Gal . 3: 23 (CO 50, 220) .
    145. Comm. 1 Peter 1:12 (CO 55, 218). This and other passages cited above show that it is inaccurate to claim that "there was nothing 'realized' about their (the fathers') eschatology," R. S. Wallace, *Calvin's Doctrine of Word and Sacraments,* 36. There is here both a present and future aspect as in the Fourth Gospel. Cf. *Inst.* IV.14.23.
    146. *Inst.* IV.14.25. Cf . Comm. 2 Tim. 1:1 (CO 52, 345).
    147. *Inst.* II.11.4 . The "entire effectiveness *(tota efficacia)* depends *(pendet)* on the coming of Christ. Otherwise the ceremonial law is "reduced to nothing *(in nihilum rediaere),* " *Inst.* IV.14.23.
    148. Comm. Rom. 8:15 (CO 49, 149).

149. Comm. Heb. 8:10 (CO 55, 103). Cf. Comm. Isa. 54:13 (CO 37, 277); Comm. Isa. 55:1 (CO 37, 281).

150. Comm. John 7: 39 (CO 47, 182). The role of the Holy Spirit becomes even more pronounced in the antithesis between law and gospel.

151. II.9.3. On the relation between faith and hope see III.2.42,43.

152. *Inst*. II.9.3. Cf. III.2.6. Concerning the phrase in Heb. 10:1, "the good things to come," Calvin observes that they "are spoken of not only in respect to the Old Testament but because we also still hope in them" (CO 55, 121). Cf. Barth, *Church Dogmatics* I, 2, 120-1, who comments on this passage and adds an illuminating parallel from Luther.

153. For some helpful contemporary treatments of this question see O. Weber, *Foundations of Dogmatics* I. 301-8; and G. C. Berkouwer, *The Person of Christ*, Chap. 7, "Promise and Fulfillment." From a more exegetical point of view see the essay, "Promise and Fulfillment" by Walter Zimmerli in *Old Testament Hermeneutics*, edited by Claus Westermann, 112ff.

154. In the series of three articles (cited earlier) in the *Reformierte Kirchenzeitung*, Jahrgang 82, 26.

155. *Die Einheit des Bundes*, 58. Krusche, on the other hand, prefers the threefold scheme of Simon, *Das Wirken des Heiligen Geistes nach Calvin*, 192, n. 349.

156. *Inst*. IV.17.11.

157. *Inst*. III.25.6. On the eschatological relation involved in the Christian faith, see T. F. Torrance, *Kingdom and Church*, 108f. He suggests that Luther thinks of the relation between time and eternity more dialectically, whereas for Calvin it is more "a time-lag in the course of fulfillment between Christ the Head and the Church as his Body," 142.

158. Comm. Matt. 24:4 (CO 45, 650).

159. The law is compared to the gospel in terms of promise and fulfillment in the *Inst*. II.9.2 where Calvin says that "God has fulfilled what he had promised." (An almost identical parallel is found in the *Argumentum* of the Commentary on the Harmony of the Gospels, CO 45,1). But the verb translated as "fulfill" here is *praesto*, which has a very broad meaning. In any case, this reference must be interpreted in the light of the remarkable statement that "God does not fulfill what he had promised under Christ's kingdom, since men are not capable of receiving so great a kindness," Comm. Jer. 31:12 (CO 38, 662).

160. Comm. Mark 13.3 (CO 45, 649).

161. Comm. Matt. 13:31f. (CO 45, 372). Here he is commenting on the parable of the mustard seed. A few lines later he adds: "The Lord begins his reign with frail and contemptible beginnings (*tenuibus et contemptis principiis*) for the express purpose that his power may be more fully illustrated by its unexpected progress."

162. Whereas earlier we saw that he likened the law to the sowing of

the seed and the gospel to the harvest (note #112), when he compares the commencement of Christ's kingdom with the manifestation of its glory he also says of the preaching of the gospel that it is "like sowing the seed." The Christian is to wait patiently for the time of reaping. And again, believers now obtain only a taste of those blessings (peace, righteousness, joy etc.) which will be enjoyed fully only in the future, Comm. Mark 13:4 (CO 45, 650). Cf. Comm. Jer. 31:12 (CO 38, 662); Comm. Matt. 13:43 (CO 45, 371).

163. Comm. Rom. 15: 8 (CO 49, 273).

164. Comm. Mark 15:43 (CO 45, 788, 789). In view of this further development it would be justified to speak of a fourfold development: a. rough sketch in black and white; b. the finished portrait in color; c. the manifestation of the reality in humility; d. the manifestation of the reality in glory. The latter two distinctions are between the nature of the kingdom under the first and second comings of Christ. Cf. Comm. 1 Pet. 1:10 (CO 55, 216).

165. Dowey, op. cit., 165.

166. So H. H. Wolf, op. cit., 45. He also cites Barth's description of this difference as that between "promise and fulfilled promise", *Weihnacht*, 45.

167. *Inst.* II.9.4. Cf. Comm. Ezek. 15:51 (CO 40, 395); Comm. Dan. 9:25 (CO 41, 182).

168. Comm. Ezek. 16:61 (CO 40, 395).

169. *Inst.* II.9.2.

170. Comm. Heb. 2:1 (CO 55, 21). However, the kingdom of Christ also has two states: that of concealment and that of the full manifestation, Comm. Matt. 24: 26, 29 (CO 45, 664, 666). For other references and parallels see Torrance, op. cit., 110.

171. Comm. 1 Pet. 1:12 (CO 55, 219). Or the "testimony" of the law finds its "complete declaration" (*matura praedicatio*) in the gospel, Comm. Heb. 3:5 (CO 55, 37, 38). Cf . Comm. 1 Pet. 1:10 (CO 55, 216) where the gospel is described as the explanation, revelation, confirmation, exhibition, and manifestation of the law!

172. Op. cit., 172, 173.

173. Comm. John 4:20 (CO 47, 85). "It is clear that the word 'gospel' applies properly to the New Testament and that those writers who say that it was common to all ages and suppose that the prophets equally with the apostles were ministers of the gospel are guilty of a lack of precision," Arg. to Genesis (CO 45, 2).

174. *Inst.* II.11.13.

175. J. S. Whale, *The Protestant Tradition*, 164.

176. Seeberg, *History of Doctrines*, 416. Paul Wernle, on the other hand, who is often critical of Calvin's treatment of the law, refers to Calvin as a "powerful Paulinist," op. cit., 23.

177. Comm. John 1:17 (CO 47, 18). Calvin understands by law in

this text primarily the ceremonial law. Cf. *Inst.* II.7.16. However, in a reference to this text in his Comm. on Rom. 10:5 (CO 49, 197, 198), he suggests that the law in this case applies to the teaching of Moses as well.

178. Comm. Rom. 4:15 (CO 49, 78).

179. Comm. Rom. 5:20 (CO 49, 102). Similarly in his exegesis of Rom 7:2, 3 Calvin cautions that "Paul is referring here only to that part of the law which is peculiar to the ministry of Moses," (CO 49, 120). In distinctions like this Calvin's exegesis differs from Luther's. Luther usually does not bother to define his terms in this way.

180. Comm. Rom. 5:30 (CO 49, 102).

181. Comm. Gal. 3:19 (CO 50, 215, 216).

182. Comm. Gal. 2:19 (CO 50, 197, 198). Cf. my essay, "Luther and Calvin on Law and Gospel in Their Galatians Commentaries," in *Reformed Review* 37/2 (Winter, 1984) 69-82.

183. *De spiritu et littera.*

184. Comm. 2 Cor. 3:6 (CO 50, 39).

185. Comm. 2 Cor. 3:6 (CO 50, 39, 40). Cf. *Inst.* II.11.7,8.

186. Comm. 2 Cor. 3:7 (CO 50, 41, 42).

187. Herein lies a crucial difference between Calvin and Barth on the interpretation of law and gospel. Cf. Barth's monograph, "Gospel and Law" in *Community. State and Church* (Garden City, N.Y.: Doubleday Anchor Books, 1960). Both Wolf, op. cit., 45-52, and Krusche, op. cit., 202, tend to blunt the sharp edge of this antithesis in their interpretations of Calvin on this question. The influence of Barth here is unmistakable.

188. Cf. *Inst.* II.7.6-8 for a description of the punitive function of the law. A good illustration of Calvin's "preaching the law" (as the Lutherans put it) is found in his sermon on Isa. 53:11 where he poses sharply the antithesis of law and gospel. "The law only begets death; it increases our condemnation and inflames the wrath of God . . . . The law of God speaks, but it does not reform our hearts. God may show us: 'This is what I demand of you,' but if all our desires, our dispositions and thoughts are contrary to what he commands, not only are we condemned, but, as I have said, the law makes us more culpable before God . . . . For in the gospel God does not say: 'You must do this and that,' but 'believe that my only Son is your Redeemer; embrace his death and passion as the remedy for your ills; plunge yourself beneath his blood and it will be your cleansing . . . " (CO 35, 668, 669).

189. Cf. Comm. Ps. 19:7, 8 (CO 31, 199-201); Comm. Acts 7:30 (CO 48, 151); Comm. 2 Cor. 3:6-10 (CO 50, 39-43); 3:1417 (CO 50, 44-46).

190. Comm. Lev. 26:9 (CO 25, 15); Comm. 2 Cor. 3:14 (CO 50, 44).

191. Comm. Ex. 19:1 (CO 24, 193). Cf. John 16:10 (CO 47, 360). This point will be taken up again in the section on the *usus elenchticus* in the next chapter.

192. Comm. Ex. 19:6 (CO 24, 201). Cf. Comm. Heb. 4:12 (CO 55, 49-51).

193. Comm. John 7:7 (CO 47, 166, 167).

194. Comm. Rom. 10:5 (CO 49, 197).

195. Comm. Ex. 19:1 (CO 24, 193).

196. Ibid. (CO 24, 193, 194).

197. "The End and Use of the Law" (CO 24, 727, 728). Christ made an end of the ministry of Moses insofar as its own peculiar properties distinguished it from the gospel . . . . I take the abolition of the law (in Jer. 31:32, 33) which is in question here, to apply to the whole of the Old Testament in so far as it is opposed to the gospel . . . ", Comm. 2 Cor. 3:7f. (CO 50, 42, 43).

198. Comm. Rom. 7:2 (CO 49, 120).

199. Comm. Rom. 10:5 (CO 49, 198).

200. Comm. Ex. 19:1 (CO 24, 193). Fom the law we "receive nothing but condemnation, for there God demands what is due to him, and yet gives no power to perform it. But by the gospel men are regenerated and reconciled to God by the free remission of sins, so that it is the ministry of righteousness and consequently of life itself," Comm. 2 Cor. 3:7 (CO 50, 42).

201. Comm. Deut. 7:12 (CO 25, 20, 21). However, Calvin adds: "Still we must remember what we have seen elsewhere, that after God has so covenanted with them, in order that the promise may not be made ineffectual, he descends to the free promise of forgiveness whereby he reconciles the unworthy to himself."

202. Comm. Lev. 18:5 (CO 25, 7); Comm. Acts 15:11 (CO 48, 351); Comm. Rom. 3:21 (CO 21 (CO 49, 58); *Inst.* II.9.4. Calvin warns, however, against drawing the false conclusion that the law is contrary to faith. Were that the case, God would be unlike himself! The contradiction between the law and faith lies only in the matter of justification, for the method of justifying in the law is completely at variance with faith, Comm. Gal. (CO 50, 209).

203. *Inst.* III.11.17.

204. *Inst.* III.17.6. Cf. Rom. 10:5, 6 (CO 49, 197, 198).

205. Comm. Ex. 24:5 (CO 25, 76). Again we encounter the *usus elenchticus* of the law. Cf. Comm. Acts 15 :11 (CO 48, 352); *Inst.* III.19.9.

206. Comm. Jer. 31:33 (CO 38, 691).

207. Comm. Deut. 30:11 (CO 24, 258).

208. *Inst.* II.11.3. It is just as though the same Lawgiver were "assuming a new character," II.11.8.

209. Comm. Lev. 26:3 (CO 25, 13). "God, having broken the chains of the law, governs his church in a more tender manner and does not lay on us such severe restraint." Comm. Gal. 4:1 (CO 50, 225) .

210. *Inst.* II.7.8. "The reconciliation obtained through Christ makes God, as it were, more gracious to us," Comm. Isa. 25:9 (CO 36, 420).

211. Comm. Deut. 30:11 (CO 24, 258). In the law are impossible conditions; under the gospel, conditions which are easily performed, *Inst.* II.5.12.

212. Comm. Heb. 12:19 (CO 55, 182) .

213. Comm. Ex. 19:1 (CO 25, 13).

214. Comm. Lev. 26:3 (CO 25, 13).

215. Comm. Ex. 19:1 (CO 24, 194). Cf. *Inst.* II.11.3; II.7.8.

216. Comm. 2 Cor. 3:6 (CO 50, 39).

217. Ibid. (CO 50, 40).

218. *Inst.* II.11.7. The grace of regeneration which the fathers enjoyed under the law "was transferred (*fuisse translatum*) to them from another source." Comm. Jer. 31:33 (CO 38, 691). It could not be ascribed to the law as such that God regenerated the elect in the Old Testament, because the Spirit of regeneration was from Christ and thus from the gospel. "Therefore, if the law is considered in itself, the promise of the new covenant will not be found in it," Comm. Ezek. 16:61 (CO 40, 396).

219. Comm. Jer. 31:34 (CO 38, 697). Cf. notes #139-141; Comm. Ex. 19:1 (CO 24, 193); *Inst.* IV.14.24-26.

220. Quoted in *Inst.* II.7.7. "The law only increases transgressions (due to our sin) until the Spirit of regeneration comes who writes it on the heart." However, "that Spirit is not given in the law, but is received by faith," Comm. Gen. 3:19 (CO 50, 215, 216).

221. Comm. 2 Cor. 3:6 (CO 50, 40). Cf. Comm. Jer. 31:34 (CO 38, 697).

222. The "papists" used passages such as Deut. 30:15-20 in order to justify free will and merits. Calvin retorts: "When Moses speaks of keeping the commandments, he does not exclude the two-fold grace of Christ, that believers, being regenerated by the Spirit, should aspire to the obedience of righteousness, and at the same time should be reconciled freely to God through the forgiveness of sins," Comm. Deut. 30: 19 (CO 25, 56).

223. "The End and Use of the Law" (CO 50, 40). Cf. Comm. Deut . 30:19 (CO 25, 56).

224. Comm. Acts 7:38 (CO 48, 151). Cf . Comm. Deut. 6:20 (CO 24, 225).

225. *Inst.* III.17.7. Cf. Comm. Jer. 31:32 (CO 38, 690).

226. Comm. Lev. 18:5 (CO 25, 7). Cf. Comm. Rom. 8:3 (CO 49, 138).

227. Comm. Lev. 26:9 (CO 25, 15). In order that the new covenant might "remain firm and effectual, it was not only necessary that the law should be engraved on our hearts, but also that God should add another grace and not remember our iniquities," Ibid.

228. Comm. Deut. 7:12 (CO 25, 20).

229. Sermon, Isa. 53:11 (CO 35, 668).

230. "Si nobis constaret pura naturae integritas . . .," Comm. Rom. 7:19 (CO 49, 133). This phrase is reminiscent of the words which are so pivotal in the first five chapters of the *Institutes:* "Si integer stetisset Adam (if Adam had remained upright)," *Inst.* I.2.1.

231. *Inst.* II.7.7.

232. Comm. Gal. 3:10 (CO 50, 208). "On the other hand, it is not true of the gospel that it always kills, because in it the righteousness of God is revealed from faith to faith," Ibid. Cf. Comm. Rom. 7:10 (CO 49, 126); Comm. 2 Cor. 3:7f. (CO 50, 42).

233. *Inst.* II.7.7.

234. In Rom. 7:21f. Calvin finds a fourfold law (CO 49, 133). However, he does not identify "the law of sin and death" in Rom. 8:2 with the law of God (CO 49, 137). Most commentators concur in this interpretation.

235. Comm. Ezek. 20:11 (CO 40, 483).

236. *Inst.* II.7.8.

237. *Inst.* II.7.7.

V

THE END AND USE OF THE LAW

In his *Harmony of the Four Last Books of Moses,* after his exposition of the decalog and the two great commandments, Calvin considers the end and use of the law.[1] The same subject matter is dealt with in Book II.7. 6-13 of the *Institutes* where there is a brief analysis of the three uses or functions of the law.

This aspect of the law has been touched on before in the preceding chapters, but never in a formal and systematic fashion. The first use of the law, the *usus elenchticus* or *theologicus,* was apparent in the last chapter.[2] The *usus politicus,* or second use of the law, has not been so prominent, but it was implied in chapter two which touched on God's providential ordering of society and its preservation through law and civil government. The third, and for Calvin the principal, use of the law, the *usus in renatis* or *usus didacticus* (the law as a guide for believers), has been alluded to frequently; however, Calvin surprisingly makes fewer specific references to this use than the first, which is to bring people to a knowledge of sin.

Nevertheless, in the survey of the meaning of the law (Chapter One, C) it was seen that the most common designation of the law was as a "rule." This was in effect a reference to the third use of the law. Again, in the study of the decalog we saw how Calvin, interpreting the law in the light of the Sermon on the Mount, related the ten commandments to the Christian life by showing their inner, positive, and universal scope. Consequently, with the exception perhaps of the political use of the law, we have already seen in various ways the end and use of the law.

However, it is necessary to consider these three functions as

Calvin develops them more technically and also to see precisely what is meant by the word law when it is a rule and guide in the Christian life. Unless this is understood, there will inevitably be criticism of the so-called third use of the law. Although the doctrine of the *triplex usus legis* (threefold use of the law) is usually attributed to Melanchthon, and thus is not unique to Calvin, this is generally considered a hallmark of Reformed theology. Historically, in Methodism as, well there has been a stress on the role of the law in sanctification.[3] Nevertheless, in the history of Christian thought Calvin is usually given the credit—or blame—for emphasizing this use of the law. Along with this, there has been a tendency to trace the legalism which has been characteristic at times of Reformed churches and Puritanism to Calvin's understanding of the law.

The whole question of the third use of the law is again in the forefront due to the debate about law and gospel which has been raging on the continent. One result has been that many Lutheran scholars, partially in reaction to Barth, have opposed as very un-Lutheran the idea of a third use of the law. Melanchthon is accordingly rejected for having polluted Luther's theology in this regard. They concede that Luther does not totally deny the function of the law in the Christian life. Luther, it should be recalled, also opposed antinomianism and was as enthusiastic as Calvin about the importance of the decalog.[4] But it is maintained at the same time that a critical analysis of Luther's writings reveals that he never taught a third use of the law as such.[5]

Several German Lutheran scholars have taken a mediating position in this regard. While rejecting the third use of the law, they recognize that the divine claim (*Anspruch*) and imperative still play a significant role in Luther's theology. Their solution is either to substitute the word "command" for "law,"[6] or to speak of "admonition" (*Parainese*) or "exhortation" (*Paraklese*) in the life of the Christian.[7] It may be questioned whether these distinctions are motivated by biblical research or by a confessional aversion to the word "law." Interestingly, the net result is not too different from Calvin's understanding of the third use of the law. In the last analysis, the difficulty here may be more semantic than theological.

I. USUS ELENCHTICUS

A. *The Law as a Mirror*

For Calvin, the first use of the law is the pedagogical or theological·[8] In this capacity it unmasks us, exposes our sin, and moves us to seek salvation in Jesus Christ. In explaining this function Calvin uses one of his favorite metaphors, that of a mirror. For in the commandments of the law we have "a mirror of perfect righteousness."[9] In this mirror "we contemplate our weakness, then the iniquity arising from this, and finally the curse coming from both—just as a mirror shows us the spots on our face."[10] Only as we are confronted with this mirror can we take stock of ourselves and see ourselves as God sees us.

In a sermon on Galatians 3:19 Calvin illustrates this point. "Through the law," he observes, "God completely awakens us and leads us to a recognition of the curse upon us. In short, it is as if some one's face were all marked up (*machure*) so that everybody who saw him might laugh at him. Yet he himself is completely oblivious of his condition. But if they bring him a mirror, he will be ashamed of himself, and will hide and wash himself when he sees how filthy he is."[11]

To change the figure, only when the law makes us aware of our disease can the medicine of the gospel prove helpful. For the maladies which afflict all people are self-deception, confidence, pride, and vanity. The first function of the law, therefore, is to vanquish these deadly ills so that the heavenly physician may perform his gracious work in us.

> For man, blinded and drunk with self-love, must be compelled to know and confess his own feebleness and impurity. If man is not clearly convinced of his own vanity, he is puffed up with insane confidence in his own mental powers, and can never be induced to recognize their poverty (*tenuitate*) as long as he measures them by a measure of his own choice . . . . Likewise, he needs to be cured of another disease, that of pride . . . . So long as he is permitted to stand upon his own judgement, he passes off hypocrisy as righteousness . . . . But after he is compelled to weigh his life in the scales (*trutina*) of the law, laying aside that presumption of fictitious righteousness, he discovers that he is a long way from

holiness, and is in fact teeming with a multitude of vices, with
which he previously thought himself undefiled.[12]

The disease—self-sufficiency, pride, arrogance—is common
to all people. But their reaction, when confronted with God's will as revealed in the law, is not uniform; for the law comes to two classes of
people. Its effect differs accordingly. With unbelievers the only result is
that they are thus deprived of any excuse before God (Rom. 3:3). In this
case the law is what Paul calls a ministry of death and condemnation
(2 Cor. 3:7). But with believers there is also a positive result.

> While they learn from it that they are unable to obtain righteous-
> ness by works, they are thus instructed in humility; and this is in-
> deed a true preparation for seeking Christ. Second, as it exacts
> much more of them than they are able to offer, it moves them to
> seek strength from the Lord; and at the same time reminds them
> of their perpetual guilt, lest they presume to be proud. Finally, it
> is a kind of bridle upon them, holding them in the fear of God.[13]

In this distinction between two classes of people, note that in
the initial stage both are sinful and lack faith in Christ. The law brings
about a different reaction in these two, however, because the one class,
being reprobate, will not and cannot respond in repentance and faith
and thus avail themselves of the remedy of the gospel. The others Calvin calls the "godly" and the "faithful," i.e., the elect, but this terminology is misleading if it is taken to mean that the godly and faithful are
already recipients of forgiveness and the gift of the Spirit. For when
this is the case, the third use of the law comes into operation although
the third function of the third use of the law, *viz.*, to act as a curb or a
bridle upon those who are already converted, is practically the same as
the second use.

By this terminology Calvin means that by virtue of their being
this in principle, one can speak of them as the faithful or godly even
prior to their conversion. Not that Calvin pretended to know or would
have us seek to know who the two classes are. Only in retrospect, and
then only superficially, is it possible to determine who they are by observing their reaction to the law. Hence Calvin is thinking of sinful humanity in general when he says that the end or function of the law is to
lead people to Christ by showing them their iniquity, condemn them,

and awaken them to the fearful judgment of God.[14] Through the law we see hell wide open before us and God as an armed enemy standing before us.[15] The function of the law in reference to sin is thus a killing one, although the death which it inflicts is life-giving.[16]

For the children of God the law even in this accusing, killing capacity is not given to cause them "to fall down in despair or, completely discouraged, to rush headlong over the brink—provided that they really profit from the testimony of the law." As the apostle Paul testifies in Romans 3:19 and 11:32, we are indeed condemned by the judgment of the law, for "God has shut up all men in unbelief," but not in order to destroy them and let them perish but "that he may have mercy upon all."

Then, in a moving passage which is reminiscent of Luther, Calvin comments:

> This means that dismissing the stupid opinion of their own strength, they [the children of God] come to realize that they stand and are upheld by God's hand alone; that naked and empty handed, they flee to his mercy, repose entirely in it, hide deep within it, and seize upon it alone for righteousness and merit. For God's mercy is revealed in Christ to all who seek and wait upon it in true faith. In the precepts of the law, God is but the rewarder of perfect righteousness, which all of us lack, and conversely, the severe judge of evil deeds. But in Christ his face shines, full of grace and gentleness, even upon us poor and unworthy sinners.[17]

In short, "the function (*officium*) of the law, then, is to uncover the disease; it gives no hope of its cure. It is the function of the gospel to bring healing to those who are without hope."[18] The law is thus a *praeparatio ad evangelium* in that it "bids us, as we try to fulfill its requirements and become wearied in our weakness under it, to know how to ask the help of grace."[19] Despite our rebellion and sin, God uses the law for our salvation and his glory.

Thus far there is nothing particularly difficult or unusual about Calvin's elucidation of the *usus elenchticus* or "theological use of the law." There are nuances which may be peculiar to Calvin, but in general he holds the traditional view of this use of the law. Although the treatment here has been brief, this use of the law plays an important role in Calvin's theology, as was already apparent at the end of the last chapter.

B. The Origin of the Knowledge of Sin

Two questions, however, require further clarification: in what way does the law bring people to a knowledge of sin? That is, what is the origin of the conviction of sin? The other question is a refinement of the first: what is the relation between the law, repentance, and faith? The first question is particularly relevant in view of Barth's treatment of this theme. The answer to the second provides an illuminating contrast with Lutheran theology.

1. Barth's Critique of the Reformers

In his *Church Dogmatics* IV., 1, pp. 358ff. Barth develops the theme, "The Man of Sin in the Light of the Obedience of the Son of God." In contrast to the usual approach in theology where the doctrine of sin is treated before Christology and soteriology, Barth takes as his starting point the obedience of Jesus Christ. The knowledge of sin, he maintains, does not precede the knowledge of Christ but is rather derived from it. Here Barth is not quite satisfied with the reformers. To be sure, they were good theologians in that they held that we learn the nature of sin from the Word of God. But their appeal to the Word was not explicitly to its center, Jesus Christ. They did not specifically relate the knowledge of sin to the knowledge of Christ as such. Instead they referred generally to the knowledge of God the Creator and Lord in his majesty and holiness. Barth concedes that they avoided the pitfall of "the abstract God of an abstract law," because even though they used biblical texts in a haphazard way when developing their doctrine of sin, they still had the right presupposition, namely, that God's covenant of grace and the redeeming work in Christ is the substance of the Bible. But they were not consciously and explicitly Christological in their thinking. Their whole theology "did not allow for any radical consideration of the meaning, importance and function of Christology in relation to all Christian knowledge."[20] Barth then specifically cites Calvin as an example of failing to be truly biblical in his approach. For Calvin, according to Barth, sometimes employed Scripture without referring to its center, Jesus Christ. The prime example is the opening chapter of the *Institutes* in which Calvin states that we can only come to a true knowledge of ourselves when we look at God and then descend to consider ourselves. Only when we contemplate God, Calvin maintains, do we become aware of our own wickedness, folly, and impotence. This was the experience of all the great saints in the Old Testament when they were confronted with the majesty of God. "As a consequence," he concludes, "we must infer that man is never sufficiently touched and affected by the awareness of his lowly state until he has compared himself with God's majesty."[21]

Barth acknowledges that Calvin says elsewhere, "The light of the Lord alone can open our eyes to behold the foulness which lies concealed in our flesh."[22] But, as Barth points out, in the opening chapters of the *Institutes* where Calvin limits himself to the knowledge of God the Creator, Calvin deliberately uses almost exclusively illustrations from the Old Testament. "It never seems to have struck him," says Barth, "that the 'lux Domini' has truly and decisively shone upon us and exposed us in man's confrontation by God in the crucified and risen Jesus Christ, not even when he came to discuss this part of the New Testament. There is simply a general antithesis: God on the one hand and man on the other."[23]

What can be said in answer to this charge—or is there no answer? Some Calvin scholars, under the influence of Barth but writing before the appearance of this volume of the *Church Dogmatics*, assure us that in Calvin's theology "it is Christ who first discloses to us the truth about our human situation."[24] Or, "Calvin forms his doctrine of man's present depravity only as a corollary of grace . . . . There can be no doubt, therefore, in the mind of Calvin, that from the view of salvation in Christ faith must speak of fallen man in total terms."[25] Barth refers to this thesis of Torrance's—that for Calvin the doctrine of human corruption is a corollary of the doctrine of grace—but he confesses that much as he would like to believe this, he finds it difficult to agree that this is actually the case. Nor would he be any more convinced by the first statement of Niesel's.

From one standpoint, Niesel and Torrance are right. Calvin recognizes no other God than the one revealed in Jesus Christ. All true knowledge of God begins and ends with him. Therefore, it may be legitimate to infer that when Calvin refers to the experience of God's majesty by Abraham, Elijah, and Job, they in effect derived this knowledge of their nothingness from Jesus Christ. For Calvin had a strong sense of the trinitarian character of God's revelation. Actually, in Chapter Three I have gone farther than either Niesel or Torrance in this respect by bringing together various passages which relate to this question and show that regardless of what Calvin's explicit reference may be, he always has no other God in mind than the Creator who is always and at the same time the Redeemer who can only be known through the Son and the Spirit. In this sense it can hardly be claimed that Calvin has an abstract concept of God.

Barth knows this, although he does not concede the force of this evidence. Were Calvin writing today, he might have well written his *Institutes* in such a way that the Christological character of his theology would be more clear-cut. But it is extremely fanciful to speculate as to what he might have done and even less justifiable to reconstruct his theology according to what we think he should have done.

The fact remains, however, that despite Calvin's hermeneutical principles and presuppositions, he did not choose to develop his *Institutes* in an explicitly and systematically Christological manner. The first book of the *Institutes* is sufficient proof of this. His doctrine of the knowledge of sin would seem to provide further confirmation of this. Barth's contention, therefore, is not basically affected by the argument of the previous paragraph. From this standpoint he is correct as over against Niesel and Torrance.

2. The Relation of Self-Knowledge, Humility, and the Law

But all the evidence is not in yet! This question can be examined from various perspectives which may shed new light on this problem. The question is still that of how we come to recognize our predicament. Is it the law alone, or something else which brings us to a recognition of our failure and guilt and forces us to look to God's grace in Christ for succour and salvation?

One perspective is that of self-knowledge, which for Calvin is closely related to the theological use of the law. This comes out clearly in one of his earliest writings, the 1537 Catechism. In section six, on "Sin and Death," he writes:

> Being sinners from our mothers' wombs, we are all born subject to the wrath and retribution of God. And, having grown up, we pile upon ourselves an ever heavier judgement of God. . . . What

can we expect in the face of God, we miserable ones who are oppressed by such a great load of sins and soiled by an infinite filth, except a very certain confusion such as his indignation brings? Though it fells man with terror and crushes him with despair, yet this thought is necessary for us in order that, being divested of our own righteousness, having given up faith in our own power. . . we may learn from the understanding of our poverty, misery and infamy, to prostrate ourselves before the Lord and, by the acknowledgement of our iniquity, powerlessness and utter ruin, may give him all glory of holiness, might, and deliverance.[26]

Note that nowhere in this quotation is Christ or the law mentioned. Nevertheless, this description of self-knowledge which results from being confronted with the justice of God, even "the face of God," is very similar to that which is produced when we are placed before the mirror of the law. Granted, it is impossible to stand in the presence of God without being confronted at the same time with his image, Jesus Christ. Moreover, we cannot perceive the glory of God "until it shines forth in Christ."[27] The point remains, however, that Calvin here has spoken of our misery and despair without referring either to the law or Christ.

Equally interesting is the fact that the next section in this Catechism is entitled, "How We Are Delivered and Restored to Life;" but again there is no mention of Christ. And although there are almost verbal parallels to this early catechism in certain chapters of the final edition of the *Institutes*, some of which deal with the law, there is no mention of the law until the last line.

If this knowledge of ourself, which shows us our nothingness, consciously enters into our hearts, an easy access of having the true knowledge of God is made to us.[28] Or rather, God himself has opened to us, as it were, a first door to his kingdom when he has destroyed these two worst pests, which are self-assurance in front of his retribution and false confidence in ourselves.[29]

I break the paragraph at this point in order to point out that the second sentence of this paragraph is developed in the 1559 *Institutes,* not in Book I but in Book II. In Book II.1.1-3 Calvin takes up again the theme of the knowledge of God and of ourselves. The two terrible "pests" of self-assurance and false confidence are the same as those

vanquished by the law, according to its first use. This we saw earlier in
the quotation from II.7.6. But this is not the end of the matter. The
whole of chapter 12 of Book III is essentially a treatment of the same
theme from a slightly different viewpoint. This is clearly an aspect of
Calvin's thought which permeates his whole theology.

But the remainder of this paragraph from the 1537 Catechism
also merits attention. After God "has destroyed these two worst pests"
(by the knowledge of ourselves)

> we begin then to lift our eyes to heaven, these eyes that before
> were fixed and stepped on earth. And we, who once rested in our-
> selves, long for the Lord. On the other hand, though our iniquity
> should deserve something quite different, this merciful Father yet,
> according to his unspeakable kindness, shows himself voluntarily
> to us who are thus afflicted and perplexed. And by such means
> which he knows to be helpful in our weakness, he recalls us from
> error to the right way, from death to life . . . . As the Lord has
> therefore established this first preparation for all these whom he
> pleases to reestablish as heirs to heavenly life--that is, these who
> distressed by conscience and burdened by the weight of their sins
> feel themselves stung in the heart and stimulated reverently to
> fear him--God then first [N.B.!] places his law before us in order
> that it exercise us in this knowledge.[30]

Then follows section eight, "The Law of the Lord," which is
an exposition of the decalog. Similar to the pattern in his Harmony of
the Pentateuch, Calvin then has a section on the summary of the law
which is followed by two sections, "What Comes to us From the Law
Alone," and "The Law is a Preparation to Come to Christ." These two
paragraphs correspond to the section in the Harmony called "The End
and Use of the Law"--with one significant exception: both of these sections deal with the first use of the law. There is no treatment of the second (civil) use of the law. The discussion of the third use does not follow immediately, but comes after several sections on election and
faith.[31]

Several things call for comment:

a) Although Calvin makes a distinction between the knowledge of ourselves derived from the knowledge of God, especially of his

majesty, and the knowledge of his will presented to us in the law which convicts us of iniquity and transgression, the effect is the same. There is no real difference between the two.

b) He nevertheless speaks of a knowledge of self which results from a prior knowledge of God which is "a first preparation" for all those (i.e., "the faithful") to whom God grants renewal and eternal life. Note that it is only after they are aware of the burden of their sins and reverently fear God that he gives them his law to "exercise" them in this knowledge. But this comes close to one function of the third use of the law, that is, to be "a constant sting or spur" (*assiduus aculeus*) even to "a spiritual man who is not yet free of the weight of the flesh."[32] Granted, Calvin has not mentioned the law prior to this; moreover, he discusses both the first and third use of the law later. But a comparison with the later Geneva Catechism (1545) tends to confirm this conjecture. For in the latter he says that believers learn three things from the law.[33]

1. First, there is humility, "a true preparation for seeking Christ." This corresponds exactly with the first use of the law in 1537 Catechism which follows the exposition of the decalog.

2. Believers also learn from the law to seek strength from God in view of their own helplessness, and at the same time are continually kept humble by the reminder of their guilt. There is no particular parallel for this in the 1537 Catechism, but there are similar emphases in the *Institutes*, II.7.6, which concerns the first use of the law, and II.7.12, which is about the third use of the law!

3. The final use of the law for believers is that of a "bridle" (*frenum*) to keep them in the fear of God. This corresponds to the function of the law mentioned at the end of the paragraph from the 1537 Catechism, namely, to continue to exercise believers in the reverent fear of God. Again there is a lack of clarity, however, for in the *Institutes* he uses the figure of a "bridle" three times in discussing the law, and in each case it is in connection with the second (civil) use of the law! The first illustration in II.7.10 clearly does not apply, for Calvin is here speaking of unjust, lawless people who only obey the law out of fear and constraint. In II.7.11, however, he is dealing with unregenerate people who are restrained by the law, as by a bridle, prior to their conversion. If this is a legitimate parallel, it would appear that this is the one and only—and extremely oblique—reference to the *usus po-*

liticus in either of his Catechisms.

c) Clearly, Calvin neither consistently nor systematically worked out this relationship. It is not only difficult to determine when he is talking about the knowledge of ourselves in general and when he is thinking of the knowledge of one's sinfulness gained specifically through the law. It is almost as difficult to discern when he passes from the first to the third uses of the law, particularly in the Geneva Catechism.

We would expect that this lack of precision in the Catechisms would be cleared up in the final edition of the *Institutes*, concerning which Calvin himself expressed satisfaction as far as its order was concerned.[34] At first glance this appears to be the case, for in chapter seven of Book II he discusses the end and use of the moral law and lists precisely and in order the three uses of the law. Yet within this treatment of each use of the law Calvin makes so many distinctions, such as between the effect of the law on the reprobate and the elect and then upon the latter before and after their conversion, that the matter becomes rather complicated.

Moreover, when we inquire into what kind of knowledge is gained through the law according to its first use, it proves very difficult to limit this knowledge only to a function of the law. For the basic thing we learn is humility, which is the first step toward being restored to God's favor. The close relation between humility and self-knowledge is one of Calvin's favorite themes. Like the monastic and scholastic moralists, he "regards pride as the chief of vices and humility as the preeminent virtue."[35] For him the "first, second and third precepts of the Christian religion" are humility.[36]

But how do we learn humility? Through the law, as we have seen,[37] but above all through the contemplation of God himself which results in an intense examination of one's self. Calvin characteristically describes this as "descending" into ourselves." This theme Calvin discusses not only in Book I of the *Institutes,* which deals with God the Creator,[38] but also in Book II, dealing with God the Redeemer,[39] and in Book III which is concerned with the Holy Spirit's application of the grace of Christ in the lives of believers.[40] As was noted before, this contemplation of God which produces humility results particularly from being confronted with God's majesty.[41] This awareness comes to us in various ways, but above all through our conscience which forces us to appear before the judgment seat of God. Through our consciences we have a sense of divine judgment which does not allow us to hide our "sins from being accused before the Judge's tribunal."[42] "In order that we may rightly examine ourselves, our consciences must necessarily be called before God's judgment seat. For there is need to strip entirely bare the secret places of our depravity, which otherwise are too deeply hidden."[43]

Although our conscience by itself leaves us with a sense of guilt and anxiety and acts as a constant "inner witness and monitor of what we owe to God," because of our dullness and arrogance[44] we will never take seriously the Heavenly Judge until we envisage him "not as our minds naturally imagine him, but as he is depicted to us in Scripture."[45] "Lurking and lagging consciences" will be awakened only when they are thus forced to compare all human works with the purity and righteousness and glory of God.[46] The "rigor of this examination" will result in our being completely stricken with an awareness of our misery and want, thus preparing us to receive Christ's grace.[47] This condition finally can be described as "perfect humility" which opens "the gateway to salvation."[48]

> For we will never have enough confidence in him [Christ] unless we become deeply distrustful of ourselves; we will never lift up our hearts enough in him unless they are previously cast down in us; we will never have consolation enough in him unless we have already experienced desolation in ourselves. Therefore we are ready to grasp God's grace when we have utterly cast out confidence in ourselves and rely only on the assurance of his goodness—"when," as Augustine says, "forgetting our own merits, we embrace Christ's gifts."[49]

This analysis reveals something of the breadth and diversity of Calvin's understanding of how people come to recognize their sinfulness and need of a Saviour, but at the same time it tends to confirm Barth's contention that Jesus Christ or the Gospel are never the focal point for Calvin's doctrine of the knowledge of sin. For Calvin does not say that we are stripped of our pride, self-confidence, and self-righteousness by the preaching of the gospel, as such, nor by a confrontation with the cross of Christ. This is accomplished, according to Calvin, primarily by the law and a consciousness of God's judgment. This consciousness comes, as we have seen, from the knowledge of God's character and will as revealed in the Word in general.

Calvin, of course, never thinks of the law or the Word apart from Christ, who is the soul and life, the end and goal of both. Apart from him--and the Holy Spirit--they are dead and meaningless. The fact remains, however, that in all the references cited thus far Calvin never specifically connects the knowledge of sin with the knowledge of Christ. He refers instead to the majesty of God, the judgment of God, the prospect of eternal death, etc.[50] According to Calvin, God uses every means to move people to seek his grace. For Calvin, the whole Word of God is the means by which God awakens slumbering consciences, hails them before his judgment seat, and thus causes people to flee to the grace offered in the gospel.

3. Election and the Holy Spirit

But we still have not come to the heart of the problem as far as Calvin is concerned. For the question remains: what is it that specifically moves people to seek God's grace in Christ? How is it that some people, when crushed by the law and God's judgment, flee to the haven of the gospel for rescue, whereas others, when condemned by the same law, resist God's free offer of salvation? The answer, for Calvin, is to be found ultimately in God's election. Recall that Calvin said that the law comes to two classes of people, potential believers and the impious, i.e., the elect and the reprobate. The former are led by the law to go beyond it and implore God for help. The latter are only deepened in their guilt thereby. The former are attracted by the promises connected to the law and cling to them. The latter spurn the promises and continue even fiercer in their opposition to God.[51]

Consequently, to be confronted with either the law or the gospel does not lead to an ultimately beneficial killing of the soul and to a true knowledge of oneself.

> The Word of God is not equally efficacious in everyone. In the elect it exerts its own power to humble them by a true knowledge of themselves so that they flee to the grace of Christ. This can never happen unless the Word penetrates to the depths of the heart . . . . This sort of thing does not apply in the case of unbelievers; for they carelessly disregard God speaking to them, and

thus mock him, or clamor against his truth and obstinately resist it. Just as the Word of God is like a hammer, so their hearts are like the anvil whose hardness withstands all blows, however forceful.[52]

In short, the knowledge of sin is fundamentally not a result of being confronted with the Word as such. The same is true even when people are confronted by Jesus Christ himself. The rich young ruler, to whom Jesus recited the law, did not see that he was liable to the judgment of God because "he did not know himself thoroughly." The bare words of the law did not really affect him and convict him of guilt even though he was confronted by the Son of God himself![53] Even the living Word is insufficient unless people are "truly instructed by his Spirit."[54]

It is well known that Calvin emphasized the unity of the Spirit and the Word[55] as well as the work of the Spirit in the application of the benefits of Christ.[56] But the following remarks concerning the Spirit are found in the context of a discussion about the law: "The Lord does all things through his Spirit . . . .God works within his elect in two ways: within, through his Spirit; without, through his Word . . . .When he addresses the same Word to the reprobate, though not to correct them, he makes it serve another use: today to press them with the witness of conscience, and in the Day of Judgement to render them the more inexcusable."[57] Then Calvin alludes to 2 Cor. 2:15, 16: "For we are the aroma of Christ to God among these who are being saved and among these who are perishing, to one a fragrance from death to death, to the other a fragrance from life to life." The word of the gospel only gives life and hope to those who have first been "violently slain by the sword of the Spirit."[58]

C. *The Nature of Repentance*

Any discussion of the *usus elenchticus legis* must also take into account the doctrine of repentance, for here most of the previous elements will be brought into focus. In contrast to the Lutheran position, where repentance is separated from faith,[59] Calvin maintained that repentance is derived from faith and a participation in Christ. He insists that "repentance not only constantly follows faith, but is also born of faith."[60] Yet when he defines repentance, he describes it as "the true turning of our life to God, a turning that arises from a pure and earnest fear of him . . . . "[61] Such "pure and earnest fear" results from reflection on the judgment of God. "For, before the mind of the sinner inclines to repentance, it must be aroused by thinking upon divine judgment . . . . For this reason the Scripture often mentions judgment when it urges us to repentance . . . ." (then Calvin cites Jer. 4:4 and Acts 17:30, 31).[62]

Calvin distinguishes further between two types of fear and correspondingly two kinds of repentance. A fear not "pure and earnest" can be called the repentance of the law. In this case sinners acknowledge their sin and fear God's wrath; but since they conceive of God only as an Avenger and a Judge, their repentance is "nothing but a sort of entryway to hell." Gospel repentance, on the other hand, takes place where not only the sting of sin is felt but also where God's mercy arouses trust and gives refreshment.[63] Therefore, "the beginning of repentance is a sense of God's mercy, i.e., when men are persuaded that God is ready to grant pardon, they then begin to gather courage to repent. Otherwise, perverseness will ever increase in them, for no matter how much their sin may frighten them, they will still never return to the Lord."[64]

This is by no means a complete presentation of Calvin's view of repentance. Our primary concern here, however, is to see it in its relationship to the law. The first thing that strikes one in reading Calvin's comments on repentance is that the law rarely enters directly into the discussion. When it does, it is usually the third use of the law that is mentioned. Repentance in such instances is equivalent to conversion, which for the reformers was a life-long process.[65] There is no reference at all to the accusing and condemning function of the law in the discussion of repentance in the *Institutes*. Nevertheless, the reality is there though explicit mention is missing.

The same ambiguity we saw earlier in regard to the knowledge of self and the knowledge of sin occurs again here. After stating that repentance stems from faith, Calvin then defines the "earnest fear of God", which is the second point in his definition of repentance, in terms almost the same as those used to describe the reaction effected by the first use of the law.[66] The same thing is true when he goes on to distinguish between two stages in gospel repentance. The first step is when people feel how grievously they have offended God. The second step is the consoling and cheering word that God is waiting for us and "desires nothing more than to see men willing to be reconciled to him."[67] This first step is for all practical purposes the same as that humility which is characteristic of true self-knowledge and the sense of unworthiness which is produced by being confronted with the demands of the law.

On the basis of this distinction between two stages in repentance, Seeberg submits that Calvin teaches an antecedent fear (*timor initialis*) which precedes repentance. There is "always in Calvin's mind," he maintains, "a state of conscious condemnation under the law as an experience preparatory to evangelical repentance."[68] But Seeberg fails to see that the two stages in repentance are both genuine parts of repentance. The same Spirit who slays the old Adam and gives life to the new person in Christ also "urges us to repentance."[69] The beginning of repentance, which is the hatred of sin,[70] is no less a gift of the Holy Spirit than the ensuing reformation of life by which the image of God is restored in us.[71] Unlike Melanchthon and others of that time, as well as ours, Calvin did not distinguish between repentance as the initial sorrow for sin and the subsequent renewal of the inner nature by the Holy Spirit.

This becomes very clear in his commentary on Matthew 11:28: "Come to me, all who labor and are heavy laden, and I will give you rest." Calvin first observes that "there are various methods by which God humbles his elect." This is an illustration of one of these means. For Christ, Calvin avers, is alluding to those "whose consciences are distressed by their exposure to eternal death and who are inwardly so pressed down by their miseries that they faint." This fainting "prepares them for receiving his grace." Then follows the important conclusion which contradicts Seeberg's allegation. "Although this preparation for coming to Christ makes them as dead men, yet it ought to be observed that it is the gift of the Holy Spirit, because it is the commencement of repentance to which no man aspires in his own strength."[72]

It is significant that even the preparatory stage in repentance and conversion is a gift of God and an act of the Holy Spirit. More importantly, Calvin here departs from the common Lutheran law-gospel approach; for it is the gospel not the law which leads to repentance![73]

"Repentance is preached in vain unless men entertain the hope of salvation."[74] In the last analysis, the preaching of grace subdues people to fear God.[75] For "all would flee from God if he did not attract them by the sweetness of his grace . . . . The first thing to know about God is that he is kind and forbearing (*beneficus et liberalis*)."[76] "These two things cannot be divided, namely, the testimony of grace and the doctrine of repentance."[77]

In all these references there is a noteworthy omission: the law is nowhere mentioned. Accordingly, it might appear that Calvin sees no direct connection between the first function of the law and repentance. Yet the law is often implied in these discussions. Moreover, when Calvin discusses the law and its uses he clearly alludes to its role in awakening a sense of sin or arousing the fear which is characteristic of the first stage of repentance although he rarely spells out their precise relationships.

A case in point is his commentary on Genesis 18:19:

> The judgement of God is proposed, not only in order that those who by their negligence please themselves in their vices, may be taught to fear, and that being thus constrained they may sigh for the grace of Christ; but also to the end that the faithful themselves, who are already endued with the fear of God, may advance more and more in the pursuit of piety.[78]

The familiar themes are here: judgment, the fear of God, a longing for grace, and growth in piety. This description of the origin and continuance of the Christian life is so general that Calvin could be discussing here either the twofold knowledge of God and self or repentance and conversion. But then he adds after a few lines, "The law thus avails not only for the beginning of repentance (*resipiscentiae*), but also for our continual progress."[79] There is a definite reference here to both the first and third uses of the law.

Another instructive passage in this connection is found in the commentary on Romans 10:5. Calvin refers here to Moses as "a herald (*praeconem*) of the gospel,"[80] since he performed a greater service than that which was peculiar to his ministry. For in addition to placing before the people God's requirements in precepts which included punishments and rewards, he also taught his people "the true rule of piety" which meant preaching repentance and faith. "But faith is not taught without offering promises, the free promises of divine mercy." A few lines later we come to a definite description of repentance in terms of the law: "In order to teach the people repentance, it was necessary for him to instruct them as to what kind of life (*quae vivendi ratio*) was acceptable to God. He included this in the precepts of the law."[81]

D. Summary and Critique

This survey has revealed that Calvin's soteriology is surprisingly complex and dialectical. Even when he explains a doctrine or series of doctrines in a rather systematic fashion, he sometimes fails to develop his points as we might expect. For one who is renowned for his systematic prowess, this seems very strange. A possible explanation is that Calvin was first of all a biblical theologian who in practice as well as in theory spurned dogmatic, metaphysical speculation.[82] As a student of the Scriptures, he apparently found it impossible to dissect the reality of knowing God and the experience of salvation in a neat, logical fashion. The knowledge of sin, repentance, conversion, and faith do not admit of cold, rational analysis. Calvin, in any case, attempted nothing of this kind. When theologians of a later generation developed a systematic *ordo salutis,* they moved beyond the reformers.[83]

Nevertheless, certain motifs have been prominent in this discussion. The law warns, informs, and convicts all people of unrighteousness and thus moves some to look to God's grace. The first step in this experience is to recognize oneself as a lost, miserable sinner, worthy only of condemnation. This state of humility is achieved particularly by the thought of the divine judgment. Yet sinners will not repent or believe, after having been so humbled, unless they are attracted by God's benevolence and mercy. Though it is our misery which drives us to seek Christ, no one would flee to him unless we were assured of God's good will toward us.

This whole process is a part of faith. And faith is only possible because of the gift of the Holy Spirit. The Spirit through the Word both kills and makes alive. He does this through both the law and the gospel. The Spirit is the bond by which Christ effectually unites us to himself and bestows his blessings on us.

The main elements here are clear, but this summary also points up some unresolved difficulties. For the inner relationship between the various phases or aspects of the way of salvation is not always clear. This is especially true of the precise function of the first use of the law. It appears to be the presupposition or background for much of what Calvin says about self-knowledge and conversion. The same is true of his numerous references to the judgment seat of God. But it is difficult to see how he reconciles this emphasis with that of the positive stress on the necessity of knowing God's offer of free grace in Christ. If repentance is born of faith and faith begins with the promise, i.e., with the gospel and not with the law, what are we to make of the theme of judgment? For, as we have seen, a genuine fear of God—not only in the sense of love and reverence but first of all as an apprehension of the judgment which we all deserve—is an indispensable component in the beginning of the Christian life.

The problem, in short, is that despite his relating repentance to an assurance of God's benevolence, Calvin does not sufficiently show the connection between the law and the gospel in this experience. He comes close to suggesting that it is only the gospel which can show us what the law is and how serious sin is, but this is never made explicit. He never quite says that we come to know ourselves as sinners and come to realize the gravity of our plight not through the law alone, but through the law as seen in Jesus Christ. This can be inferred from several passages cited earlier, but Calvin himself does not make this clear.

E. Law and Gospel or Gospel and Law?

Does one begin then with the law or with the gospel when preaching repentance and faith? The traditional Lutheran answer is an unhesitating, "with the law!" On the other side, many recent theologians—especially Barth and his followers—would reply emphatically, "with the gospel!" And Calvin . . . ? He did not think in these terms, but his answer would probably be both-and.[84] He obviously knows nothing of a strict "preaching of the law," for he also stresses that no one will turn to God in repentance and faith except they are drawn by a love of righteousness and the sweetness of God's grace. On the other hand, he maintains that this must be preceded by a sense of humility and unworthiness which is usually the result of being confronted with God's righteousness, wrath, and judgment, i.e., the law.

Calvin falls somewhere between Luther and Barth in respect to preaching the law and the gospel. He clearly sees a place for the law in its accusing, damning function. The advent of Jesus Christ does not transform the demands of the law, the "you must", into a promise, "you shall be," or the imperatives into indicatives.[85] Nevertheless, neither in theory nor in practice does he exhibit a doctrinaire method of using the law. He apparently would not insist that we must always preach the law before we preach the gospel.[86] In Book III of the *Institutes*, where he takes up soteriology and describes in effect the first use of the law, he generally avoids the word law and shows surprising flexibility in describing the experience of salvation.

It is difficult to determine why Calvin rarely refers to the *usus elenchticus* in this context. The reason seems to be that for Calvin the law, even when directed to the unconverted, is essentially the Word in its totality, just as it was for the Psalmist. Unlike Luther, he does not call every exhortation or commandment in the Bible the law. God's gift and demand, promise and claim (*Zuspruch und Anspruch*) are inseparable. God is both holy and gracious, just and merciful. One can no more divide up God than divide or compartmentalize his Word. This does not mean that we should confuse God's holiness and his grace any more than we should confuse the law with the gospel. But it also means that we should not pit the one against the other. God's will is one; therefore his Word is ultimately one, not the word of the law and the word of the gospel, but the one Word of the law and gospel. The law is included in the gospel; but the gospel is also included in the law. For Calvin it was axiomatic that "the law in all its parts has reference to Christ."[87] Therefore, the one must never be separated from the other.

It is possible, however, to make a distinction between the objects of faith and repentance, when each is viewed according to its peculiar properties, and say that "as a general rule, Calvin relates faith and repentance to different aspects of the Word of God."[88] That is, faith is related to the gospel, the gracious aspect of the Word, repentance to the law, to the demands and threats of judgment. Often this holds true, but there are almost as many exceptions. Fear, arising from an apprehension of God's judgment does not become passé once a person becomes a believer. This fear of God's wrath and continual reflection on the future judgment does not vitiate the confidence which is necessary for true faith but rather serves to strengthen it![89]

Calvin can say of repentance that it "proceeds from an earnest fear of God" on one occasion and then assert that "the beginning of repentance is a sense of God's mercy." The same is true of faith. In the same paragraph where he speaks of the promise of mercy as "the proper goal of faith" he can immediately add, "As on the one hand believers ought to recognize God to be Judge and Avenger of wicked deeds, yet on the other hand they properly contemplate his kindness, since he is so described to them as to be considered as 'one who is kind' (Ps. 86:5), and 'merciful' (Ps. 103:8), 'far from anger and of great goodness' (Ps. 103:8), 'sweet to all' (Ps. 145:9), 'pouring out his mercy on all his works' (Ps. 145:9)."[90]

This may seem very inconsistent, for Calvin joins together as necessary corollaries fear and faith, law and gospel, God's wrath and love, judgment and mercy. For Calvin, there is no contradiction here. This polarity is necessary, not because these seeming antitheses stand either in a balanced relationship or in an ontological tension. The "sum of blessedness (*summa beatitudinis*)" does not consist in any such balance or tension, but in the grace of God alone.[91] But the believer has not been removed from the conflict; the devil is yet at work. Hence a divine dialectic is necessary and desirable because of human frailty.

> Therefore the godly heart feels in itself a division because it is partly imbued with sweetness from its recognition of the divine goodness, partly grieves in bitterness from an awareness of its calamity; partly rests upon the promise of the gospel, partly trembles at the evidence of its own iniquity; partly rejoices at the expectation of life, partly shudders at death. This variation arises from the imperfection of faith . . . . [92] For not only does piety beget reverence toward God, but the very sweetness and delightfulness of grace so fills a man who is cast down in himself with fear, and at the same time with admiration, that he depends upon God and humbly submits himself to his power.[93]

This does not mean that there is a constant alternation between hope and fear, faith and unbelief, in the life of the believer. The experience of fear, doubt, and dread all take place within the realm of faith, for the believer belongs to Christ. "Since Christ has been so imparted to you with all his benefits that all things are yours, that you are made a member of him, indeed one with him, his righteousness overwhelms your sins; his salvation wipes out your condemnation; with his worthiness he intercedes that your unworthiness may not come before God's sight."[94] In this union with Christ the assurance of faith rests.

II. USUS POLITICUS

The second use or function of the law is to maintain and preserve external discipline and order in society.[95] This is known as the "political use" (*usus politicus*) or "civil use" (*usus civilis*) of the law, although the word "political" has a much broader connotation than is usually understood today.

A. *Principally for Unbelievers*

According to Calvin, the second function of the law is this:

> At least by fear of punishment to restrain certain men who are untouched by any care for what is just and right unless compelled by hearing the dire threats of the law. But they are restrained, not because their inner mind is stirred or affected, but because, being bridled, so to speak, they keep their hands from outward activity, and hold inside the depravity that otherwise they would have wantonly indulged. Consequently, they are neither better nor more righteous before God . . . . But this constrained and forced righteousness is necessary for the public community of men, for whose tranquility the Lord herein provided when he took care that everything be not tumultuously confounded.[96]

The second use of the law thus applies primarily to unbelievers. They obey the laws of the community and state, but not because of a genuine love of justice and a concern for the welfare of their neighbors. "The more they restrain themselves, the more strongly they are inflamed; they burn and boil within, and are ready to do anything or burst forth anywhere—but for the fact that this dread law hinders them." More seriously, they not only hate the law but also the Lawgiver and would do away with him if they could.[97]

But for believers also, prior to their conversion, the civil use of the law serves as a necessary deterrent. Recall that when Calvin spoke of the first use of the law, he referred to two classes of people. Now he distinguishes further and divides the elect or believers into two states: their pre- and post-conversion existence.

> Even for the children of God, before they are called and while they are destitute of the Spirit of sanctification, so long as they live lewdly in the folly of the flesh, it is profitable for them to undergo this tutelage (*paedagogia*). While by the dread of divine vengeance they are restrained at least from outward wantonness, with minds yet untamed they progress but slightly for the present,

yet become partially broken in by bearing the yoke of righteousness. As a consequence, when they are called, they are not utterly
untutored and uninitiated in discipline as if it were something unknown.[98]

In this formal explanation of the *usus politicus* Calvin does not
indicate how the Mosaic or moral law is related to the secular or civil
laws of the state. He deals with this, however, in Book IV (Chapter 20)
when he discusses civil government.

B. Only a Twofold Use of the Law?

Before turning to this matter, it is necessary to consider a
viewpoint which undercuts this use of the law. A. Göhler, in his book
on Calvin's doctrine of sanctification, takes the position that Calvin actually teaches only a double use of the law. He acknowledges that Calvin teaches the threefold use of the law in the final edition of the *Institutes*, but he still maintains that "a closer examination reveals that we
have here . . . a twofold relationship. The order and public communal
life is not coordinated with the other two forms of the use of the law.
He merely designates special application of the *usus normativus* (third
use) to the ordering of society . . . . Consequently, relative to our problem, the *usus civilis* should be considered together with the *usus normativus*."[99]

This theory has been accepted by several other Calvin scholars,[100] but it still remains highly questionable. The origin of this misunderstanding lies in Göhler's erroneous interpretation of an expression in
the 1545 Catechism, namely, "the double office of the law" (*duplex legis officium*). In this passage Calvin is explaining that just as there are
two kinds of people (believers and unbelievers) so there is also a double office of the law. Göhler concludes from this that there is therefore
only a twofold function of the law[101]—despite Calvin's clear statement
to the contrary in the *Institutes*.

What Calvin is saying here is that the law is not only relevant
to believers but also to unbelievers. The primary reference here is to the
usus theologicus. Unbelievers are thereby rendered more inexcusable,
whereas believers are provided with "a true preparation for seeking
Christ," and are moved to "seek strength from the Lord." This corre-

sponds precisely to the two functions of the law described in the *Institutes* within the first use of the law.[102]

Göhler fails to see that the first use of the law primarily has to do with potential believers, the third use with believers after they have been effectually called and have been regenerated. An understanding of the double use of the word "believer" in this connection is crucial to distinguishing between the various functions of the law. Moreover, a careful comparison of the Geneva Catechism (1545) with the *Institutes* shows that where there are parallels, whether in terms of Scripture references or the metaphors used, more overlapping occurs between the first and third uses of the law than the second and third.

Calvin is admittedly unclear in his designation of the various functions of the law within each of the three principal uses, but the evidence in any case does not warrant subsuming the *usus civilis* under the *usus normativus*. Had the doctrine of the threefold use of the law been inserted only in the last edition of the *Institutes*, it might be possible to play off one edition against another (a dubious practice). But the second use of the law is set forth unambiguously in every edition from 1536 to 1559.[103]

Nevertheless, it must be conceded at the same time that the civil use of the law receives far less attention, outside of the *Institutes*, than the other two uses. In the section on the end and use of the law in his commentary on the Pentateuch there is not even an indirect allusion to this use. This in itself, however, is not too significant since even the third use of the law, or *usus normativus* which is the principal one, receives scant attention there. We have seen several times already that the failure to make explicit reference to something does not necessarily mean that the reality is absent in Calvin's thinking.

The key text for this use of the law is 1 Timothy 1:9, 10: "The law is not laid down for the just but for the lawless and disobedient, for the ungodly and sinners, for the unholy and profane."[104] In his commentary on this text Calvin warns that it is not the apostle's intention here "to set out all the functions that the law fulfills; his argument is rather directed 'ad homines,' to those with whom he was dealing."[105] Paul was dealing with insolent men and therefore warns them that the

> law is, as it were, God's sword to slay them, while he and those like him have no reason to fear or hate the law, since the law is no enemy to just men, i.e., to those who are godly and who freely

worship God . . . . Paul is taking for granted the common saying
that good laws spring from bad morals and holds that God's law
was given to restrain the licentiousness of the ungodly, for those
who are good of their own accord do not need the law to control
them.[106]

There is a rather close connection between this function of the
law and the role of the law of nature, even in fallen humanity. Just as
God in his grace has left fallen humanity with some notion of good and
evil, truth and order, justice and equity lest they destroy themselves, so
also the written moral law acts as a brake against the innate criminal
tendencies in humankind. To live in a society without any laws, morals,
or any established order would be anarchy. For Calvin, nothing is more
dangerous or destructive than this.[107] "To introduce anarchy is to violate charity."[108] Love and order go together. The law was given to foster love; therefore, to introduce disorder is to strike at the heart of the
law which is love. The law is indispensable to order and thus also to
love.

The opposite is also true; for the law is not truly observed
where willing and spontaneous obedience, i.e. love, is lacking. But this
is only possible in lives where the Spirit rules. Nevertheless, even
where there is no recognition of God as Lord, the grace of God is at
work restraining excesses and outbreaks and preserving order through
magistrates and governments. God does this not only for the church,
which requires law and order in the civil realm for its welfare and existence, but also for the sake of humanity in general.[109] This is an aspect
of God's providence.

Calvin cites Romans three as an illustration of the terrible possibilities of sinful humanity. The grace of God alone prevents human
beings from realizing their potentialities for evil. Whereas God works
in the elect inwardly, others must be restrained by outward means. This
is the service the law performs, for it acts as a check to control unregenerate people and thus preserves a degree of order in society. "Thus God
by his providence bridles the perversity of nature that it may not break
forth into action; but he does not purge it within."[110]

God's providence manifests itself further in the establishment
of political order through governments. A well-ordered society needs
not only just laws. Leaders are equally indispensable to administer
them and governments to enforce them. Hence there is a definite place

for civil government in God's gracious and orderly will. For "empires did not spring up by chance or from men's mistakes but were appointed by the will of God, who wishes political order to flourish among men and that we should be governed by right and by law (*iureque ac legibus*)."[111] As McNeill points out, "In his warm admiration for political government, Calvin does not for a moment regard it as a realm of mere secularity. It is God-given, a 'benevolent provision' for man's good, and for it men should give God thanks."[112]

C. *Law and Civil Government*

This brings us to the monumental chapter on civil government in Book IV of the *Institutes*. The subject of the state as such is beyond the limits of this study. Even the more limited question of the relation of natural law or the moral law to civil (or positive) law is too complicated a subject to be considered in detail here.[113] However, several points which Calvin makes in regard to the law call for special mention.

He divides his discussion of civil government into three parts: "the magistrate, who is the protector and guardian of the laws; the laws, according to which he governs; and people, who are governed by the laws and obey the magistrate."[114]

The most striking thing in the discussion of this subject in sections 14-16 is the simple, non-technical way in which Calvin relates civil laws to the moral law of the Old Testament, and that in turn to natural law and conscience. For one trained in jurisprudence this is hardly what we would have expected.[115] He even says that he "would have preferred to pass over this matter (i.e., concerning the best kind of laws) in utter silence"! He nevertheless takes up the subject very briefly because it is just at this point where "many go dangerously astray."[116]

Calvin notes in the first place that laws are "the stoutest sinews of the commonwealth."[117] Following Plato and Cicero, he goes on to depict the interdependence of laws and magistrates by the phrase, "the law is a silent magistrate; the magistrate a living law."[118] His next point, however, comes as somewhat of a surprise, for in view of Calvin's esteem for the Mosaic law, one might anticipate an immediate relating of civil laws to the law of Moses. But he does just the opposite and warns against the notion that a government is only legitimate (from a Christian viewpoint) when its laws are based on the political system of Moses. To attempt this, Calvin insists, is "perilous and seditious . . .

false and foolish."[119] It is highly significant, if not ironical, that the man who allegedly made Geneva into a theocracy based on the Old Testament denies vigorously that the Mosaic law should be taken as the model of all subsequent legislation![120]

Like Aquinas and Melanchthon, Calvin divides the Mosaic law into three parts: moral, ceremonial, and judicial.[121] Only the first, he says, is universally applicable; for "it is the true and eternal rule of righteousness, prescribed for men of all nations and times who wish to conform their lives to God's will."[122] The whole ceremonial system, on the other hand, has been superseded by the coming of Christ. The judicial system was designed only for Israel's particular situation and thus applies nowhere else.[123]

Then follows the crucial deduction: "If this is true," Calvin contends, "surely every nation is left free to make such laws as it foresees to be profitable for itself."[124] This is a remarkable application which reveals great tolerance and latitude. Here something of Calvin the humanist comes to the fore. But he quickly adds, "Yet these must be in conformity to that perpetual rule of love, so that they indeed vary in form but have the same purpose."[125]

Calvin can take such a flexible position not only because of his high view of civil government, but even more because he bases both state constitutions and civil laws on natural law and the providence of God. Nations are free not only to formulate whatever laws may be necessary and appropriate for their particular needs, but also the particular kind of government which suits them best.[126] For in all laws, Calvin concludes, we should examine two things: "the constitution of the law and the equity (*aequitas*) on which its constitution is itself founded and rests. Equity, because it is natural, cannot be the same for all, and therefore this same purpose ought to apply to all laws, whatever their object."[127]

Calvin thus descends from the revealed law of God to the varied forms of positive law, which in turn are based on a concept of natural equity. Here Calvin, like Luther, is employing a classical medieval distinction between positive law (*iustum*), which strictly judges according to the letter of the law, and equity or natural law (*aequum*), "in which the spirit of the law softens and qualifies the rigid application of the letter of the law when its strict enforcement would do more harm than good in a concrete case."[128]

The problem here is to determine more precisely what the relationship is between God's revealed law and natural law or equity. Calvin states his position clearly enough in the following key passage, but what is presupposed here remains problematic.

> It is a fact that the law of God which we call the moral law is nothing else than a testimony of natural law and of that conscience which God has engraved upon the hearts of men. Consequently, the entire scheme (*ratio*) of this equity of which we are now speaking has been prescribed in it. Hence this equity alone must be the goal and rule and limit of all laws. Whatever laws shall be framed to that rule, directed to that goal, bound by that limit, there is no reason we should disapprove of them, howsoever they may differ from Jewish law, or among themselves.[129]

D. *Criticisms of the "Usus Politicus"*

With this quotation we are confronted again by the whole problem of natural law in Calvin's theology. But now a new aspect of this problem becomes apparent. For the objection has been raised–not only against Calvin but against all the reformers–that this represents a confusion of civil and moral law. According to this view, the whole idea of an *usus politicus legis* is illegitimate. Some maintain that the reformers' use allows for no definite criterion by which to distinguish clearly between these two distinct spheres.[130] Wernle, for example, finds it "amazing" that Bucer and Calvin could trace not only civil law but even criminal law back to the moral law, i.e., the double commandment of love, "as if love and equity were not two completely different things."[131]

Wernle, in contrast to critics such as Lobstein and Simon, finds some comfort in the fact that he feels Calvin tends to "correct himself." By this he means that whereas Calvin refers to the two tables of the law as the final norm in IV.20.9, 15 of the *Institutes*, in IV.20.16 he no longer speaks so much about love as the end toward which all laws must aim, but rather about equity as the only goal, rule, and limit of all laws.[132] This switch from love to equity (and justice) in the realm of positive law is credited to Calvin's "thoroughly practical nature." That is, when it came to the point where Calvin was confronted with concrete issues, he was too sensible to keep talking about love. As if love had anything to do with justice![133]

Wernle's criticism of Calvin has a direct bearing on the recent debate about this issue. Barth, Brunner, Reinhold Niebuhr, and Paul Tillich have all dealt with, and have sometimes debated with each other concerning, the issue of the relation of love and justice and the related question about the nature of the state.[134] As far as Calvin is concerned, it is interesting to observe that while both Barth and Brunner find much of value in the chapter on civil government at the close of the *Institutes*, they do so for quite different reasons. (This is not the first time that the two great Swiss theologians have exegeted Calvin differently.) Barth finds Calvin's position acceptable as far as it goes, and thus implicitly the *usus politicus* as a particular ordinance of divine providence. But characteristically he feels that Calvin and the other reformers failed to provide a firm and truly Christian basis for civil law and the state by not relating them to the gospel. Barth wants to go beyond a general divine providence to a concept which is directly related to Christ and justification.[135]

Brunner, on the other hand, rejoices in the fact that Calvin did not do this. For Brunner, the realms of justice and the state are orders of creation and therefore are not to be related to Christology. Unlike Barth, he approves of Calvin's use of natural law and distinguishes it from the Stoic and modern concepts of natural law.[136] But Brunner, along with Lobstein and Wernle, maintains that the reformers were not clear about the connection between justice and love. His objection is precisely the same as Wernle's, namely, that the principle of *equitas* merges into the principle of love.[137] His view is basically that of the Lutheran antimony between the social and personal spheres of ethics where love is limited to personal relationships alone. Hence, for him, "the law of justice is quite different form the commandments of brotherly love." The latter cannot form the basis of justice.[138]

On this point, however, more contemporary theologians would follow Calvin than Brunner. Calvin rightfully distinguished between love and justice, moral law and positive law; but he did not separate them or view them antithetically. They are integrally related in that love is the fulfillment of justice and equity, not its substitute. Justice, on the other hand, is a necessary instrument of love. But it is difficult to maintain these distinctions and it is legitimate to query whether Calvin in practice was faithful to his principles in Geneva. As Dowey points out,

Although the separation between the natural law and the specific constitution was maintained in theological principle, in actual fact both Geneva and succeeding Calvinistic societies tended to identify the particular laws of their community with the law of God itself. This was a great danger to them, partly because the tradition of natural law remains strong both in Luther and in Calvin as a way of understanding secular society, and thus was always available for this kind of misuse.[139]

However, his principles were sound. By refusing to take Old Testament legislation as a norm for civil government he made a radical and significant break. Whether it was due to biblical or legal insight – or the exigencies of his situation—he recognized that we must not seek for absolute expressions of the law of God in state constitutions. The forms of civil law are necessarily relative. But he did not therefore resign himself either to quietism or ethical relativism. The state must always recognize its inability and failure to express adequately the absolute command. But the standard and goal remains, which is inescapable and uncompromising.[140]

E. *The Goal: the Reestablishment of God's Order*

On the other hand, unlike the Anabaptists of his day and individualistic Protestants in our own, Calvin would not separate these realms. Spiritual government and civil government are distinct. Yet the Kingdom of God and the kingdoms of this world do not exist as contrary entities; nor is their relationship even a neutral one. The state no less than the church is an ordained means of God.[141] "Man is under a twofold government" (*duplex in homine regimen*).[142] The one complements the other. Zeal for the Kingdom of God must not lead to indifference to social behavior and civil justice.[143]

For Calvin, justice and love are not irreconcilable, but he does not conceive of the former as abstract and coldly legal or the latter as only emotional and individual. For him, *caritas* and *aequitas* ultimately serve the same end, namely, order, whether it be the well-ordered life or the well-ordered state. For both serve to restore that order which was disturbed by sin. Disorder is a characteristic and sign of sin. God's reordering of his world assumes a different form on the personal level than on the socio-political level, but in both cases the goal is the same:

the coming of the Kingdom of God.

> The opposite of the Kingdom of God is complete disorder (*ata-raxia*) and confusion; for order (*ordinatum*) is nowhere found in the world except when he regulates by his hand the schemes and dispositions of men. Hence we conclude that the beginning of God's reign in us is the destruction of the old man and the denial of ourselves, that we may turn to newness of life.

Had Calvin been a pietist or fundamentalist, he might have stopped here. The kingdom of God comes when God's rule becomes actualized in the lives of individual men and women. But Calvin shows his "catholic"[144] concern by adding immediately,

> There is still another way in which God reigns; and that is when he overthrows his enemies and compels them, with Satan as their head, to yield a reluctant subjection to his authority, "until they be made his footstool" (Heb. 10:13). The substance of this prayer is that God would enlighten the world by the light of his Word, would form the hearts of men unto the service of his justice by the inspiration (*afflatu*) of his Spirit, and by his guidance would restore to order whatever has been dispersed (*dissapatum*) in the world.[145]

Thus the prayer for the coming of God's Kingdom comprehends more than isolated individuals; the social order and the state in their own sort of way must also acknowledge the Lord. The law, therefore, as an expression of God's will for order in the creation cannot be abstracted from the realm of constitutions and governments. However infrequent the specific references to the *usus politicus* may be in Calvin's writings, his theology as a whole and his life work reveal how important this function of the law was for him. Thus those who have suggested Calvin actually recognized only two uses of the law have greatly underestimated his profound interest and concern in this realm.

As Robert Gessert points out, the law for Calvin

> in relation to man signifies governance in several respects. God's reign through law over fallen man is like the reign of a strong monarch over a traitorous people; every law seems to be a sedition law. His reign in his elect is like a loyal constitutional repub-

lic . . . . It is primarily the principle of sovereignty that allows Calvin to use the term law when speaking of other things than the revealed divine law. Positive or civil law still partakes of the nature of the law for Calvin, even when it does not clearly express good intention or righteousness, because it always explicitly expresses governance—God's mysterious governance as well as man's.[146]

God's rule—God's order: this is what Calvin is trying to express in his concept of law. This rule and order manifest themselves as much in God's providential governance of nations as in his redemptive reign in Christ in the lives of his children. There are these two distinct realms, but there is only one God, one Kingdom, one Mediator, and ultimately only one law. Therefore, the three uses or functions of the law are in the last analysis inseparable. The law is a unity even in its three distinctive functions. Confusion of these functions would be fatal, but severance of any one use from the others will also result in damage to the whole concept of the law.[147]

Calvin, unfortunately, does not always indicate clearly these inter-relationships. We saw earlier the close connection between the *usus politicus* and *usus elenchticus*. To a lesser extent the same is true of the *usus politicus* and the *usus tertius*. Calvin can pass almost imperceptibly from one function to another. This makes for confusion at times, but it also underscores the unity of the law. This becomes quite apparent in an important passage from one of his commentaries. Here the close relationship between the second and third functions becomes clear, although the accent is on the *usus politicus*.

> It would be better for us to be wild beasts and to wander in forests than to live without government or laws, for we know how furious the passions of men are. Therefore, unless there is some restraint, the condition of wild beasts would be better and more desirable than ours. Liberty would then always bring ruin with it if it were not bridled and joined to moderation.

But now a transition takes place so that the *usus in renatis* (third use) moves into the foreground, yet without supplanting the *usus politicus*. Notice again the relation between law and liberty.

> Thus it is a true and genuine happiness, not only when liberty is

granted to us but also when God prescribes a certain rule and ar-
ranges for a certain public order (*aliquem statutum*) among us
that there may be no confusion . . . . Now this subjection is better
than all the ruling powers of the world, i.e., when God is pleased
to rule over us, undertakes the care of our safety and performs the
office of a governor. [148]

Almost all of the motifs, so characteristic of Calvin's concept
of the law, and particularly of his understanding of the *usus politicus*,
find expression in the exposition of Jeremiah 33:15. Here we have
God's government and rule, the judging and restraining aspect of the
law, both spiritual and civil government, the Kingdom of Christ and the
rule of the Spirit. The text reads: "In those days and at that time I will
cause a righteous Branch to spring forth from David; and he shall exe-
cute judgement and justice in the land." Concerning the last phrase Calvin comments:

By these words the ideal government (*optima gubernatio*) is de-
noted; for when these two words [judgement and justice] are
joined together, justice refers to the defense of the innocent, and
judgement to the punishment by which the wickedness of those is
curbed who, unless they are restrained by fear of the law would
violate all order. Indeed judgement by itself indicates rectitude.
But as I have already said, justice and judgement include the protection of those who are good and also the restraint of the wicked
who do not become obedient willingly or of their own accord.[149]

Thus far we have only a description of the *usus politicus*, although Calvin characteristically makes no specific mention of it. As he
continues, he makes a transition similar to the one noted above, but this
time he makes a clear-cut distinction between the second and third uses
of the law. Behind even this diversity, however, there is an underlying
unity.

In the meantime, however, it is necessary to return to the nature
of Christ's kingdom which, as we know, is spiritual. Yet it is here
depicted under the image of an earthly or political government.
For whenever the prophets speak of Christ's kingdom, they
present us with an earthly image because spiritual truth, without
any metaphor, was incapable of being sufficiently understood by

an uncultivated people in their childhood. . . .Therefore since the judgement and justice of which the prophet speaks is spiritual, they do not pertain only to the political and external order but even more to the rectitude by which men are reformed according to God's image, which is in righteousness and in truth. Hence Christ is said to reign over us in justice and judgement, not only because he keeps us in subjection, preserves the good and innocent, and represses the audacity of the wicked, but also because he rules us by his Spirit.[151]

III. USUS IN RENATIS

A. *The Third Use and the Holy Spirit*

The reference to the rule of the Spirit in the last quotation leads us to the heart of Calvin's understanding of the third use of the law, the *usus normativus* or, as Calvin preferred, *usus in renatis*. For this use is connected in a special way with the work of the Holy Spirit. When the law is separated by sin from Christ, its heart and goal, it is devoid of the Spirit. But when the law is viewed and experienced according to its original purpose, i.e., as a gift and guide to God's children, then it is a peculiar organ of the Holy Spirit for renewing and reforming people in the image of God. Hence its chief function is for those who have been regenerated by the Spirit of God.[152]

Thus the three uses of the law correspond roughly to the three persons of the Godhead and their respective offices: the *usus politicus* and God the Creator; the *usus elenchticus* and God the Redeemer: the *usus in renatis* and God the Sanctifier. However, whereas the first two functions of the law are essentially negative in that they either restrain, condemn, or reveal the nature and power of sin, the "third and principal use pertains more closely to the proper purpose of the law," for it "finds its place among believers in whose hearts the Spirit of God already lives and reigns."[153]

This emphasis on the role of the law in the Christian life is a corollary of Calvin's accent on sanctification. As Barth has pointed out, Calvin recognized the basic, critical importance of the doctrine of justification. Yet "one thing is certain—that if the theology of Calvin has a center at all, it does not lie in the doctrine of justification." Calvin refers to two main gifts which the Christian receives from Christ and the

Holy Spirit: justification, or the forgiveness of sins, and sanctification or renewal (*renovatio*) which is indissolubly connected with it. But an examination of Book III of the *Institutes* shows that it is the second of these gifts, "the question of the development and formation of the Christian life and therefore of sanctification, . . . which controls and organizes his thinking."[154]

Just as God redeemed Israel to the end that they might be forever bound to him,[155] so we have been redeemed by Christ to the end that we may be wholly devoted to God. For Christ died and rose again for this purpose—that he might be the Lord of the living and the dead.[156] The blessing of the forgiveness of sins would be a passing (*evanidum*) thing if God did not at the same time keep us in subjection to his law. Therefore "he regenerates by his Spirit unto righteousness all those whose sins he pardons."[157] This was why God gathered to himself a church—"that those whom he has called may be holy. The foundation, indeed, of the divine calling is a free promise, but the immediate consequence of this is that those whom God has chosen as a peculiar people to himself should devote themselves to the righteousness of God."[158] "To serve God is the purpose for which we were born, and for which we are preserved in life."[159]

The whole of the Christian life proceeds by a double process: the negative aspect is mortification, the putting off of the old Adam; the positive side is vivification, our consecration to the Lord whereby we are renewed in the image of God.[160] In both of these processes—which are simultaneous—the Holy Spirit works through the instrument of the law. Also—and this is fundamental—"both things happen to us by participation in Christ,"[161] for he is "the root and seed of heavenly life in us."[162]

Calvin thinks of the Christian life in terms of growth or as a race. There are setbacks, and progress may be painfully slow, but with the law as our norm and with the Spirit of Christ as our source of power, we make progress toward the goal.[163]

> We confess that while through the intercession of Christ's righteousness God reconciles us to himself, and by free remission of sins accounts us righteous, his beneficence is at the same time joined with such a mercy that through his Holy Spirit he dwells in us and by his power the lusts of our flesh are each day more and more mortified; we are indeed sanctified, that is, consecrated to

the Lord in true purity of life, with our hearts formed to the obedience to the law. [164]

B. *The Necessity for a Norm and Guide*

In the passage quoted above a few allusions to the law implied that the Christian needs the law in order to make progress in the Christian life. But it is often objected that the Christian is a new person in Christ, who lives by grace, not by the law. Believers possess the righteousness of faith and therefore need no longer strive for the righteousness of works. As children of God they are united by faith to Christ and are led by the Spirit. Why then talk about the law? Do the redeemed need anything besides the wisdom and riches that are theirs in Christ and the Holy Spirit?

Calvin answers: "Even though they [believers] have the law written and engraved on their hearts by the finger of God (Jer. 31:33; Heb. 10:16), that is, have been so moved and quickened through the directing of the Spirit that they long to obey God, they still profit by the law in two ways."

> Here is the best instrument (*organum*) for them to learn more thoroughly each day the nature of the Lord's will to which they aspire, and to confirm them in the understanding of it. It is as if some servant, already prepared with all earnestness of heart to commend himself to his master, must search out and observe his master's ways more carefully in order to conform and accommodate himself to them. And not one of us may escape from this necessity. For no man has heretofore obtained such wisdom as to be unable, from the daily instruction of the law, to make fresh progress toward a purer knowledge of the divine will.[165]

This is the first way in which the law assists Christians in living out the grace they have experienced in Christ. It gives a clearer understanding of God's will for our lives. No believers are so mature that they can presume to know perfectly what form their gratitude toward God should take.

The second reason is actually an extension of the *usus theologicus*, for the believer is never free from the temptations of sloth, self-centeredness, pride, and hypocrisy.

Again, because we need not only instruction but also exhortation, the servant of God will also avail himself of this benefit of the law: by frequent meditation upon it to be aroused to obedience, be strengthened in it, and be drawn back from the slippery path of transgression. In this way the saints press on; for however eagerly they may strive in accordance with the Spirit toward God's righteousness, the listless flesh always so burdens them that they do not proceed with due readiness. The law is to the flesh like a whip to an idle and balky ass, to arouse it to work. Even for a spiritual man not yet free of the weight of the flesh the law remains a constant sting that will not let him stand still.[166]

Calvin concludes this section by noting that it was this use of the law to which David referred when he sang the praises of the law in Psalms 19 and 119. This is significant, for Calvin was quite aware of the fact that the law which was the object of David's rejoicing was not just the decalog but the whole of God's Word which was available to him. Hence the law in this case means simply God's revelation. Yet this should not be taken to imply that Calvin has forgotten his stress on the importance and sufficiency of the decalog. In the very next section he warns against those who would "bid farewell to the two tables of the law."[167]

C. Calvin and Luther

Once again we are confronted with the crucial question of what Calvin means by the law. The answer must be deferred at this point, but it is at least clear that law here does not refer primarily to a set of statutes or list of rules and regulations. He has something much broader in mind than that. Otherwise David and the Apostle Paul would then be found in opposition.

But here the prophet [viz., David in Psalms 19 and 119] proclaims the great usefulness of the law: the Lord instructs by their reading of it those whom he inwardly instills with a readiness to obey. He lays hold not only of the precepts, but also the accompanying promise of grace, which alone sweetens the bitter. For what would be less lovable than the law if, with importuning and threatening alone, it troubled souls through fear, and distressed them through fright? David especially shows that in the law he apprehended the Mediator without whom there is no delight or sweetness.[168]

This point is extremely important for understanding the real import of Calvin's concept of the role of the law in the Christian life. Nothing could be further from Calvin's intention than to introduce by the back door a disguised legalism via the *usus tertius*; for the law in question here is the law in the context of the covenant of grace, the promises, and Jesus Christ himself. If Calvin sounds different from Luther here, it is largely because he is talking about a different law.[169] Luther knew this law also, but the third use was illogical and untenable for Luther as long as he emphasized the bare, abstract law which cannot be a vessel of grace but must rather stand in opposition to it. Of *this* law Calvin also says that it is bitter and unrelenting, only demands and threatens, and causes fear and death.

But when the law is viewed from the perspective of its original context, where the promise precedes and accompanies the demand, when it is seen in the light of the new covenant where it is written on the heart by the Holy Spirit, then the law should be welcomed by the believer and used in gratitude for the gift already received. That gift, as we have seen, is the Mediator who must be "apprehended" in the law.

Luther, on the other hand, following the negative strictures of the Apostle Paul in his controversies against the Judaizers, saw the law primarily as a corollary of sin, death, and the devil. Calvin too recognized this law, just as Luther also acknowledged with Paul that the law was holy and good. But each reformer reflects his own experience and situation in stressing that function of the law which he saw as the central one.

At this point it may be helpful to turn to two excellent analyses of the difference between Calvin and Luther in this regard.

> The Lutheran conception of the law is distinguished above all by the way in which the Pauline passages in which the law is thought of as a correlate of sinfulness are utilized and emphasized much more strongly than by Calvin . . . . The occasion for this lies incontestably in the basic conception of Luther's that the peculiar attribute of the law is its condemning work and that where this attribute of the law is lacking, it is no more the law in its proper sense. Where Luther finds a free acquiescence in the law, the law for him completely disappears or at least it assumes a form to

which the universal concept of the law is no longer suitable. Calvin, on the contrary, conceives of the law according to two diverse characteristics, namely, both with and apart from its condemning work. The law itself is not abolished for the believer,
but only the *maledictio legis* . . . . Thus, while for Luther the *usus
praecipius* of the law is intended for the sinner, for Calvin the law
is related above all to believers for whom, however, the *maledictio* is removed.[170]

    The other comparison by Doumergue begins with a contrast of
the Lutheran and Reformed types of faith. "For the Lutheran, faith is a
mystical union which assures the union of the believer with God in
such a way that the believer finds the rule and impetus of his action
within himself and thereby does not require to receive anything from
outside. The law is no longer something outside of him and foreign to
his will for his will has assimilated the law to itself. Thus the law has
become an internal impulse, stemming from his love which has been
aroused by the Holy Spirit."

    Doumergue then illustrates his point by citing a passage from
Luther's *Table Talk* where the reformer maintains that to say a Christian must do good works is like saying that God must do good and the
sun must shine. For Luther, good works are a "necessary consequence"
of faith; they follow naturally without any commandment or law. Christians spontaneously do good works because they possess a new nature.
Good works come as a matter of course, just as a good tree produces
fruit.

    "For the Reformed also, faith is a union of the human and the
divine, but this unity is only the beginning. The complete realization of
this union is far away in the future. In so far as this union is already realized through the Holy Spirit, faith produces the will, desire, effort and
general tendency to do good. But the rule for this faith and for individual wills continues to be the divine will which is above the individual believer . . . . "

    As an illustration of this, Doumergue points to Calvin's Gene-
va Catechism where the minister says to the child: The law "shows us
the mark at which we ought to aim and the goal to which we must
strive that each of us, according to the measure of grace bestowed upon
him, may try to conform his life to the highest rectitude, and by assidu-
ous care make more and more progress."[171]

Luther, however, "in his ecstasy (*eblouissement*) at having dis-
covered the gospel, considers only the ideal. Calvin, being more experienced and knowing the human condition better, considers reality. Each
conception, in a sense, is both true and dangerous." The dangers in the
Lutheran conception, according to Doumergue, are a tendency toward
subjectivism, quietism, and even license. The Calvinistic conception,
on the other hand, can develop into a servile legalism. Doumergue adds
that in neither Luther nor Calvin did these extreme consequences manifest themselves. Nevertheless, in their disciples the faults of the masters
are exaggerated and sometimes revealed.[172]

D. *Freedom from the Law*

Several features of Calvin's understanding of the third use of
the law must still be examined to avoid misunderstanding. One is his
emphasis on the freedom of the believer from the curse of the law. Calvin devoted a whole chapter to the subject of Christian freedom in the
third book of the *Institutes*.[173] Over half of this chapter deals with freedom from the law and freedom of conscience. Nevertheless, within his
discussion of the *usus tertius* in Book II he gives more attention to a
discussion of the abrogation of the law and the Christian's freedom than
he does to the positive explication of the meaning of the law for the
Christian. This is noteworthy, for it indicates that Calvin was concerned
lest he be misunderstood at this point. He might merely have referred
his readers to the chapter in Book III dealing with this subject. But instead, before advancing to the exposition of the decalog in the following chapter, he apparently wants to make it clear that the decalog is ultimately only useful for the Christian who is a free person in Christ.

1. Freedom From the Absolute Demands and Curse of the Law

It is important to see first the sense in which a Christian is free
from the law. Paul clearly teaches the abrogation of the law in passages
like Romans 7:6, observes Calvin.[174] However, it would be a terrible
mistake to draw the conclusion "that the righteousness which God approves in his law is abolished, when the law is abrogated. This abrogation, however, does not at all apply to the precepts which teach us the

right way to live, for Christ confirms and sanctions these. The proper solution to the objection is that the only part of the law which is removed is the curse, to which all men who are beyond the grace of Christ are subject.[175] Consequently, when Paul says that we are dead to the law (Rom. 7:14) he is referring here

> only to that part of the law which is proper to the ministry of Moses. We must never imagine that the law is in any way abrogated in regard to the ten commandments, in which God has taught us what is right and has ordered our life; for the will of God must stand forever. The release here mentioned (in Rom. 7:2), we must carefully notice, is not from the righteousness which is taught in the law, but from the rigid demands of the law and from the curse which follows from its demands. What is abrogated, therefore, is not the rule of living well, which the law prescribes, but that quality which is opposed to the liberty which we have obtained through Christ, namely, the demand for absolute perfection.[176]

In short, the law is abolished once and for all, *insofar as* it is able to bind the conscience with the threat of a curse. The believer has been freed from the burden of the "unending bondage" of a conscience agonizing with the fear of death.[177] This is one of the major differences between the old and new dispensations. Under the old, "consciences were struck with fear and trembling," but a benefit of the new is that "they are released unto joy. The old held consciences bound by the yoke of bondage; the new by its spirit of liberality emancipates them unto freedom."[178] Peace of conscience is "the chief source (*primum caput*) of a happy life."[179]

The removal of the curse of the law and the concomitant blessing of peace of conscience is possible only because Christ, the Son of God, who had the right to claim exemption from every kind of subjection, voluntarily became subject to the yoke of the law. He did this in our place in order to obtain freedom for us.[180] "He was set under the law (Gal. 4:4), although he was not debtor to the law but himself had the right of ruling and was the one to whom all submission was due. But he put himself into that lowly degree to set us free form the law's intolerable yoke."[181] Thus the "bond which stood against us with its legal demands" was canceled. Through the blood of Christ not only are our sins blotted out, but we also obtain "full liberty." For "as he fastened to the cross our curse, our sins and also the punishment due to us, so also that bondage of the law and everything that tends to bind consciences."[182]

Therefore, we must rely not on our works or efforts but on Christ alone, for in him we obtain complete redemption. In him "there is found everything necessary for setting consciences at peace.[183] Just as we have nothing more to do with the law as far as justification is concerned, so too our consciences must "embrace God's mercy alone, turn our attention from ourselves and look only to Christ . . . . The consciences of believers, in seeking assurance of their justification before God, should rise above and advance beyond the law, forgetting all law righteousness."[184]

This is the first aspect of Christian freedom, which is largely negative. Believers are freed from the harsh requirements and the curse of the law in order that they might serve God in peace and joy through the law which no longer holds any terrors for them. They are freed from the law of sin and death and are thereby made free for the law of the Spirit of life in Christ Jesus. This freedom is not a bare, negative thing. It is completely different from the modern concept of the autonomous person who assumes freedom as an innate right. Freedom is rooted in God and must be directed to him.

2. Freedom to Serve God

Therefore, the second aspect of freedom "is that consciences observe the law, not as if constrained by the necessity of the law, but that freed from the law's yoke they willingly obey God's will. For since they dwell in perpetual dread so long as they remain under the sway of the law, they will never be disposed to obey God with eager readiness unless they have already been given this sort of freedom."[185] Only the truly free person can obey God.

In the previous chapter we saw that the difference between the ministry of the law and that of the gospel was that under the gospel perfect obedience is no longer required. The will to obedience suffices because Christ by his perfect obedience has fulfilled the requirements of the law. Hence, if we are in Christ, it is enough "if we strive after the form of living" presented in the law. For "even if we are wide of the mark, i.e., of perfection, the Lord forgives what is lacking."[186] The criterion is simply whether our works and activities "proceed from the love of Christ." Since we "keep his commandments only insofar as we love him, it follows that a perfect love of him can be found nowhere in the world, since there is no man who keeps his commandments perfectly. But God is pleased with the obedience of those who sincerely aspire to this goal."[187]

This is the glory of the freedom of the gospel. For our works are no longer measured by the strict requirements of the law but are judged leniently by a gracious God. Without this comfort and assurance no one would strive to serve God with much enthusiasm. But if believers "hear themselves called with fatherly gentleness by God from this severe requirement of the law, they will cheerfully and with great eagerness answer and follow his leading."[188]

In this spirit and on this basis Calvin teaches the third use of the law. The only obedience and service which is acceptable to God is that which is spontaneous and free. Unless it springs from love and gratitude, it is not the obedience of faith. Christians obey God and seek to do his will not because they must, but because they want to do so. This joyous obedience is only possible because they are freed from the constraint and bondage of the law. Now, being truly free, they are free to love, free to obey, free to submit to the rule and leading of the Spirit.

Freedom is not autonomy or anarchy but finding one's true master. In the words of the hymn, "Make me captive Lord, and *then* I shall be free." Or, as Calvin puts it, the freedom of the Christian is "a free servitude and a serving freedom."[189] True freedom is freedom in obedience. Only "those who serve God are free . . . We obtain liberty in order that we may more promptly and more readily obey God."[190]

3. The Role of the Spirit

Sincere, willing obedience, however, only issues from a heart that is governed by the Holy Spirit. And this is precisely the "peculiar office (*proprium munus*)" of the Holy Spirit, namely, to engrave the law on our hearts and inculcate in us a spirit of obedience. Our wills, being depraved, naturally incline to sin, but God through his Spirit changes them so that they seek after righteousness. "From this arises that true freedom which we obtain when God frames our hearts, which before were in thraldom to sin unto obedience to himself."[191]

Therefore, when Paul says, "If you are led by the Spirit, you are not under the law" (Gal. 5:18), according to Calvin, the meaning is that the Spirit frees us from the *yoke* of the law. If you walk according to the Spirit, "you will then be free from the dominion of the law, which will only be a liberal teaching (*liberalis doctrina*) to advise you. It will no longer hold your consciences in bondage."[192] Governed now by the grace of the Holy Spirit, the commandment is no longer "above us" (Deut. 30:11). Freed from the yoke of the law, we "perceive how sweet the yoke of Christ is, and how light his burden is" (Matt. 11:30). Since the rigor of the law has been taken away, "the instruction of the law will not only be tolerable, but even joyful and pleasant; nor must we refuse the bridle which governs us mildly and does not urge us more severely than is expedient.[193]

The real test of Christian freedom is whether it turns believers back upon themselves or outward in the service of God and neighbor. "Christ does not reconcile believers to the Father that they may indulge themselves with impunity, but that by governing them with his Spirit, he may keep them under the hand and rule of his Father. From this it follows that Christ's love is rejected by those who do not prove by true obedience that they are his disciples."[194] Consequently, believers rejoice not only in the liberty which is granted to them, but also in the fact that God prescribes "a certain rule" for them. It would be no blessing to be left in uncertainty as to what the Lord's will is. Hence this subjection is not a burden but "a true and real happiness.[195]

In the above paragraphs almost all of the main elements in Calvin's doctrine of the didactic or third use of the law have emerged. Christians are free, not from the abiding meaning of the law, but from the rigid requirements, curse, and consequent burden of the law. By faith and union with Christ, who has borne that burden and suffered that curse in their place, believers have become children of God. Since they are children and not servants, they enjoy the freedom of the Spirit. The special office of the Spirit is to mold and re-make them according to the image of God. The Spirit does this by means of the law, which is no longer an external accusing power but a helpful friend implanted in their being.

Thus through the Spirit believers seek more and more to do God's will, not their own. In joyful gratitude they seek to serve their rightful Lord in whom they find perfect freedom. They rejoice in their new-found power through the Spirit to obey the will of their Father.

They also give thanks that they are not left to guess as to this will and what is pleasing to their Lord, but that some direction, a rule of life, has been given them. They recognize their inability and failure to measure up to that standard of loving God and their neighbor with their whole being. Yet they do not despair because they rest finally in the grace and mercy of their Lord.

This in summary is Calvin's understanding of the role of the law in the Christian life. Several matters, however, require further clarification. It is still not altogether clear how Calvin reconciles his high view of the ten commandments with his general references to following the will of God in all things. He insists that "a certain rule" is necessary in order to do God's will, but it is sometimes not clear as to what the precise content of that rule is. This is a rather complicated matter, for Calvin's view of the law turns out to be surprisingly dynamic. This question, therefore, must be dealt with in the final chapter.

NOTES

1. *"Finis et Usus Legis,"* CO 24, 725f. For some reason the English translator chose to omit the first word, so that the English reads simply, "The Use of the Law."

2 For Luther and Melanchthon, this is the second use, with the *usus politicus* being first. It is not clear why Calvin did not follow this order.

3. See Harald Lindström, *Wesley and Sanctification* (London: The Epworth Press, 1950), chapter two.

4. 5ee Luther's Preface to the Large Catechism, *The Book of Concord*, Edited by Theodore G. Tappert (Philadelphia: Fortress Press, 1959), 359-361; and the conclusion of his exposition, ibid., 407-411; cf. "Against the Heavenly Prophets" in *Luther's Works*, Vol. 40.

5. See Werner Elert, *The Christian Ethos* (Philadelphia: Muhlenberg Press, 1957) 294-303; also Gerhard Ebeling, "On the Doctrine of the *Triplex Usus Legis* in the Theology of the Reformation," in *Word and Faith* (Philadelphia: Fortress Press, 1963).

6. So Paul Althaus in *Gebot und Gesetz*, and Emil Brunner in his *Dogmatics* Vol., III, chapter 22.

7. The subtitle of W. Joest's important book, *Gesetz und Freiheit* is "Das Problem des tertius usus legis bei Luther und die neutestamentliche Parai-

nese." He also discusses "Gesetz und Paraklese im Leben des Christen" in chapter three. Cf. E. Schlink's essay in *Antwort*, "Gesetz und Paraklese." Wingren, in his essay in the same volume, does likewise (320), but he also uses the German equivalent, *Ermahnungen* (321).

8. Calvin does not use the usual expression, *usus elenchticus* (the pedagogical use; cf. Gal. 3:24), either in the *Institutes* or in his commentaries or catechisms. He seems to prefer the terminology, *usus theologicus*, which he uses in his commentary on the Pentateuch (CO 24, 725).

9. *Inst.* III.18.9. Cf. Comm. Gal. 3:24 (CO 50, 220).

10. *Inst.* II.7.7.

11. CO 50, 535.

12. *Inst.* II.7.6.

13. Geneva Catechism (CO 6, 80). Cf. *Inst.* II.7.8,9; II.5.10.

14. Comm. Rom. 3:31 (CO 49, 68); 5:20 (CO 49, 120); 10:4 (CO 49, 196); Comm. Gal. 3:19 (CO 50, 215).

15. Sermon Gal . 3 :1-3 (CO 50, 466).

16. "The End and Use of the Law" (CO 24, 726) .

17. *Inst.* II.7.8.

18. Comm. 2 Cor. 3:7 (CO 50, 42). The law pricks and stings our consciences with an awareness of sin. By faith we are made sure and certain of the forgiveness of sins, *Inst.* III.17.1.

19. *Inst.* II.7.9. Calvin is here quoting Augustine.

20. C.D. IV, 1, 366.

21. II.1.3.

22. Comm. Rom. 6:21 (CO 49, 117).

23. Op. cit., 367. "Thus we are always in the sphere of the biblical concept of God, even though we are not at the center . . . . We find the same methodological weakness but unmistakable practical strength of presentation in Luther, Zwingli, the younger Melanchthon, and to a large extent the older Orthodoxy. When in the application of the method the thinking and teaching are biblicist if not biblical, by a happy inconsistency they could and can produce serious results," ibid.

24. W. Niesel, *The Theology of Calvin*, 90. His quotations from Calvin which follow hardly support this statement.

25. T. F. Torrance, *Calvin's Doctrine of Man*, 85, 87. Torrance's references are somewhat more apropos, especially the one from the Comm. on Rom. 6:21, but his contention is still questionable. True, the awareness of God's wrath makes us thankful for his love manifest in Christ's redemption. Moreover, except we look on Christ we cannot be assured of God's favor toward us (*Inst.* II.16.1-3, one of Torrance's references); but the question at issue remains unanswered: what is it that brings us to an awareness of our existence as sinners under the wrath of God?

26. O. S. I., 382.

27. Comm. Heb. 1:3 (CO 55, 12).

28. A parallel to this sentence, and an elaboration of it, is found in the *Inst.* I.6.1. where Calvin describes the two kinds of knowledge of God. One is a general knowledge of God as the Creator and Lord of the universe. The other is an "inner knowledge" of God as Redeemer in Jesus Christ.

29. O. S. I., 382.

30. Ibid.

31. In neither the Harmony nor the 1537 Catechism is there any mention of the *usus politicus.* This point will be discussed later.

32. *Inst.* II.7.12.

33. C.O. 6, 80. All three things, however, pertain to the first use of the law. In the following question he seems to take up the third use as such.

34. The Harmony of the Pentateuch, completed four years later (1563), offers no help in this regard. Although he has a separate section devoted to the use of the law, he begins with the third use (which he does not label as such). Barring two or three sentences interjected incidentally, most of the rest of the discussion deals exclusively with the first use. At the end of the section he refers his readers to his discussion in the *Institutes* for a further explanation of this subject. Apparently practical motives underly this emphasis, but it is still noteworthy that in his final writing on this subject he hardly touches the third and "principal" use of the law and omits the second use altogether.

35. LCC edition of the *Inst.* 269, n. 50.

36. *Inst.* II.2.11.

37. Recall that according to the Geneva Catechism, this is the first thing we learn from the law. Likewise, according to the Harmony of the Pentateuch, the law was given to people who are "puffed up with vain confidence" and imagine that they are righteous. Cf. *Inst.* II.7.11.

38. See I.1.2 and I.5.3, 10.

39. See II.2.10, 11; II.8.1, 3 (this is another discussion of the first use of the law); II.16.1.

40. See III.2.23; III.12, 2, 5, 6, 8. In IV. 17.40, in connection with the Lord's Supper, Calvin interprets 1 Cor. 11:28 as meaning that each person should "descend into himself."

41. Cf. also III.2.23.

42. *Inst.* III.19.15. Cf. I.3.2,.3; II.8.3; Comm. Gen. 4:9 (CO 23, 91, 92); Comm. Rom. 2:15 (CO 49, 38, 39). A perceptive discussion of the role of the conscience in Calvin's theology is found in Dowey, op. cit., 56-65. Cf. the unpublished dissertation by David L. Foxgrover, *John Calvin's Understanding of Conscience* (Claremont Graduate School, 1978).

43. *Inst.* II.12.5.

44. *Inst.* II.8.1. Cf. II.2.22.

45. III.12.1. Later in the same section we are told that we will not have a sufficient awareness of God's judgments unless "our life is examined according to the standard of the written law."

46. III.12.4.

47. III.12.5.

48. III.12.6.

49. III.12.8.

50. The emphasis is the same in the commentaries and sermons. "The gospel [note!] cannot be preached aright without summoning the whole world as guilty to the judgement seat, that flesh and blood may be crushed and reduced to nothing . . . " Comm. John 7:7 (CO 47, 166). Cf. Comm. Gen. 18:19 (CO 23, 259); Comm. Ex. 19:16 (CO 24, 201); Comm. John 4:15 (CO 47, 83); Comm. Rom. 5:13 (CO 49, 96). "Until God has summoned men before him and drawn them there as by force, they are so drunken with boldness that they cannot recognize themselves as they are . . . . Man would never recognize himself as long as he looked only at himself or as long as he compared himself with his neighbors; but this comes only when we have raised our eyes on high and we consider that we must come before the judgement seat of him who knows everyone . . .," Sermon on Job 25:1-6 (CO 34, 414). Cf. Sermon on Job 31:1-4 (CO 34, 634-5).

51. *Inst*. II.5.7.

52. Comm. Heb. 4:12 (CO 55, 49, 50).

53. Comm. Matt. 19:18 (CO 45, 539).

54. *Inst*. III.12.2. An Old Testament parallel is found in the story of Hagar. God had to humble her through affliction, but she "was not reduced to order by stripes only—a heavenly vision was added." In other words, without the addition of the positive grace of the Spirit, her knowledge of self (and her sin) would have been of no avail. Calvin then applies this truth to us. "The same thing is necessary for us, namely, that God while chastising us with his hand, also produces gentleness with his Spirit," Comm. Gen. 16:14 (CO 23, 232).

Krusche, therefore, errs in asserting that the *usus elenchticus legis* is not understood pneumatologically by Calvin, *Das Wirken des Heiligen Geistes nach Calvin,* 200. This can be said only of its effect on the unbeliever for whom the bare law means only greater condemnation. For the believer, however, both law and gospel perform their function by virtue of the work of the Holy Spirit.

55. See *Inst*. I.7.4.

56. See *Inst*. III.3.8.

57. *Inst*. II.5.5.

58. *Inst*. III.3.8. "Among all the vices of men, the chief and most destructive is haughtiness and arrogance. The Spirit alone softens us to bear re-

proofs patiently and so to offer ourselves willingly to be slain by the gospel,"
Comm. John 7:7 (CO 47, 157).

    59. See the excellent essay by H. Gollwitzer, "Zur Einheit von Gesetz
und Evangelium," in *Antwort*, 306-7.

    60. *Inst.* III.3.1. But he also warns against confusing them in III.3.5.

    61. *Inst.* III.3.5. Cf. III.3.7; Comm. II. Cor. 7:10 (CO 50, 89).

    62. *Inst.* III.3.7.

    63. *Inst.* III.3.4.

    64. Comm. Hos. 6:1 (CO 42, 463). Cf. Comm. Joel 2:13 (CO 42, 544,
545). A favorite text of Calvin's in this regard is Ps. 130:4: "There is forgiveness with thee that thou mayest be feared."

    65. "Repentance is nothing else but a reformation of the whole life
according to the law of God," Comm. Hos. 12:6 (CO 42, 463). Cf. Comm. Lk.
15:10 (CO 45, 506); *Inst.* III.3.8, 16. Cf. Luther's first thesis: "Our Lord and
Master Jesus Christ when he said 'repent' (*poenitentiam agite*) willed that the
whole life of believers should be repentance," *Luther's Works*, Vol. 31 (Philadelphia: Muhlenberg, 1957), 25.

    66. See *Inst.* III.3.7.

    67. Comm. Joel 2:14 (CO 42, 547).

    68. *The History of Doctrines*, 403.

    69. *Inst.* III.3.16.

    70. *Inst.* III.3.20. Later in this section Calvin almost repeats the words
of the early Luther: "No one ever hates sin unless he has previously been seized
with a love (*amore*) of righteousness."

    71. *Inst.* III.3.9.

    72. CO 45, 321. "Repentance is a singular gift of God," *Inst.* III.3.21.

    73. *Inst.* III.3.19.

    74. Comm. Joel 2:13 (CO 42, 544). God's "mercy ought to be a cause
for men to repent," *Inst.* III.3.20.

    75. Comm. Gen. 18:19 (CO 23, 259).

    76. Comm. Jer. 9:24 (CO 38, 52).

    77. Comm. Ezek. 16:63 (CO 40, 398).

    78. CO 23, 259.

    79. Ibid. Note that the word translated "repentance" in this quotation
is not the usual expression, namely, *poenitentia*. However, *resipiscentia* expresses the biblical idea of repentance better than *poenitentia*, for it means to
come to one's right mind, to recover one's senses.

    80. CO 49, 197. The new English translation by R. Mackenzie in the
Torrance Edition mistakenly refers this phrase to Paul rather than Moses.

    81. Ibid. We find the same thing in the *Institutes*. The first use of the
law is hardly alluded to in the chapter on repentance. In the chapter on faith
(III.2.1) Calvin notes that his description of faith cannot be understood apart

from what he wrote earlier (cf. II.8.3) about the moral law. Thus he bases repentance on faith, and faith in turn on the preparatory work of the law. Still, Göhler is correct in observing: "It is clear that the law does not serve justification directly as it does sanctification, but only indirectly afterwards prepares men to expect God's justification from his grace alone," *Calvin's Lehre von der Heiligung*, 114.

82. Referring to his soteriology, Bauke comments: "We see here again that Calvin is throughout a stranger to real metaphysical speculation," *Die Probleme der Theologie Calvins*, 74. Doumergue comes to a similar conclusion concerning Calvin's treatment of the knowledge of sin: "The great logician intrepidly stops short of the inferences of his dialectic. It is a fact, and a fact of experience which is simple and universal. And the fact says to the dialectic: 'Stop here—you cannot go beyond this point!'" *Calvin* IV, 173.

Even of Calvin's doctrine of reprobation, which would seem to contradict this thesis, Dowey says: "I here disagree with a majority of contemporary theologians who see a predominant speculative and metaphysical motif in Calvin's formulation of the doctrine of reprobation," *The Knowledge of God in Calvin's Theology*, 218.

83. "There is a profound difference between sixteenth century theology and later theology in their manner of speaking about the way of salvation . . . . It is not possible to deduce a fixed ordo from the words of Scripture and their order," G. C. Berkouwer, *Faith and Sanctification*, 27, 31.

84. In my essay, "Law and Gospel or Gospel and Law?" in *Calviniana*, I suggested that Calvin's approach might be described as law-gospel-law; law in the first instance being the law of creation, op. cit., 32. The redemption of Israel, which is the backdrop for the giving of the ten commandments, would then be the gospel.

85. Cf. Barth, "Gospel and Law" (in *Community, State and Church*), 78, 87.

86. As far as I know, there is no treatment of how Calvin preached the law except by Benjamin Farley in the Introduction to his translation of Calvin's *Sermons on the Ten Commandments*, and a brief discussion by J. Plomp, *De Kerkelijke Tucht bij Calvijn* (Kampen: J. H. Kok, 1969), 324 ff.; but neither writer discusses the law-gospel question. The latter simply points out that in his preaching of the law Calvin sometimes stresses the second use, other times the third use. In the latter case, "the law is now welcome. For the believer it is the good law of God," ibid., 326.

87. "Lex omnibus suis partibus in Christum respiciat," Comm. Rom. 10:4 (CO 49, 196).

88. Wallace, *Calvin's Doctrine of the Christian Life*, 97. But he concedes a few lines later, "It must not be thought, however, that in Calvin faith is exclusively thought of as the response of grace, and repentance as exclusively

attached to wrath and judgement . . . . After all, we are here dealing with a realm of personal encounter and personal response where the action of God and the response of men cannot possibly be systematically analyzed and neatly summarized, and Calvin is too great a thinker to attempt such exact systematization."

89. See *Inst.* III.2.15, 16, 21-23.

90. *Inst.* III.2.30.

91. *Inst.* III.2.28.

92. *Inst.* III.2.18.

93. *Inst.* III.2.23. The last statement is based on Hosea 3:5.

94. *Inst.* III.2.24.

95. In Lutheran theology this is the first use. Wesley also teaches three uses of the law, but his first and second uses are both aspects of the *usus elenchticus*. Like Calvin he emphasized the third use, which means that he omitted the *usus politicus*. Cf. Harald Lindström, *Wesley and Sanctification* (London: Epworth, 1950), 81.

96. *Inst.* II.7.10. Cf. Comm. Acts 9:6 (CO 48, 203).

97. Ibid.

98. Ibid. Calvin's terminology here raises the question whether the children of God, prior to their actual conversion, are totally "destitute of the Spirit of sanctification." To deal with such questions, however, is beyond the scope of our present concern.

99. *Calvins Lehre von der Heiligung*, 117,118. Göhler does not mention Lobstein, but this thesis was first propounded by him. There are even verbal parallels in their discussions. Cf. Lobstein, *Die Ethik Calvins*, 53.

100. Cf. Niesel, *Theology*, 96, and H. H. Wolf, *Die Einheit des Bundes*, 52. Both of them give Göhler rather than Lobstein the credit for this suggestion.

101. CO 6, 80.

102. II.7.6-9. Cf. Ii.5.10 and II.8.3.

103. 5ee the first edition, O.S.I., 61: "Ex his colligi potest, quale officium et quis sit usus legis. Tribus autem partibus continetur."

104. The only reference to this text in the *Institutes* is in II.7.10, where the second use of the the law is under discussion. Calvin observes that in this passage "the apostle seems especially to have alluded to this function of the law."

105. CO 52, 255.

106. Ibid. Calvin then explains that not even believers are exempt from the law, for they are not perfect. Paul, according to Calvin, uses the word "righteous" in a relative sense to describe "those who aim at what is good as the chief desire of their hearts, so that their godly desire is like a voluntary law that needs no external pressure or restraint . . . whose whole life was exhibiting the

genuine rule (*veram regulam*) of the law."
    107. Comm. Gen. 18:27 (CO 23, 264).
    108. Comm. Rom. 13: 8 (CO 49, 253).
    109. *Inst.* IV.20.3; Comm. Lev. 26:14 (CO 25, 23).
    110. *Inst.* II.3.3. Cf. Comm. Acts 15:10 (CO 48, 348).
    111. Comm. John 10:35 (CO 47, 2 52). Cf. *Inst.* IV.20.2. Here Calvin's position stands in sharp contrast to Luther's. For as Bohatec points out, a statement such as the following from Luther could never be found in Calvin. "Secular government is the lowest and least of God's governments" (W. A. 23, 514), *Calvin und das Recht*, 59. This is also a theme of Troeltsch, who refers to Luther's "attitude of pessimism and mere toleration" of the state, law, and economics, *Social Teaching*, 615.
    112. J. T. McNeill, *Introduction to John Calvin on God and Political Duty*, xiii. "The state in particular . . . is never regarded as a mere antidote to the fallen state and a penalty for evil, but is always chiefly regarded as a good and holy institution, appointed by God himself," Troeltsch, op. cit., 613.
    113. Bohatec has investigated this problem with his characteristic thoroughness in *Calvin und das Recht*, 97-129. He treats the same subject more briefly in *Calvins Lehre von Staat und Kirche*, 27-35. Cf. Troeltsch's fascinating but not altogether reliable generalizations in his *Social Teaching*, 599ff, 896ff.
    114. *Inst.* IV.20.3
    115. As McNeill laments, "It is to be regretted that the one major Reformer who was trained in law left no systematic treatise on natural and positive law," "Natural Law in the Teaching of the Reformers," in *The Journal of Religion* (July, 1946), 179.
    116. IV.20.14.
    117. "Validissimi rerum publicarum nervi," Ibid. Cf. IV.12.1 where Calvin uses the same metaphor in describing church discipline.
    118. IV.20.14.
    119. Ibid. Again in IV.20.16 Calvin refers to some who felt that "the law of God given through Moses is dishonored when it is abrogated and new laws preferred to it." Calvin's opponents here are apparently some of the *Bundesgenossen* of the Peasant Revolt who wanted to replace the "heathen" laws of the state with the law of Moses. On the other side, Calvin had to counter the anarchistic Anabaptists. For references see Bohatec, op. cit., 123.
    120. "Calvin wholly rejects the notion of a theocracy based on the judicial laws of the Old Testament," LCC *Inst.*, 1502, n. 36.
    121. IV.20.14.
    122. IV.20.15.
    123. The opposite view is being espoused today by a group variously known as Theonomists or Christian Reconstructionists who believe that the

Mosaic Law offers a blueprint for rebuilding modern society. See Rousas John Rushdoony's *The Institutes of Biblical Law*, 2 vols. (Nutley, N.J.: Craig Press, 1973). Other leaders in the movement are Gary North and Greg Bahnsen.

124. *Inst*. IV.20.15.

125. Ibid. Presupposed, however, is Calvin's definition of the function and purpose of the state given earlier in this chapter: "Civil government has as its appointed end . . . to cherish and protect the outward worship of God, to defend sound doctrine of piety and the position of the church, to adjust our life to the society of men, to form our social behavior to civil righteousness, to reconcile us with one another, and to promote general peace and tranquility" (IV.20.2). Again later: "No government can be happily established unless piety is the first concern; and that those laws are preposterous which neglect God's right and provide only for men" (IV.20.9). The freedom, therefore, which Calvin grants to the state must be viewed against this background.

126. "Divine providence has wisely arranged that various countries should be ruled by various kinds of government," IV.20.8.

127. IV.20.16. There is a difference between constitutions and civil laws, however, in that the former are of direct, divine appointment, whereas the latter are made by the government which results from the constitution. Thus their authority "is divine only at first remove," R. E. Davies, *The Problem of Authority in the Continental Reformers*, 134. Cf. Niesel, *The Theology of Calvin*, 237.

128. Lazareth, *Luther on the Christian Home*, 122. Cf. *Inst*. III.5.7 (and note in LCC ed., 677) and IV.20.11.

129. *Inst*. IV.20.16. On the surface there are undeniable similarities between certain phrases of Calvin's and the classic definition of natural law given by Cicero: "The true law, which accords with the nature common to all is constant and eternal . . . It is no different in Rome or in Athens, in the present or later. It is for all nations, in all times, and it will remain eternal and immovable," quoted in Doumergue, *Calvin* V, 455.

130. So Lobstein, *Die Ethik Calvins*, 52, 57-59. Also M. Simon, "Die Beziehung zwischen Altem und Neuem Testament," 20: "A certain lack of clarity undeniably remains here and thus the danger of a confusion of moral norms and legal ordinances, of morality and legality, of the first and the second uses of the law."

131. *Calvin*, 149.

132. Wernle complains, however, that Calvin "remains silent about the difference between love and equity. He says nothing about the fact that whereas criminal law is concerned with acts, the moral law is concerned with the intention; and that no human justice can ever be maintained by asserting the love-commandment for the intention," ibid., 150.

133. Ibid.

134. Cf. Reinhold Niebuhr, *The Nature and Destiny of Man*, Vol. II (1943), Chapter IX; Brunner, *Das Gebot und die Ordnungen* (1932; E.T., *The Divine Imperative*), Chapters XVIII. and XXII; *Gerechtigkeit* (1943; E.T. *Justice and the Social Order*); Barth's two important monographs, "Rechtfertigung und Recht" (1938) and "Christengemeinde und Bürgergemeinde" (1946), both translated in *Community, State and Church*, edited by Will Herberg; and Tillich, *Love, Power and Justice* (1953).

135. "Church and State" (E.T. of "Rechtfertigung und Recht") in *Community, State and Church*, 102-5. Cf. the sharp critique of the Reformers by a jurist who is very close to Barth, Jacques Ellul, *The Theological Foundation of Law*, 376f., 60ff.

136. See *Justice and the Social Order*, Chap. 12; and *The Divine Imperative*, 269ff., 627ff.

137. *Justice and the Social Order*, 266, n. 19.

138. Ibid., 48, 50. "Love is concrete and personal, nondeliberate, nongeneral. Justice, on the other hand, is general, lawful, deliberate, impersonal and objective, abstract and rational," *The Divine Imperative*, 450. Reinhold Niebuhr, who otherwise is much closer to Brunner than to Barth in the realm of ethics, is critical of this divorce by Brunner. Cf. his essay in *The Theology of Emil Brunner*, 270-1, and *The Nature and Destiny of Man*, 251.

139. "The Third Use of the Law in Calvin's Theology," in *Social Progress* (Nov., 1958), 26.

140. For Calvin, "positive laws are neither a copy nor an imitation of the absolute principle as Plato meant, but only relative expressions of the absolute moral law. This expression, since it is local, temporal and conditioned by the creative order, always remains relative. Natural law becomes an authoritative ordinance, though relative and adapted to historical reality, only through a combination of the essential and the peripheral, the *aequitas* and the *constitutio*," Bohatec, *Calvin und das Recht*, 128-9.

141. *Inst.* IV.20.2. Concerning civil magistrates Calvin writes: "They have a mandate from God, have been invested with divine authority, and are wholly God's representatives, acting as his vicegerents (cuius vices quodammodo agunt)." Authority is given to kings and rulers not by chance but "by divine providence and holy ordinance . . . . Accordingly, no one ought to doubt that civil authority is a calling, not only holy and lawful before God, but also the most sacred and by far the most honorable of all callings in the whole life of mortal men," IV.20.4.

142. *Inst.* IV.20.1.

143. *Inst.* IV.20.2.

144. "The greatness of Calvin consists in the fact that he cannot think one thought about God and his Kingdom without immediately thinking also of the state. This is the catholic in him as a reformer. He does not neglect one bit

of reality; he is never one-sided. He always strives for the all-embracing synthesis," A.A. van Ruler, in *Calvin Studien* 1959, 92. Fundamentally this is a true statement, but van Ruler claims too much when he says that Calvin never thinks about the Kingdom of God without thinking at the same time of the state. Cf. *Inst.* II.2.12; II.10.7; III.3.19.

145. Comm. Matt. 6:10 (CO 45, 197). Cf. M. Eugene Osterhaven, "John Calvin: Order and the Holy Spirit," Chapter 14 in *The Faith of the Church* (Grand Rapids: Eerdmans, 1982).

146. "The Integrity of Faith," in *Scottish Journal of Theology*, Sept., 1960, 257.

147. Cf. Paul Jacobs, *Grundlinien christlicher Ethik*, 478; and Dietrich Bonhoeffer, *Ethics* (London: SCM Press, 1955), 271-285. Bonhoeffer deals primarily with the *usus politicus* in the Lutheran symbolic writings, but his analysis and critique applies to Calvin as well.

148. Comm. Jer. 30:9 (CO 38, 617). Later in his discussion of this same text Calvin comes specifically to the church and observes: "God would not govern his church except by a king . . . . God is not our king, however, unless we obey Christ whom he has set over us and by whom he would have us to be governed . . . . If this is true that God, therefore, will not rule over us in any other way than by Christ, even to the end of the world, let us obey him and offer ourselves in submission to him," (CO 38, 618, 619).

149. Comm. Jer. 33:15 (CO 39, 66).

150. Note that this is the second time in this passage that the word "rectitude" has occurred. T. F. Torrance has pointed out the importance of this concept for Calvin: "In many ways the governing thought in Calvin's teaching [about the order of the church] is rectitude, which describes the order and government of creation within which man is placed and within which he is made to reflect the image and glory of God in such a way that the divine order is manifest," *Kingdom and Church*, 150. Cf. also 151-153.

151. Comm. Jer. 33:15 (CO 39, 66-7). Cf. Comm. Gen. 18:19 (CO 23, 259).

152. The designation *usus in renatis* means literally the use of the law for those who are regenerate. *Renatio* comes from the verb *renascor* which means "to be born again."

153. *Inst.* II.7.12. Because Luther applied the two key adjectives in this sentence (*praecipuus* and *proprius*) to the *usus elenchticus*, Werner Elert has made the claim that Calvin here "is waging a polemic against Luther with deliberate sharpness," *Zwischen Gnade und Ungnade* (1948), 166. This is highly unlikely, for there is no evidence that Calvin and Luther had any difficulty about this question. The conflict between Lutheran and Reformed theologians about law and gospel is a later development.

154. *Church Dogmatics* IV., 1, 525. Van Ruler, who interprets Calvin

quite differently from Barth, nevertheless concurs with Barth's evaluation at this point. According to van Ruler, "Calvin is concerned about the daily life of the Christian in the world. This means that he is concerned about *pietas*, godliness, reverence and sanctification. The justification of the sinner, the gospel, which Luther had again made central, is the firm point of departure. To this point every Christian must return daily. It is the anchor to which one commits himself. But it is only a means to an end. God is not concerned about his grace but about holy living in the world. Justification is the means, sanctification is the goal," op. cit., 86.

     155. Comm. Hosea 12:9 (CO 42, 466).

     156. Comm. Hosea 12:10 (CO 42, 648); Comm. Hosea 13:5 (CO 42, 479)

     157. Comm. Deut. 30:15 (CO 25, 55). "Christ regenerates to a blessed life those whom he justifies and, rescuing them from the dominion of sin, hands them over to the dominion of righteousness, transforms them into the image of God and trains them by his Spirit unto obedience to his will . . . ", "Reply to Sadolet" (OS I, 470).

     158. Comm. Gen. 17:1 (CO 23, 235). "As the efficient cause of human salvation was the undeserved goodness of God, so its final cause is that by a godly and holy life men may glorify his name. We ought to make a special note of this that we may remember our calling and so learn to apply the grace of God to its proper use," Comm. Lk. 1:74 (CO 45, 49).

     159. Comm. Ps. 111:10 (CO 32, 170).

     160. See *Inst*. III.3.3-8.

     161. *Inst*. III.3-9.

     162. *Inst*. III.1.2.

     163. "This restoration does not take place in one moment or one day or one year; but through continual and sometimes even slow advances God wipes out in his elect the corruptions of the flesh, cleanses them of guilt, consecrates them to himself as temples renewing all their minds to true purity that they may practice repentance throughout their lives and know that this warfare will end only at death," *Inst*. III.3.9.

     164. *Inst*. III.14.9. In his concern for practical holiness and progress in the Christian life Calvin is closer to Wesley than Luther. A Wesley specialist concludes: "In comparing Wesley with the Reformers we note that he is closer to Calvin than Luther in regard to sanctification and empirical righteousness . . . Luther suspects all forms of piety to be some sort of works—legalism; hence all true righteousness is in Christ rather than the Christian . . . . In Calvin and Wesley, however, sanctification is said to bring about a definite moral growth in man, the life of man being actually changed by the work of the Holy Spirit," Lycurgus M. Starkey, Jr., *The Work of the Holy Spirit*, (Nashville: Abingdon Press, 1962), 135-137. There is a major difference between Calvin and Wesley,

however, on the matter of Christian perfection. Cf. Starkey, ibid., 56-7.

165. *Inst.* II.7.12.

166. Ibid. Cf. the discussion of the necessity and nature of church discipline in IV.12.1. Calvin uses almost the same metaphors here as in II.7.12 where he discusses the third use of the law. Discipline, e.g., is likened to a bridle or spur and also to a father's rod. The object of this discipline is to chastise "mildly and with the gentleness of Christ's Spirit those who have more seriously lapsed."

167. II.7.13. According to the note in the LCC tr. of the Inst., "This is probably directed not only against the libertine sect but also against John Agricola, who broke from Luther and began the Antinomian Controversy (1537), denying all Christian obligation to fulfill any part of the Old Testament Law," 361.

168. *Inst.* II.7.12.

169. "That Calvin praises the law more highly than does Luther is not indicative, of itself, that he is more 'legalistic,' because he and Luther used the term with different meanings," Dowey, op. cit., 223.

170. Lobstein, op. cit., 55-56.

171. Geneva Catechism (CO 6, 82). The parallel to this statement in the *Institutes* is found in II.7.13: "In this perfection to which it exhorts us, the law points out the goal toward which we are to strive throughout life."

172. *Calvin* IV, 195-196. John Dillenberger and Claude Welch give a similar analysis in their *Protestant Christianity Interpreted Through its Development* (New York: Charles Scribner's Sons, 1955): "While Calvin's position on the transforming power of Christ is essentially the same [as Luther's], there are important nuances of difference which it is important to note. Luther speaks with great exuberance about the presence of Christ and almost regrets the necessity of the law within the Christian life. Calvin too, stresses the new life in Christ, but he is sober rather than ecstatic in his account. Whereas Luther spoke of the qualitatively new and decisive redirection of the Christian life, Calvin preferred usually to speak of the path in which the Christian walks and in which, with diligence, he can make some progress" 37.

173. He begins by saying, "We must now discuss Christian freedom. He who proposes to summarize the gospel teaching ought by no means to omit an explanation of this topic . . . . For unless this freedom be comprehended, neither Christ nor the truth of the gospel, nor inner peace of soul, can rightly be known," III.19.1. Concerning this chapter Wernle comments enthusiastically: "This short section on Christian freedom is a jewel in Calvin's *Institutes* . . . . How many words about Calvin's legalism would have remained unspoken if this chapter had been read more widely," op. cit., 131.

174. *Inst.* II.7.14.

175. Comm. Rom. 6:15 (CO 49, 113, 114).

176. Comm. Rom. 7:2 (CO 49, 120, 121). Cf. Comm. Gal. 4:4 (CO 40, 227).

177. *Inst.* II.7.14, 15.

178. *Inst.* II.11.9. "As under the law there was the spirit of bondage which oppressed the conscience with fear, so under the gospel there is the spirit of adoption, which gladdens our souls with the testimony of our salvation," Comm. Rom. 8:15 (CO 49, 149).

179. Comm. Ps. 119 :165 (CO 32, 289). "'Peace of conscience' is, in the language of the sixteenth century, the goal of all moral and religious striving," Edward Dowey, in *Social Progress*, op. cit., 23.

180. Comm. Gal. 4:4 (CO 50, 227).

181. Sermon Isa. 52:13-53:1 (CO 35, 597). Cf. *Inst.* II.16.5 .

182. Comm. Col. 2:14 (CO 52, 108, 109). Cf. *Inst.* II.7.17.

183. Comm. Heb. 9:15 (CO 55, 112).

184. *Inst.* III.19.2. "The gospel delivers us from anxiety and frees us from the stings of conscience; for all must necessarily tremble and finally be overwhelmed by despair, who seek salvation by works. For peace and rest exist only in the mercy of God," Comm. Ex. 19:1 (CO 24, 194).

185. *Inst.* III.19.4.

186. Geneva Catechism (CO 6, 80). Cf. *Inst.* III.6.5; III.19.5.

187. Comm. John 14:22 (CO 47, 33).

188. *Inst.* III.19.5 The basis for this confidence and cheerfulness is the knowledge that "not only we ourselves but our works as well are justified by faith alone," *Inst.* III.17.10. "This doctrine of 'justification of works' (which was developed in the Reformed Church) is of the greatest consequence for ethics. It makes it clear that the man who belongs to Christ need not be the prey of continual remorse. On the contrary, he can go about his daily work confidently and joyfully," Niesel, *The Gospel and the Churches*, 221.

189. "Est libera servitus, et serva libertas," Comm. 1 Pet. 2:16 (CO 55, 246).

190. Ibid. Cf. *Inst.* III.17.1.

191. Comm. Ps. 40:7 (CO 31, 412). Commenting on King Agrippa's reaction to Paul's proclamation of the gospel, Calvin concludes: "From this we see how great the pride of men's nature is until it is subdued to obey by the Spirit of God," Comm. Acts 26:28 (CO 48, 548).

192. Comm. Gal. 5:18 (CO 50, 218).

193. Comm. Acts 15:10 (CO 48, 351).

194. Comm. John 15:10 (CO 47, 343). "We are adopted for this end that God might have us as his obedient children," Comm. 1 Pet. 1:14 (CO 55, 221). Cf. *Inst.* III.17.6.

195. Comm. Jer. 30:9 (CO 38, 617). "Christian freedom is not the antithesis to authority, but consists rather in the Lordship of Christ so that the will

of the Lord becomes one with our wills," Kolfhaus, *Vom christlichen Leben nach Calvin,* 139.

VI

CONCLUSION: CALVIN'S DYNAMIC UNDERSTANDING OF THE LAW

I. INTRODUCTION

Calvin was indeed a man of the law, but not in the negative sense suggested by certain Reformation scholars of a past generation. For Calvin, as we have seen, the law is a dynamic entity primarily expressive of the gracious will of God for the benefit of his people. Because of sin it can also play a negative role, but even then the ultimate goal is the redemption of individuals and the restoration of order in the church and the cosmos. Only when sin intervenes and the law is separated from the promises of the gospel, which find their culmination in Christ, is the law antithetical to the gospel.

Properly understood and applied, law and gospel complement each other. Each has its distinctive role in God's economy of salvation. Hence they must not be confused. Here Calvin was as concerned as Luther to avoid any notion of works righteousness or form of legalism which would in any way undermine the precious gift of Christian freedom. At the same time, however, Calvin was equally concerned about pitting the gospel against the law as if one of them could stand alone. There is a "sacred tie" *(sacrum nexum)* between law and gospel, he insists, although "many erroneously try to break it. It has no small effect on consolidating our faith in the gospel," he adds, "if we hear that it is no other than the complement *(complementum)* of the law, both in mutual agreement claiming God as their common author."[1]

Moreover, it has also become apparent that law for Calvin connotes far more than the ten commandments, although the moral law finds its classic expression therein. Since the principal purpose of the law is to instruct us in godly living and guide us in the ways of right-eousness, veritably the whole of Scripture can serve that purpose.[2] Yet behind the words of Scripture lies the living and active will of God. This connection is crucial to understanding the dynamic character of Calvin's concept of the law, for it is ultimately to God himself, and not simply to any precepts or commandments that we owe our allegiance.[3] This linking of the law to the will of God is one of the factors that pre-cludes a literalistic understanding of the various commandments and guards against a possible legalism. Calvin's concerns are practical and ethical, not philosophical and abstract, as was the case with the nomin-alists.[4]

This is not the only dimension, however, which gives to Cal-vin's concept of the law its dynamic character. There are at least three other themes which further illustrate the dynamic nature of the law in Calvin's theology:

1. Christ as the exemplar and image of the law.
2. The guidance and leading of the Holy Spirit in understand-ing and living out the law.
3. The goal of the law: the restoration of the image of God.

II. CHRIST AS THE "EXEMPLAR" OF THE LAW

If we "desire to order our life by God's will," which consists of renouncing our past life[5] and true repentance, then "our life must be conformed to the example of Jesus Christ."[6]

As was noted earlier,[7] this is the theme of Chapters VI and VII of Calvin's treatment of the Christian life in Book III. He begins each of those chapters with a reference to the law and then quickly moves on to a more specific and concrete "plan for the regulation of life (*rationem vitae formandae*)."[8] That "plan" consists not only of a collection of var-ious New Testament texts which exhort us to live a holy life and pro-vide the motivation to do so, but ultimately points to Jesus Christ the "example (*exemplar*) whose image (*formam*; French, *l'image*) we ought to express in our life."[9]

In the seventh chapter, Calvin follows much the same proce-dure. After a reference to the law, he proceeds to a more precise princi-ple for living the Christian life. For "even though the law of the Lord provides the finest and best disposed method of ordering a man's life, it seemed good to the Heavenly Teacher to shape his people by an even more exact plan (*accuratiore etiamnum ratione*) to that rule (*regulam*) which he had set forth in his law."[10]

The beginning of this plan (*principium rationis*) is Romans 12: 1-2, a text which for Calvin has programmatic significance. Then he elaborates the nature of the Christian life in terms of a well-known contrast: "We are not our own . . . we are the Lord's," derived from Romans 14:8 and 1 Corinthians 6:19. This is Calvin's "Christian philosophy" (*Christiana philosophia*) which "bids reason give way to, submit and subject itself to the Holy Spirit so that man himself may no longer live but hear Christ living and reigning within him (Galatians 2:20)."[11]

This is the plan by which God would "shape" (*formare*) his people. The framework of that plan is provided in the law, but the Christian must move beyond that to that exemplar or image to which God would have us conform, viz., Jesus Christ.[12] This becomes particularly clear in the commentaries where Calvin frequently makes this point. He uses a variety of words to indicate that Christ is the one to whom our lives must be conformed or shaped; for Christ is the image (*imago; l'image*) example (*exemplum/exemplar*) and pattern (*patron*).[13]

In one case, it is "the example (*exemplum*) of *God* [which] is set for us to follow,"[14] but given the fact that God's image is found in Jesus Christ, it is not surprising that Calvin would appeal generally to the example or image of Christ. In his exposition of Romans 8:29, for example, he notes that the Apostle "did not simply say that they should be conformed to Christ, but to the image of Christ, in order to teach us that in Christ there is a living and conspicuous example (*exemplar*) set before all the sons of God for their imitation."[15] Later, in the same context, Calvin adds that the heavenly Father "wants all those whom he adopts as heirs of his kingdom to be conformed to his example (*eius exemplo conformes fieri*).[16]

There are similar exhortations in the sermons, especially in those on Ephesians. "The fathers that lived in the time of the law," Calvin points out, "already perceived that it behoved them to be conformed to the image and pattern (*conformassent a l'image et patron*) of our Lord Jesus Christ, who was their head . . ."[17] "Let us know that our Lord Jesus Christ is given us for a pattern and example (*pour exemple et patron*). . . . "[18] Being conformed to Christ and his image, however, does not mean a literal and superficial imitation of Christ. Referring back to the comments on Romans 8:29, when Calvin stated explicitly that Christ was set before us as "a living and conspicuous example" for our "imitation," he notes that this imitation consists not in a slavish imitation of Christ's activities, but in "our conformity to the humility of Christ."[19] In John 13:14, where Jesus exhorts his disciples to follow his example in washing Peter's feet, Calvin, in a polemical aside against the Roman practice, says that the "papists" "ought to have followed Christ," but instead "were copying rather than imitating him."[20] A key passage in this connection is 1 Peter 2:21: "For to this you have been called, because Christ also suffered for you, leaving you an example, that you should follow in his steps." Calvin comments:

> Since he [Peter] is speaking of imitation, it is necessary to know what Christ has set before us as our example (*exemplum*). He walked dry-shod on the sea, He cleansed the leper, He raised the dead, He restored sight to the blind. If we try to imitate Him in these things, it would be absurd . . . . What He had in view was something quite different [viz. to be humble and to be willing to suffer for Christ's sake].[21]

All of this fills out the brief but very significant statements in the beginning of the discussion of the Christian life in the *Institutes* III.6 where Calvin quickly moves from the law to Christ, who "has been set before us as an example whose pattern we ought to express in our life."[22]

It would be quite false to conclude from all this that Calvin has left the law behind as antiquated and irrelevant now that we have the example and model of Christ. The law has not been rendered obsolete with the advent of Christ. Nor should we oppose Christ to the law, as has been done by situational ethicists in our own time.[23] Calvin does not have two norms for the Christian life but one.[24]

This becomes apparent in a passage from one of his commentaries where he passes quickly from the law to the image of God. "The sum of the whole law and of all that God requires of us has this end in view, that his image should shine forth in us . . . ."[25]

Note that whereas Calvin normally understands "the sum of the law" to mean the two great love commandments, here he states that it requires that God's image "shines forth in us"; and that image is revealed in Jesus Christ. But again, there is no contradiction here, for in discussing the two great commandments, Calvin makes a very similar assertion to that just cited:

> Now it will not be difficult to decide the purpose of the whole law; the fulfillment of righteousness to form human life to the archetype (*exemplar*) of divine purity. For God has so depicted his character in the law that if any man carries out in deeds whatever is enjoined there, he will express the image of God, as it were, in his own life.[26]

For Calvin, then, there is no inconsistency in affirming that the sum of the law is love or that the sum of the law is encapsulated in God or God's image in Christ. The law provides the framework, the concrete guidelines for living according to God's will. But Jesus Christ is the "best interpreter" of the law,[27] the fulfillment of the law,[28] and in his own person is the exemplar and the Spirit of the law.[29]

Here Calvin fits nicely in almost all of the categories James M. Gustafson employs in his *Christ and the Moral Life*:[30] Jesus Christ as "The Lord Who Is Creator and Redeemer"; "Jesus Christ, the Sanctifier"; "Jesus Christ, the Justifier" (Gustafson's order); "Jesus Christ, the Pattern"; and "Jesus Christ, the Teacher." In relation to this subdivision, however, the category that applies most directly is that of "Jesus Christ, the Pattern." Gustafson points out that one does not follow Christ as a moral ideal or heroic image, "but as the Son of God who came in lowliness and humility, who was obedient unto death, who suffered at the hands of the world. It is the obedient one, the suffering Christ, the lowly Christ who calls you to be his disciple, to follow him."[31]

This is practically a paraphrase of Calvin's position. For one of the motifs in Calvin's discussion of the Christian life is "bearing the cross" as "a part of self-denial."[32] In fact, Gustafson then summarizes Calvin's understanding of the Christian life and interjects his own comment: "The Christian's conformity to Christ has a deeper mark of Christ's own life, namely, bearing the cross."[33]

R. C. Doyle, an Australian Calvin scholar, comes to a similar conclusion in an essay related to this theme: "The ethical system thrown up by Calvin's writings is christologically homothetical. That is, in *Jesus Christ*, and in him alone, we perceive that God our Father benevolently orders our lives, directs us by his Word and Spirit as law."[34]

III. THE GUIDANCE AND LEADING OF THE SPIRIT

Doyle does not develop his last point, namely, that God "orders our lives [and] directs us by his Word and Spirit"; nor, in fact, has anyone else, with the exception of Werner Krusche.[35] That God guides us by the Word, more particularly the law, is obvious, but the question remains, How does God guide or direct by his Spirit?

Calvin gives no detailed or formal answer to this question, but he refers again and again to the guidance, rule, direction, and governing of the Holy Spirit in the life of the believer. It is this aspect of Calvin's doctrine of the Holy Spirit which has been almost totally overlooked or ignored by Calvin scholars.[36]

In perusing this usage it must be kept in mind that Calvin strongly stressed the unity of Word and Spirit, although he allowed for more freedom of the Spirit than did Luther. Nevertheless, Calvin would not countenance any notion of new revelations of the Spirit or any leading of the Spirit that would run counter to the Scriptures.

> For by a kind of mutual bond (*mutuo nexu*) the Lord has joined together the certainty of his Word and of his Spirit so that the perfect religion of the Word may abide in our minds when the Spirit, who causes us to contemplate God's face, shines; and that we in turn may embrace the Spirit with no fear of being deceived when we recognize him in his own image, namely, in the Word.[37]

Nevertheless, the Spirit, according to Calvin, also assists believers by granting them not only understanding of God's Word but also additional guidance in concrete situations. Most of the references to the leading of the Spirit are made in the context of the doctrine of regeneration and sanctification. The role of this special work of the Spirit is to implement and assist the life-long process of mortification and vivification, which for Calvin are the chief components of conversion or repentance.[38] Representative are the following: "God regenerates and governs his own people by the influence of the Spirit";[39] and "The Lord by his Spirit *directs*, *bends*, and *governs* our heart and *reigns* in it as his possession. . . . It is obviously the privilege of the elect that, regenerated through the Spirit of God, they are *moved* and *governed* by his leading"[40] (italics mine).

Passages where Calvin explicitly relates this leading or guidance of the Spirit to the law, however, are few. In a sermon on Ephesians 2:8-10, Calvin says that God must not only teach us what is good through the Scriptures, but must also "reform us and so govern and guide us by his Holy Spirit that there may be agreement (*accord*) between our life and his law."[41] He concludes this sermon with the prayer: May God "so uphold us and govern us by his Holy Spirit that our whole endeavor may be nothing else than to frame our lives after his holy law."[42]

Although such passages are rare, most of the references to the guidance and leading of the Spirit apply to the law. It is not enough to have the various commandments, however specific they may be. Without the aid of the Spirit we will lack the motivation, the power, and the specific sense of what to do in a given situation. As the editors of the LCC edition of the *Institutes* put it in their caption for II.2.25, "Every day we need the Holy Spirit that we may not mistake our way."[43] In this section Calvin quotes the words of Psalm 119:10: "With my whole heart have I sought thee; let me not wander from thy commandments." Then Calvin adds, "Although he [David] had been reborn and had advanced to no mean extent in true godliness, he still confesses that he needs continual direction (*assidua directione*) at every moment."[44] In one of his commentaries Calvin expresses the same idea in a slightly different fashion. "In order that our zeal may be approved by God, it must be tempered by spiritual prudence and directed by his authority; in a word, the Holy Spirit must go before (*praeire*) and dictate what is right."[45]

Thus, the law in itself is insufficient. Its directives must be filled out by the example of Christ and explicated by a special grace of the Spirit. The goal of every Christian should be: 1. to be "so totally resigned to the Lord that he permits every part of his life to be governed by God's will";[46] and 2. that our life "be so regulated that whatever we say or do may be wholly governed by the authority of Christ (*totum regatur auspiciis Christi*), and may look to his glory as its aim."[47]

IV. THE ULTIMATE GOAL OF THE CHRISTIAN LIFE—
THE RESTORATION OF THE IMAGE OF GOD

In the above discussions there have been several references to the goal of the Christian life. One way of describing it is that we do everything to the glory of God (as noted above). Another way is to think of the goal of the life-long process of regeneration as the restoration of the image of God in the life of the believer.[48] This is accomplished, albeit imperfectly, by the renewing work of the Holy Spirit as believers respond in gratitude to God's will for their lives as expressed in the law and in Jesus Christ.

Calvin expresses this idea in a variety of ways. He begins his chapter on the Christian life with the following lines:

> The object of regeneration . . . is to manifest in the life of believers a harmony and agreement between God's righteousness and their obedience, and thus to confirm the adoption they have received as sons [Gal. 4:5; cf. 2 Peter 1:10].
> The law of God contains in itself that newness by which his image can be restored in us.[49]

Here he is simply reiterating a point he has made several times earlier in the *Institutes*. In a passage cited above, he writes: "God has so depicted his character in the law that if any man carries out in deeds whatever is enjoined there, he will express the image of God, as it were, in his own life."[50] In his discussion of repentance he adds: "I interpret repentance as regeneration, whose sole end is to restore in us the image of God that had been disfigured and all but obliterated through Adam's transgression."[51]

Similar statements abound in the commentaries.

> The sum of the whole law and all that God requires of us has this end in view, that his image should shine forth in us, so that we should not be degenerate children. This cannot happen unless we are renewed and put off the image of the old Adam.[52]

"The end to which we are called," Calvin says in reference to the Sermon on the Mount, is that "with the image of God restored in us, we are to live a godly and holy life."[53] The sum of the gospel, in short, as understood by the Apostle Paul, is this:

> . . . that the Messiah was promised to make atonement for the sins of the world by the sacrifice of his death, to reconcile God to men, to procure eternal righteousness, to regenerate men by his Spirit and fashion (*formaret*) them according to the image of

God, and, finally, to make his faithful ones heirs with him of the life of heaven; and that all these things have been fulfilled in the person of Jesus Christ, crucified.[54]

SUMMARY

"For Calvin, the law in its richest meaning is synonymous with the Word of God, and grace with the Spirit. Their objective unity is found in Christ, the Mediator; in faith the subjective unity becomes our 'purity of heart'."[55]

We have seen this illustrated in countless ways. God is Lord and therefore the rule of his law is manifest everywhere—in providence, in the secret work of his Spirit in the reprobate, in the calling of his children, in their sanctification and restoration to his image, in his governance of nations, and finally in the coming of his kingdom. The scope of the work of the law is as broad as the activity of God himself. The law is not the gospel, but it serves the gospel; it is an indispensable part of the gospel. In a sense, it is prior to and more comprehensive than the gospel, for it was the mode of God's relationship to humanity prior to and apart from sin.

The ultimate meaning of the law, therefore, is not to be found simply in individual commandments, not even in the ten commandments, where the essence and sum of the law is expressed. The idea of the law behind its accommodated form as it has come to us in the decalog is that God might be preeminent.[56] "We must not play with God!"[57] is the constant reminder provided by the law. This was true of Adam before the fall. It is true of those who have been reconciled to God in Christ. For the law was given on the one hand that God might maintain the right due to himself, and on the other hand that people might know that God rules over them.[58] God wants us to regard him as the master and guide of our lives.[59]

God, however, rules only in his Son. Through the Word, which witnesses to Christ, its center and life, and the Spirit, whom he gives to those who are united to him by faith, Christ so rules our wills and affections that God's will is done through our wills. Thus God restores in us that rectitude which was lost in Adam. The Spirit, who writes the law in our minds and engraves it on our hearts remakes us af-

ter the image of him who is the true man. We have been adopted on this
condition—that our life express Christ.[60] But this is only accomplished
insofar as we seek to put off the old Adam, crucify the old nature, and
let Christ's life master ours. For the life of a Christian is "a continual effort and exercise in the mortification of the flesh till it is utterly slain
and God's Spirit reigns in us."[61]

The law is thus a constant reminder of the truth—"We are not
our own. . . . We are God's." The law finally has nothing else to say but
this. "We are God's: let us therefore live for him and die for him. We
are God's: let all the parts of our life accordingly strive toward him as
our only lawful goal [Rom. 14:8; cf. 1 Cor. 6:19]."[62]

> O how much has that man profited who, having been taught that
> he is not his own, has taken away dominion and rule from his
> own reason that he may yield it to God! For, as consulting our
> self-interest is the pestilence that most effectively leads to our de-
> struction, so the sole haven of salvation is to be wise in nothing
> through ourselves but to follow the leading of the Lord alone.
>
> Let this, therefore, be the first step, that a man depart from him-
> self in order that he may apply the whole force of his ability in
> the service of the Lord. I call "service" not only what lies in obe-
> dience to God's Word but what turns the mind of man, empty of
> its own carnal sense, wholly to the bidding of God's Spirit. While
> it is the first entrance to life, all philosophers were ignorant of
> this transformation, which Paul calls 'renewal of the mind' [Eph.
> 4:23]. For they set up reason alone as the ruling principle in man,
> and think that it alone should be listened to; to it alone, in short,
> they entrust the conduct of life. But the Christian philosophy bids
> reason give way to, submit and subject itself to, the Holy Spirit,
> so that the man himself may no longer live but hear Christ living
> and reigning within him [Gal. 2:20].[63]

NOTES

1. Comm. Mt. 5:17 (CO 45, 172).
2. "I understand by the word 'law' not only the Ten Commandments

which set forth a godly and righteous rule of living, but the form of religion (*forma religionis*) handed down by God through Moses," *Inst.* II.7.1.

"Under the word 'law' Christ embraces the whole teaching by which God governed his ancient people. For since the prophets were simply expounders of the Law, the Psalms were also regarded as an appendage (*accessio*) to the Law," Comm. John 10:35 (CO 47, 252-3). Moreover, "The gospel was not given to add anything to the law and the prophets," Sermon 2 Tim. 3:16-17 (CO 32, 294). Cf. Comm. 2 Tim. 3:17 (CO 52, 384).

3. See Chapter One, II A.

4. See Chapter One, II B.

5. "Short Treatise on the Holy Supper of Our Lord. . . ." *Library of Christian Classics*, Vol. XXII, 150 (0S, I, 512).

6. ". . . nostre vie sort faicte conforme a l'example de Jesus Christ," Ibid., 151 (0S, I, 513).

7. See Chapter One, II D and Three, I D. I have developed this point in more detail in an essay contributed to the posthumous Festschrift for Ford Lewis Battles edited by Brian Gerrish, *Reformatio Perennis*: "Christ, the Law, and the Christian: An Unexplored Aspect of the Third Use of the Law in Calvin's Theology" (Pittsburgh: Pickwick Press, 1981), 11-26.

8. *Institutes* III.6.1.

9. *Institutes* III.6.3. Beveridge translates *exemplar a*s "model." Such references are fairly common in the commentaries and sermons. Ronald Wallace notes that "throughout his sermons he [Calvin] frequently refers to Christ as the "'*patron*" (i.e., "pattern") after which the children of God must be modeled (*configurez*) or to which they must be conformed (*conformez*), *Calvin's Doctrine of the Christian Life*, 41.

10. *Institutes* III.7.1.

11. Ibid.

12. In at least one place Calvin speaks of the law as an *exemplar* of the Christian life: "Now it will not be difficult to decide the purpose of the whole law: the fulfillment of righteousness to form human life to the archetype (*exemplar*; Allen tr.: 'example'; Beveridge, 'model') of divine purity," i.e., the law, *Institutes* II.8.51.

13. These words are not always translated consistently by the various translators. As we saw in note 12 (above) *exemplar* was translated by Battles as "archetype" and by Allen as "example." *Imago* is translated as "image" in some of the commentaries and as "likeness" by Battles in one place in the *Institutes* (III.6.3). The meaning is not affected, however, by these variations.

14. Comm. Mt. 5:45 (CO 45, 189).

15. Comm. Rom. 8:29 (CO 49, 160).

16. Ibid.

17. Sermon on Eph. 4: 7-10 (CO 51, 545). Cf. Sermon on Eph. 4:23-

26 (CO 51, 619): "Just as our Lord Jesus Christ is the second Adam, so he must be like a pattern (*patron*) to us, and we must be fashioned after him and his image (*image*), that we may be like him."

18. Sermon on Eph. 4:23-26 (CO 51, 623). Calvin then continues, "and moreover, that it is his [Christ's] office so to reform us by the Spirit of God his Father, that we may walk in newness of life and become God's creatures. . . . "

19. Comm. Rom. 8:30 (CO 49, 160).

20. Comm. John 13:14 (CO 47, 309).

21. Comm. 1 Pet. 2:21 (CO 55, 249-250). "Since the godly, from the first to the last, are made to be associates (*socii*) in bearing the cross of Christ, and to be conformed to his example (*imaginem*), there is no reason for any of us to shun his lot," Comm. Mal. 3:17 (CO 44, 483). "Why should we exempt ourselves from the condition to which Christ our Head had to submit, especially since he submitted to it for our sake to show us an example of patience for himself?" *Institutes* III.8.1.

22. III.6.1.

23. Cf. my essay, "Christ, the Law and the Christian," op. cit.

24. Contra Hugo Röthlisberger, *Kirche am Sinai*, op. cit., 130ff.

25. Comm. 1 Peter 1:14 (CO 55, 221).

26. *Institutes* II.8.51. The last phrase goes: " . . . imaginem Dei quodammodo sit in vita expressurus."

27. *Institutes* II.8.7.

28. "Every doctrine of the law, every command, every promise, always points to Christ. We are, therefore, to apply all its parts to him," Comm. Rom. 10:4 (CO 49, 196). Cf. *Institutes* II.7.2.

29. *Institutes* II.7.2.

30. New York: Harper & Row, 1968.

31. Ibid., 163.

32. The title of Chapter VIII of Book III.

33. Op. cit., 165.

34. "John Calvin, His Modern Detractors and the Place of Law in Christian Ethics," *The Reformed Theological Review*, Vol. 41 (1982), 83.

35. See *Das Wirken des Heiligen Geistes*, 288ff. Cf. also the appendix to Benjamin Milner's *Calvin's Doctrine of the Christian Life* on a related theme, "the secret impulse of the Spirit (*arcano spiritus instinctu*)," Leiden: E. J. Brill, 1970), 197ff.

36. I have tried to fill that lacuna with a paper given at the Davidson College Calvin Studies Colloquy in January, 1990, "Governed and Guided by the Spirit—A Key Issue in Calvin's Doctrine of the Holy Spirit." This was reproduced, along with the other papers given at that colloquy, in a volume entitled *Calvin Colloquy V*, edited by John H. Leith (Davidson, N.C.: Davidson

College Presbyterian Church, 1990), 29-40.

37. *Institutes* I.9.3. Cf. IV.8.13; ". . . the Spirit wills to be conjoined with God's Word by an insoluble bond (*individuo nexu*)."

38. See *Institutes* II.2.25; Geneva Catechism Q. 128 (O.S. II, 96); Comm. 1 John 3:23 (CO 50, 345); Sermon on Eph. 4:20-24 (CO 51, 613).

39. Comm. 2 Cor. 5:16 (CO 50, 69).

40. *Institutes* II.3.10.

41. CO 51, 384.

42. This prayer is not included in the *Calvini Opera* edition but is contained in the English translation by Arthur Golding (revised), *John Calvin's Sermons on Ephesians*, 168.

43. Vol . I, 284.

44. *Institutes* II.2.25. "The good works which we perform by the guidance and direction (*ductu ac directione*) of the Holy Spirit are the freely granted fruits of adoption, " Comm. Gal . 6: 8 (CO 50, 262).

45. Comm. Numbers 25:7 (CO 25, 299). Stanley Hauerwas, in his otherwise perceptive treatment of Calvin's understanding of the law in relation to sanctification, errs in concluding that "Calvin gives little help in this matter," i.e., in knowing how to "carry out in deeds whatever is enjoined in there [the law]." Hauerwas adds, Calvin "just seems to have assumed if one were a Christian, one would know how this was done," *Character and the Christian Life: A Study in Theological Ethics* (San Antonio: Trinity University Press, 1975), 207, n. 48. As we have seen in the passages cited in the text, Calvin does not assume that the believer will automatically or easily always understand what the law may dictate in a given situation. This is why Christians need the help of the Spirit to lead, guide, or direct where God's revealed will may not be clear.

46. *Institutes* III.7.10. "What we should be striving to reach all through our lives is the will of God," Comm. 1 Cor. 8:11 (CO 49, 435).

47. Comm. Col. 3:17 (CO 52, 125). "Ever since the Holy Spirit dedicated us as temples to God, we must take care that God's glory shine through us. . . . " *Institutes* III.6.3. Cf. *John Calvin's Doctrine of the Christian Life* by John H. Leith, Chapter I, A: "The Glory of God" (Louisville, Ky.: Westminster/John Knox, 1989).

48. On a broader scale, the goal for the whole created order is the restoration of order, the results of sin being conceived of as disorder. In addition to passages cited earlier on this theme, see the exposition of the petition, "Thy kingdom come." The opposite of the kingdom of God is complete *ataraxia* (disorder) and confusion. . . . So the sum of this supplication is that God will illuminate the heart by the light of his Word, bring our hearts to obey his righteousness by the breathing of his Spirit, and restore to order at his will, all that is lying waste upon the face of the earth," Comm. Matt. 6:10 (CO 45, 197).

49. *Institutes* III.6.1. After this last statement Calvin proceeds to de-

scribe "the pattern for the conduct of life," based largely on the New Testament, which complements the law.

50. *Institutes* II.8.51.

51. *Institutes* III.3.9 . A few lines later he adds: " . . . the closer any man comes to the likeness of God, the more the image of God shines in him." In this section he also explains that "this restoration [of the image of God] does not take place in one moment or one day or one year; but through continual and sometimes even slow advances God wipes out in his elect the corruptions of the flesh. . . . " Cf. III.17.5.

52. Comm. 1 Peter 1:14 (CO 55, 221).

53. Comm. Matt. 5:45 (CO 45, 189).

54. Comm. Acts 28: 22 (CO 48, 568-9).

55. R. A. Gessert, "The Integrity of Faith, " op. cit., 260.

56. Comm. Psalm 81:9 (CO 31, 763).

57. "Discamus non esse cum Deo ludendum, " Comm. Lev. 22 :19 (CO 24, 541).

58. Comm. Gen. 2 :16 (CO 23, 45). "Let this be a general proposition, that the law was given for no other end but to regulate the present life," Comm. Rom. 7:1 (CO 49, 119).

59. *Institutes* IV.10.7.

60. *Institutes* II.6.3.

61. *Institutes* III.3.20.

62. *Institutes* III.7.1.

63. Ibid.

BIBLIOGRAPHY

PRIMARY SOURCES

Ioannis Calvini opera quae supersunt omnia. Edited by G. Baum, E. Cunitz, E. Reuss. 59 vols. (Corpus Reformatorum, vols. xxix f.) Brunswick: C.A. Schwetschke, 1863-1900.

Calvini opera selecta. Edited by P. Barth and W. Niesel. Vols. I-V. München: Kaiser, 1926-1936.

Jean Calvin, *Institution de la Religion Chrètienne.* Edition Novelle Publiee par La Societe Calviniste de France. Ed. Jean Cadier. Vols. 1-4. Geneva: Labor et Fides, 1955-1958.

TRANSLATIONS

Calvin: Commentaries. Edited by Joseph Haroutunian. Library of Christian Classics, vol. 23. Philadelphia: Westminster, 1958.

Calvin: Theological Treatises. Edited by J.K. S. Reid. Library of Christian Classics, Vol. 22. Philadelphia: Westminster Press, 1954.

Calvin's New Testament Commentaries. Edited by D.W. Torrance and T.F. Torrance. Grand Rapids: Eerdmans, 1960-1972.

The Commentaries of John Calvin. 46 vols. Calvin Translation Society Edition. Grand Rapids: Eerdmans, 1948-1950.

Concerning the Eternal Predestination of God. Translated with an Introduction by J.K.S. Reid. London: James Clarke, 1961.

Institutes of the Christian Religion. Trans. by John Allen. 8th ed., revised. 2 vols. Grand Rapids: Eerdmans, 1949.

Institutes of the Christian Religion. Edited by John T. McNeill. Translated by Ford Lewis Battles. Library of Christian Classics, Vols. 20, 21. Philadelphia: Westminster Press, 1960.

Institution of the Christian Religion: 1536 Edition. Translated and annotated by Ford Lewis Battles. Grand Rapids: Eerdmans, 1986.

Instruction in Faith (1537 Catechism). Trans. by Paul T. Fuhrmann. Philadelphia: Westminster, 1949.

John Calvin: Catechism 1538. Translated and annotated by Ford Lewis Battles. Pittsburgh: Pittsburgh Theological Seminary, 1972.

John Calvin's Sermons on Ephesians. Revision of Arthur Golding's translation by Leslie Rawlinson and S.M. Houghton. Edinburgh: The Banner of Truth Trust, 1973.

John Calvin's Sermons on the Ten Commandments. Edited and translated by Benjamin W. Farley. Grand Rapids: Baker, 1980.

John Calvin's Tracts and Treatises. Trans. by Henry Beveridge. 3 vols.. (Reprint of Calvin Translation Society Edition, 1851). Grand Rapids: Eerdmans, 1958.

Sermons on Isaiah's Prophecy of the Death and Passion of Jesus Christ. Trans. by T.H.L. Parker. London: James Clarke, 1956.

SECONDARY SOURCES

Adams, James Luther. "Rudolph Sohm's Theology of Law and Spirit," in *Religion and Culture—Essays in Honor of Paul Tillich.* Edited by Walter Leibrecht. New York: Harper, 1959.

Althaus, Paul. *Die christliche Wahrheit.* Fünfte durchgesehene Auflage. Gutersloh: Gerd Mohn, 1959.

_____. *Gebot und Gesetz.* Gutersloh: Gerd Mohn, 1952.

Aquinas, Thomas. *Summa Theologiae.* Blackfriars edition. New York: Mac Graw, 1966.

Asmussen, Hans, and Sartory, Thomas. *Gespräch zwischen den Konfessionen.* Frankfurt am Main: Fischer Bucherei, 1959.

Augsburger, Daniel. "Calvin and the Mosaic Law." Ph.D. dissertation, Strasbourg University, 1976.

Aulen, Gustaf. *The Faith of the Christian Church.* Translated from the fourth Swedish edition by E.H. Walhstrom and G.E. Arden. Philadelphia: Muhlenberg, 1948.

Barrois, Georges. "Calvin and the Genevans," *Theology Today* 21/4 (January 1965), 458-465.

Barth, Karl. "Calvin als Theologe," *Reformatio* VIII. Jahrgang 5/6 (Juni 1959), 317-18.

_____. *Church Dogmatics,* Vols. I.2-IV.2. Zollikon. Edinburgh: T & T Clark, 1956-1959.

_____. *Christengemeinde und Bürgergemeinde.* München: C. Kaiser Verlag, 1946. (E.T. in *Community. State, and Church*, edited by Will Herberg. New York: Doubleday: Anchor Books, 1960).

_____. "Der Heilige Geist und das christliche Leben," in *Zur Lehre vom Heiligen Geist*, by K. and H. Barth. München: Kaiser, 1930.

_____. *Evangelium und Gesetz.* Theologische Existenz Heute, Heft 50. München: C. Kaiser Verlag, 1956. (E.T. in *Community. State, and Church.*)

_____. *The Faith of the Church.* Trans. by Gabriel Vahanian (A commentary on the Apostle's Creed according to Calvin's Catechism). New York: Meridian Books, 1958.

_____. *Rechtfertigung und Recht.* Theologische Studien No.1.. München: C. Kaiser Verlag, 1938. (E.T. in *Community, State, and Church.*)

Barth, Peter. *Das Problem der naturlichen Theologie bei Calvin. Theologische Existenz Heute*, Heft 18. München, 1935.

Battles, Ford Lewis. *The Piety of Calvin: An Anthology Illustrative of the Spirituality of the Reformer*, Grand Rapids: Eerdmans, 1978.

Bauke, Hermann. *Die Probleme der Theologie Calvins.* Leipzig: J.C. Hinrchs'schen Buchhandlung, 1922.

Baur, Jurgen. *Gott. Recht und weltliches Regiment im Werke Calvins.* Bonn: H. Bouvier, 1965.

Bavinck, Herman. *Our Reasonable Faith.* Trans. by Henry Zylstra; from *Magnalia Dei.* Grand Rapids: Eerdmans, 1956.

Berger, Heinrich. *Calvins Geschichts Auffassung.* Zurich: Zwingli-Verlag, 1955.

Berge, Wolfgang. *Gesetz und Evangelium in der neueren Theologie.* Berlin: Evangelische Verlagsantalt, 1958.

Berkouwer, G.C. *Divine Election.* Trans. by Hugo Bekker. Grand Rapids: Eerdmans, 1960.

_____. *Faith and Justification.* Trans. by Lewis B. Smedes. Grand Rapids: Eerdmans, 1954.

_____. *Faith and Sanctification.* Trans. by John Vriend. Grand Rapids: Eerdmans, 1952.

_____. *General Revelation.* Grand Rapids: Eerdmans, 1955.

_____. *The Person of Christ.* Trans. by John Vriend. Grand Rapids: Eerdmans, 1954.

_____. *The Triumph of Grace in the Theology of Karl Barth.* Trans. by Harry R. Boer. Grand Rapids: Eerdmans, 1956.

Beyerhaus, Gisbert. *Studien zur Staatsanschauung Calvins mit besonderer Berucksichtigung seines Souveranitatsbegriffs.* Berlin: Trowitzsch, 1910.

Biéler, André. *La Pensée Économique et Sociale de Calvin*. Genève: Librairie de L'université, 1959.

Bohatec, Joseph. *Calvin und das Recht*. Feudigen in Westphalen: H. Boehlaus, 1934.

Bonhoeffer, Dietrich. *Ethics*. London: SCM Press, 1955.

The Book of Concord. Translated and edited by Theodore G. Tappert. Philadelphia: Fortress, 1959.

Bornkamm, Heinrich. *Luther und das Alte Testament*. Tübingen: J.C.B. Mohr, 1948.

Bouwsma, William J. *John Calvin. A Sixteenth Century Portrait*. New York: Oxford U. Press, 1988.

Bring, Ragmar. "Preaching the Law," *Scottish Journal of Theology*, Vol. 13, No. 1 (March, 1960), 1-32.

Brunner, Emil. *The Christian Doctrine of Creation and Redemption*. Dogmatics Vol. II. Trans. by Olive Wyon. London: Lutterworth, 1952.

_____. *The Christian Doctrine of the Church. Faith and the Consummation*. Dogmatics Vol. III. Philadelphia: Westminster, 1962.

_____. *The Divine Imperative*. Trans. by Olive Wyon; from *Das Gebot und die Ordnungen: Entwurf einer protestantisch theologischen Ethik*. London: Lutterworth, 1937.

_____. *Justice and the Social Order*. Trans. by Mary Hottinger; from *Gerechtigkeit*. New York: Harper, 1945.

_____. *Man in Revolt*. Trans. by Olive Wyon; from *Der Mensch im Widerspruch*. London: Lutterworth, 1953.

_____. *Revelation and Reason*. Trans. by Olive Wyon. London: Lutterworth, 1947.

_____. *The Scandal of Christianity*. Philadelphia: Westminster, 1951.

_____. *Vom Werk des Heiligen Geistes*. Zürich: Zwingl Verlag, 1935.

_____. Brunner, Peter. *Vom Glauben bei Calvin*. Tübingen: J.C.B. Mohr (Paul Siebeck), 1925.

Büsser, Fritz. *Calvins Urteil über sich Selbst*. Zürich: Zwingli Verlag, 1950.

Carré, Meyrick H. *Realists and Nominalists*. Oxford: Oxford U. Press, 1946.

Come, Arnold B. *Human Spirit and Holy Spirit*. Philadelphia: Westminster, 1959.

Dankbaar, W.F. *Calvin, sein Weg und sein Werk*. Trans. by H. Quistorp; from *Calvijn, ziin Weg en Werk*. Neukirchen Kr. Moers: Neukirchener Verlag, 1959.

Davies, Rupert E. *The Problem of Authority in the Continental Reformers*. London: Epworth Press, 1946.

de Quervain, Alfred. *Calvin. sein Lehren und Kämpfen*. Berlin: Furcheverlag, 1926.

_____. *Die Heiligung*. Zollikon-Zürich: Evangelischer Verlag, 1942.

Dillenberger, John, and Welch, Claude. *Protestant Christianity Interpreted Through its Development*. New York: Scribners, 1955.

Doumergue, E. *Jean Calvin, les hommes et les choses de son temps..* Paris: G. Bridel & Co., Vol. IV, 1910; Vol. V, 1917.

Dowey, Edward A., Jr. *The Knowledge of God in Calvin's Theology*. New York: Columbia U. Press, 1952.

_____. "Law in Luther and Calvin," *Theology Today*, Vol. 41, No. 2 (1984), 146-153.

_____. "The Third Use of the Law in Calvin's Theology," *Social Progress*. Vol. XLIX, No. 3 (November, 1958), 20-27.

Doyle, R.C. "John Calvin, His Modern Detractors and the Place of the Law in Christian Ethics," *The Reformed Theological Review*. XLI/2 (1982), 74-83.

Durant, Will. *The Reformation*. ("The Story of Civilization") Vol. VI. New York: Simon and Schuster, 1957.

Ebeling, Gerhard. "Geist und Buchstabe," in *Religion in Geschichte und Gegenwart* (3.Auflage), III Band. Tübingen: J.C.B. Mohr, 1959.

_____. *Word and Faith*. Philadelphia: Fortress, 1963.

Eichrodt, Walter. *Theology of the Old Testament*, Vol. I. Philadelphia: Westminster, 1961.

Eire, Carlos M.N. *War Against Idols. The Reformation of Worship from Erasmus to Calvin*. Cambridge: Cambridge U. Press, 1986.

Elert, Werner. *Der christliche Glaube*. Berlin: Furche-Verlag, 1940.

_____. *The Christian Ethos*. Philadelphia: Muhlenberg, 1957.

Ellul, Jacques. *The Theological Foundation of Law*. Trans. by Marguerite Wieser from *Le Fondement Theologique du Droit*. New York: Doubleday, 1960.

Engel, Mary Potter, *John Calvin's Perspectival Anthropology*. Atlanta: Scholars Press, 1988.

Flückiger, Felix. "Vorsehung und Erwählung in der reformierten und in der lutherischen Theologie," *Antwort* (Festschrift zum 70. Geburtstag von Karl Barth). Zollikon-Zürich: Evangelischer Verlag, 1956, 509-526.

_____. *Geschichte des Naturrechts.* Band 1. *Altertum und Früh-mittelalter.* Zollikon-Zürich: Evangelischer Verlag, 1954.

Foxgrover, David. "John Calvin's Understanding of Conscience." Ph.D. dissertation, Claremont Graduate School, 1978.

Ganoczy, Alexandre. *The Young Calvin.* Philadelphia: Westminster, 1987.

Gerrish, Brian A. *Grace and Reason. A Study of the Theology of Luther.* Oxford: Clarendon Press, 1962.

Gessert, Robert A. "The Integrity of Faith—An Inquiry into the Meaning of the Law in the Thought of John Calvin," *The Scottish Journal of Theology.* Vol. 13, No. 3 (Sept. 1960), 247-261.

Gloede, Gunter. *Theologia Naturalis bei Calvin.* Stuttgart: N. Kohlhammer, 1935.

Göhler, Alfred. *Calvins Lehre von der Heiligung.* München: N. Kohlhammer, 1934.

Gollwitzer, Helmut. "Zur Einheit von Gesetz und Evangelium," in *Antwort,* 287-309.

Harkness, Georgia. *John Calvin. The Man and His Ethics.* Nashville: Abingdon, 1958.

Hauerwas, Stanley. *Character and the Christian Life: A Study in Theological Ethics.* San Antonio: Trinity U. Press, 1975.

Heideman, Eugene P. *The Relation of Revelation and Reason in E. Brunner and H. Bavinck* (Diss. Utrecht). Assen: van Gorcum, 1959.

Heintze, Gerhard. *Luthers Predigt von Gesetz und Evangelium.* München: Chr. Kaiser, 1958.

Hendry, George. *The Westminster Confession for Today.* Richmond, Va: John Knox Press, 1960.

Henry, Carl F. *Christian Personal Ethics.* Grand Rapids: Eerdmans, 1957.

Hesselink, I. John. "Calvin and Heilsgeschichte," in *Oikonomia. Heilsgeschichte als Thema der Theologie.* Hrsg. von Felix Christ. Hamburg-Bergstedt: Herbert Reich, 1967.

_____. "Christ, the Law, and the Christian: An Unexplored Aspect of the Third Use of the Law in Calvin's Theology," in *Reformatio Perennis.* Edited by B.A. Gerrish. Pittsburgh: Pickwick Press, 1981, 11-26.

_____. "The Development and Purpose of Calvin's Institutes," *The Reformed Theological Review* (Oct. 1965), 65-72.

_____. "Governed and Guided by the Spirit - A Key Issue in Calvin's Doctrine of the Holy Spirit," *Calvin Studies V.* John H. Leith, editor. Davidson, NC: Davidson College Presbyterian Church, 1990.

_____. "Law and Gospel or Gospel and Law? Calvin's Understanding of the Relationship," in *Calviniana, Ideas and Influence of John Calvin*. Edited by Robert B. Schnucker. Kirksville, Mo: Sixteenth Century Journal Publishers, 1988.

_____. "Luther and Calvin on Law and Gospel in Their Galatians Commentaries,"*Reformed Review* 37/2 (Winter, 1984), 69-82.

Holl, Karl. *The Cultural Significance of the Reformation*. Trans. by Karl and Barbara Hertz and John H. Lichtban. New York: Meridian, 1959.

Hunt, R.N. Carew. *Calvin*. London: The Centenary Press, 1933.

Hunter, A.M. *The Teaching of Calvin*. London: James Clarke, 1950.

Jacobs, Paul. *Grundlinien christlicher Ethik*. Witten: Luther-Verlag, 1959.

_____. *Prädestination und Verantwortlichkeit bei Calvin*. Kassel: Oncken, 1937.

_____. *Theologie reformierter Bekenntnisschriften*. Neukirchen Kr. Moers: Neukirchener Verlag, 1959.

Jewett, Paul K. *The Lord's Day. A Theological Guide to the Christian Day of Worship*. Grand Rapids: Eerdmans, 1971.

Joest, Wilfried. "Gesetz und Evangelium, dogmatisch," in *R.G.G*. 3. Auflage, Bd.2, 1526-1531.

_____. *Gesetz und Freiheit—Das Problem des tertius usus legis bei Luther und die Neutestementiliche Parainese*. 2. Auflage. Göttingen: Vandenhoeck & Ruprecht, 1956.

Keesecker, William F. "John Calvin's Mirror," *Theology Today*, Vol. XVII, No. 3 (Oct. 1960), 288-289.

Klempa, William. "Calvin and Natural Law," *Calvin Studies IV*. Edited by John H. Leith and W. Stacey Johnson. Davidson, NC: Davidson College Presbyterian Church, 1988.

Koehler, Ludwig. *Old Testament Theology*. London: SCM Press, 1957.

Kolfhaus, D. Wilhelm. *Vom christlichen Leben nach Johannes Calvin*. Neukirchen Kr. Moers: Buchhandlung des Erziehungsvereins, 1949.

Köstlin, J. "Calvins Institutio nach Form und Inhalt, in ihrer geschichtlichen Entwicklung," *Theologische Studien und Kritiken*, 1868, 6-62, 410-486.

Kreck, Walter, "Die Eigenart der Theologie Calvins," *Calvin Studien 1959*. Hrsg. Jürgen Moltmann. Neukirchen Kreis Moers: Neukirchener Verlag, 1960, 26ff.

Krusche, Werner. *Das Wirken des Heiligen Geistes nach Calvin*. Göttingen: Vandenhoeck & Ruprecht, 1957.

Kuizenga, Henry. "The Relation of God's Grace to His Glory in John Calvin," *Reformation Studies*. Edited by Franklin H. Littell. Richmond, Va: John Knox Press, 1962.

Lazareth, William. *Luther on the Christian Home*. Philadelphia: Muhlenberg, 1960.

Lecerf, A. *Études Calvinistes*. Neuchatel: Delachaux et Niestle, 1949.

Lehmann, Paul. "Law," in *A Handbook of Christian Theology*, edited by Marvin Halverson. New York: Meridian, 1958, 203-207.

Leith, John H. "Calvin's Polemic Against Idolatry," *Soli Deo Gloria. New Testament Studies in Honor of William Childs Robinson*. Richmond, Va: John Knox, 1968.

_____. "Calvin's Theological Method and the Ambiguity in His Theology," *Reformation Studies*. Edited by Franklin H. Littell. Richmond, VA: John Knox Press, 1962.

_____. *John Calvin's Doctrine of the Christian Life*. Louisville: Westminster/John Knox, 1989.

Lindström, Harald. *Wesley and Sanctification*. London: Epworth Press, 1950.

Little, David. *Religion Order. and Law. A Study in Pre-Revolutionary England*. New York: Harper Torchbook, 1969.

Lobstein, P. *Die Ethik Calvins*. Strasburg: C.F. Schmidt, 1877.

Luther, Martin. *Luther: Early Theological Works*. Library of Christian Classics, Vol. XVI. Philadelphia: Westminster, 1962.

_____. *Lectures on Romans*. Library of Christian Classics, Vol. XV. Philadelphia: Westminster, 1961.

_____. *Luther's Works*. American edition, Vols. 37 & 40. Philadelphia: Muhlenberg, 1957, 1958.

Mann, Ulrich. *Gottes Nein und Ja—Von Grundriss und Richtmass Theologisches Denkens*. Hamburg: Furche Verlag, 1959.

Manson, T.W. *Ethics and the Gospel*. London: SCM Press, 1960.

Maxwell, William D. *An Outline of Christian Worship*. London: Oxford U. Press, 1939.

McDonough, Thomas. *The Law and Gospel in Luther*. London: Oxford U. Press, 1963.

McGrath, "John Calvin and Late Medieval Thought," *Archiv für Reformationsgeschichte* 77 (1986), 58ff.

McNeill, John T. *The History and Character of Calvinism*. New York: Oxford University Press, 1954.

_____. *John Calvin on God and Political Duty*. The Library of Liberal Arts. New York: The Liberal Arts Press, 1950, 1956.

_____. "Natural Law in the Theology of the Reformers," *Journal of Religion*, Vol. XXVI (July, 1946), 168-182.

Melanchthon, Philip. *Melanchthon and Bucer.* Edited by Wilhelm Pauck. Library of Christian Classics, Vol. XIX. Philadelphia: Westminster, 1969.

Michalson, Carl. *The Hinge of History. An Existential Approach to the Christian Faith.* New York: Scribner, 1959.

Milner, Benjamin C., Jr. *Calvin's Doctrine of the Church.* Leiden: E.J. Brill, 1970.

Mülhaupt, Erwin. *Der Psalter auf der Kanzel Calvins.* Neukirchen Kreis Moers: Neukirchener Verlag, 1959.

Narum, William. "The Preaching of Justification," *The Lutheran World*, Vol. VI, No. 4 (March, 1960), 369-387.

Niesel, Wilhelm. *The Gospel and the Churches.* Philadelphia: Westminster, 1962.

_____. *The Theology of Calvin.* Trans. by Harold Knight from the 1938 edition. Philadelphia: Westminster, 1956.

_____. *Die Theologie Calvins.* 2. Neugearbeitete Auflage. München: C. Kaiser, 1957.

Oberman, Heiko A. *The Dawn of the Reformation.* Edinburgh: T & T. Clark, 1986.

_____. *The Harvest of Medieval Theology.* Cambridge, Ma: Harvard U. Press, 1963.

O'Connor, D.J. *Aquinas and Natural Law.* London: Macmillan, 1967.

Osterhaven, M. Eugene. *The Faith of the Church.* Grand Rapids: Eerdmans, 1982.

Parker, T.H.L. *Calvin's Doctrine of the Knowledge of God.* Revised American edition. Grand Rapids: Eerdmans, 1960.

_____. *The Oracles of God. An Introduction to the Preaching of John Calvin.* London: Lutterworth, 1947.

Partee, Charles. *Calvin and Classical Philosophy.* Leiden: E.J. Brill, 1977.

Pauck, Wilhelm. *Heritage of the Reformation.* Revised edition. Glenco: Free Press, 1961.

Pfisterer, Ernst. *Calvins Wirken in Genf.* Neukirchen Kr. Moers: Verlag der Buchhandlung des Erziehungsvereins, 1957.

Plomp, J. *De Kerkliike Tucht bij Calvijn.* Kampen: J.H. Kok, 1969.

Ramsey, Paul. "Love and Law" (in Reinhold Niebuhr's Theology), in *Reinhold Niebuhr. His Religious, Social and Political Thought*. Edited by C.W. Kegley and R. Bretall. New York: Macmillan, 1961.

Reuter, Karl. *Das Grundverständnis der Theologie Calvins*. Neukirchen: Neukirchener Verlag, 1963.

Richard, Lucien Joseph. *The Spirituality of John Calvin*. Atlanta: John Knox, 1974.

Ritschl, Otto. *Dogmengeschichte des Protestantismus*. Vol. III. Göttingen: Vandenhoeck & Ruprecht, 1926.

Rommen, Heinrich A. *The Natural Law*. St. Louis: B. Herder. 6th printing, 1964.

Röthlisberger, Hugo. *Kirche am Sinai. Die Zehn Gebote in der Christlichen Unterweisung*. Zürich: Zwingli Verlag, 1965.

Rupp, Gordon. *The Righteousness of God—Luther Studies*. London: Hodder and Stoughton, 1953.

Schellong, Dieter. *Das evangelische Gesetz in der Auslegung Calvins..* München: Chr. Kaiser Verlag, 1968.

Schlink, Edmund. "Gesetz und Paraklese," in *Antwort*, 323-335.

_____. *Theologie der lutherischen Bekenntnisschriften*. München: Chr. Kaiser Verlag, 1948.

Seeberg, Reinhold. *Lehrbuch der Dogmengeschichte*. Band IV, 1 and 2. Basel: Benno Schwabe. 6.Auflage, 1960.

_____. *Textbook of the History of Doctrines*. Trans. by C.E. Hay from the 1895-1898 edition. Grand Rapids: Baker, 1952.

Shepherd, Victor. *The Nature and Function of Faith in the Theology of John Calvin*. Macon, Ga: Mercer U. Press, 1983.

Simon, M. "Die Beziehung zwischen Altem und Neuem Testament in der Schriftauslegung Calvins," *Reformierte Kirchenzeitung* Jahrg. 82 (1932), 17-21, 25-28, 33-35.

Sittler, Joseph. "Ethics and the New Testament Style," *Union Seminary Quarterly Review*, Vol. XIII, No. 4 (May, 1958), 29-36.

Starkey, Lycurgus M., Jr. *The Work of the Holy Spirit. A Study in Wesleyan Theology*. Nashville: Abingdon, 1962

Stauffer, Richard. *The Humanness of Calvin*. Nashville: Abingdon, 1971.

Stickelberger, Emanuel. *Calvin*. Trans. by Philip E. Hughes. London: James Clarke, 1959.

Stumpf, S.E. "Natural Law," *A Handbook of Christian Theology*, New York: Meridian, 1958, 246-249.

Tillich, Paul. *A History of Christian Thought*. Edited by Peter H. John. Cambridge, Ma., 2nd ed., 1956.

_____. *Systematic Theology I*. Chicago: University of Chicago Press, 1951.

_____. *Systematic Theology II*. Chicago: University of Chicago Press, 1957.

Torrance, T.F. *Calvin's Doctrine of Man*. London: Lutterworth, 1952.

_____. *The Hermeneutics of John Calvin*. Edinburgh: Scottish Academic Press, 1988.

_____. *Kingdom and Church. A Study of the Theology of the Reformation*. Edinburgh: Oliver and Boyd, 1956.

_____. *The School of Faith. The Catechisms of the Reformed Church*. Translated and edited by T.F. Torrance. London: James Clarke, 1959.

_____. *Space, Time, and Incarnation*. New York: Oxford U. Press, 1969.

_____. *Theology in Reconstruction*. Grand Rapids: Eerdmans, 1965.

Troeltsch, Ernst. *The Social Teachings of the Christian Churches*. Two vols. London: Allen & Unwin, 1931.

Van Buren, Paul. Christ in Our Place. *The Substitutionary Character of Calvin's Doctrine of Reconciliation*. London: Oliver and Boyd, 1957.

Van Oyen, Hendrik. *Evangelische Ethik-Grundlagen*. Basel: F. Reinhardt, 1952.

_____. *Theologische Erkenntnislehre: Versuch einer dogmatischer Prolegomena*. Zürich: Zwingli Verlag, 1955.

Van Ruler, A.A. "Das Leben und das Werk Calvins," in *Calvin Studien*, 1959. Neukirchen Kr. Moers: Buchhandlung des Erziehungsvereins, 1960.

_____. *De Vervulling van de Wet*. Nijkerk: G.F. Callenbach, 1947.

_____. *Gestaltwerdung Christi in der Welt. Über das Verhältnis von Kirche und Kultur*. Neukirchen Kr. Moers: Buchhandlung des Erziehungsvereins, 1956.

_____. *Religie en Politiek*. Nijkerk: G.F. Callenbach, 1945.

Vasady, Bela. *The Main Traits of Calvin's Theology*. Grand Rapids: Eerdmans, 1951.

Verhey, Allen. "Natural Law in Aquinas and Calvin," in *God and the Good*. Clifton J. Orbeleke and Lewis B. Smedes, Editors. Grand Rapids: Eerdmans, 1975.

Wallace, Ronald S. *Calvin's Doctrine of the Word and Sacrament.* Edinburgh: Oliver & Boyd, 1959.

_____. *Calvin's Doctrine of the Christian Life.* Edinburgh: Oliver & Boyd, 1959.

Warfield, B.B. *Calvin and Augustine.* Philadelphia: Presbyterian and Reformed Publishing Co., 1956.

Watson, Philip S. *Let God be God. An Interpretation of the Theology of Martin Luther.* London: Epworth, 1947/1954.

Weber, Otto. "Calvin: Theologie," in *Die Religion in Geschichte und Gegenwart.* Band I, 3.Auflage. Tübingen: J.C.B. Mohr, 1957, 1594-1599.

_____. *Foundations of Dogmatics,* Vol. I. Grand Rapids: Eerdmans, 1981.

Welch, Claude, and Dillenberger, John. *Protestant Christianity Interpreted through its Development.* New York: Scribners, 1955.

Wendel, François. *Calvin. The Origins and Development of his Religious Thought.* New York: Harper, 1963.

Wernle, Paul. *Der evangelische Glaube nach den Hauptschriften der Reformatoren.* Band III, Calvin. Tübingen: J.C.B. Mohr, 1919.

Whale, J.S. *The Protestant Tradition.* Cambridge: University Press, 1955.

Williams, Daniel Day. *God's Grace and Man's Hope.* New York: Harper, 1949.

Wilterdink, Garret A. *Tyrant or Father? A Study of Calvin's Doctrine of God.* Bristol, In: Wyndham Hall, 1985.

Wingren, Gustaf. "Evangelium und Gesetz," in *Antwort,* 310-322.

_____. *Theology in Conflict: Nygren, Barth, Bultmann.* Trans. by Eric H. Walstrom. Philadelphia: Muhlenberg Press, 1958.

Wolf, H.H. *Die Einheit des Bundes. Das Verhältnis von Altem und Neuem Testament bei Calvin.* Neukirchen Kr. Moers: Buchhandlung des Erziehungsvereins, 1958.

NAME INDEX

Agricola, John, 274
Althaus, Paul, 262
Anderson, Bernhard W., 202
Aquinas, Thomas, 20, 51, 67, 69, 73, 82, 83, 102, 167, 244
Asmussen, H., 48
Augsburger, Daniel, 4
Augustine, St., 44, 81, 82, 159, 191, 205, 263
Aulén, G., 82, 83

Bahnsen, Greg, 270
Bainton, Roland, 47
Balke, Willem, 77
Barrois, Georges, 145
Barth, Karl, 3, 10, 14, 40, 45, 47, 57, 117, 136, 140, 148, 153, 156, 204, 210, 211, 212, 222, 223, 224, 236, 246, 267, 271, 273
Barth, Peter, 3, 57, 78
Battles, Ford Lewis 38, 39, 151, 287
Bauke, Hermann, 267
Baur, Jürgen, 4, 43
Bavinck, Herman, 85
Berge, Wolfgang, 48, 50
Berger, H., 202
Berkouwer, G.C., 44, 47, 82, 83, 84, 204, 210, 267
Beyerhaus, G., 3, 57, 78
Biel, Gabriel, 21, 41, 42, 43
Biéler, André, 6, 124

Bohatec, Josef, 3, 4, 31, 57, 74, 76, 79, 83, 84, 144, 269, 271
Bonhoeffer, Dietrich, 272
Bornkamm, Heinrich, 105, 142, 143
Bouwsma, William J., 44, 47, 83
Breen, Quirinus, 154
Bring, R., 37, 49
Bruggink, Donald J., 138
Brunner, Emil, 3, 82, 83, 136, 154, 156, 246, 262, 271
Brunner, Peter, 57
Brunstad, Friedrich, 5
Bucer, Martin, 18, 38, 116, 156, 159, 202, 206, 245
Bullinger, Heinrich, 156
Büsser, Fritz, 6, 145, 147

Cadier, Jean, 44
Carré, M., 41, 42
Chenevière, M-E, 57
Chrysostom, John, 81
Cicero, 68, 69, 83, 154, 243, 270
Cochrane, A., 57
Cranfield, C.E.B., 142
Cross, F.L. 42
Cullmann, Oscar, 209

Dankbaar, W.F., 31, 44
Davies, R.E., 270
de la Tour, Imbart, 1

SUBJECT INDEX